TOKYO
Love Story

A Manga Memoir of One Woman's Journey in the World's Most Exciting City

JULIE BLANCHIN FUJITA

English translation by *MARIE VELDE*

TUTTLE Publishing

Tokyo | Rutland, Vermont | Singapore

Contents

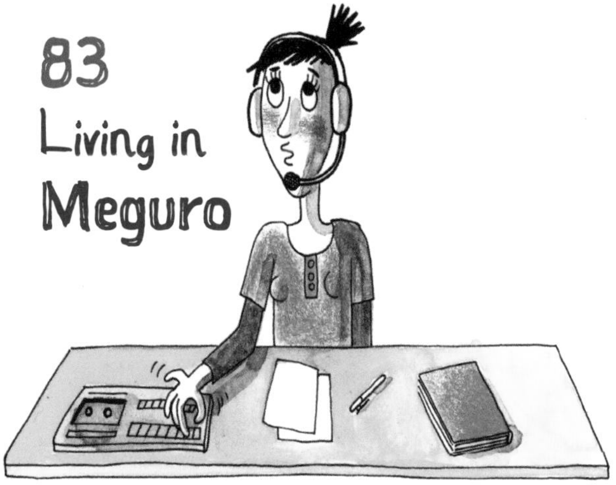

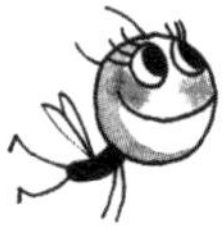

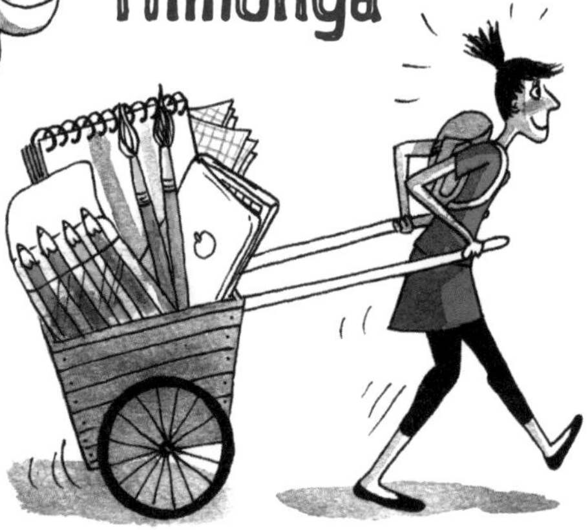

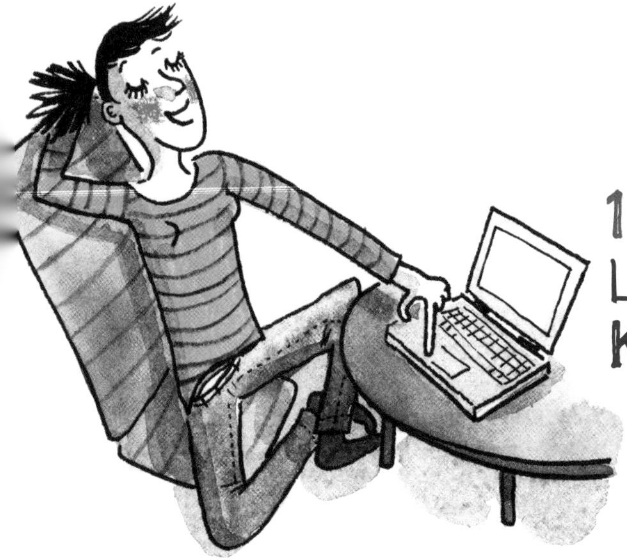

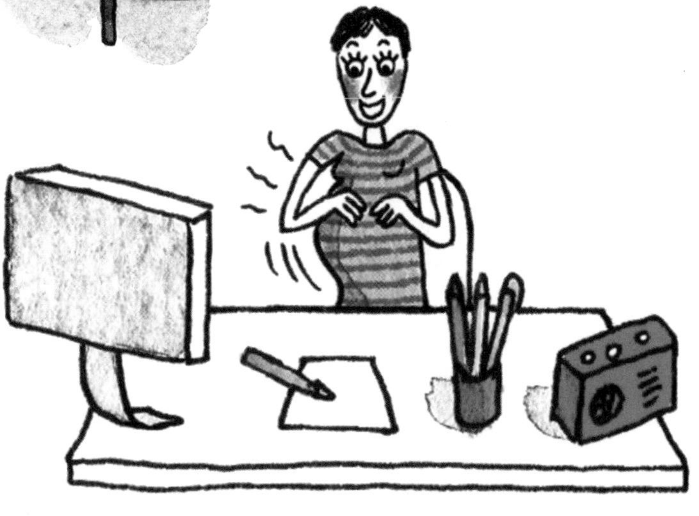

日本
Japan

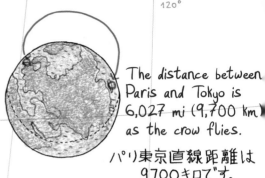

120°

The distance between Paris and Tokyo is 6,027 mi (9,700 km) as the crow flies.

パリ東京直線距離は 9700キロです。

Japan's area: 145,936 sq mi (377,915 km²)
Area of the USA: 3,797 million sq mi (9,834 million km²)

• Beijing

Pyongya

Japan's total population in 2020: 126,476,461 inhabitants.
(USA: 331,002,651)

Japan is an archipelago of 6,852 islands.
Mountains make up 78 percent of Japan's territory.

You can go practically anywhere in Japan by train.

Japan's currency is the yen, which is written 円 in Japanese.
Japan is the third-largest economic power in the world, with industrial groups such as Toyota, Fujitsu, Nissan, Honda, Mitsubishi, Canon, Panasonic, Sony, Sharp, Nintendo . . .

Shanghai •

CHINA

Life expectancy is high in Japan: 85 years (second highest in the world after Monaco).

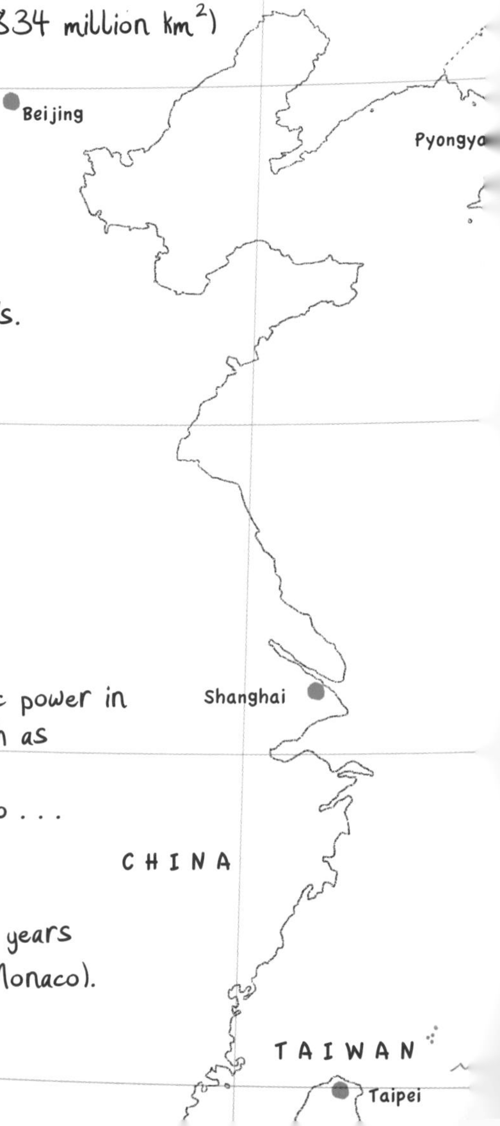

TAIWAN

• Taipei

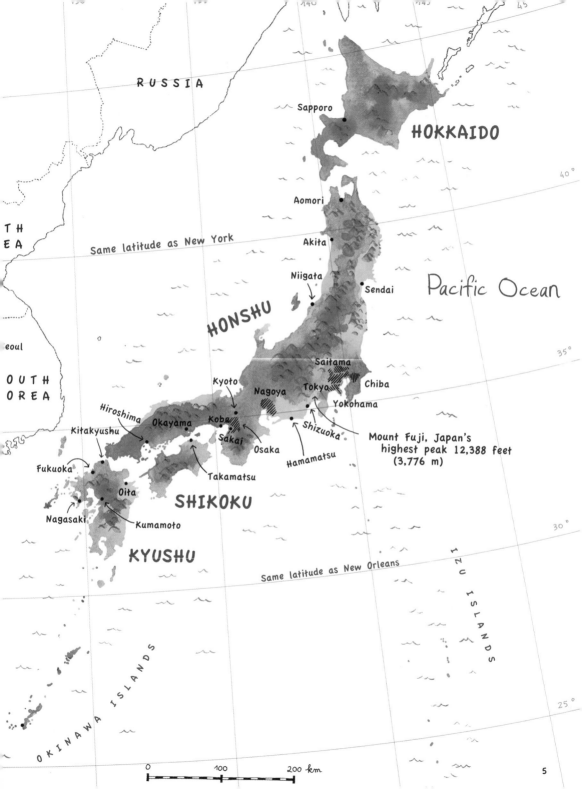

RUSSIA

Sapporo

HOKKAIDO

Aomori

Same latitude as New York

Akita

Niigata

Sendai

Pacific Ocean

HONSHU

Saitama

Kyoto

Nagoya

Tokyo

Chiba

Hiroshima

Okayama

Kobe

Shizuoka

Yokohama

Kitakyushu

Sakai

Hamamatsu

Mount Fuji, Japan's
highest peak 12,388 feet
(3,776 m)

Osaka

Fukuoka

Takamatsu

Oita

SHIKOKU

Nagasaki

Kumamoto

KYUSHU

Same latitude as New Orleans

IZU ISLANDS

OKINAWA ISLANDS

0   100   200 km

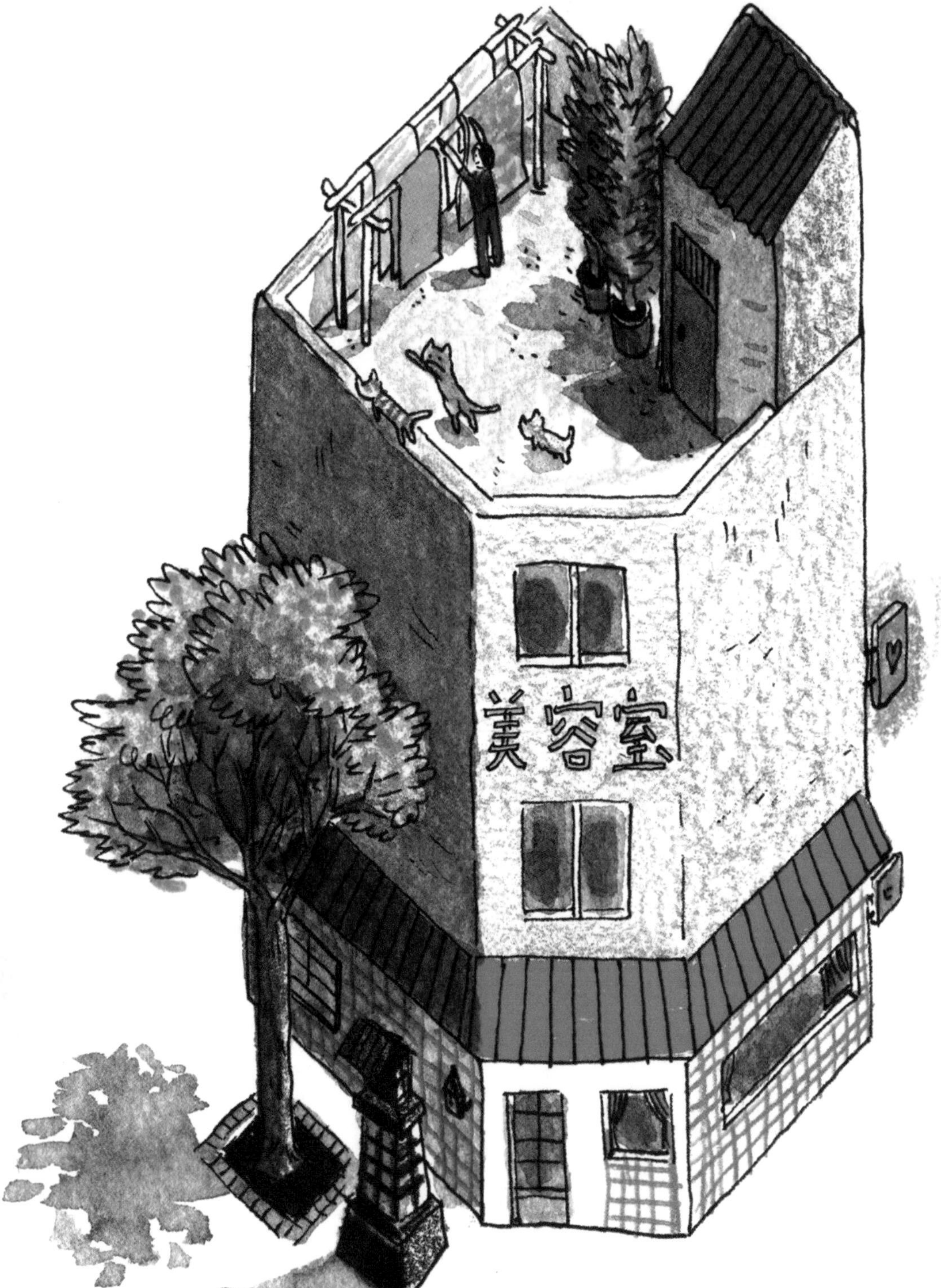
美容室

In the Beginning
とりあえず

1979-1980 年6月

I was born near La Rochelle in France. For the first few months of my life, I lived in public housing.

私はラ・ロシェルのとなりの サントで生まれます。 公団住宅で数ヶ月、 暮らします。

Come on, さぁ let's go! 始めましょう!

They're crazy, these hippies! ヒッピーだべか?

My dad, art teacher. 父は美術の先生。
My mom, painter and special 母はソーシャルワーカーで画家。
ed. teacher.

Then my parents bought an old, dilapidated house in ruins in a tiny village near La Rochelle.

While I waited for my parents to make the house livable, I stayed with my grandparents who lived on a campground in the neighboring village.

両親は近くの小さな村にある 廃屋を買います。

両親が家の基礎作りの間、 となり村のキャンプ場で、 祖父母と一緒に暮らします。

1984年

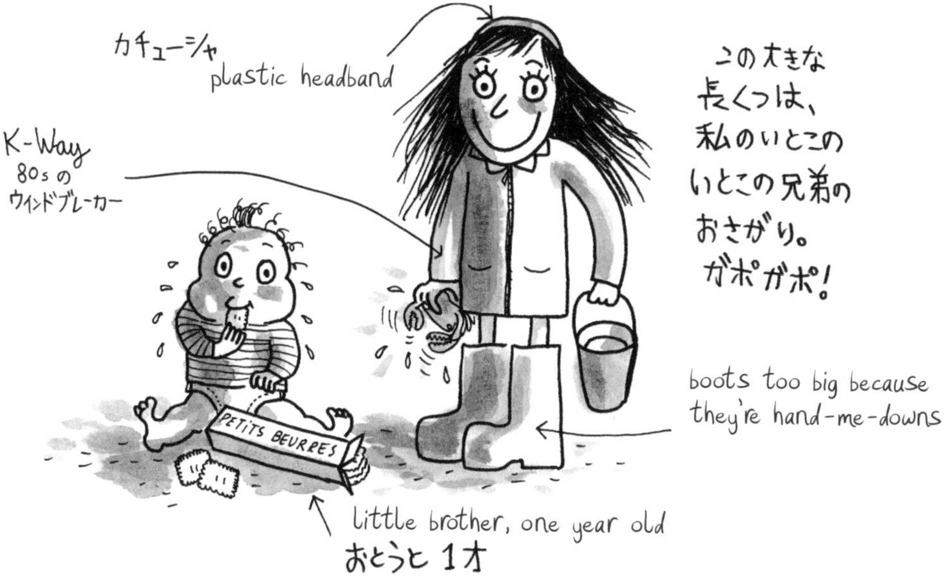
カチューシャ
plastic headband
K-Way
80sの
ウィンドブレーカー
この大きな
長ぐつは、
私のいとこの
いとこの兄弟の
おさがり。
ガポガポ！
PETITS BEURRES
boots too big because
they're hand-me-downs
little brother, one year old
おとうと 1才

1989年

My brother and I spent our time building tree houses, drawing pictures and making up stories.

いつも弟と一緒に、
秘密基地を作ったり
大きな絵を書いたり、
空想の物語を作って
遊びます。

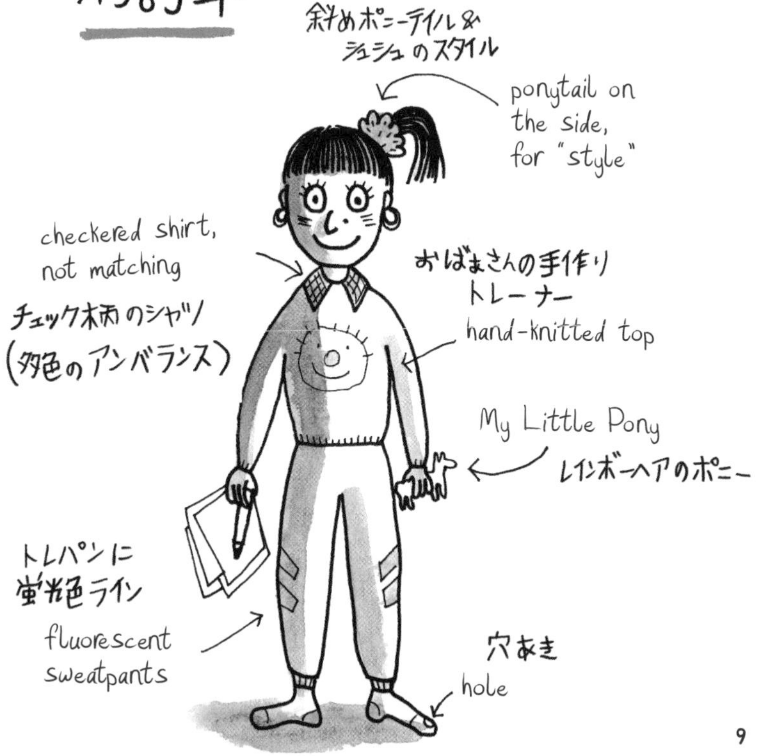
斜めポニーテイル＆
シュシュのスタイル
ponytail on
the side,
for "style"
checkered shirt,
not matching
チェック柄のシャツ
（多色のアンバランス）
おばあさんの手作り
トレーナー
hand-knitted top
My Little Pony
レインボーヘアのポニー
トレパンに
蛍光色ライン
fluorescent
sweatpants
穴あき
hole

1994年

顔にニキビ
my changing face

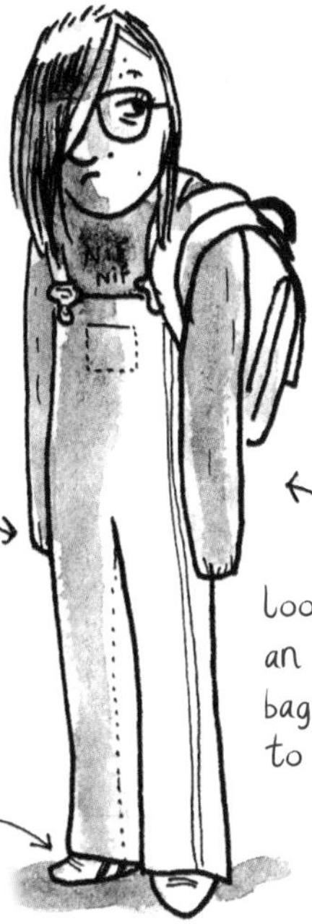

思春期。
私の興味は美術高校に
行く事だけです。両親、先生は
私には関係ないです。

Ugly teen years.
I don't care about anything (parents, teachers...) 'cause all I want to do is go to Nîmes and study Applied Arts.

手は袖の中
hands in my sleeves

Looking like an oversized bag (according to my mom)

母親の
嫌いな
スタイルをする
まるで服が
カバン

fake Adidas sneakers bought in Spain

スペインで
買ったニセ
アディダス

1997年

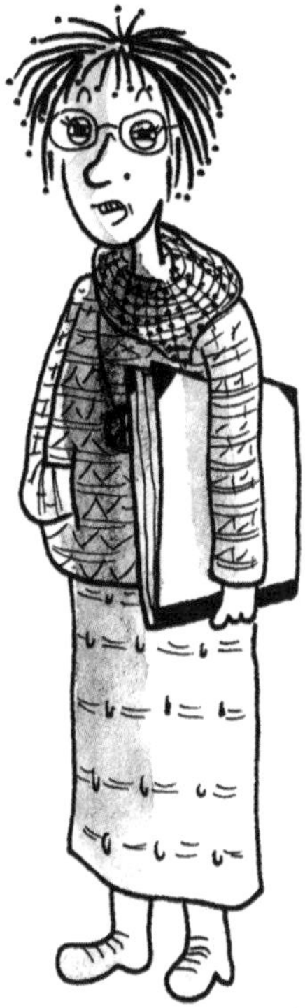
Anyway, fashion is for losers!

モードな
スタイルは
かっこよくないよね。

私はニームの美術高校にいます。
スタイルはラブ&ピース。
I made it to Nîmes, I'm studying applied art and I'm in "peace and love" mode.

1998年

トゥールーズの 美大にいます。
が、ストラスブール のアートスクールに
　行きたいので テストをします。

I'm studying art at the
University of Toulouse-Mirail. But
then I decide to take the exam
for the Strasbourg School of
Decorative Arts.

1999年

テストは合格です。
スクールが始まる前に 髪を短かく切り、
ボリビアに ボランティアをしに行きます。

I get in to Strasbourg. Before school
starts, I get a haircut and go volunteering
for a month in Bolivia.

PARIS
STRASBOURG
TOULOUSE
PERPIGNAN
SPAIN

STRASBOURG
SPECIALTIES

アルザス地方の
名物

脂100%
100% calories

BAECKEOFFE

ビール
beer

生クリーム 100%
100% cream

SAUERKRAUT

FLAMMEKUECHE

肉 100%
100% meat

December 2002 年12月

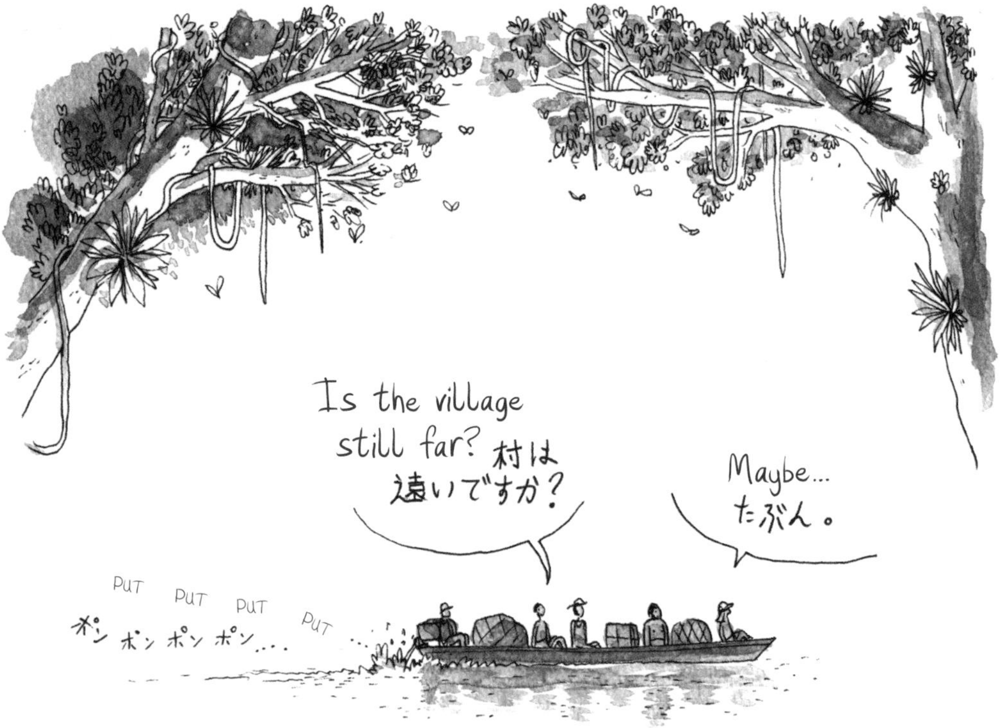

Is the village still far? 村は遠いですか？
Maybe... たぶん。
PUT PUT PUT PUT
ポン ポン ポン ポン…

I'm awarded a scholarship that lets me spend a month with a non-profit organization in the Amazon Rainforest.

ドキュメンタリーの
本の制作の為、
奨学金で
アマゾンに行きます。

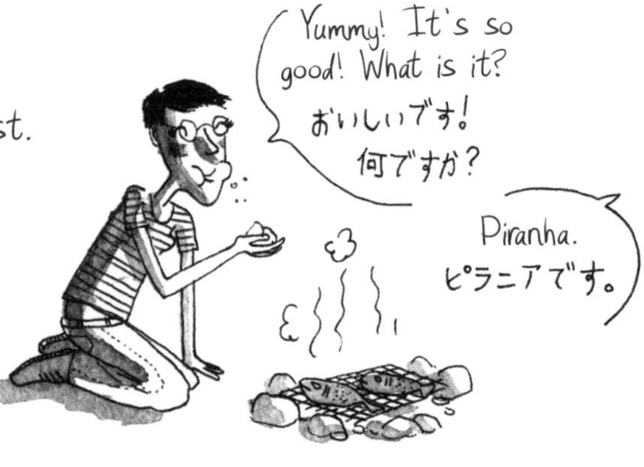

Yummy! It's so good! What is it? おいしいです！何ですか？
Piranha. ピラニアです。

I survive this project, get my master's, and enter the job market.

無事にアマゾンから戻り、
卒論に取りかかります。
これから就職活動を
します。

June 2004年6月

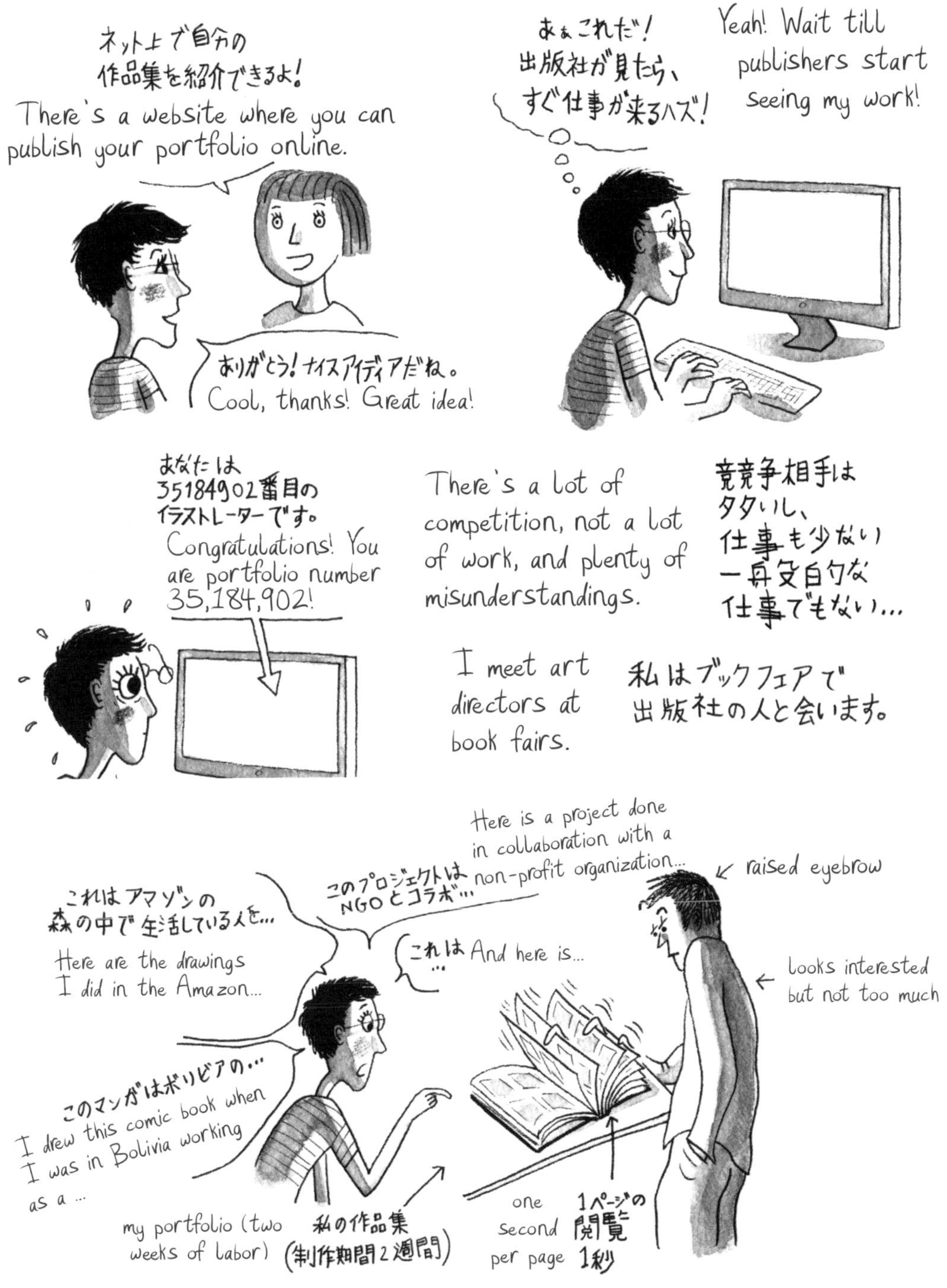
ネット上で自分の作品集を紹介できるよ!
There's a website where you can publish your portfolio online.
ありがとう! ナイスアイディアだね。
Cool, thanks! Great idea!
あぁこれだ! 出版社が見たら、すぐ仕事が来るハズ!
Yeah! Wait till publishers start seeing my work!
あなたは 35184902番目の イラストレーターです。
Congratulations! You are portfolio number 35,184,902!
There's a lot of competition, not a lot of work, and plenty of misunderstandings.
競争相手は多いし、仕事も少ない 一般的な仕事でもない…
I meet art directors at book fairs.
私はブックフェアで出版社の人と会います。
これはアマゾンの森の中で生活している人を…
Here are the drawings I did in the Amazon...
このプロジェクトは NGOとコラボ…
Here is a project done in collaboration with a non-profit organization...
raised eyebrow
これは…
And here is...
Looks interested but not too much
このマンガはボリビアの…
I drew this comic book when I was in Bolivia working as a ...
my portfolio (two weeks of labor)
私の作品集 (制作期間2週間)
one second per page
1ページの閲覧1秒

イラストレーターの 就職活動は アマゾンでの生活より 大変です。なので、生物学者と一緒に 6ヶ月間、アマゾンで 生活をします。そこで、私の 経験をもとに コミックを 作り、出版します。フレンチポリネシアの ブックフェアに ゲストとして 招待されます。

自慢します ←

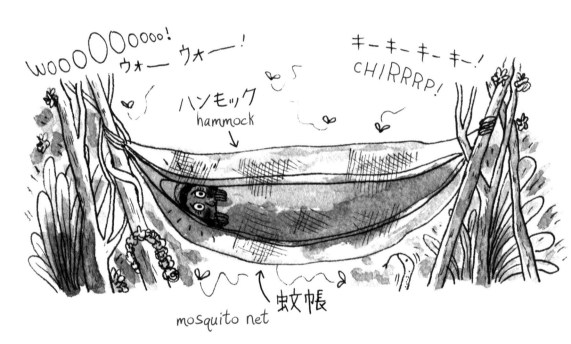

WOOOOOOOooo! ウォー ウォー！

キーキーキーキー！
CHIRRRP!

ハンモック
hammock

蚊帳
mosquito net

Being an illustrator turns out to be much more difficult than life in the Amazon. I end up spending six months on a documentary project about biologists in the jungles of French Guiana.

I publish a comic book about that adventure. In 2006, I am actually invited to the Papeete Book Fair in French Polynesia.
I take this opportunity to tour Tahiti and some of the surrounding islands for three weeks.

I'm flexing here →

2007 年

A science publisher comes across my comic book, and finds my ideas super interesting. So, with the publisher's help and accompanied by a designer friend, I go back to the Amazon Rainforest for two months to follow a team of ecologists. We publish a graphic novel about the expedition with a CD-Rom insert and I become a scientific illustrator.

コミックを出版したおかげで、学術誌の出版社から声がかかり
彼らの援助で、友達のグラフィックデザイナーと共にもう一度アマゾンへ
森林保護の技術者に会いに2ケ月間 行きます。
自伝 グラフィック ノベル を出版し学術誌系のイラストレーターになります。

アマゾン川
Amazon River

our boat
私たちのボート

I am so motivated that I come up with an idea for a huge new project—a collection of illustrated books about scientific research. I'm thinking big.

私はスーパーもチベーション。また新しいメガプロジェクトです。
自然科学の学術研究 シリーズの 制作です。
本当にスーパーメガ プロジェクトです。

November 2008 年11月

I get a few grants, enabling me to meet pygmy penguins in Australia and the ornithologists who study them.

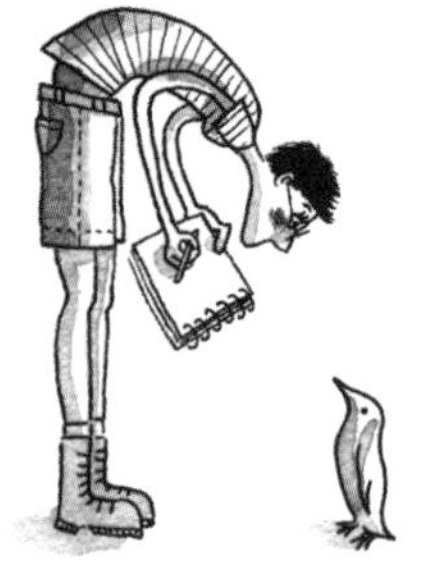

少し国から助成金をもらい、
オーストラリアにいる
コガタペンギンと鳥類学者に会います。

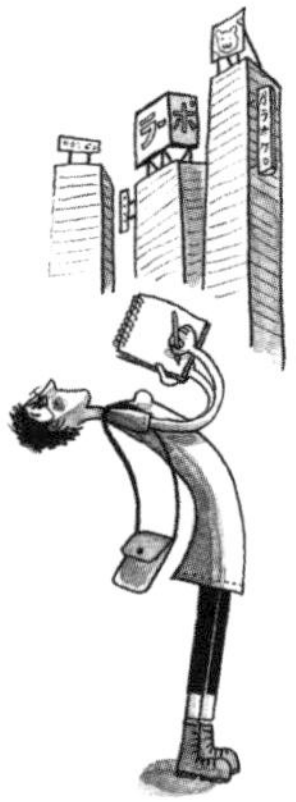

Then I go to Tokyo for 2 weeks to meet Japanese scientists who specialize in the polar regions because I hope to go with them to Antarctica.

そして東京へ。
極地研究の学者に会います。
今度は彼らに同行して
南極大陸へ足を踏み
入れたいです。

東京では2週間の滞在。国立極地研究所のメグムさん、サトシさん、カオリさんはとても素敵な人たちです。彼らに色いろ教えてもらいます。研究所の仕事内容と… 日本を。

Megumi and Satoshi from the National Institute of Polar Research introduce me to their work and to... life in Japan!

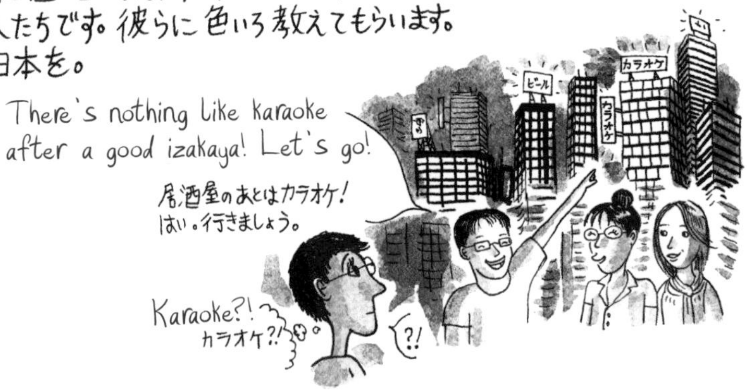
There's nothing like karaoke after a good izakaya! Let's go!
居酒屋のあとはカラオケ!
はい。行きましょう。
Karaoke?!
カラオケ?!
?!
カラオケ
ビール

後日、温泉にて。 The day after...

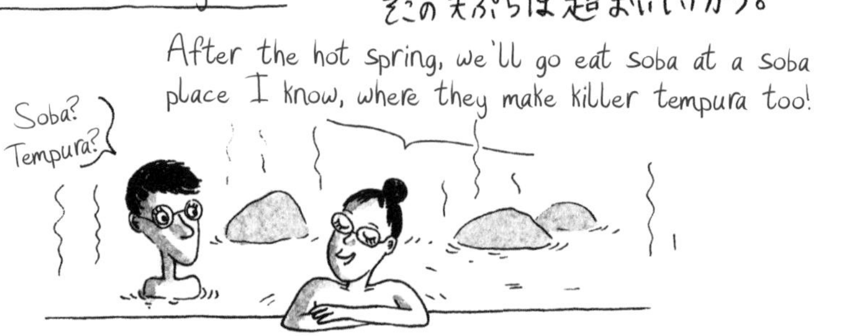
あがったら私の知っているそば屋へ行こう。
そこの天ぷらは超おいしいから。
After the hot spring, we'll go eat soba at a soba place I know, where they make killer tempura too!
Soba?
Tempura?

I am fascinated by this country I don't know much about.
日本をあまり知らなかった私。いつの間にかこの国に魅了されます。

October 2009年10月

Because I'm hoping to take part in the expedition to Antarctica aboard the Japanese icebreaker Shirase, I decide to spend a year in Tokyo so I can prepare properly.

南極観測船「しらせ」に乗るために
もう一度東京に来て1年間、その準備をします。

But alas! I don't get the grants I was expecting from important scientific organizations! And I'm already en route to Japan...

が、大惨事です！国からの助成金が下りず、私の期待を
裏切る結果となります。もう日本へ向かう飛行機に
乗っています。

So what am I going to do in Tokyo?

私は東京でどうなりますか？

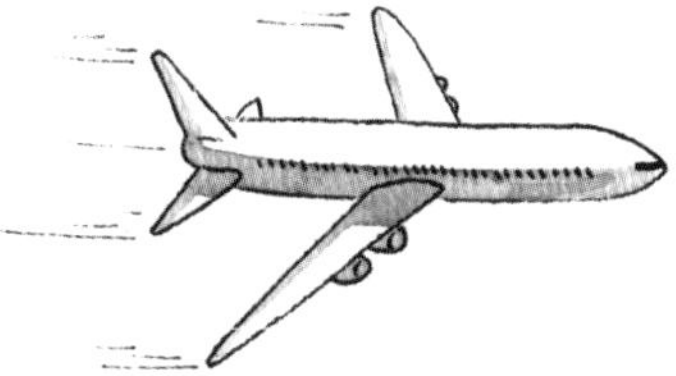

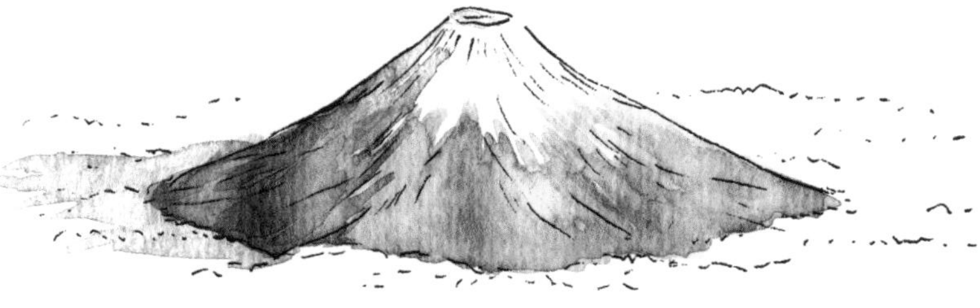

Tokyo
東京

"Greater Tokyo" (or the "National Capital Region") is the largest metropolitan area in the world, with 43 million inhabitants. Even so, living in Tokyo doesn't feel stifling.

The population density of Tokyo is 16,433 inhabitants per sq mi (6,394 per km2). New York has 27,000 people per sq mi (38,242 per km2).

It's easy to move around Tokyo using public transportation. Not counting the suburbs, Tokyo is crisscrossed by
- 31 Japan Rail (JR) lines
- 11 Tokyo Metro subway lines
- 7 Toei subway lines
- 39 private train lines (subways or above ground)

碑文谷
4. HIMONYA, NEAR GAKUGEI DAIGAKU

TAMAGAWA

玉川

LEGEND 説明
Places I've lived
住んだ場所
Important stations 大きな駅

1. TAMAGAWA GAKUEN MAE, NEAR MACHIDA 町田

0 ⊢———————⊣ 3 miles (5 km)

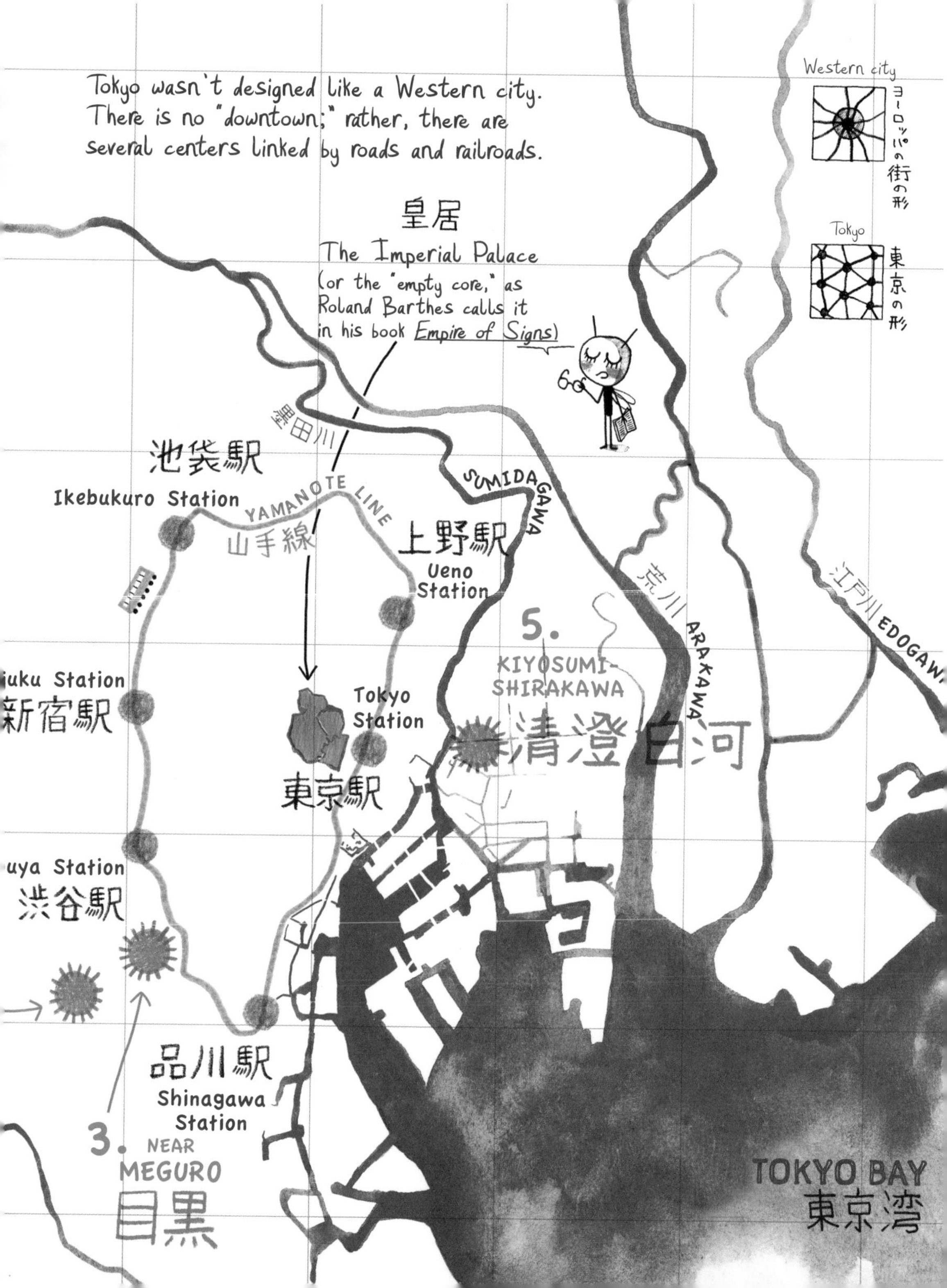

Tokyo wasn't designed like a Western city. There is no "downtown;" rather, there are several centers linked by roads and railroads.
Western city
ヨーロッパの街の形
Tokyo
東京の形
皇居
The Imperial Palace
(or the "empty core," as Roland Barthes calls it in his book Empire of Signs)
墨田川
SUMIDAGAWA
池袋駅
Ikebukuro Station
YAMANOTE LINE
山手線
上野駅
Ueno Station
荒川
ARAKAWA
江戸川
EDOGAWA
5.
KIYOSUMI-SHIRAKAWA
清澄白河
iuku Station
新宿駅
Tokyo Station
東京駅
uya Station
渋谷駅
品川駅
Shinagawa Station
3.
NEAR MEGURO
目黒
TOKYO BAY
東京湾

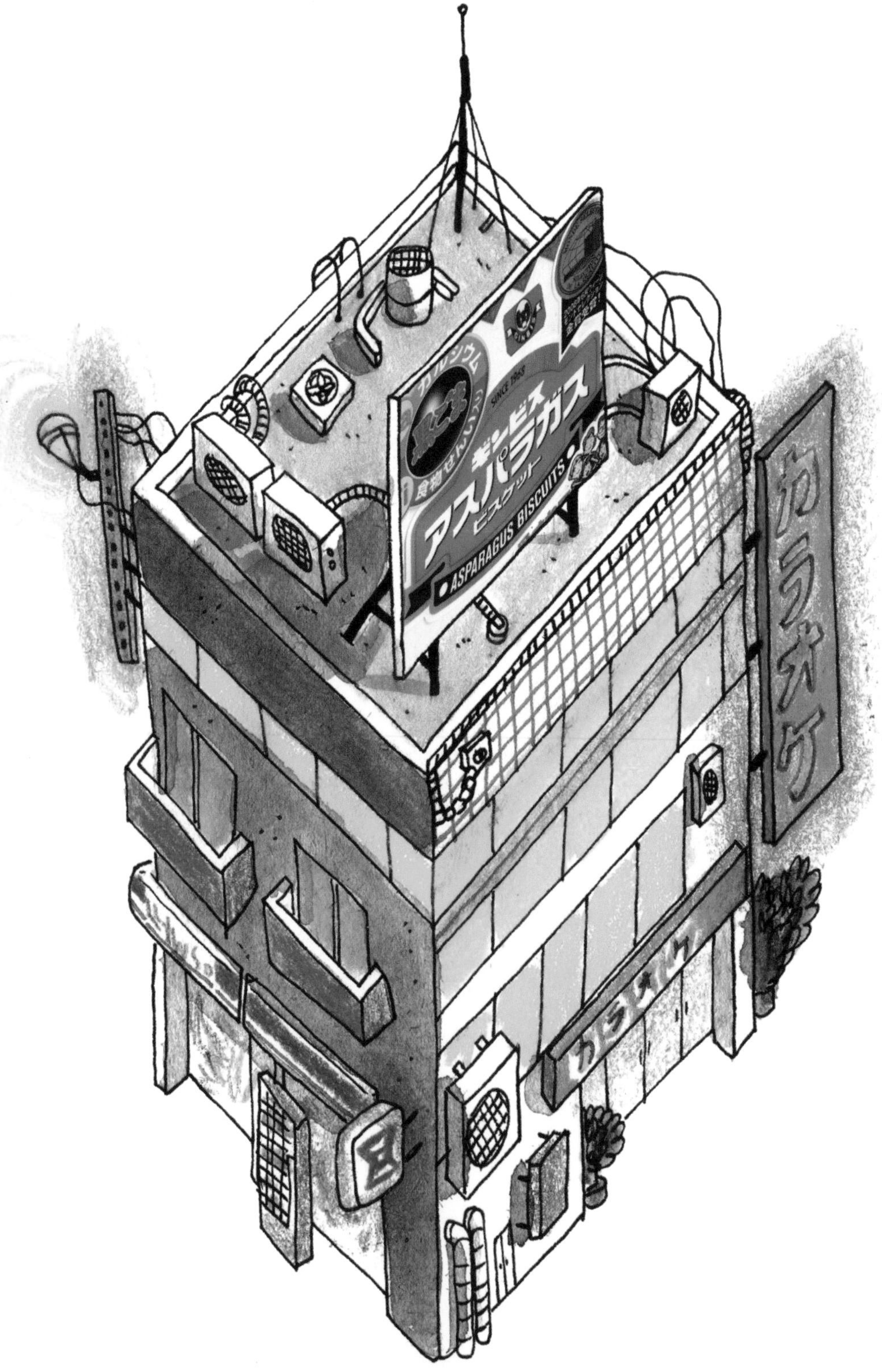

ギンビス
アスパラガス
ビスケット
SINCE 1968
ASPARAGUS BISCUITS
カラオケ
カラオケ

Living in
Machida
町田

A Room of My Own in Tamagawagakuen-mae
玉川学園前のシャールハウス

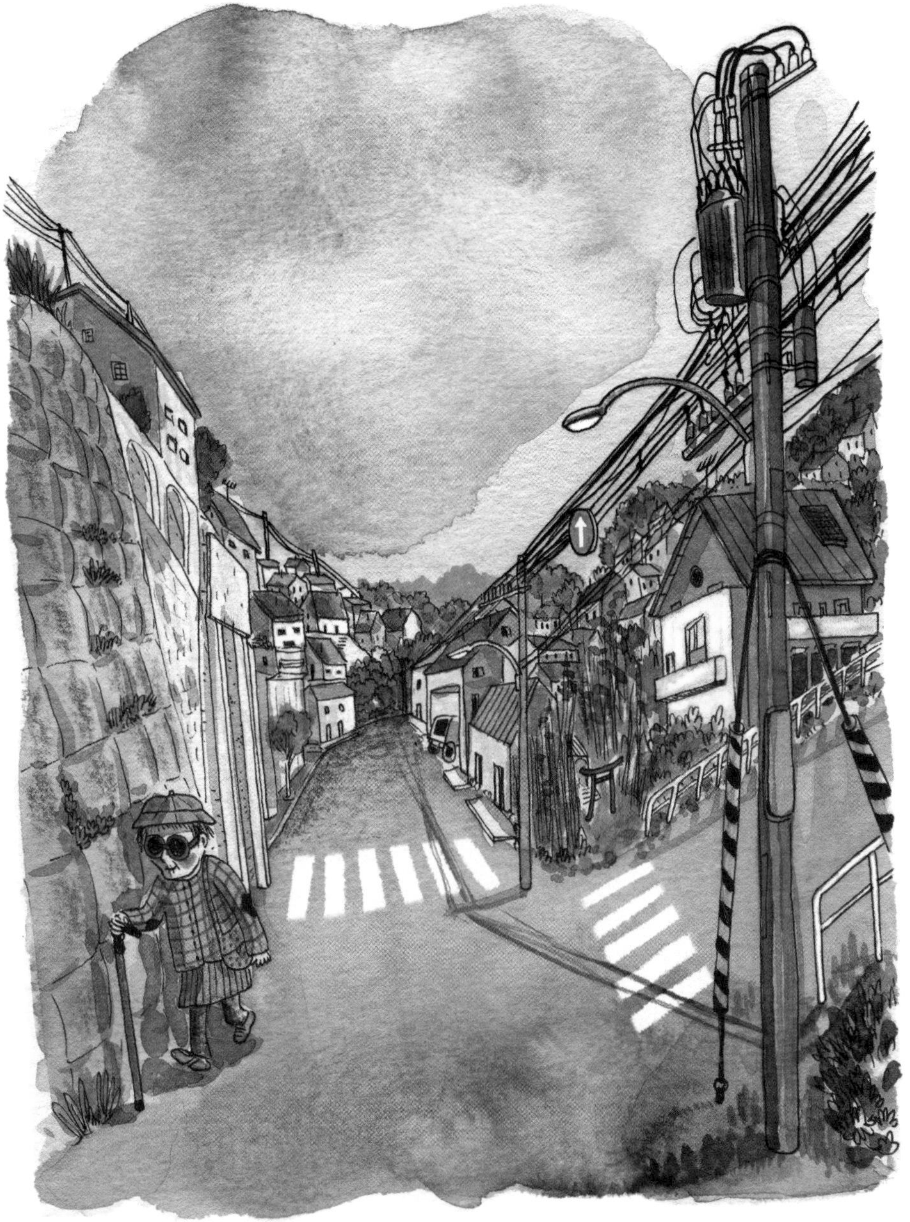

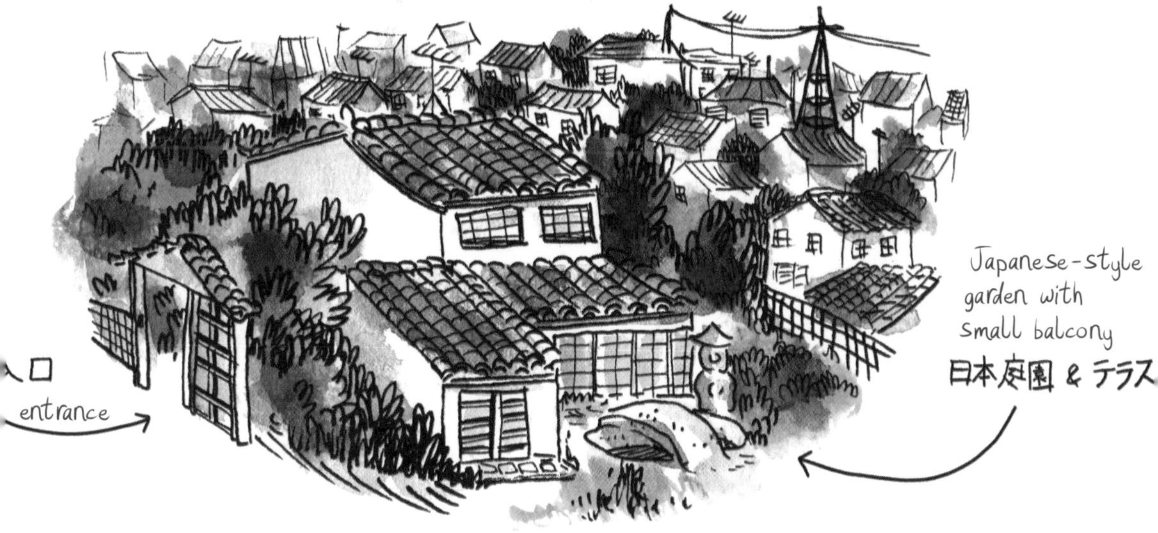
入口
entrance
Japanese-style garden with small balcony
日本庭園 & テラス

Since I don't have a lot of money, I start by sharing a rental house in a suburb west of Tokyo. It's nice there, with regular commuter trains, and we're only 30 minutes away from Shinjuku Station, one of Tokyo's huge transportation hubs.

私はリッチではないので、
都心からはなれた
シェアハウスに住みます。
この家はとても住みやすいです。
駅も近いし急行で
新宿まで30分です。

私はこの部屋が大好きです。
外国人がイメージする
これぞ日本の部屋という感じです。

My room is simply awesome, with tatami matting and shoji screen doors. I feel like I'm in an 80s deodorant ad.

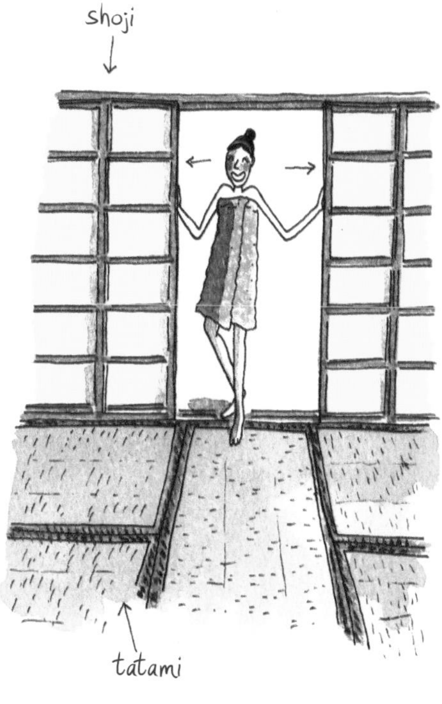
shoji
tatami

KAMPAI!

My roommates are nice too and come from all over the world—Japan, Korea, Canada, England...

私のシェアメイトは とても 良い 人達です。
いろんな 国の 出身 です。
日本、韓国、カナダ、イギリス など...

I work on a few illustration commissions, and with Rina, one of my roommates, we often organize BBQs.

私は フリーランスの イラストレーションの
仕事をしながら ときどき りなさんと
バーベキューを します。

Rina is Japanese. She's back from a year in Australia. She's unemployed right now so she has lots of free time.

りなさんは オーストラリアの
ワーキングホリデーから
帰って来たばかりです。
今は 仕事がないので 時間があります。

A big drawback with this house is its fauna.

よくない事があります。
たくさんの虫と
一緒に暮らします。

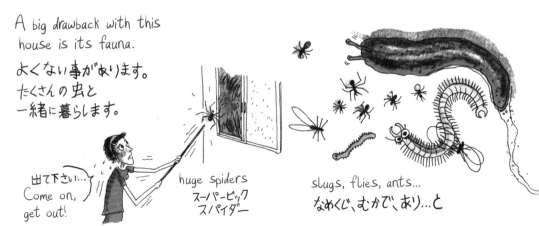

出て下さい...
Come on, get out!

huge spiders
スーパービック
スパイダー

slugs, flies, ants...
なめくじ、むかで、あり...と

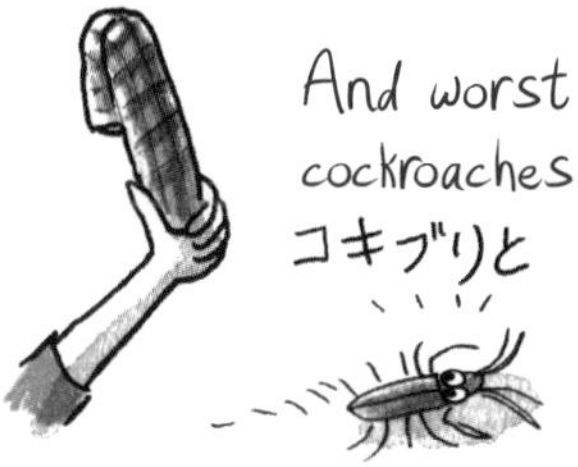

And worst of all, cockroaches.
コキブリと

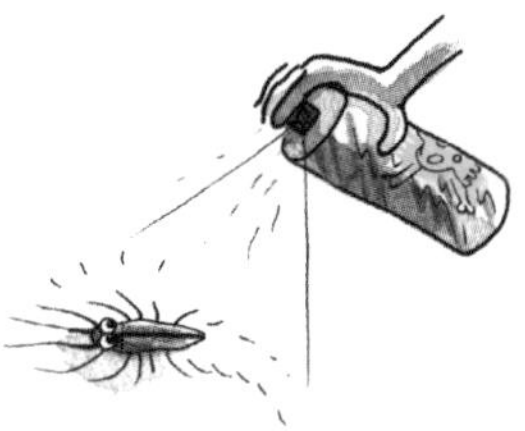

and more cockroaches.
ゴキブリです。

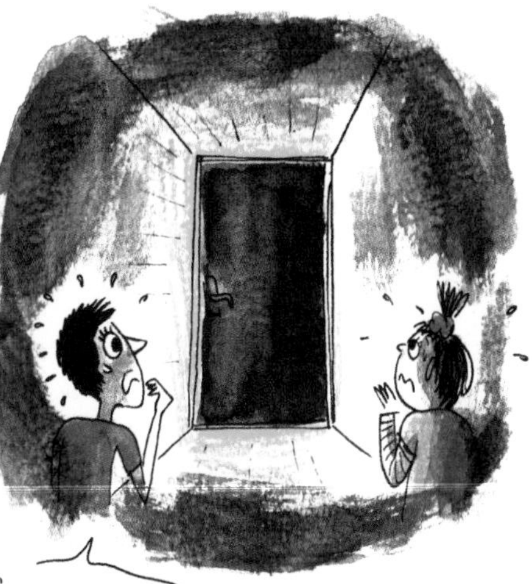
It's been a week since he locked himself in his room!
一週間以上、会っていません。

Like most Asian countries Japan is humid, so cockroaches are a fact of life. If you live in a clean and well-kept house, it's ok. But we live with the shyest guy in the universe, so shy that he never makes food in the communal kitchen or even leaves his room to take out his trash. So our house is a cockroach paradise.

世界で一番シャイなんも住んでいます。
部屋から出ません。ゴミもたまります。
ゴキブリはうれしいです。

ときどき、りなさんと出かけます。
新宿、渋谷、下北沢…
そうなると帰る方法は2つです。

I go out with Rina from time to time. We have two choices for getting back home:

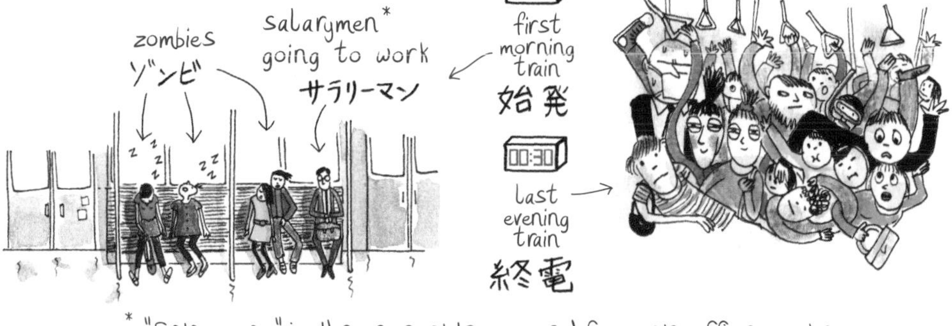
zombies
ゾンビ
salarymen* going to work
サラリーマン
05:00
first morning train
始発
00:30
last evening train
終電

* "Salaryman" is the general term used for male office workers. For women, the term "office lady" is used. Most office ladies and salarymen must obey a dress code of skirts and blazers for women and suits for men.

Ofuro (Japanese Bath)

However, one big advantage of living in a Japanese house is experiencing the joy of taking a Japanese bath every evening!

日本のお風呂のシステムはすばらしいです。外国とはちがいます。

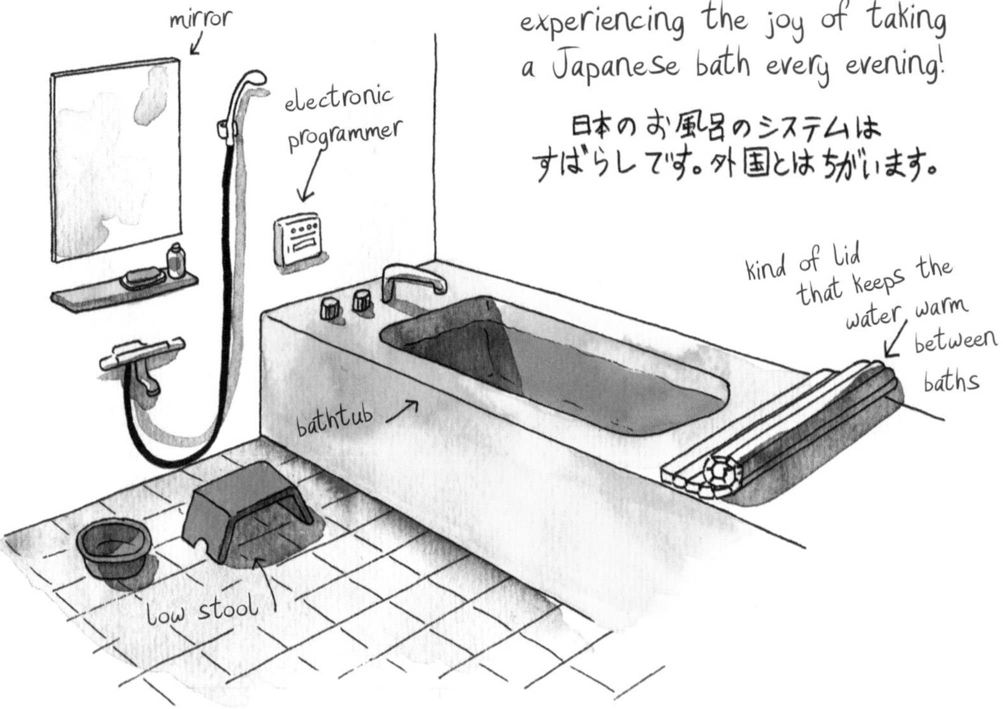

mirror
electronic programmer
kind of lid that keeps the water warm between baths
bathtub
low stool

日本のお風呂 How to Take a Japanese Bath

After showering,

最初に体を洗います。

1

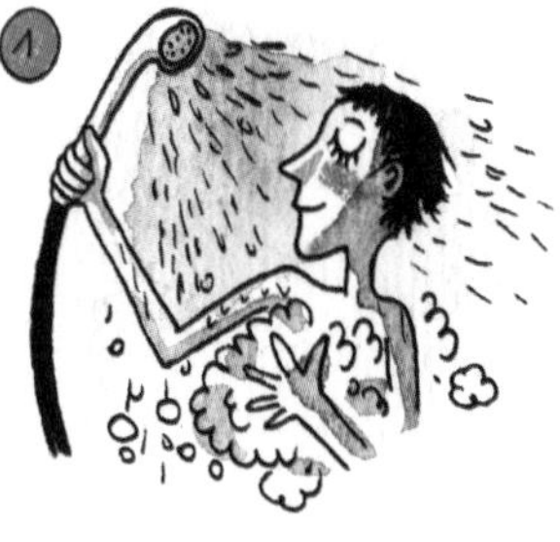

you get into the hot bath

2

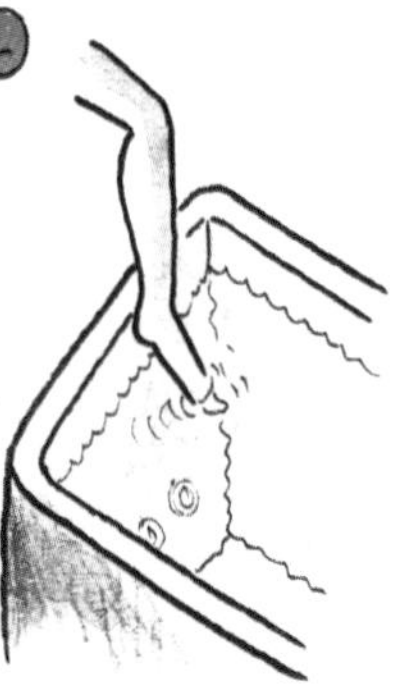

and the great thing is that the water stays clean, so you can reuse it.

3

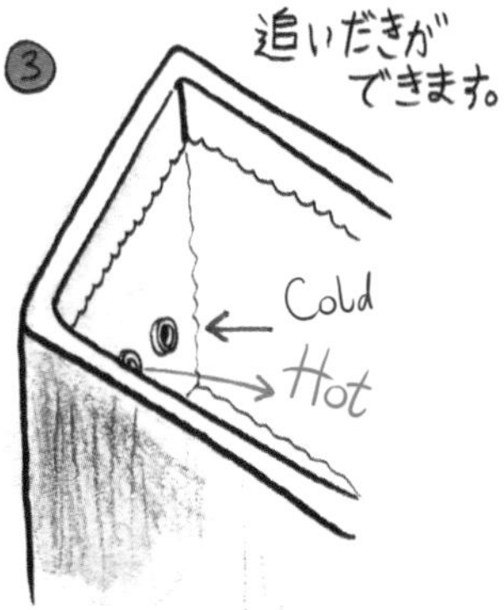

追いだきができます。
Cold
Hot

The Onsen 温泉

From youngest to oldest volcano
island forming
island island
island
island
sea
SHIFTING TECTONIC PLATE
magma
All of this happening over many thousands of years, needless to say.

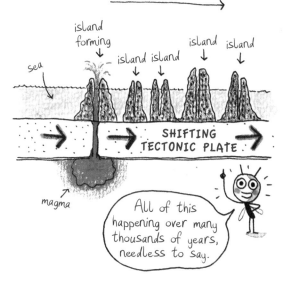

Japan is an archipelago of more than 6,800 volcanic islands situated right where several tectonic plates meet. That's why there are so many volcanoes, as well as hot springs, which are called "onsen" in Japanese.

日本人にとって温泉とその文化は一般的ですが、外国人にとっては特別なものです。

There are so many onsen that the pleasures of bathing have permeated Japanese popular culture. Nowadays, there are managed onsen everywhere; you go with your friends or family; there's often a restaurant, a hotel, gift shops... In other words, taking a trip to the onsen is a lifestyle.

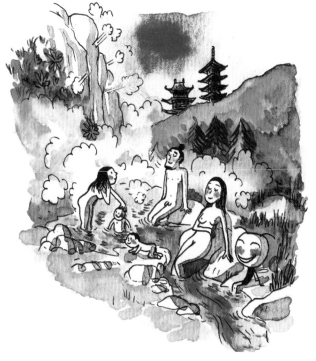

気持ちがいいので
温泉は裸で入ります。
19世紀ごろから、
宗教的な影響で
男風呂と女風呂が
分けられます。

In order to relax completely, you bathe completely naked at the onsen. In the old days, men and women bathed together, but that changed with the influence of Western culture in the 19th century. Since Westerners considered nakedness sinful, baths became segregated. This was before the days of "flower power"!

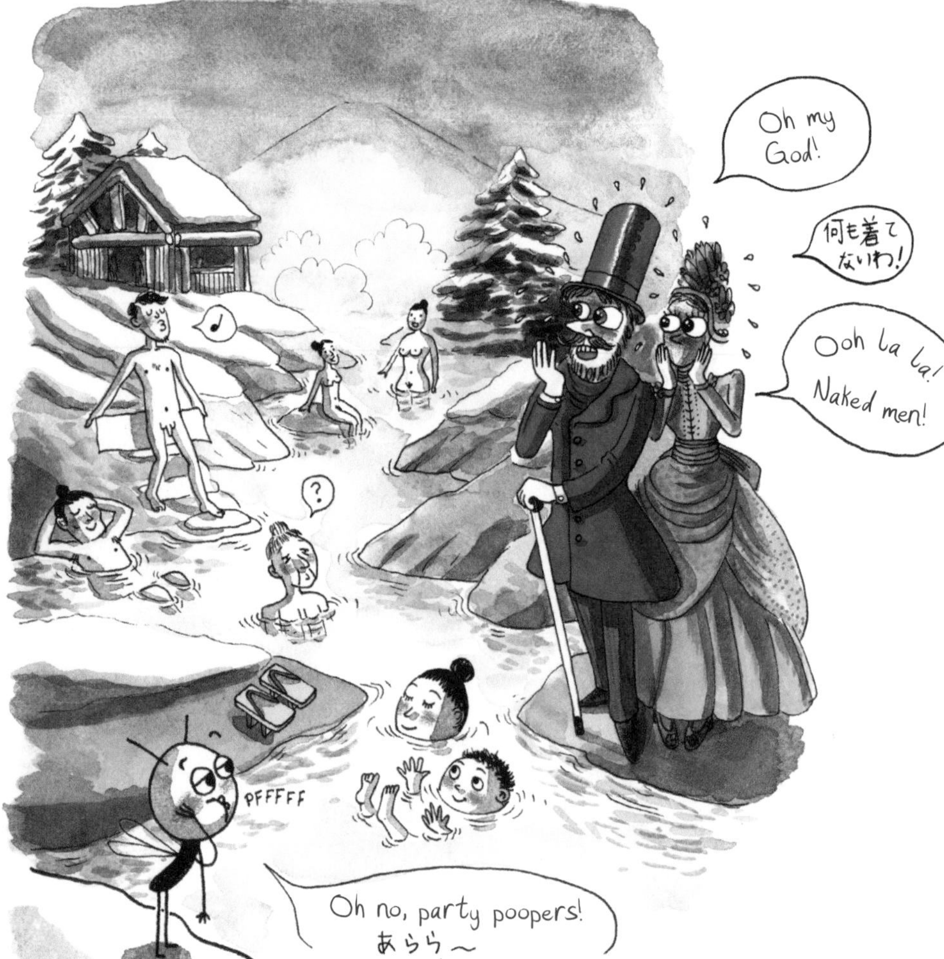
Oh my God!
何も着てないわ!
Ooh la la! Naked men!
?
PFFFFF
Oh no, party poopers!
あらら～
たいした事じゃないよ

昔話はともかく、
温泉に入ります。
So that's the history. Now, I'll give you a tour!

入り口をまちがえると、
はずかしいです。
First, use the proper door if you want to avoid embarrassing yourself.

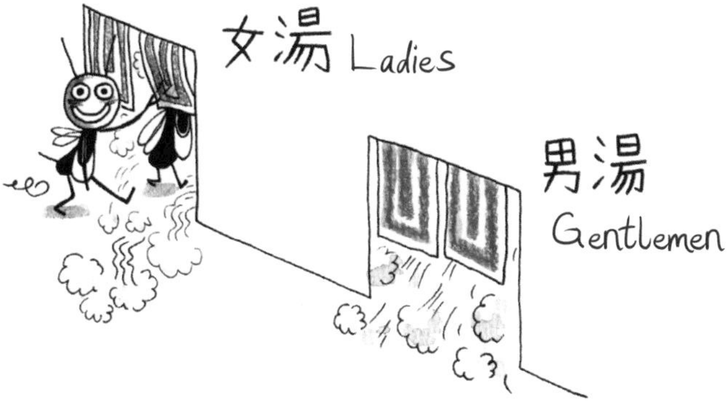
女湯 Ladies
男湯
Gentlemen

Inside, there are changing rooms.
脱衣所

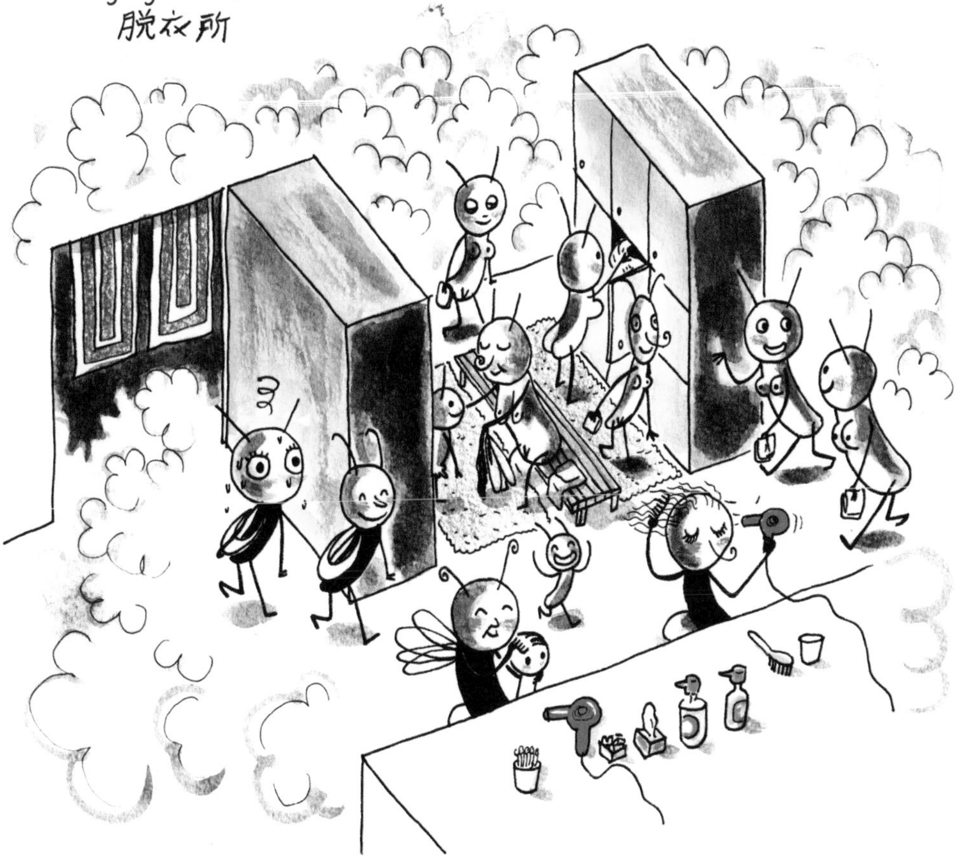

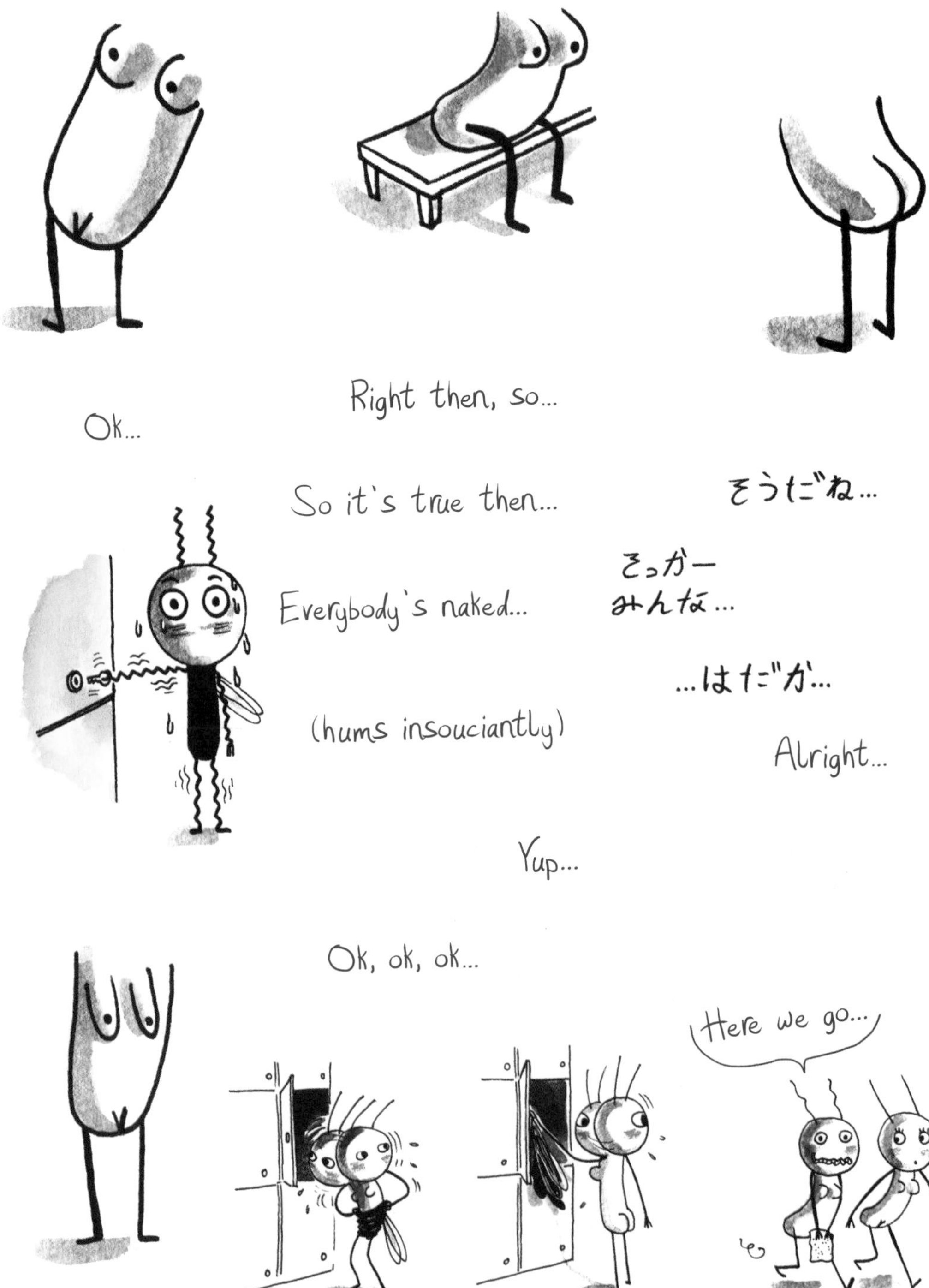

Ok...
Right then, so...
So it's true then...
そうだね…
Everybody's naked...
そっかー
みんな…
…はだか…
(hums insouciantly)
Alright...
Yup...
Ok, ok, ok...
Here we go...
?

Just like with the ofuro you wash yourself first.
温泉に入る前に…

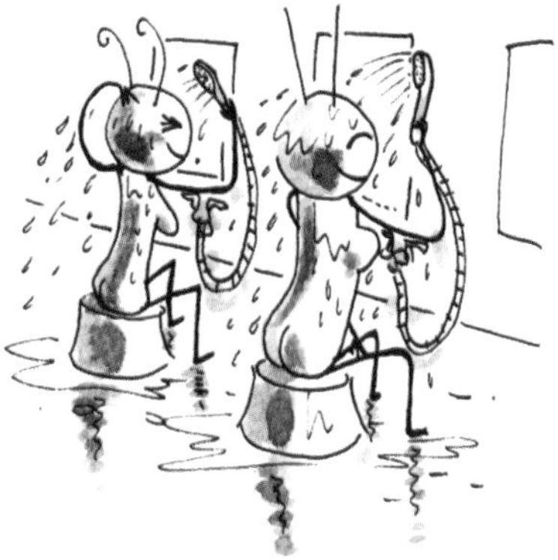

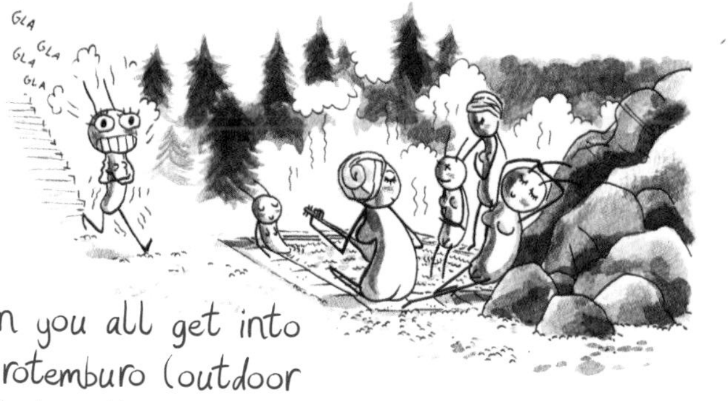
GLA
GLA
GLA
GLA

Then you all get into the rotemburo (outdoor pool) together.

すべりやすいので走るの禁止!
(No running—it's slippery!)

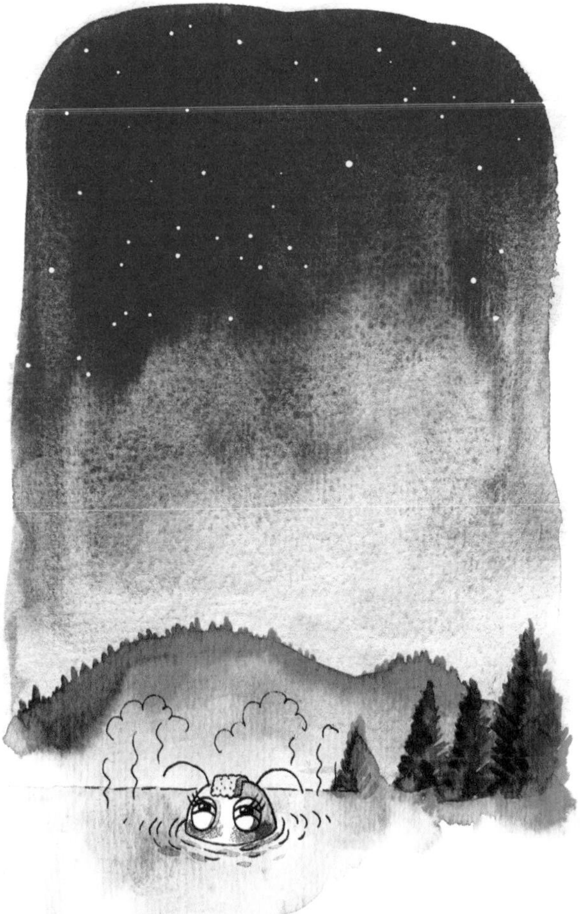

Like a newborn child
The trees beneath shining stars
It's a perfect night.

しもつきに
てぬぐいひとつ
ほしともり

The Party パーティー

土曜の夜。東京のおしゃれでクールな場所、中目黒で。

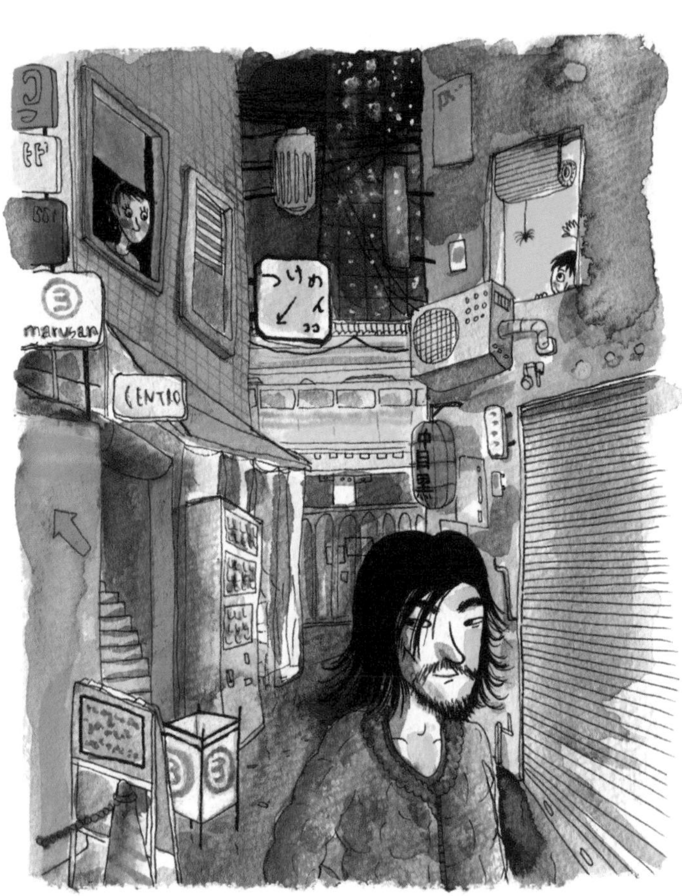

marusan
CENTRO
つけめん
中目黒

日本人アーティストに会いたいので、いろんなアートエキシビジョンへ行きます。アートプロデューサーのおかげで、今日はゲストとして入場します。

Saturday evening in Nakameguro, a cool and fashionable area of Tokyo. Since I want to meet Japanese artists, I gatecrash all the gallery openings and parties I can find. And then one day, a Japanese producer invites me to a techno party at a Nakameguro club.

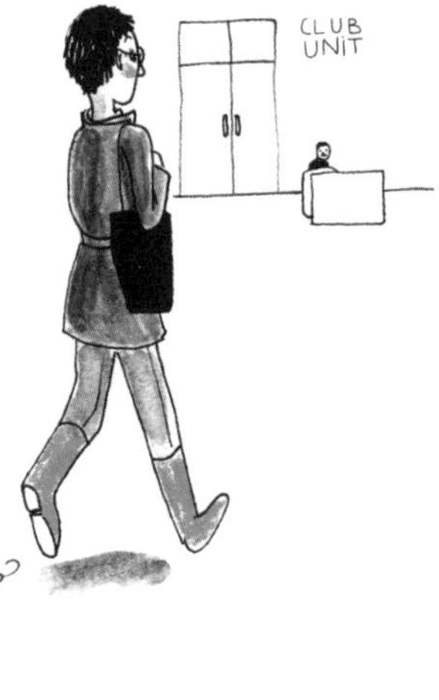

CLUB UNIT

invisible step
ここに見えない段があります。

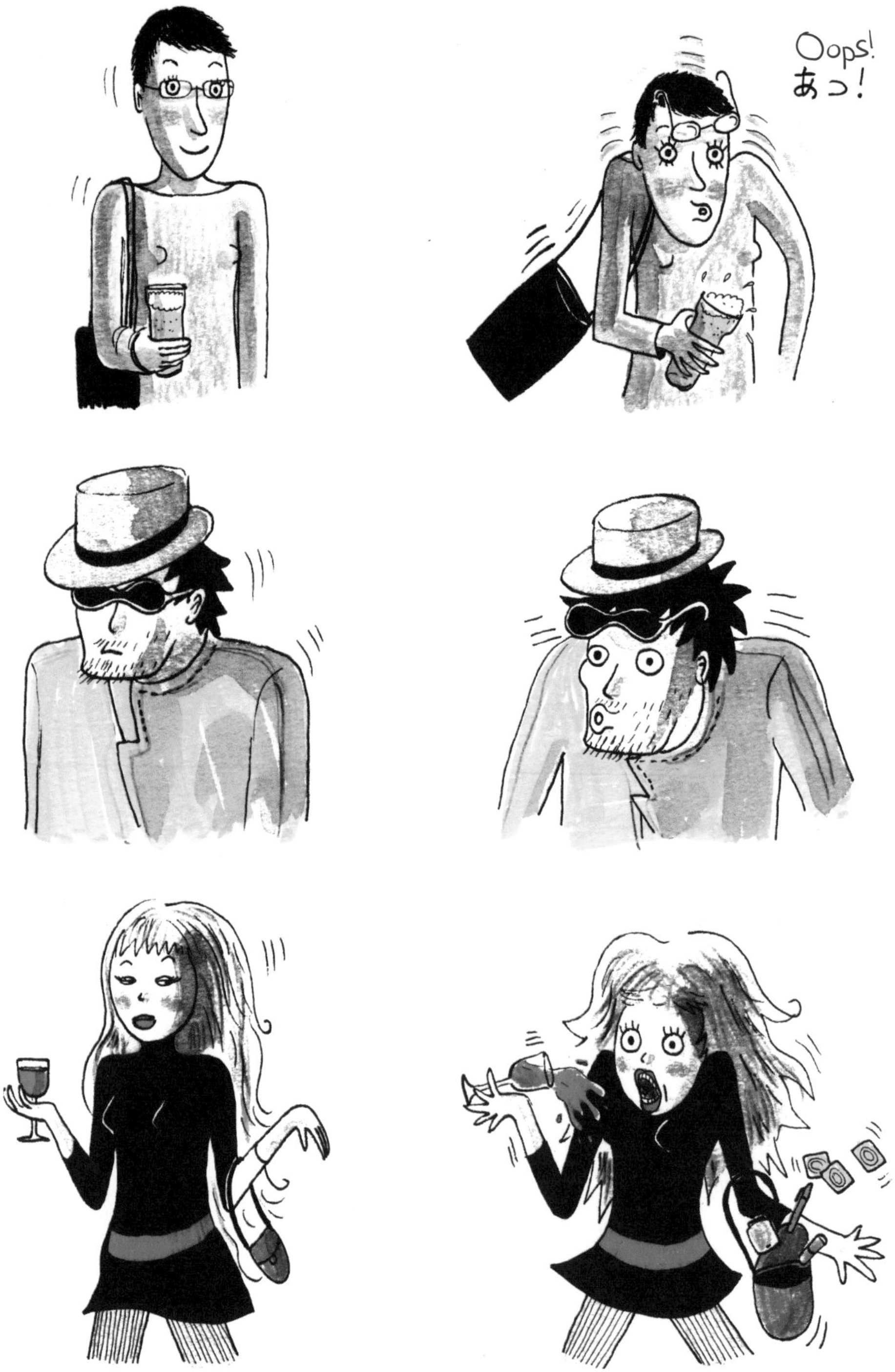
Oops!
あっ!

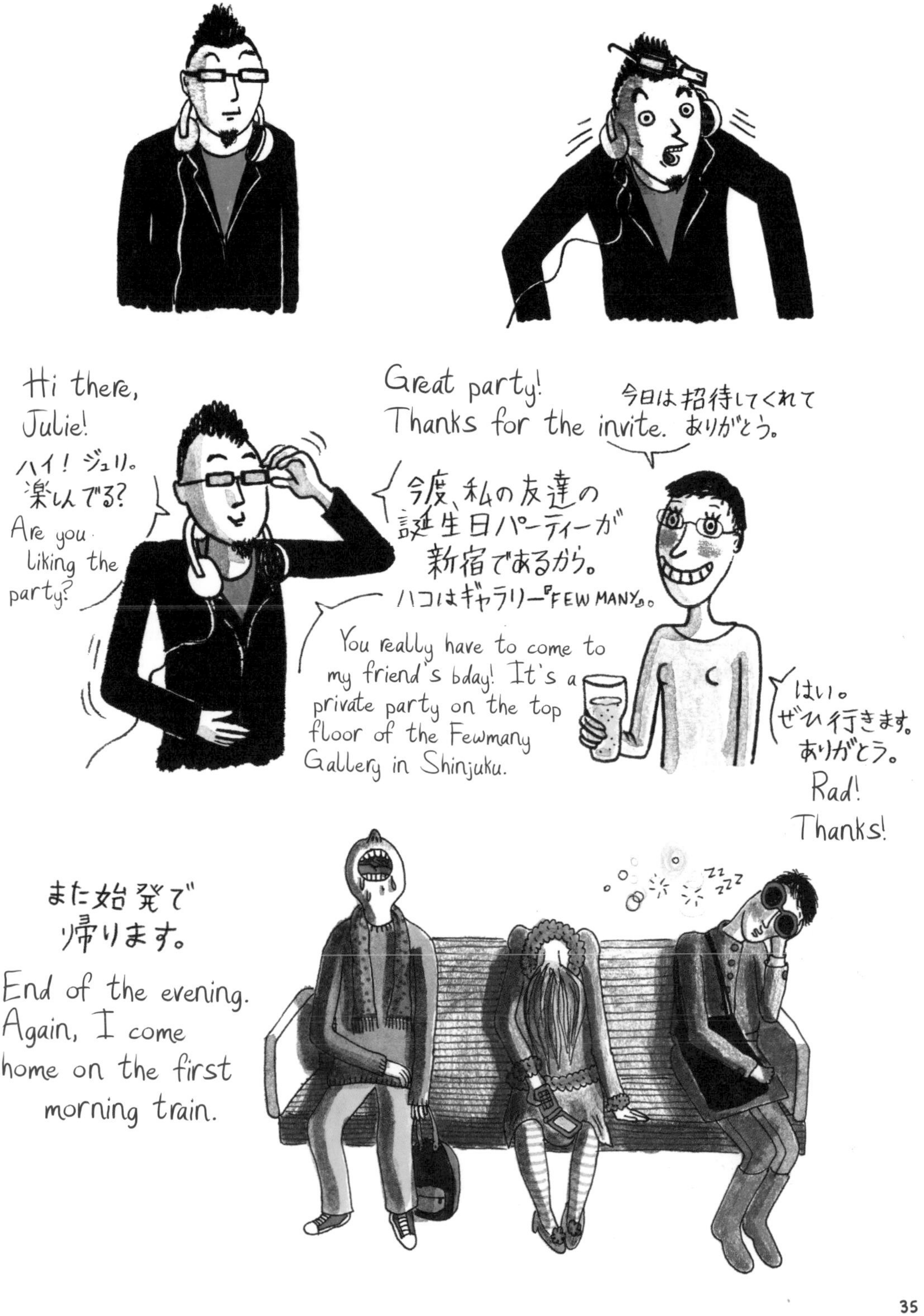

Hi there, Julie!
ハイ！ジュリ。楽しんでる?
Are you liking the party?
Great party! Thanks for the invite.
今日は招待してくれてありがとう。
今度、私の友達の誕生日パーティーが新宿であるから。
ハコはギャラリー『FEW MANY』。
You really have to come to my friend's bday! It's a private party on the top floor of the Fewmany Gallery in Shinjuku.
はい。ぜひ行きます。ありがとう。
Rad! Thanks!
また始発で帰ります。
End of the evening. Again, I come home on the first morning train.

The Gift プレゼント

Shinjuku, 6:30 pm. The course I teach on animation has just ended.

午後6時半、新宿。
私の教えるアニメのクラスも
終わり、ホッとひと息。

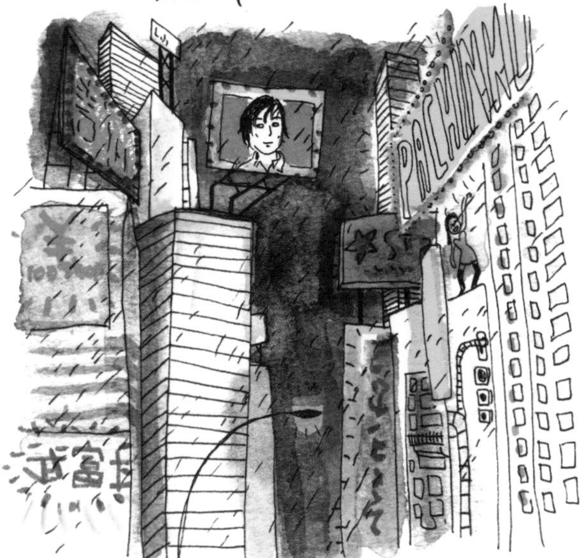
PACHINKO

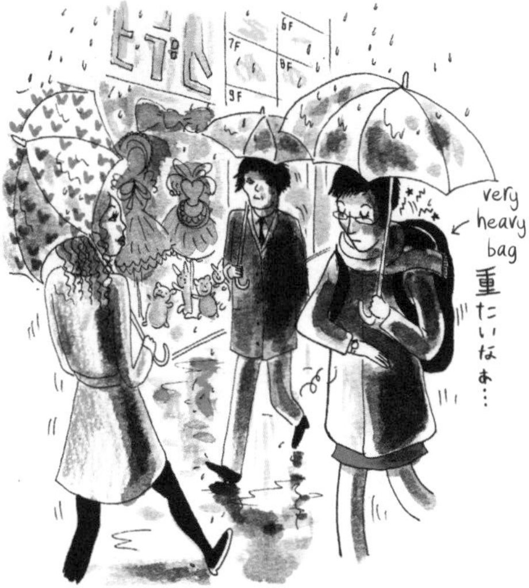
very heavy bag
重たいなぁ…

誕生日パーティーまであと1時間。
その前にプレゼントを探さなくちゃ。

I have one hour left before the party starts, just enough time to buy a gift.

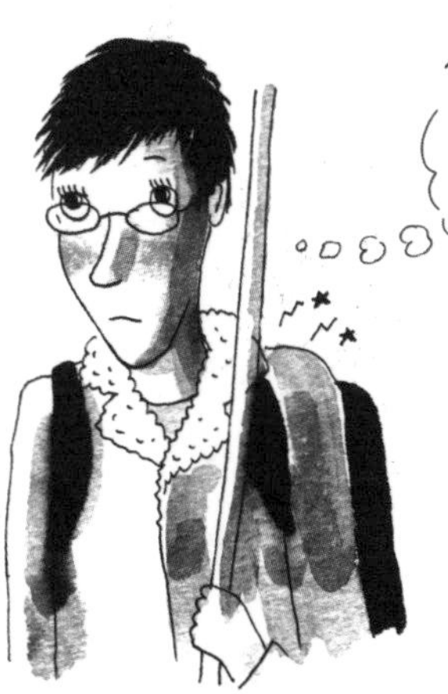
プレゼントは
何がいいかな?
What could I buy?

It needs to be something stylish since they'll all be artists...

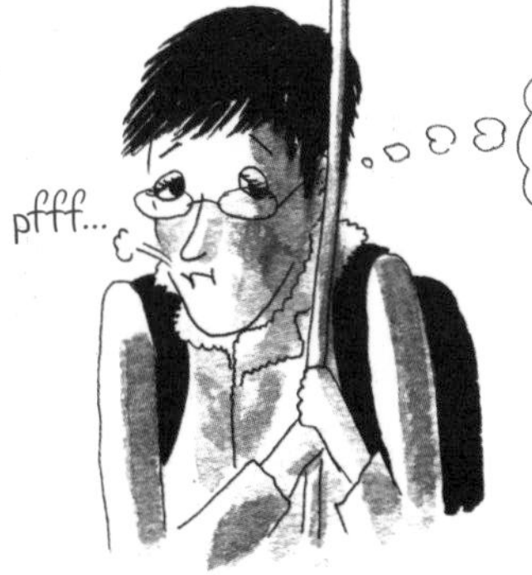
Not easy...
来る人達はみんな
アーティストばかり
だからむずかしい…
pfff...

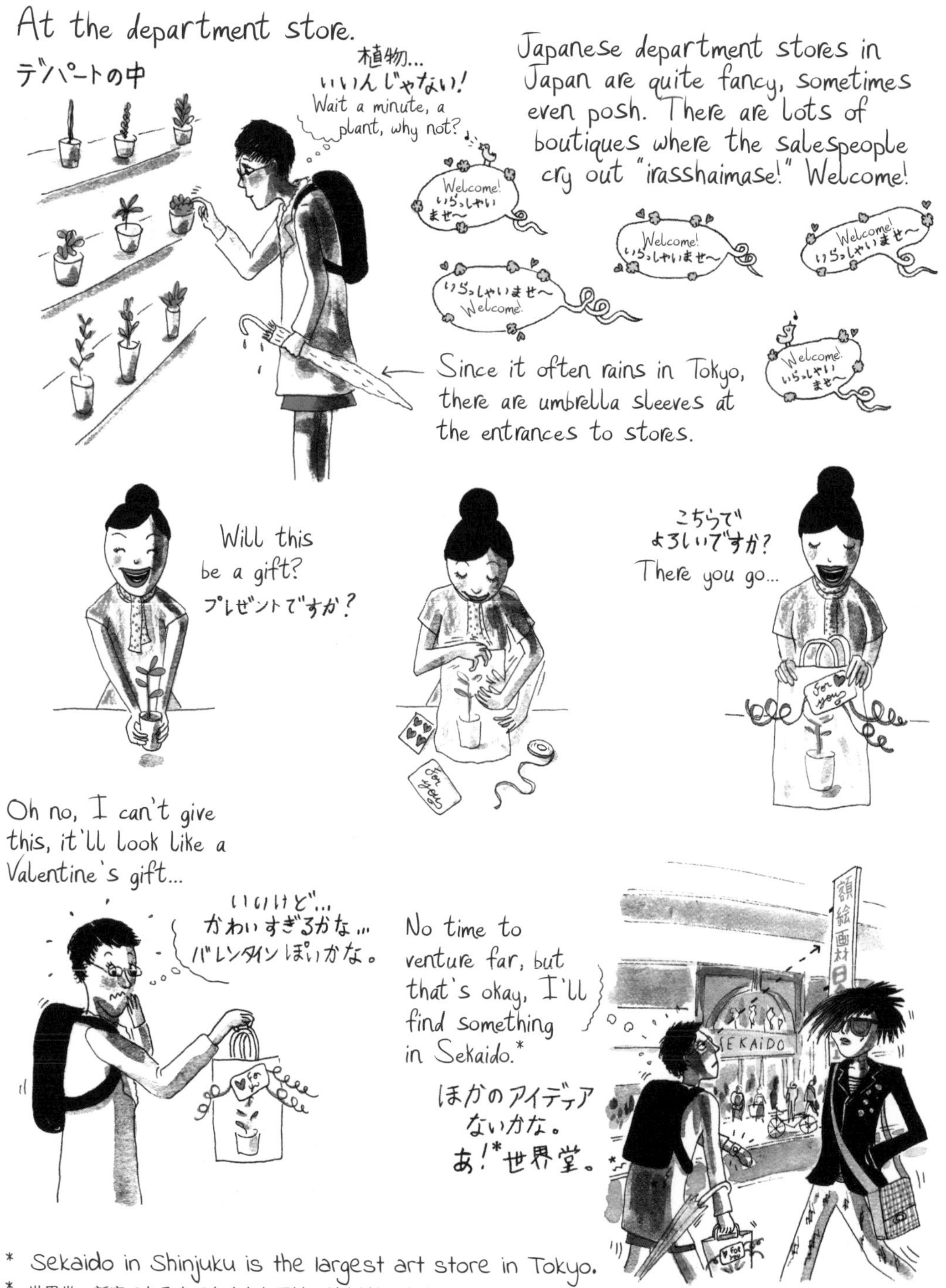
At the department store.
デパートの中
植物…
いいんじゃない!
Wait a minute, a plant, why not?
Japanese department stores in Japan are quite fancy, sometimes even posh. There are lots of boutiques where the salespeople cry out "irasshaimase!" Welcome!
Welcome! いらっしゃいませ〜
Welcome! いらっしゃいませ〜
Welcome! いらっしゃいませ〜
いらっしゃいませ〜 Welcome!
Welcome! いらっしゃいませ〜
Since it often rains in Tokyo, there are umbrella sleeves at the entrances to stores.
Will this be a gift?
プレゼントですか?
For you
こちらでよろしいですか?
There you go...
For you
Oh no, I can't give this, it'll look like a Valentine's gift...
いいけど…
かわいすぎるかな…
バレンタインぽいかな。
No time to venture far, but that's okay, I'll find something in Sekaido.*
ほかのアイデアないかな。
あ!*世界堂。
額絵画材
SEKAIDO

* Sekaido in Shinjuku is the largest art store in Tokyo.

* 世界堂：新宿にあるとても大きな画材、がくぶちのお店。

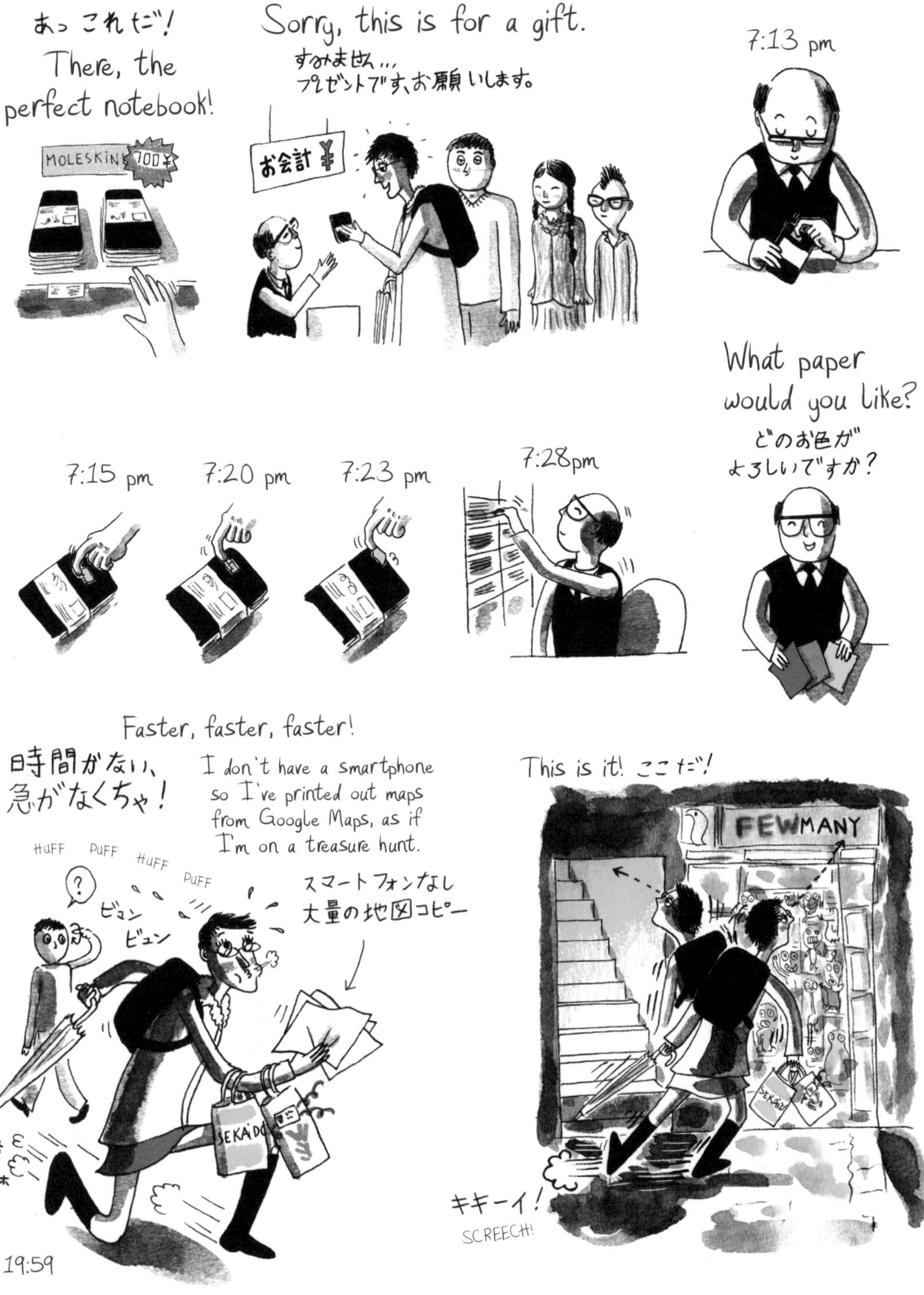
あっ これだ！
There, the perfect notebook!
MOLESKIN
700¥
Sorry, this is for a gift.
すみません…、
プレゼントです、お願いします。
お会計 ¥
7:13 pm
What paper would you like?
どのお色が
よろしいですか？
7:15 pm
7:20 pm
7:23 pm
7:28pm
Faster, faster, faster!
時間がない、
急がなくちゃ！
I don't have a smartphone so I've printed out maps from Google Maps, as if I'm on a treasure hunt.
HuFF
PuFF
HuFF
PuFF
?
ビュン
ビュン
スマートフォンなし
大量の地図コピー
エッホ
エッホ
SEKAIDO
19:59
This is it! ここだ！
FEWMANY
SEKAIDO
キキーイ！
SCREECH!

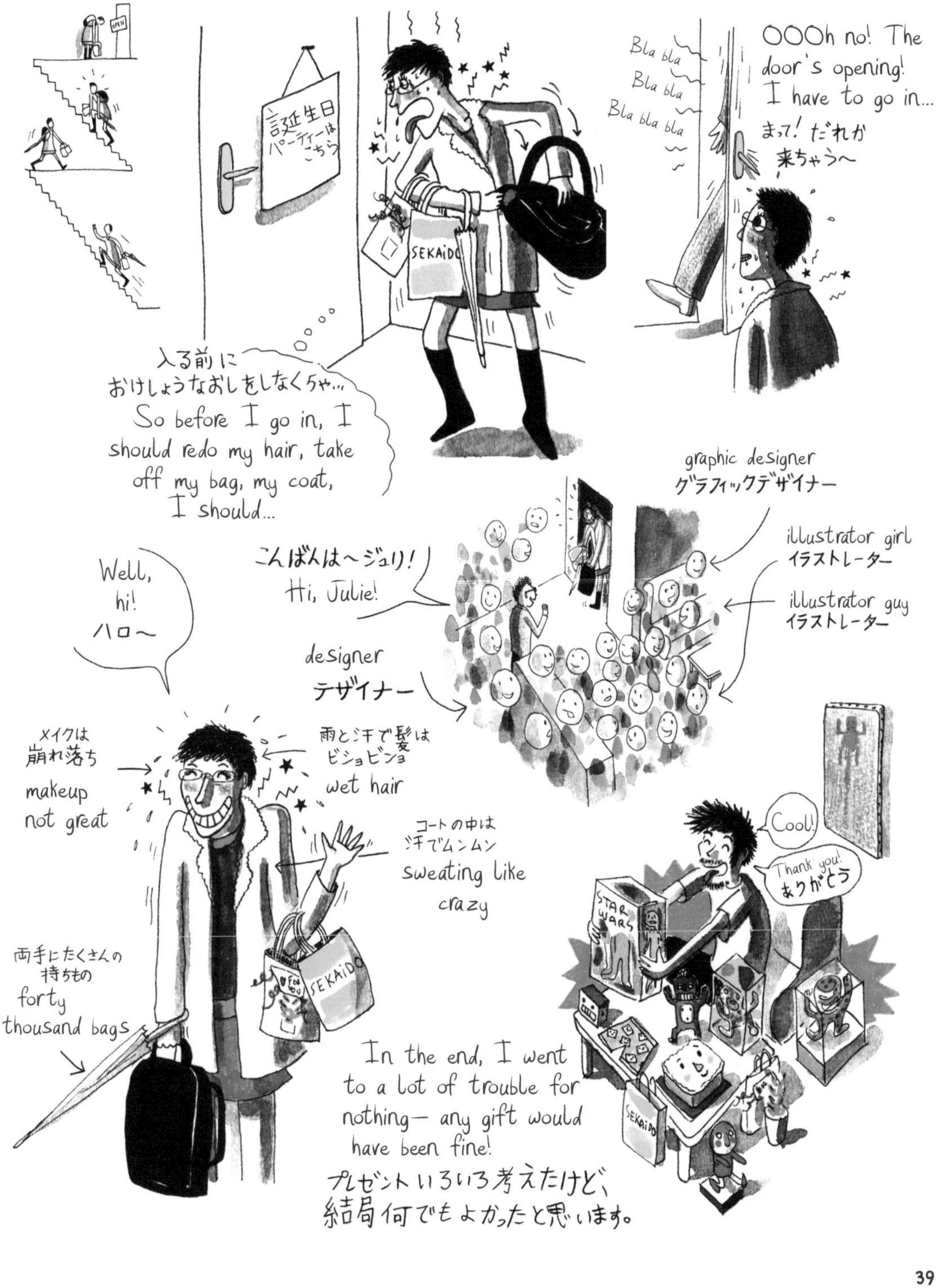

OPEN
誕生日
パーティーは
こちら
SEKAIDO
入る前に
おけしょうなおしをしなくちゃ…
So before I go in, I should redo my hair, take off my bag, my coat, I should…
Bla bla
Bla bla
Bla bla bla
OOOh no! The door's opening! I have to go in…
まって! だれか来ちゃう〜
graphic designer
グラフィックデザイナー
こんばんは〜ジュリ!
Hi, Julie!
illustrator girl
イラストレーター
illustrator guy
イラストレーター
designer
デザイナー
Well, hi!
ハロ〜
メイクは
崩れ落ち
makeup
not great
雨と汗で髪はビショビショ
wet hair
コートの中は
汗でムンムン
sweating like crazy
両手にたくさんの
持ちもの
forty thousand bags
SEKAIDO
FOR YOU
Cool!
Thank you!
ありがとう
STAR WARS
SEKAIDO
In the end, I went to a lot of trouble for nothing— any gift would have been fine!
プレゼントいろいろ考えたけど、
結局何でもよかったと思います。

XXL

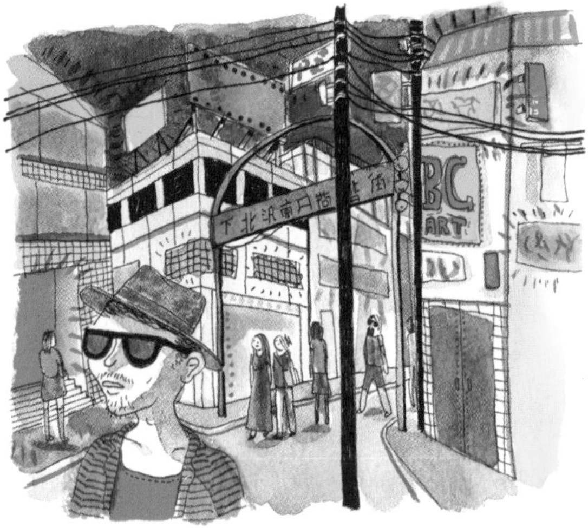

下北沢 Shimokitazawa

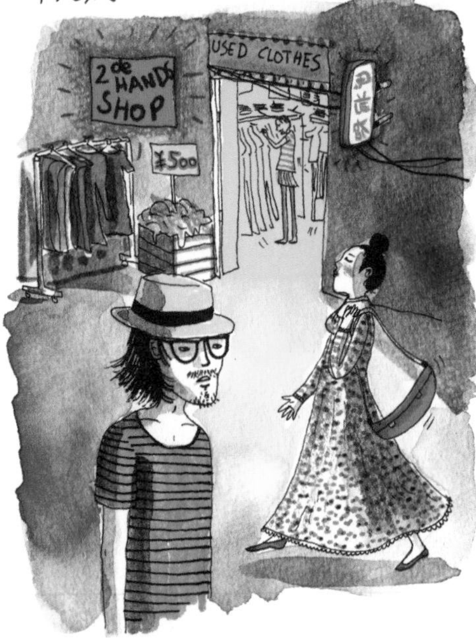
USED CLOTHES
2de HANDS SHOP
¥500

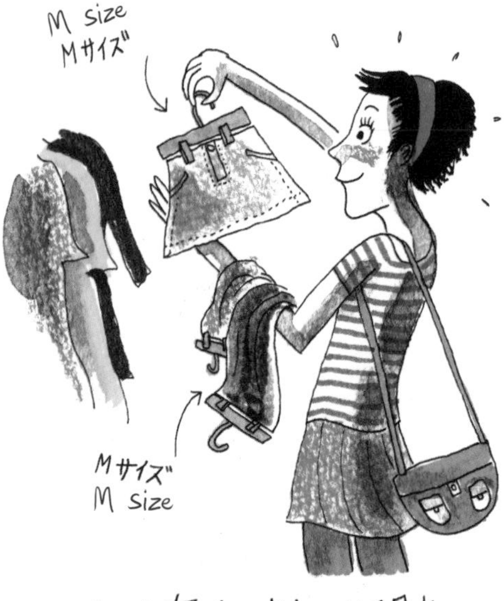
M size
Mサイズ
Mサイズ
M size

私は安くてかわいい服を
買いに行きます。
The neighborhood for
cool vintage clothing.

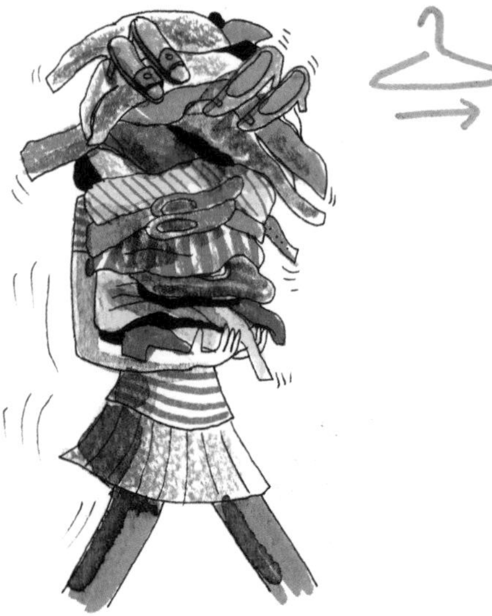

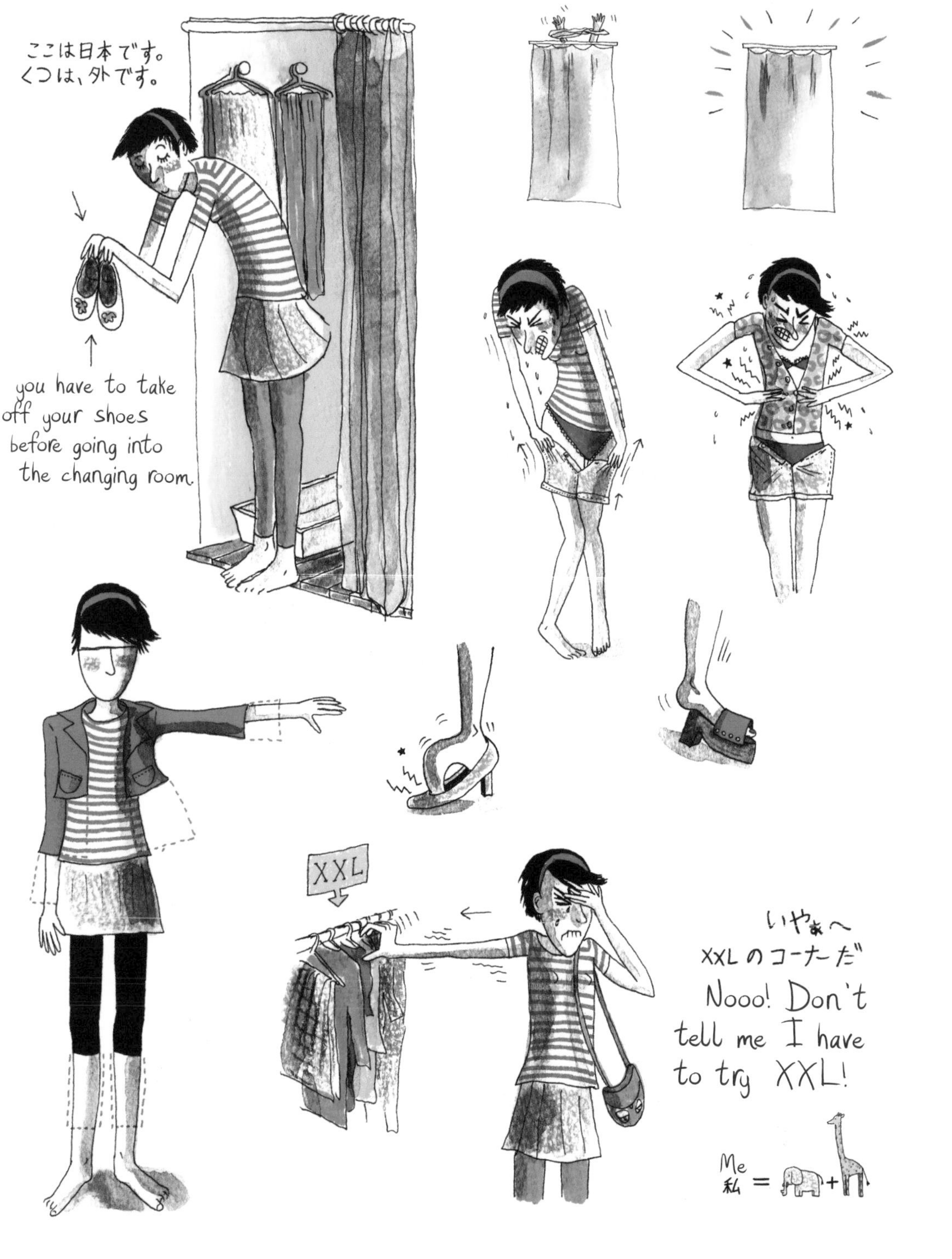
ここは日本です。
くつは、外です。
you have to take off your shoes before going into the changing room.
XXL
いやぁ〜
XXLのコーナーだ
Nooo! Don't tell me I have to try XXL!
Me
私 =

The End of the Line 終点まで

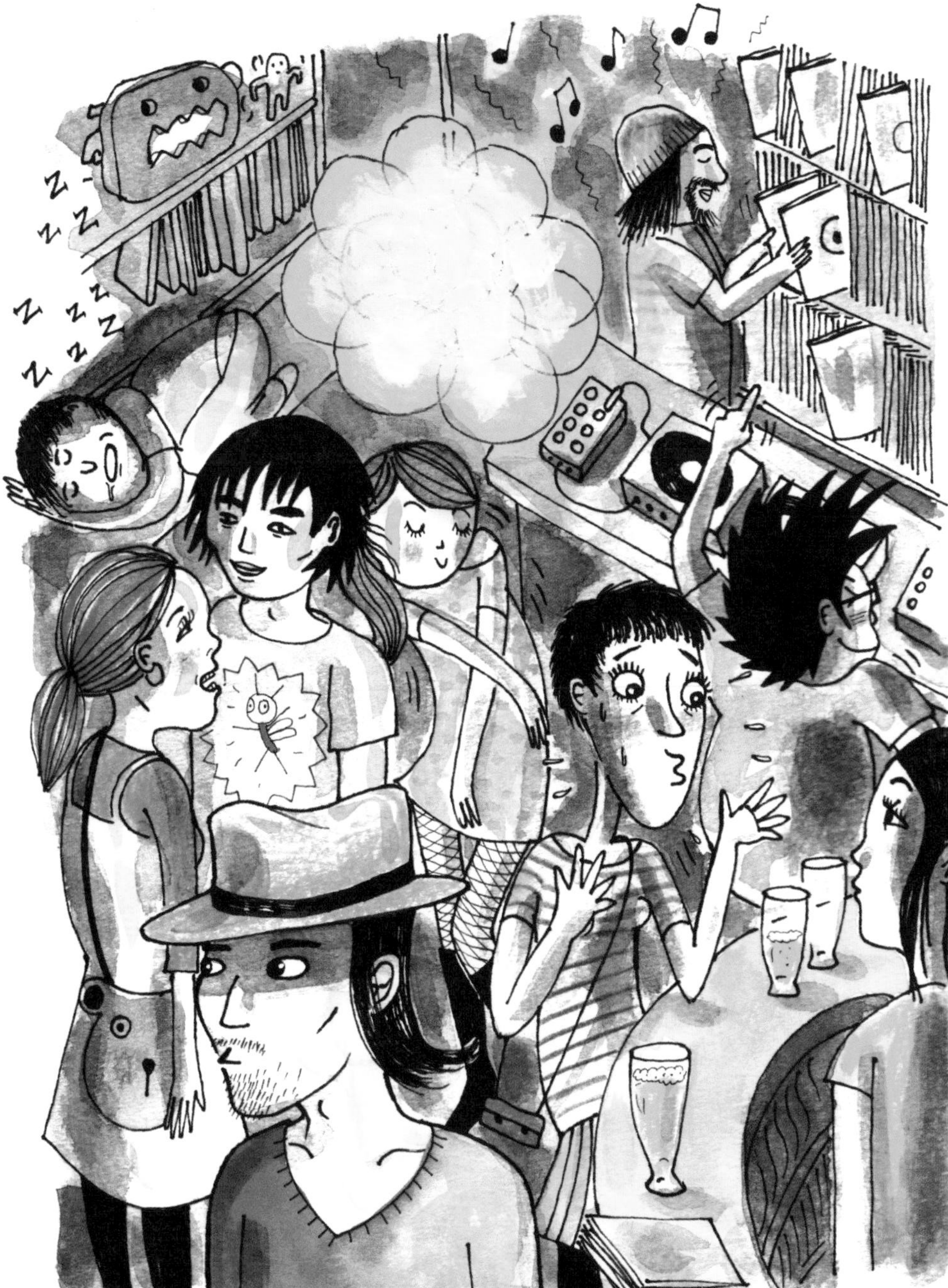

I spend the evening in a tiny underground bar in the Higashi-Koenji neighborhood. I'm trying to order a boo-ro... buro... bura... a Bloody Mary.

東高円寺の アングラなバーで
ブラッド ブラッ、ブロッディ、何とか マリーを
ブレッ たのみます。

始発で家に 帰ろうと思ったけど、 そのまま 終点まで 行ってみます。

The sand is chilly, Nina Simone is singing. Just like a painting.

I take the first morning train home, but decide to skip my stop and go to the end of the line—Katase Enoshima, at the seaside.

描かれた 景色に浸る 朝の海 風に揺れる ニナ・シモン

The Music Festival エレクトロイベント

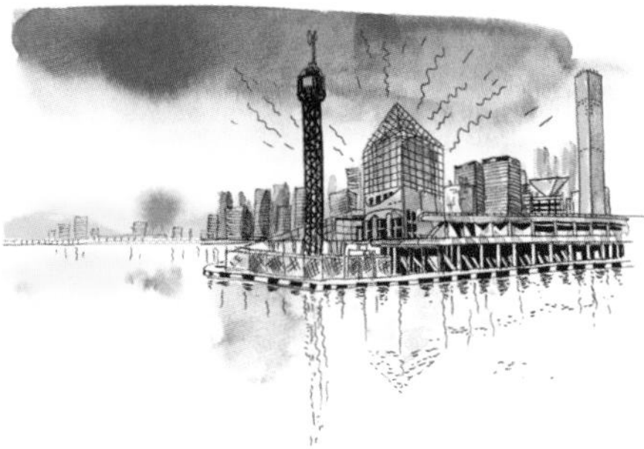

スーパーメガ高いチケットで
お台場の音楽イベントに行きます。

I go to a techno music festival on the banks of Tokyo Bay, with a super expensive ticket.

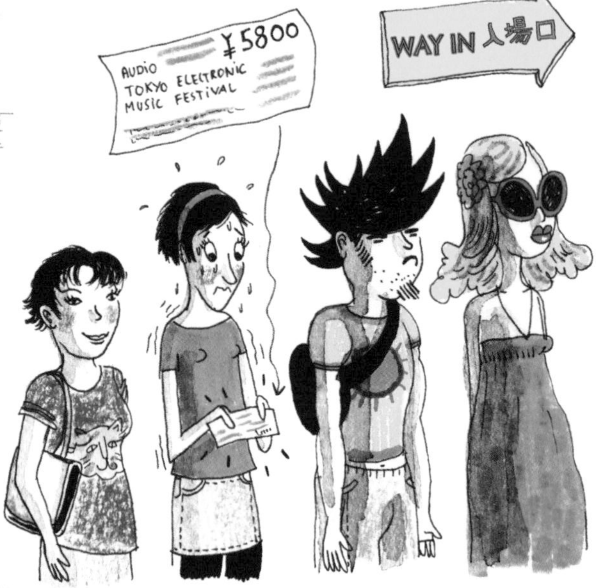
¥5800
AUDIO
TOKYO ELECTRONIC
MUSIC FESTIVAL
WAY IN 入場口

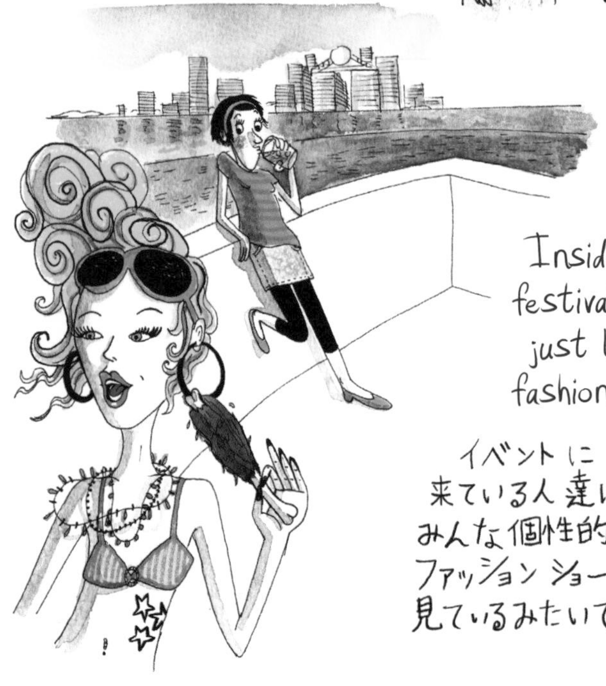

Inside the festival, it's just like a fashion show.

イベントに
来ている人達は
みんな個性的で、
ファッションショーを
見ているみたいです。

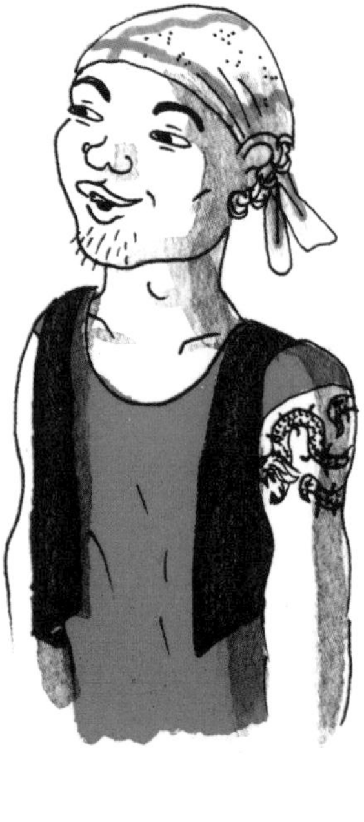

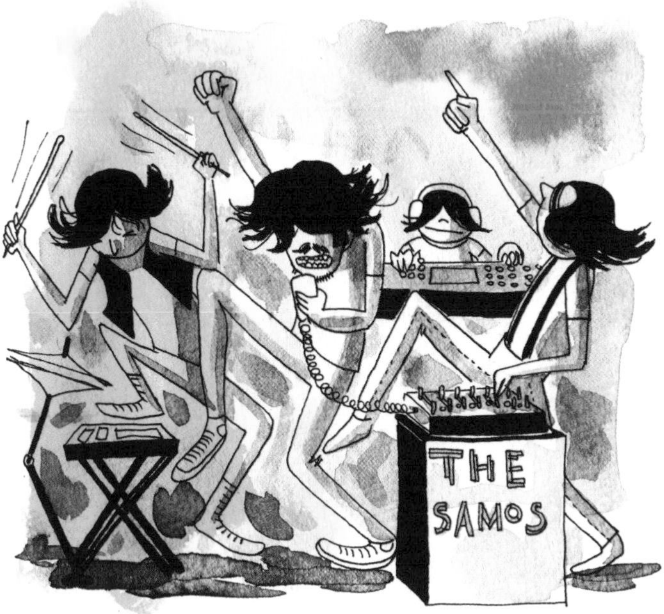
THE
SAMOS

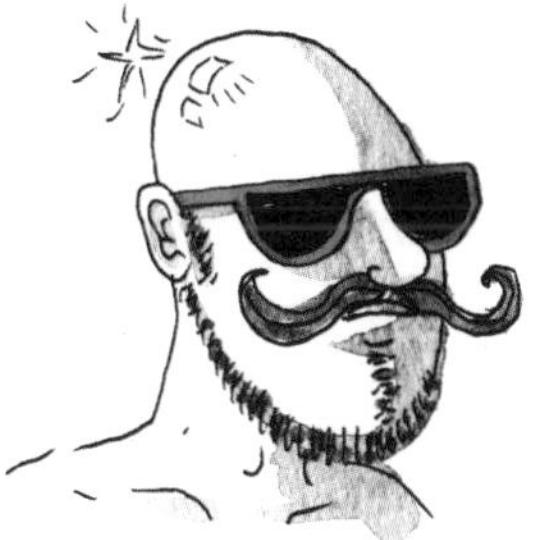

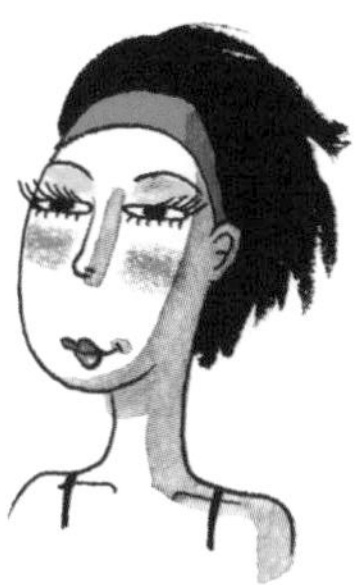

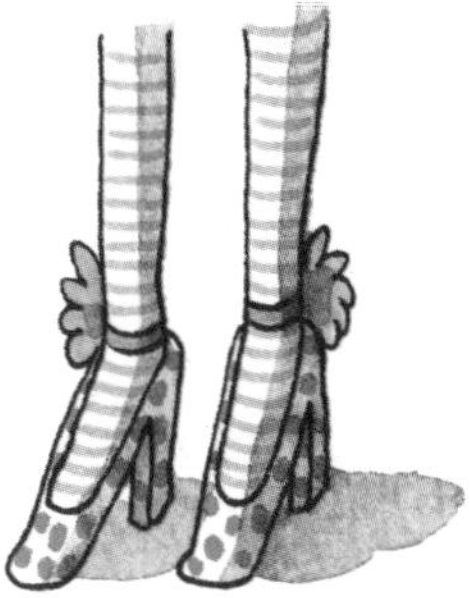

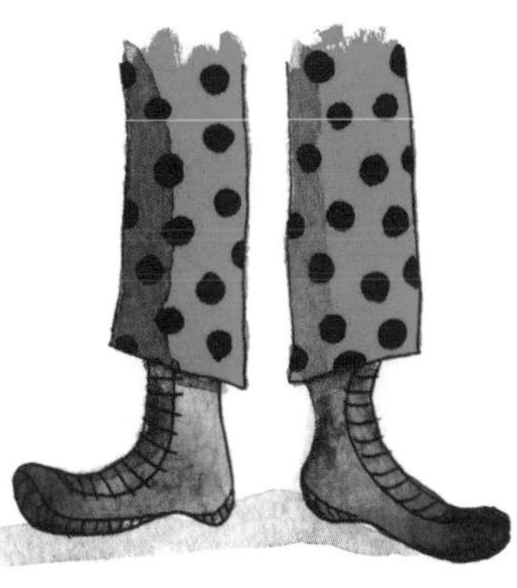

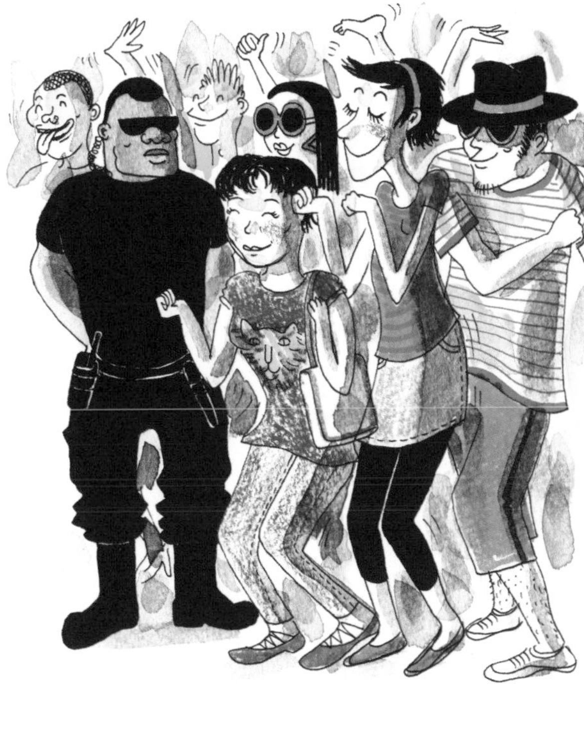

野外イベントなのに
喫煙所があるのは、
すばらしい文化です。

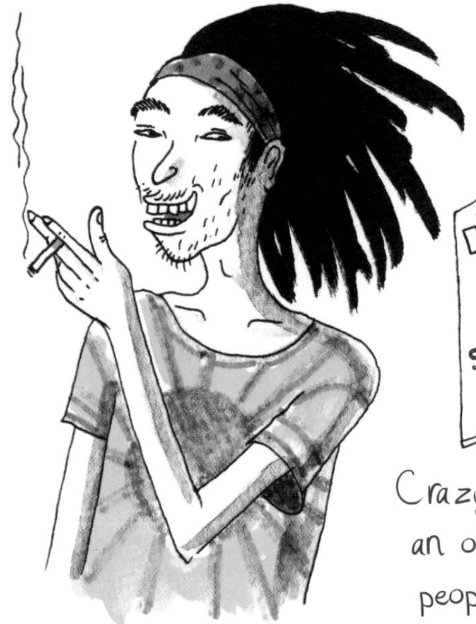

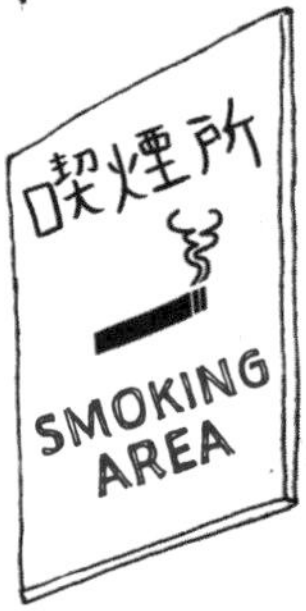
喫煙所
SMOKING AREA

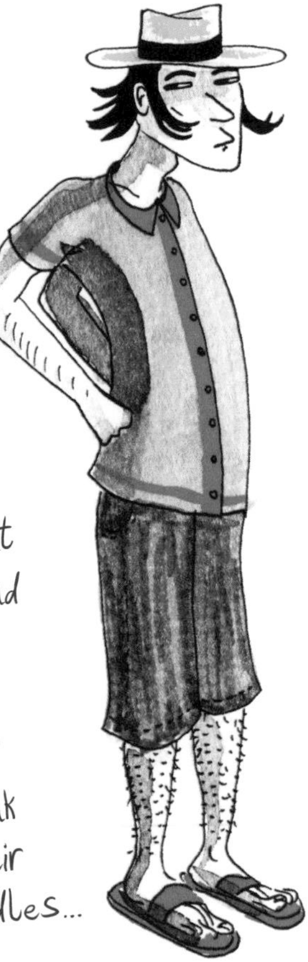

Crazy! A smoking area at an outdoor festival! And people obey!

There are always those stupid Western macho guys who think they rule the world with their body hair and their love handles...

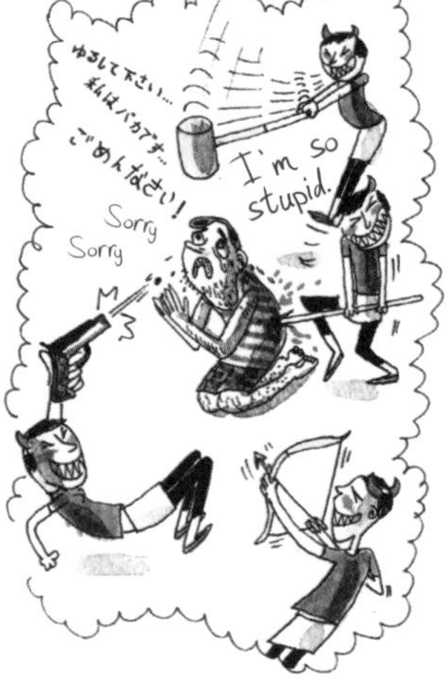
ゆるして下さい…
私はバカです…
ごめんなさい!
I'm so stupid.
Sorry
Sorry

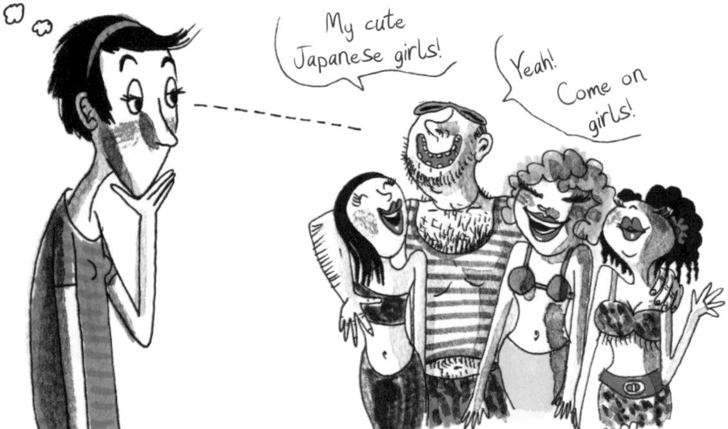
My cute Japanese girls!
Yeah! Come on girls!

こうゆう外国人男性
よくいますねぇ。

とつぜん友達が！
Suddenly, my friend appears.

ワインのにおい
smell of wine

よこ向けば
胸にマリファナ
おどる人

Seriously?
A marijuana
leaf on your
bosom? How
discreet!

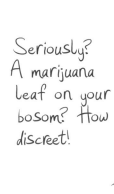

もちろん始発です。
Then the morning train again.

47

My First Tokyo Summer 初めての東京の夏

東京の夏は
あついです。

Summer in
Tokyo is hot.

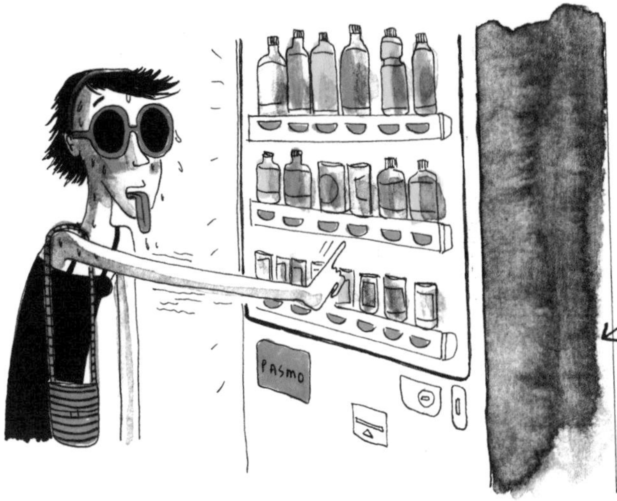
PASMO

Drink vending
machines are
everywhere.

I often go to Ishiki Kaigan with my friends; it's a nice little beach an hour away from Tokyo.

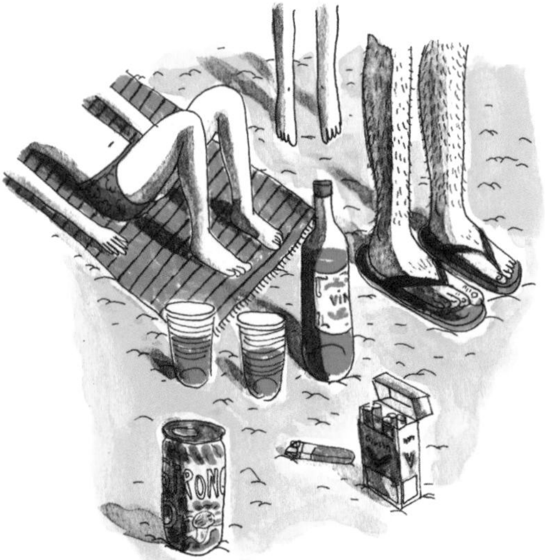
VIN

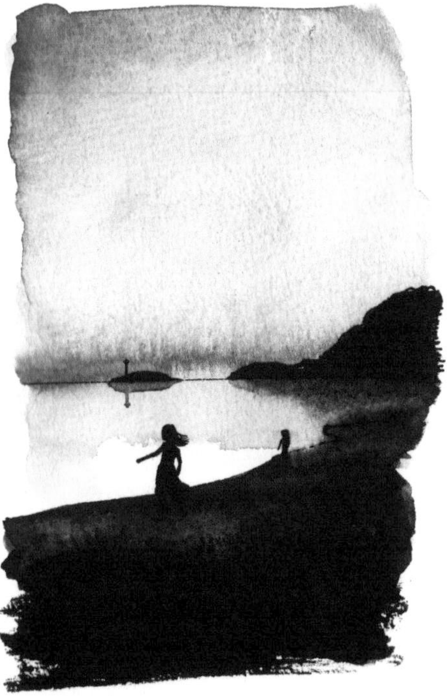

なのでよく友達と一色海岸へ行きます。

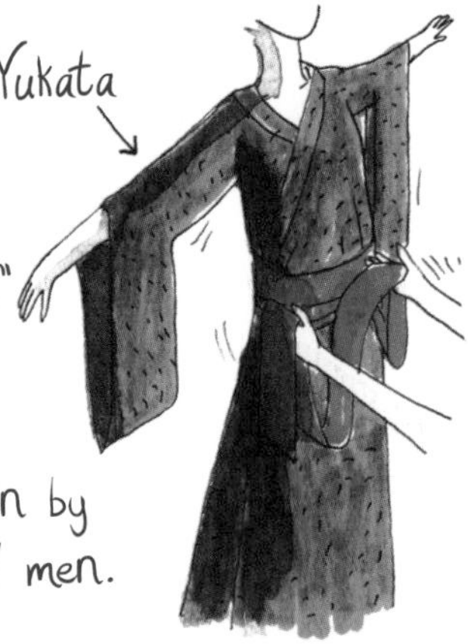
Yukata

It's like a kimono, but "summer style" as in lighter and easier to wear. It's worn by both women and men.

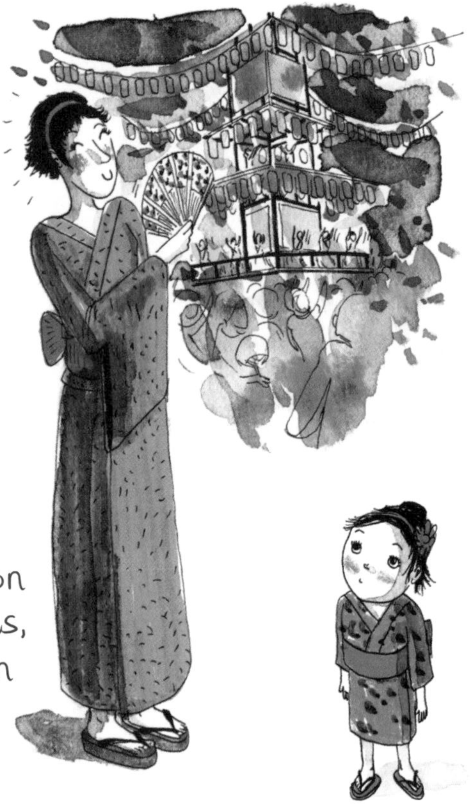

東京の夏は
きれいです。
浴衣を着て
盆おどりに
行きます。

Summer is the season for traditional festivals, like bon odori... Put on a yukata and you're ready to party!

The worst thing about public transportation is when you have to run to catch your train.

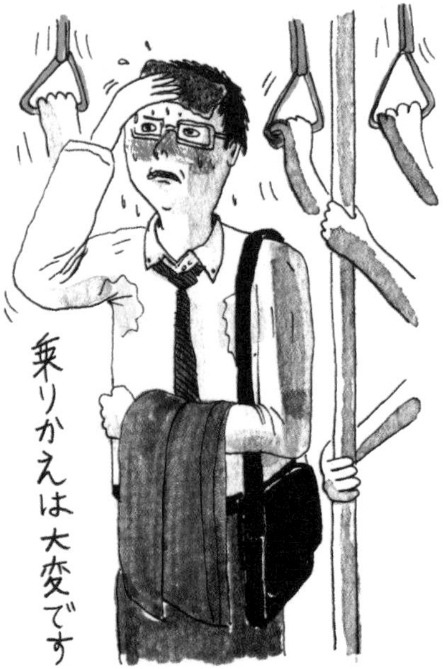

乗りかえは大変です。

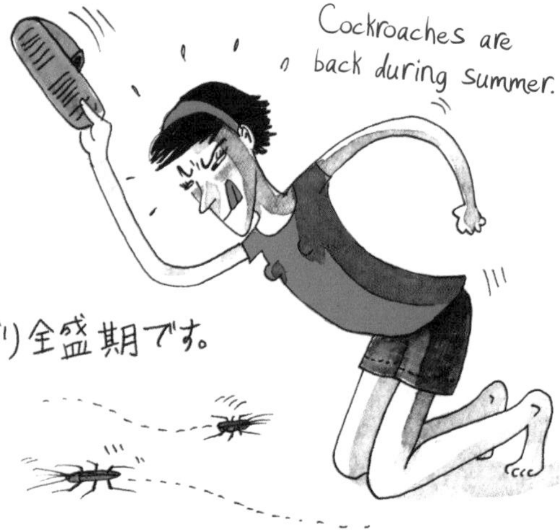

Cockroaches are back during summer.

ゴキブリ全盛期です。

ダースベイダーが
通ります。

Hey, is that Darth Vader?
No, it's just a mom
wearing sun protection.

セクシー
0%
SEXY

As in gloves that go all
the way to the armpits.

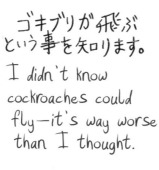

ゴキブリが飛ぶ
という事を知ります。
I didn't know
cockroaches could
fly—it's way worse
than I thought.

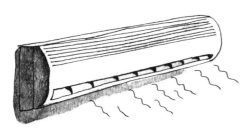

Air conditioning is not that widespread in France, but in Asia, and especially in Japan, it's been everywhere for a long time. Everyone calls it "air con," even in Japanese

BRRR
BRRR
BRRR
BRRR
BRRR
BRRR

北極です。
電車の中です。

Greenland? Siberia? No, it's only the inside of the train with the AC on full blast.

roasted barley tea (mugicha) 麦茶
むぎ茶
Japanese green tea (ryokucha) 緑茶

The Japanese have long understood that you have to hydrate properly in summer. You drink water, tea and especially mugicha, a roasted barley infusion. It's delicious!

月 火 水 木 金 土 日
lun mar mer jeu ven sam dim
Only three roaches today, that's better.
3匹。
今日は少ない方です。

The Semis 蝉

セミがいない夏は、
日本の夏じゃないです。
There's no summer in Japan
without the song of the semi.

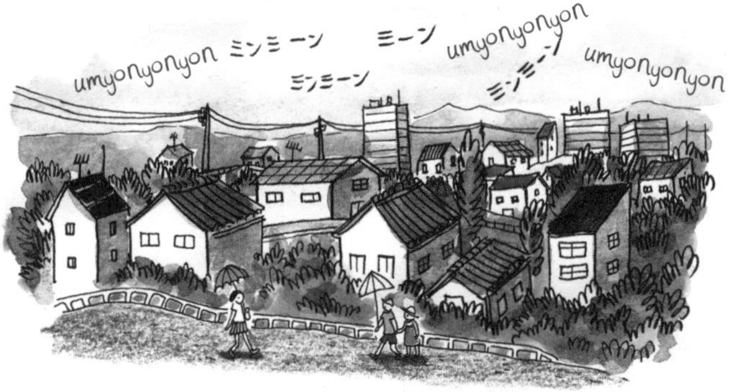

umyonyonyon
ミンミーン
ミンミーン
ミーン
umyonyonyon
ミンミーン
umyonyonyon

Semis are Japanese cicadas.

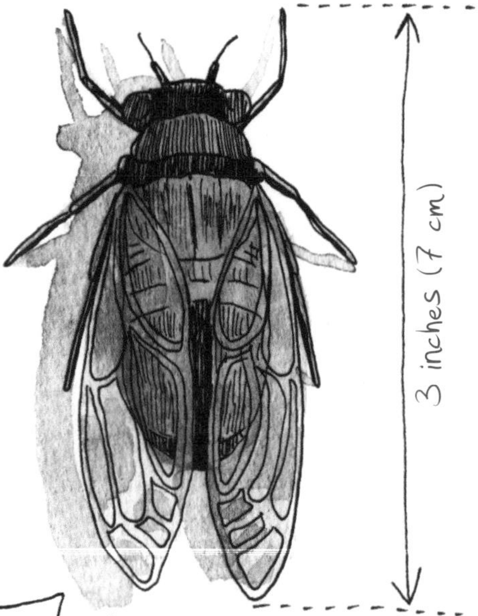

3 inches (7 cm)

Actual Size

The fabulous life cycle of the semi
素晴らしきセミの一生

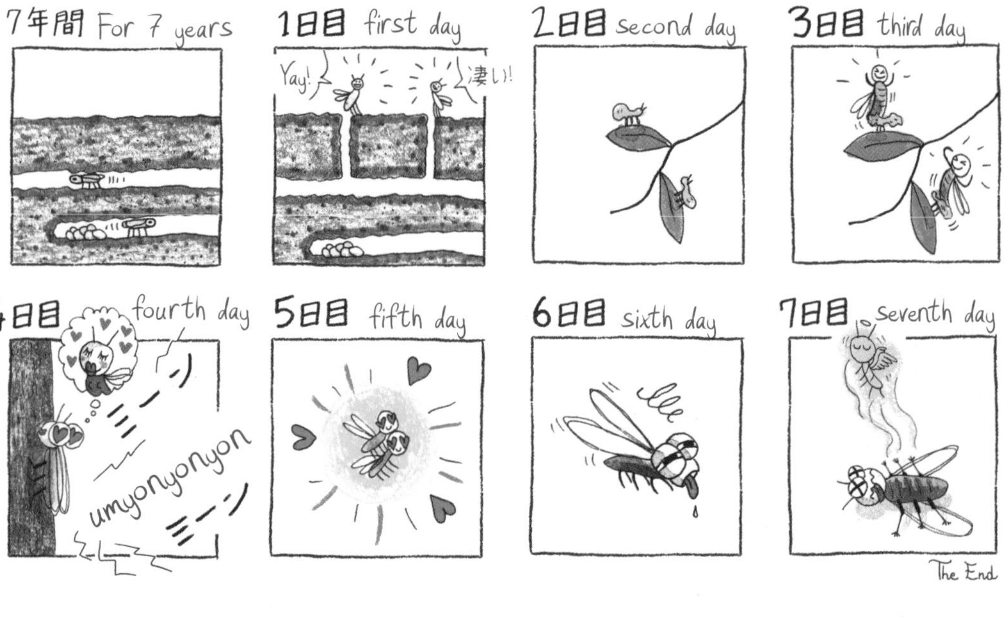

7年間 For 7 years
1日目 first day
Yay!
凄い!
2日目 second day
3日目 third day
4日目 fourth day
ミーン
ミーン
umyonyonyon
ミーン
5日目 fifth day
6日目 sixth day
7日目 seventh day
The End

This is a Japanese-style garden
こちらは
一般的な庭です。

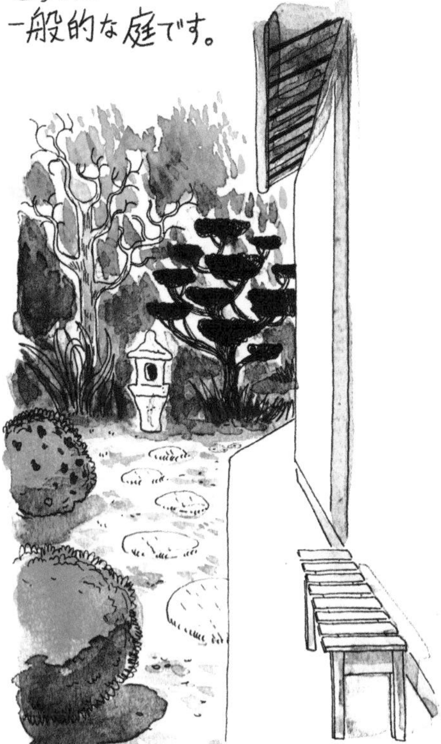

This is our house garden.
こちらは、私達の家の庭です。

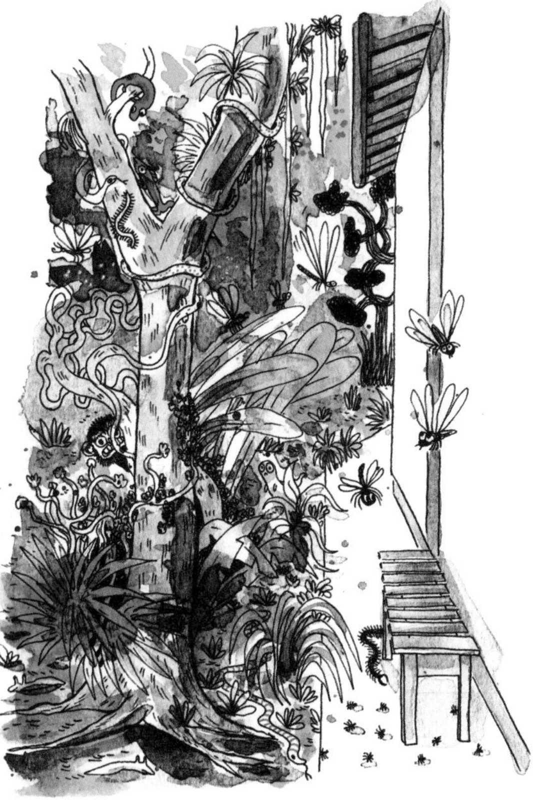

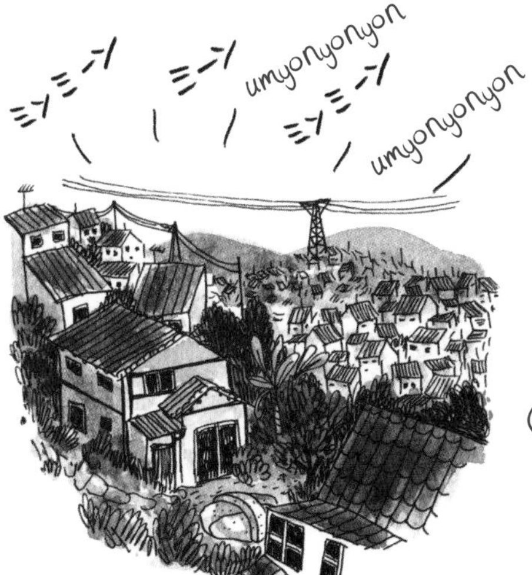
ミンミーン
ミーン
umyonyonyon
ミンミーン
umyonyonyon

セミの
パラダイスです。
Our garden is
a paradise for
semis.

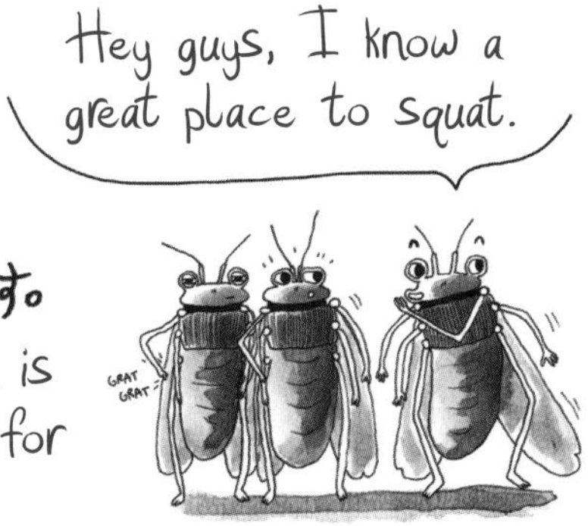
知ってる？
近くにいい庭があるよ！
Hey guys, I know a
great place to squat.
GRAT
GRAT

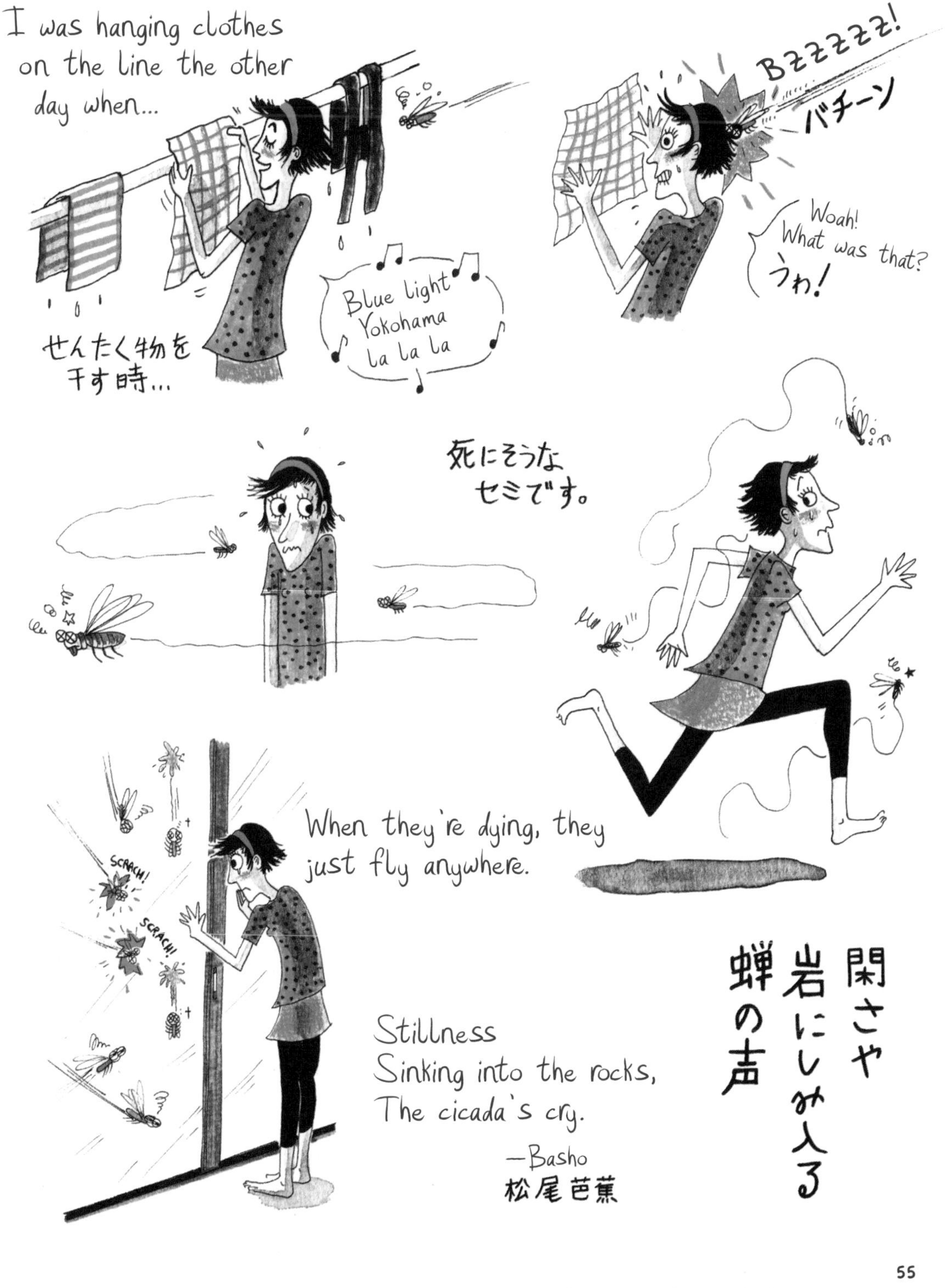
I was hanging clothes on the line the other day when...
せんたく物を干す時...
Blue light Yokohama la la la
Bzzzzzz!
バチーン
Woah! What was that?
うわ!
死にそうなセミです。
When they're dying, they just fly anywhere.
SCRACH!
SCRACH!
Stillness
Sinking into the rocks,
The cicada's cry.
—Basho
松尾芭蕉
閑さや
岩にしみ入る
蝉の声

Climbing Mount Fuji

富士山

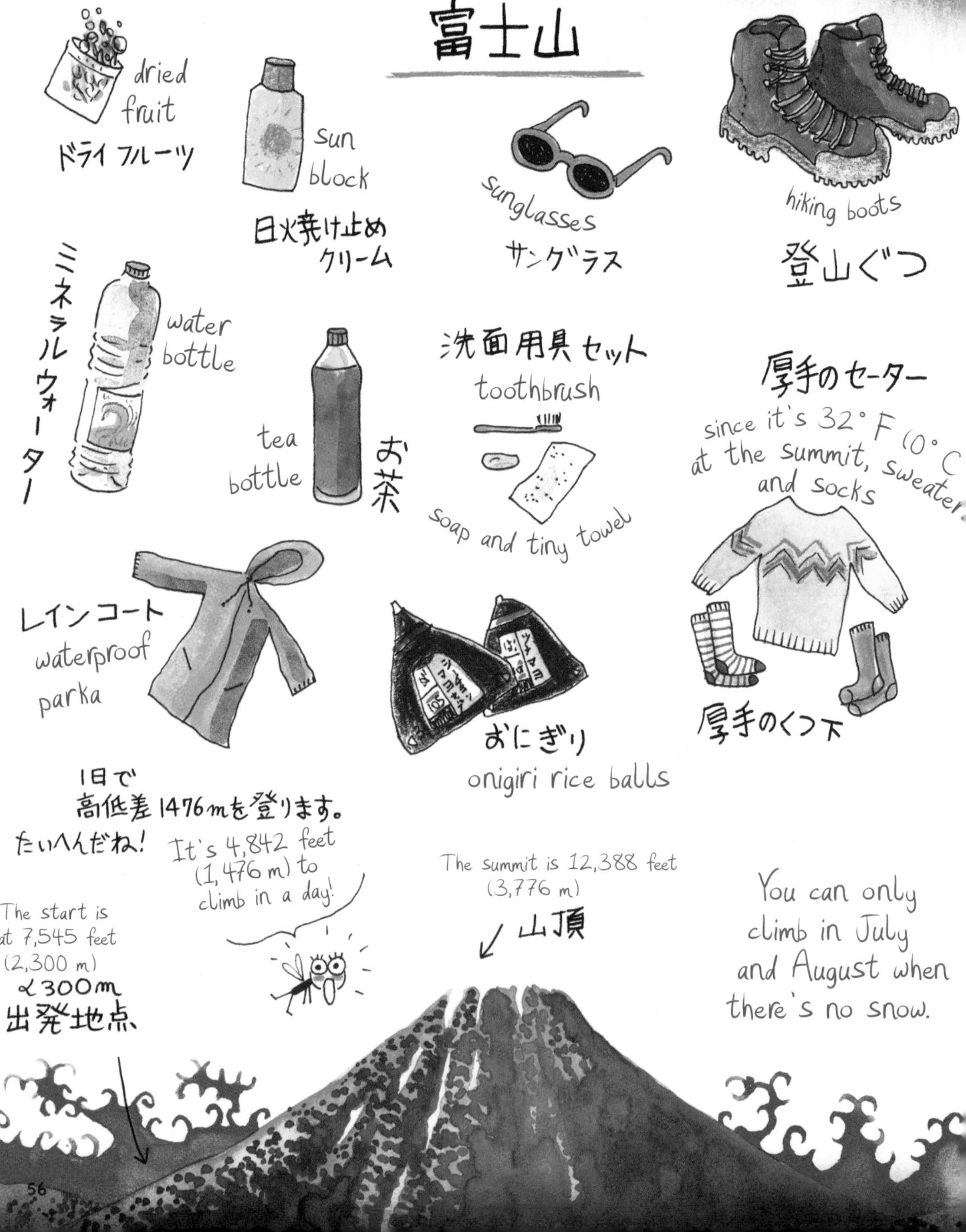
dried fruit
ドライフルーツ
sun block
日焼け止めクリーム
sunglasses
サングラス
hiking boots
登山ぐつ
ミネラルウォーター
water bottle
tea bottle
お茶
洗面用具セット
toothbrush
soap and tiny towel
厚手のセーター
since it's 32°F (0°C
at the summit, sweater
and socks
レインコート
waterproof parka
おにぎり
onigiri rice balls
厚手のくつ下
1日で
高低差1476mを登ります。
たいへんだね!
It's 4,842 feet (1,476 m) to climb in a day!
The summit is 12,388 feet (3,776 m)
山頂
The start is at 7,545 feet (2,300 m)
2300m
出発地点
You can only climb in July and August when there's no snow.

私の父と母が日本に来たので富士山に登ります。
My parents come to visit, so we
decide to climb Mount Fuji together.

Start the climb at 10 am.

他の登山者たち →
other hikers

午前10時、登山開始。

Get through the sea
of clouds at 2 pm.

他の登山者たち
other hikers

午後2時、雲海展望。

Arrive at the last shelter at
5 pm and go to bed at 7 pm

午後7時、就寝。

午後5時、山小屋到着。

Like everywhere else,
you take off your
shoes at the door.

Get up at 3 in the morning.

zzzzz....

stiff

筋肉痛

zzzzz....

午前3時、起床。

Climb the last
few hundred yards.

山頂を目指す。

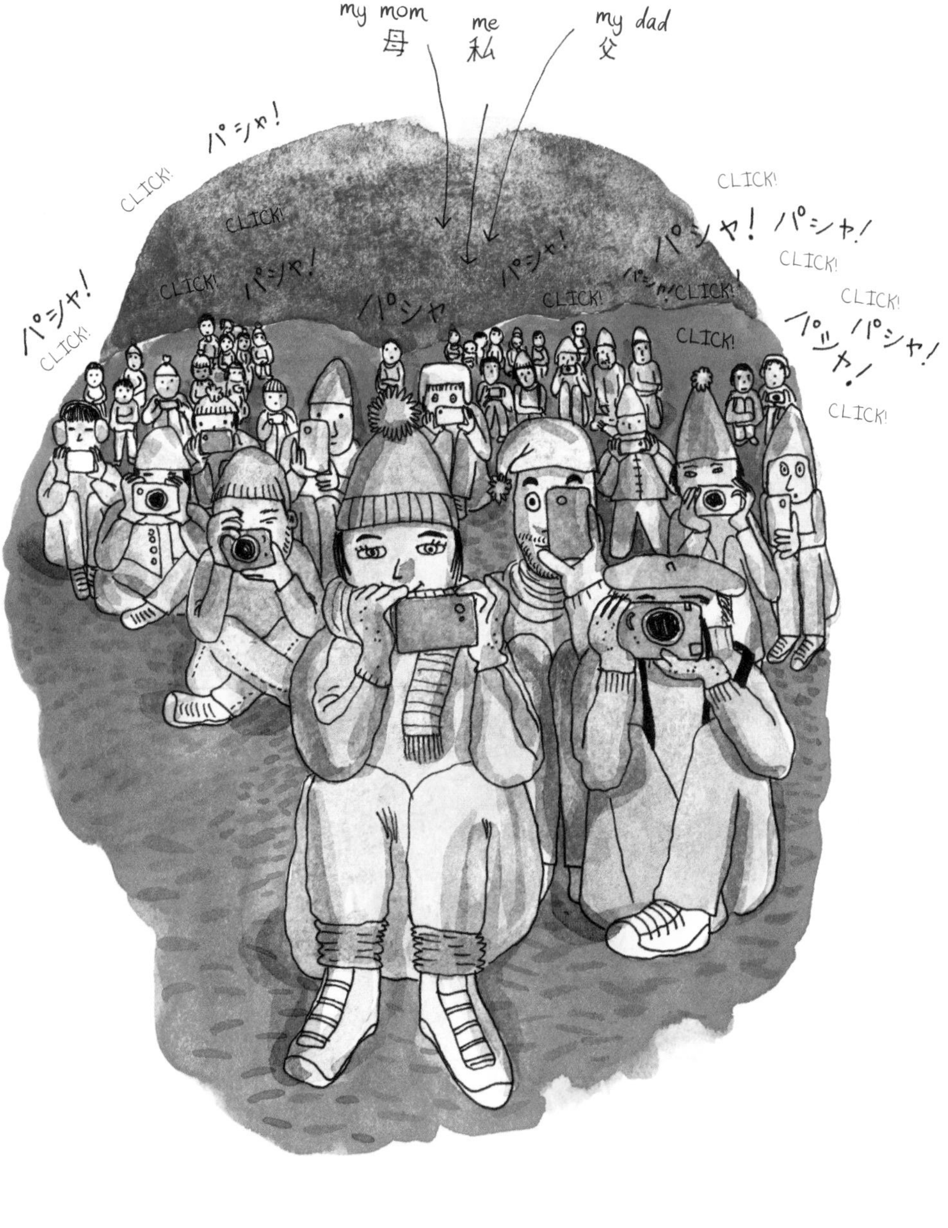
my mom
母
me
私
my dad
父
パシャ!
CLICK!
CLICK!
パシャ!
CLICK!
パシャ!
パシャ!
CLICK!
パシャ
パシャ!
CLICK!
パシャ!
CLICK!
CLICK!
パシャ! パシャ!
CLICK!
CLICK!
CLICK!
パシャ!
パシャ!
CLICK!

Watching the sun rise from Japan's highest peak.

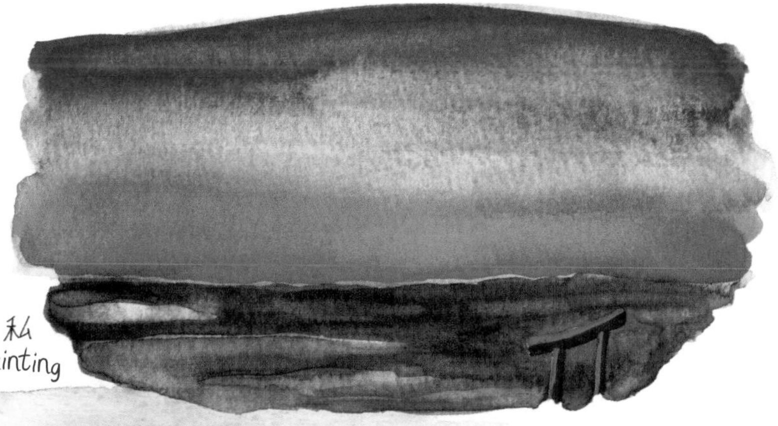

私
my painting

午前5時、富士山頂。

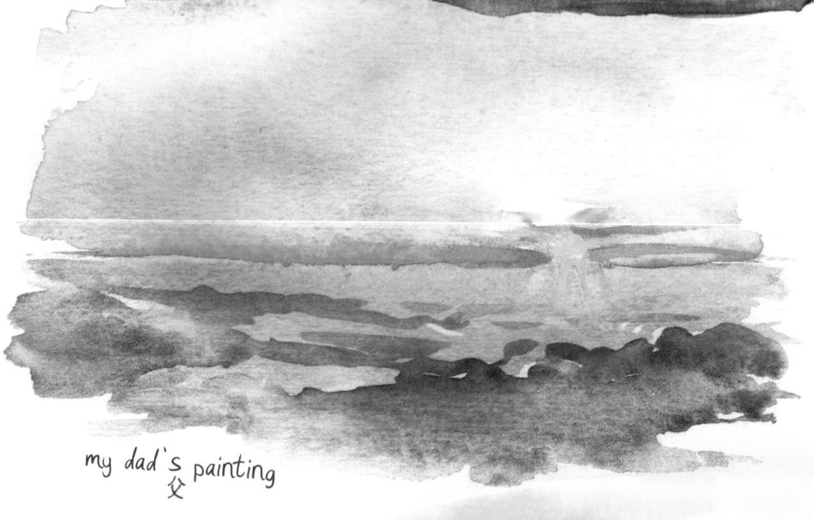

my dad's 父 painting

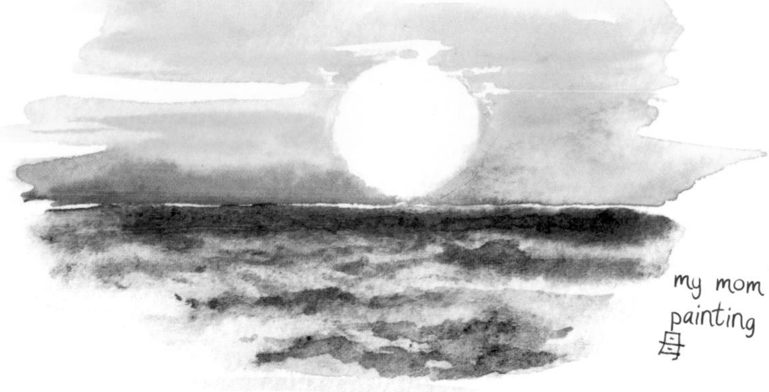

my mom's painting 母

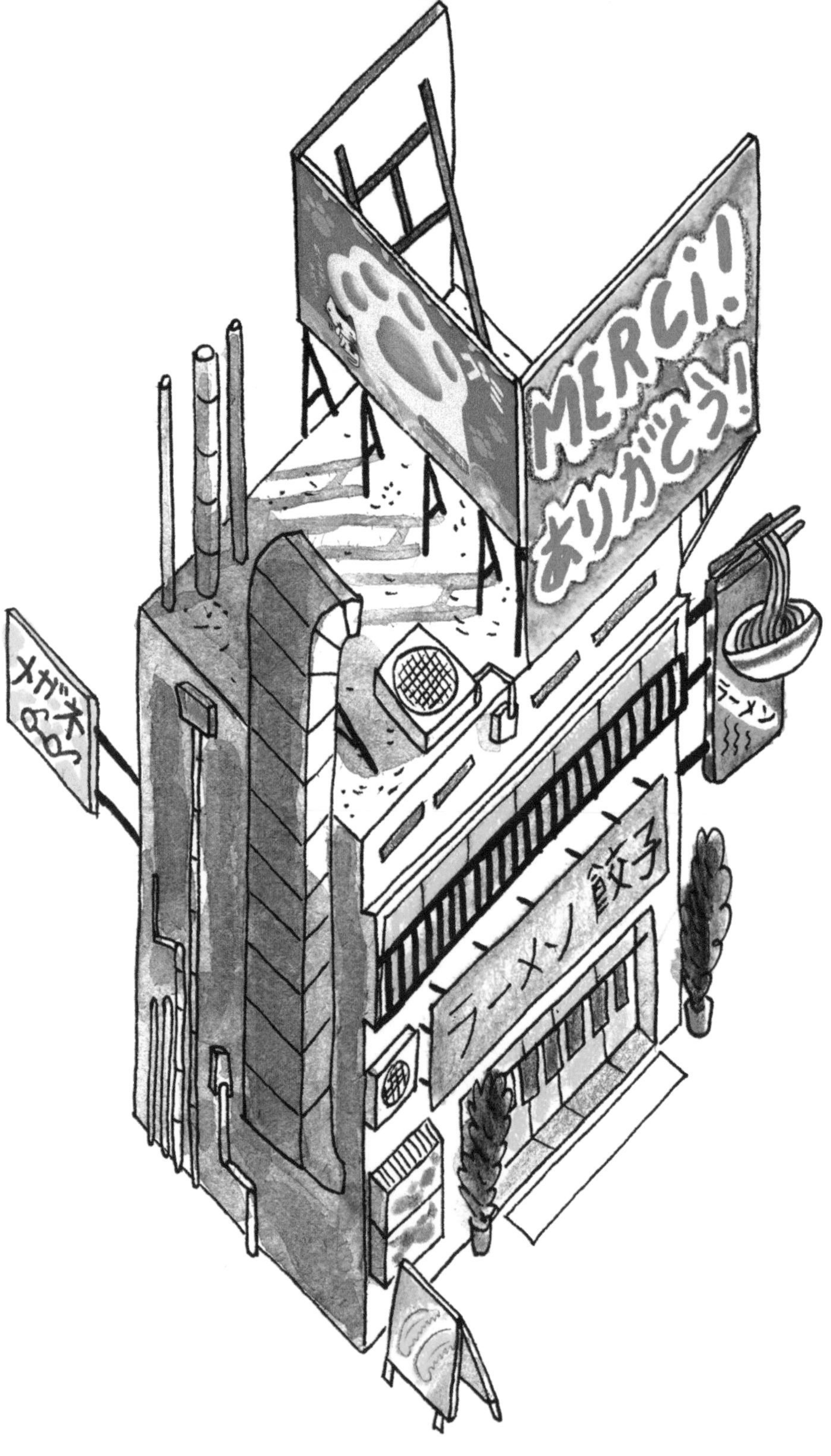
メガネ
MERCI!
ありがとう!
ラーメン
ラーメン 餃子
ラーメン

Living in
Tsuruse
鶴瀬

Tsuruse 鶴瀬

I've been living in my shared rental for one year already. It's great, but I'd like to hang out more with Japanese people and discover the country from the inside. A friend I run into at an independent publishers' fair invites me to meet Mariko, a stay-at-home mom of two who's looking for an English-speaking au pair. My English isn't the best but I meet her anyway and... Mariko is sold!

I leave my rental and move to Tsuruse.

シェアハウスでもう1年。いいけど...
もっと日本人と交流したい。もっと深く内側から日本の文化を見つめたいと思います。ある友達がマリコさんという人を紹介してくれます。彼女は専業主婦で子供が2人います。子供たちの教育の為に英語を話す外国人を家に招きたいとの事です。私の英語はパーフェクトではないけど、私の申し出をよろこんで引き受けてくれます。鶴瀬に引っ越しです！

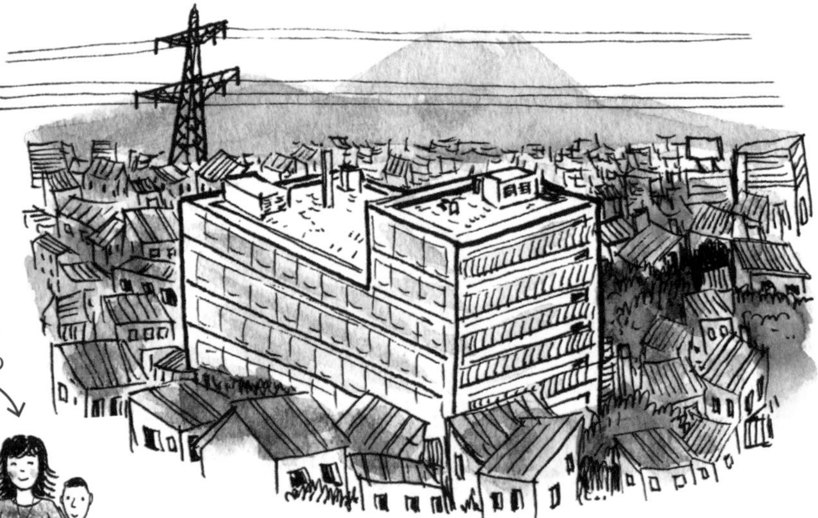

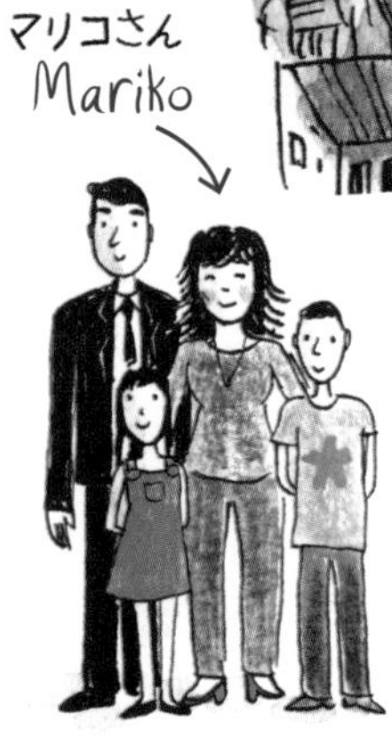
マリコさん
Mariko

お父さんは福岡に単身ふにん。息子と娘は中学生です。

The dad works in Fukuoka for the time being—he only comes home two or three weekends a month. The son and daughter both go to middle school.

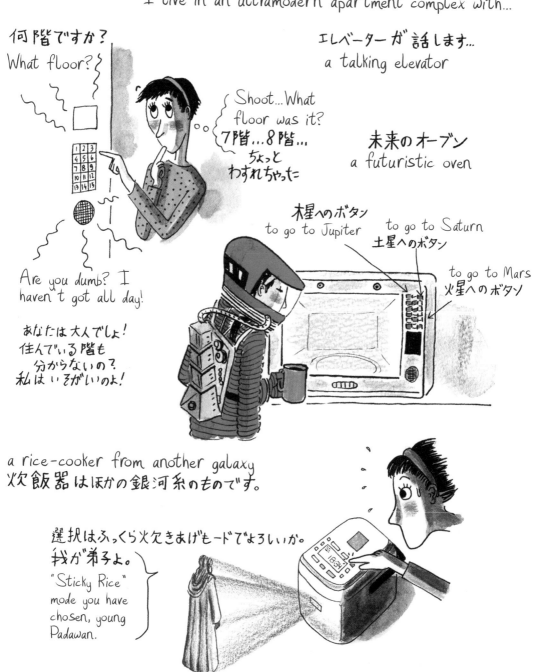

とても新しいマンションです…
I live in an ultramodern apartment complex with…

エレベーターが話します…
a talking elevator

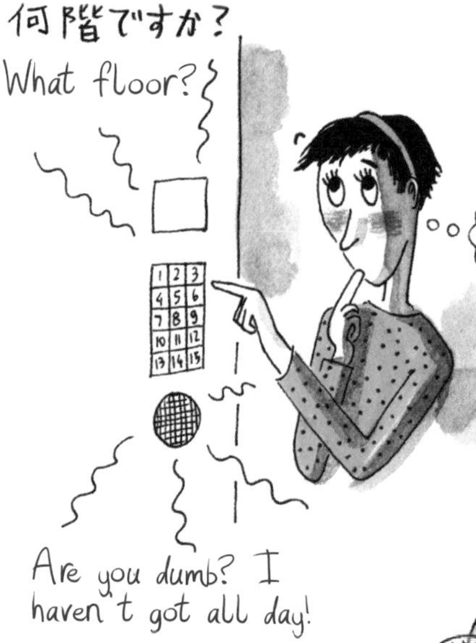
何階ですか？
What floor?
Shoot… What floor was it?
7階…8階… ちょっと わすれちゃった
Are you dumb? I haven't got all day!
あなたは大人でしょ！ 住んでいる階も 分からないの？ 私はいそがしいのよ！

未来のオーブン
a futuristic oven

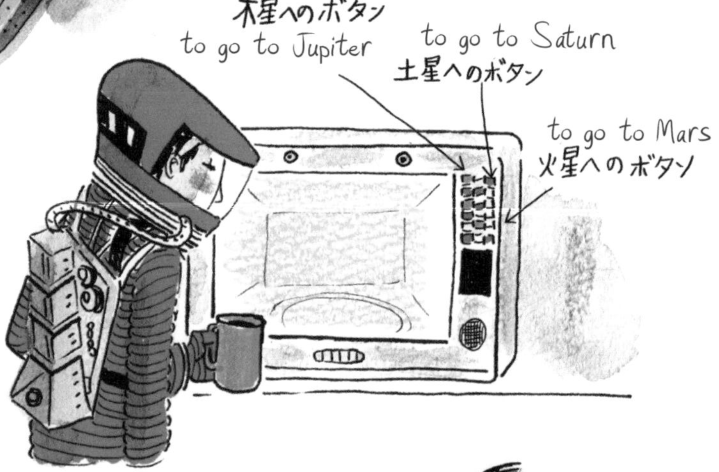
木星へのボタン
to go to Jupiter
to go to Saturn
土星へのボタン
to go to Mars
火星へのボタン

a rice-cooker from another galaxy
炊飯器はほかの銀河系のものです。

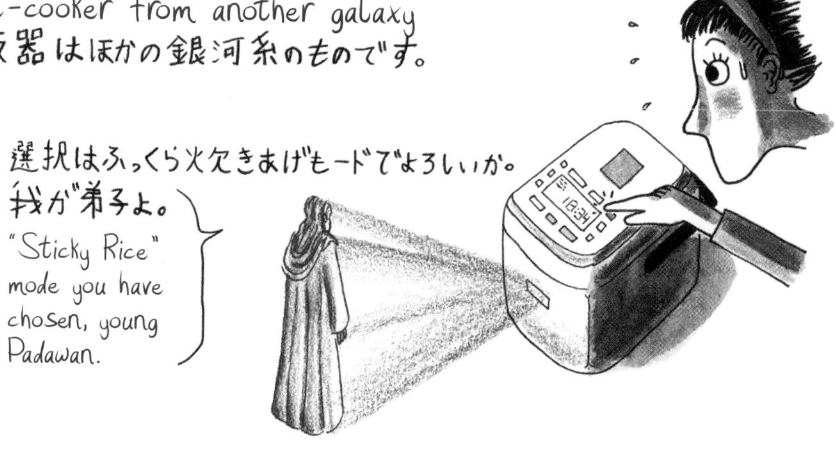
選択はふっくら炊きあげモードでよろしいか。
我が弟子よ。
"Sticky Rice" mode you have chosen, young Padawan.

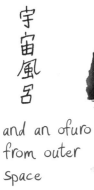

宇宙風呂

and an ofuro from outer space

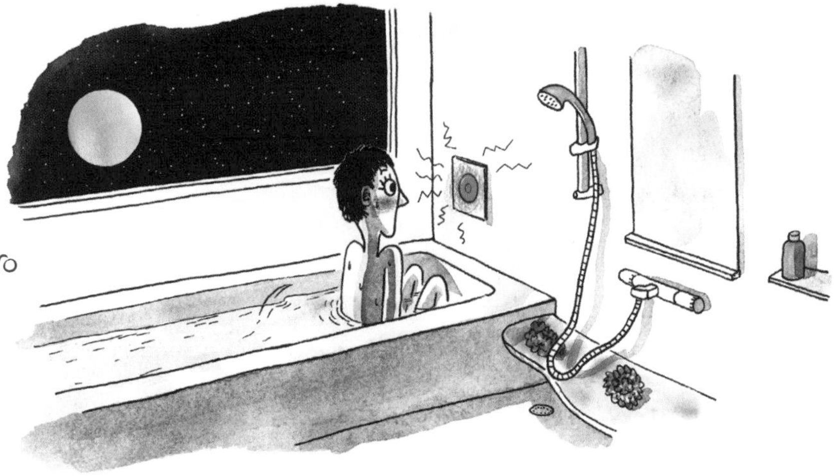

たくさんの テクノロジーに かこまれていますが、
い草のいい香りの部屋でとてもリラックスします。

Thankfully, among all this technology, there's a tatami room that smells wonderfully of rice straw.

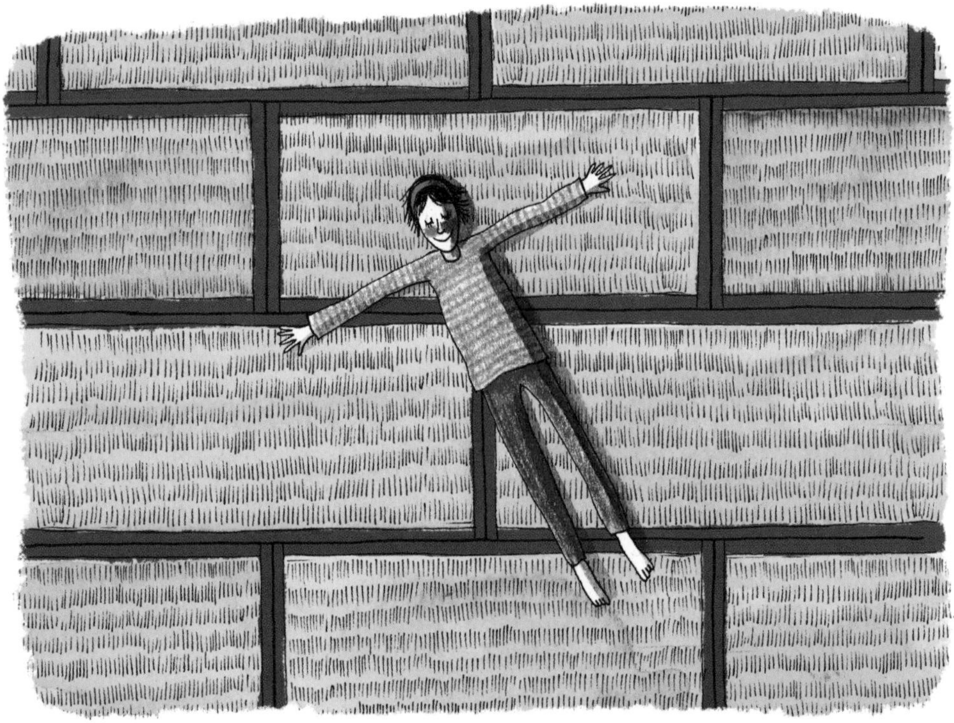

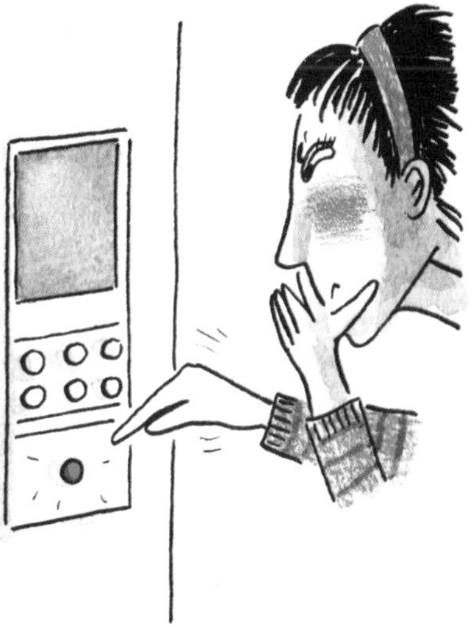
There's also a brand new intercom with a button that intrigued me so much the other day that I couldn't resist pushing it.
インターフォンの中に不思議なボタンがあります。
好奇心でおしてみます。

5分後… five minutes later…

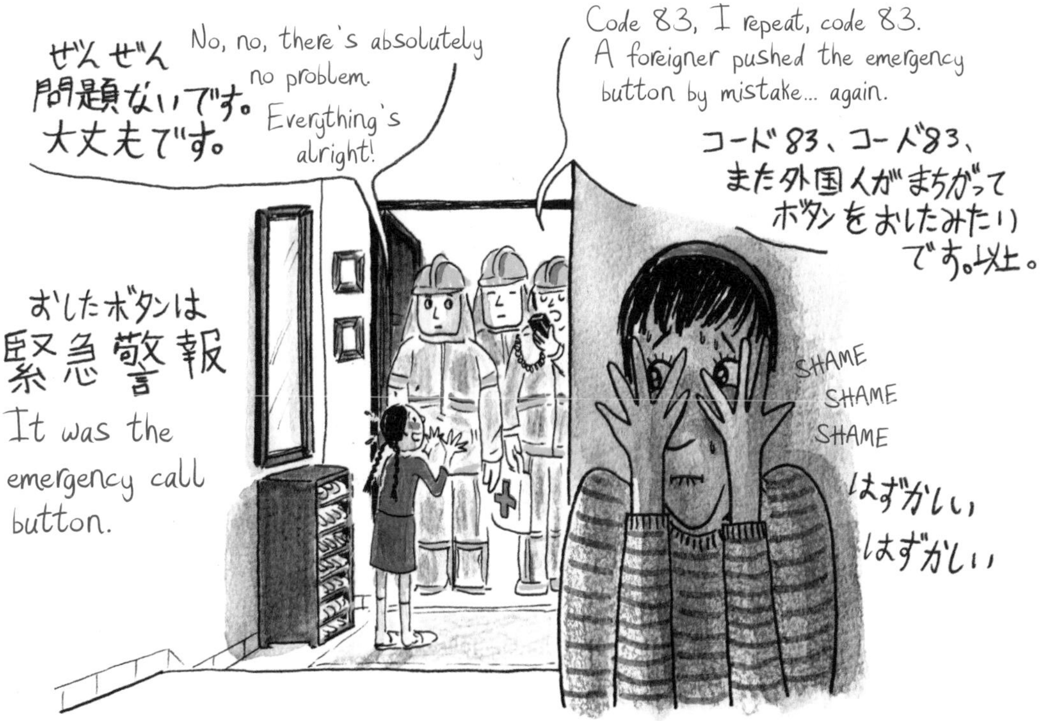
ぜんぜん問題ないです。大丈夫です。
No, no, there's absolutely no problem. Everything's alright!
Code 83, I repeat, code 83. A foreigner pushed the emergency button by mistake… again.
コード83、コード83、また外国人がまちがってボタンをおしたみたいです。以上。
おしたボタンは緊急警報
It was the emergency call button.
SHAME
SHAME
SHAME
はずかしい
はずかしい

The Bicycle 自転車

close call
at ¼ in.

In Japan...
日本では…

people ride bikes on sidewalks.
… 自転車も歩道を通ります。

一番あぶないのは重い電動ママチャリで
まわりを気にしないお母さんです。

The most dangerous are
the mamachari (very heavy electric
bikes with kids' seats and baskets) ridden
by moms who are oblivious to danger.

DANGER
LEVEL
危険度

ただちに逃げて!
Run!

非常に危険!
Immediate danger!

危険!
Look out!

注意!
Be careful!

問題なし
OK.

カゴ用バンド
kind of elastic lid so that your stuff doesn't fall off (just in case you were thinking of doing a back flip)

お年よりは すぐに止まれ ないので危ないです。
Or little old ladies who ride well but have trouble avoiding obstacles.

There are also crazy youngsters who ride in the rain while holding an umbrella and talking on the phone.

よくいる こうゆうタイプも 危ないです。

GULP!

So I keep to the "Yellow Lego Zone".

なので、 本当はだめだけど ときどき『黄色のレゴゾーン』 テクニックを使います。

点字ブロックは
レゴブロックに
にているので、
私は『黄色のレゴゾーン』
といいます。

Let me explain—in Japan there's a special strip for blind people on sidewalks. It has small knobs on it which they can follow.

It reminds me of Lego.

私も自由がほしい。
私もいろんな所へ行きたい。
自転車を買います！

Finally I make up my mind to buy a bike—I too want my freedom!

Which color would you like?

どの色がいい？

緑？ The green one?　白？ The white one?　茶？ The brown one?

The red one!
Red, the color of love,
passion and
revolution!

赤。
それは、愛、情熱そして、
革命の色！

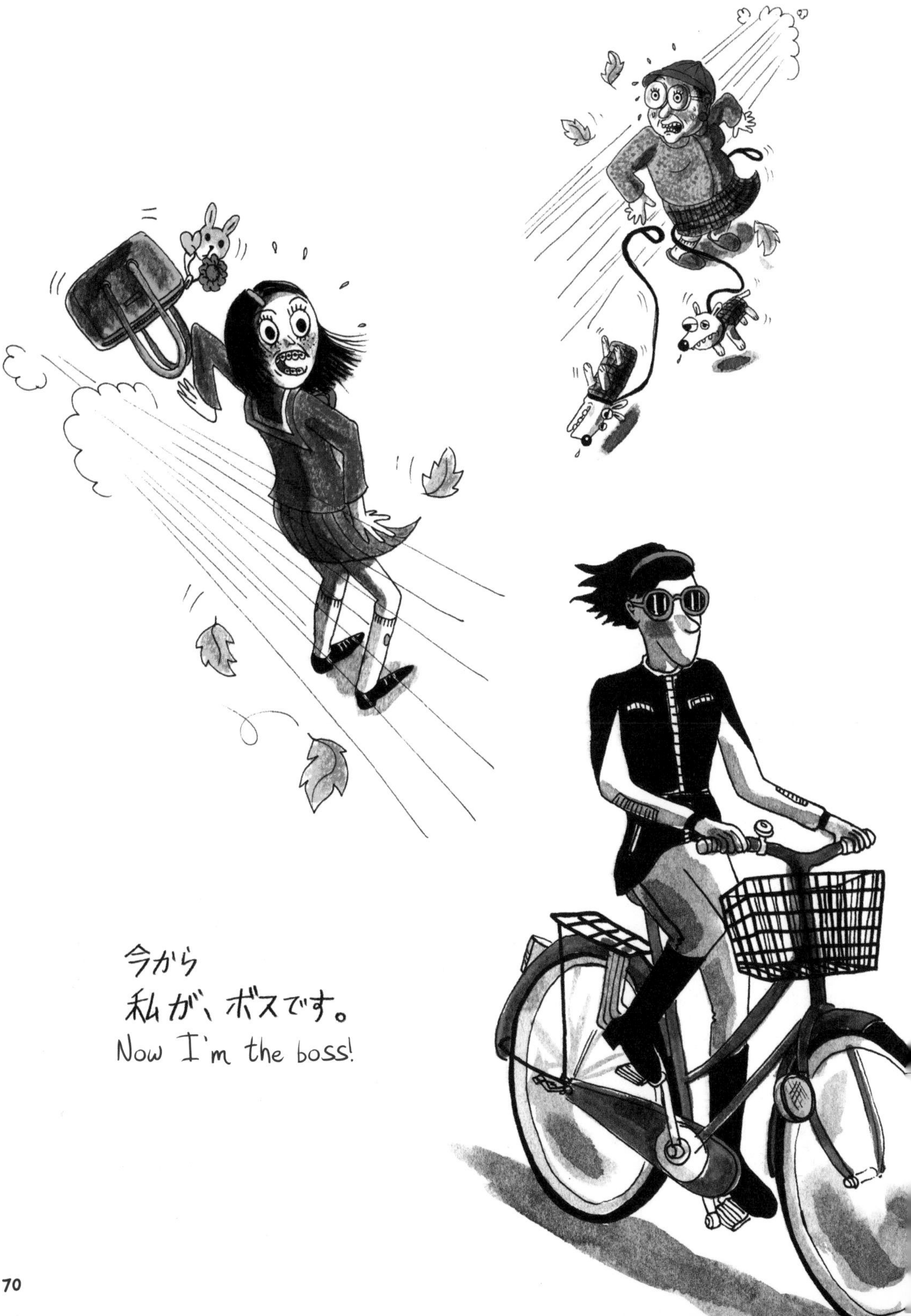
今から
私が、ボスです。
Now I'm the boss!

Around Tsuruse

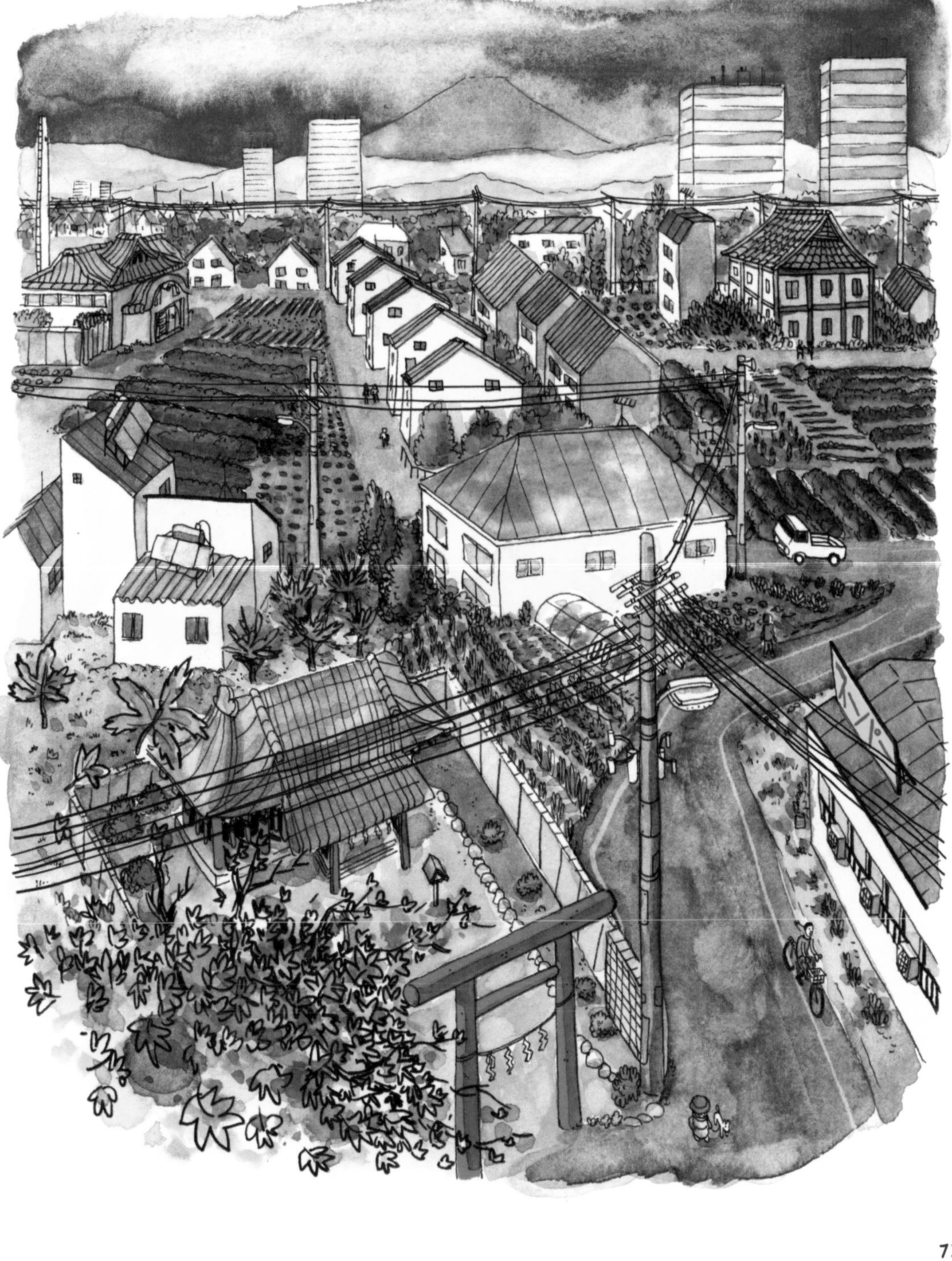
スーパー

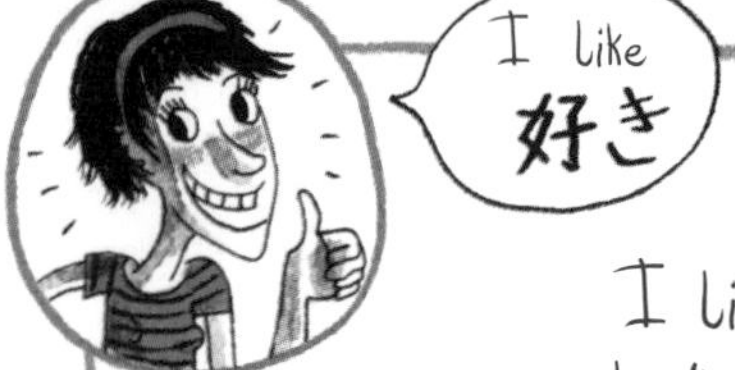
I like
好き

I like the little cushions the old ladies from the neighborhood make and attach to the seats at Tsuruse Station so that your butt is protected from the cold in winter.

鶴瀬駅のイスには
おばあさんたちが作って
くれた座布団が
あります。

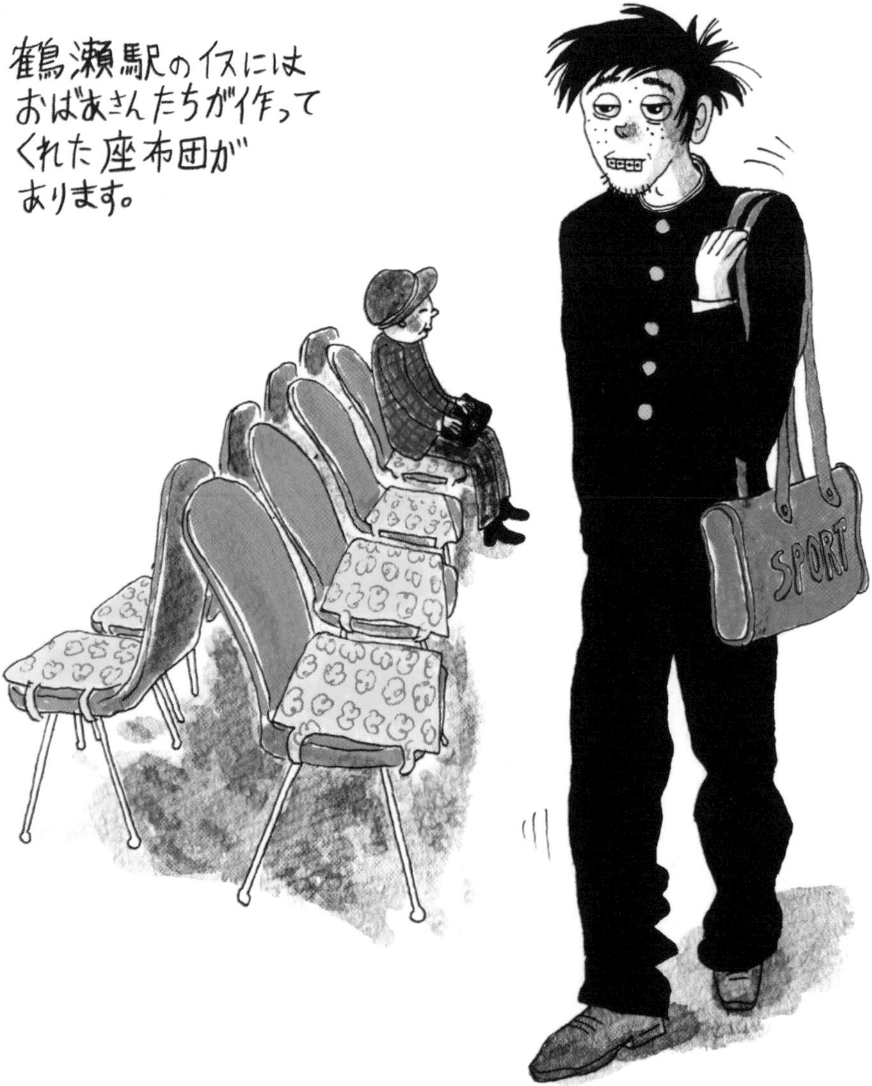
SPORT

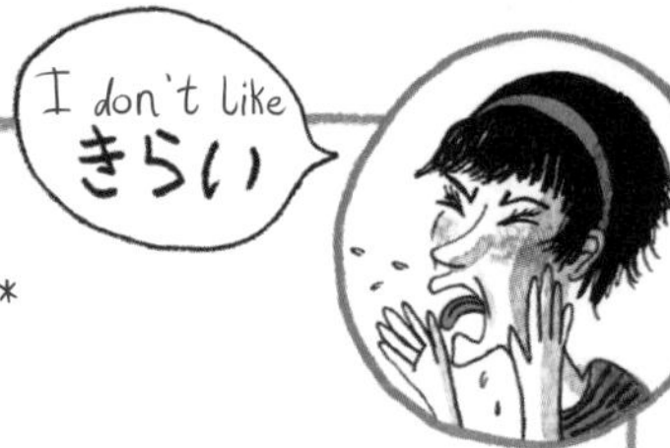
I don't like
きらい

I don't like the female-only car at rush hour.*
朝のラッシュの女性専用車両がきらいです。

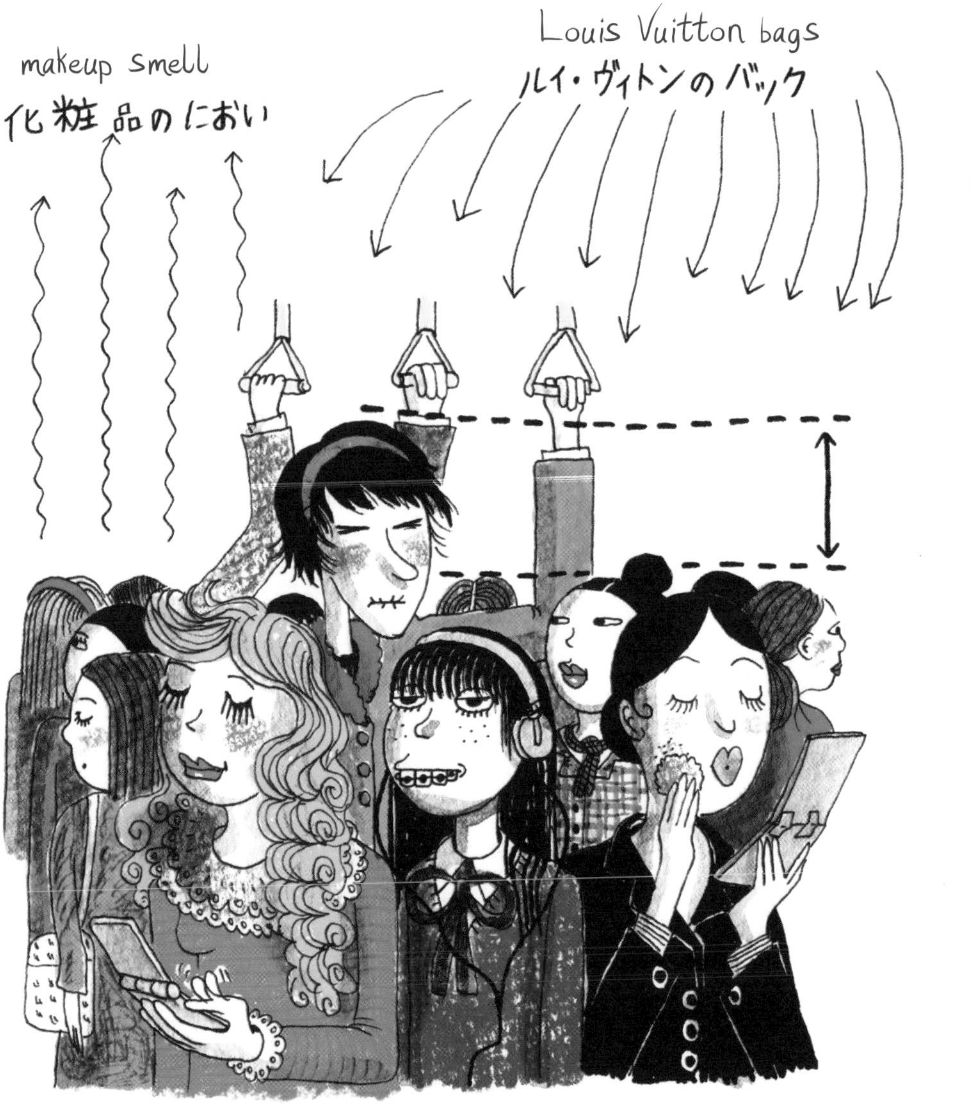
makeup smell
化粧品のにおい
Louis Vuitton bags
ルイ・ヴィトンのバック

* At rush hour, there's a special car for women in order to limit the number of molestation cases.

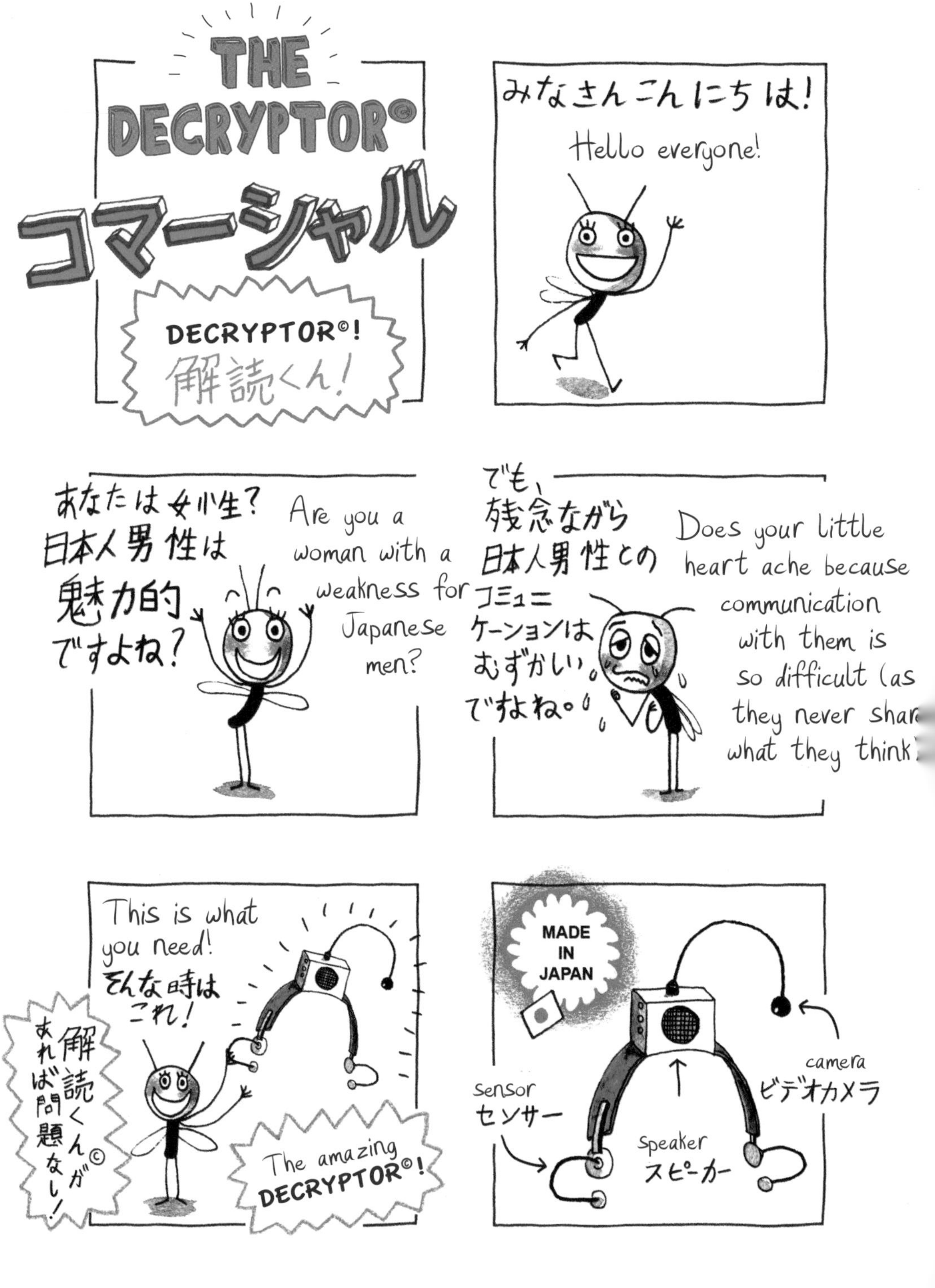
THE DECRYPTOR©
コマーシャル
DECRYPTOR©!
解読くん!
みなさんこんにちは!
Hello everyone!
あなたは女小生?日本人男性は魅力的ですよね?
Are you a woman with a weakness for Japanese men?
でも、残念ながら日本人男性とのコミュニケーションはむずかしい。ですよね。
Does your little heart ache because communication with them is so difficult (as they never shar
what they think
This is what you need!
そんな時はこれ!
解読くん©が
あれば問題なし!
The amazing DECRYPTOR©!
MADE IN JAPAN
camera
ビデオカメラ
Sensor
センサー
Speaker
スピーカー

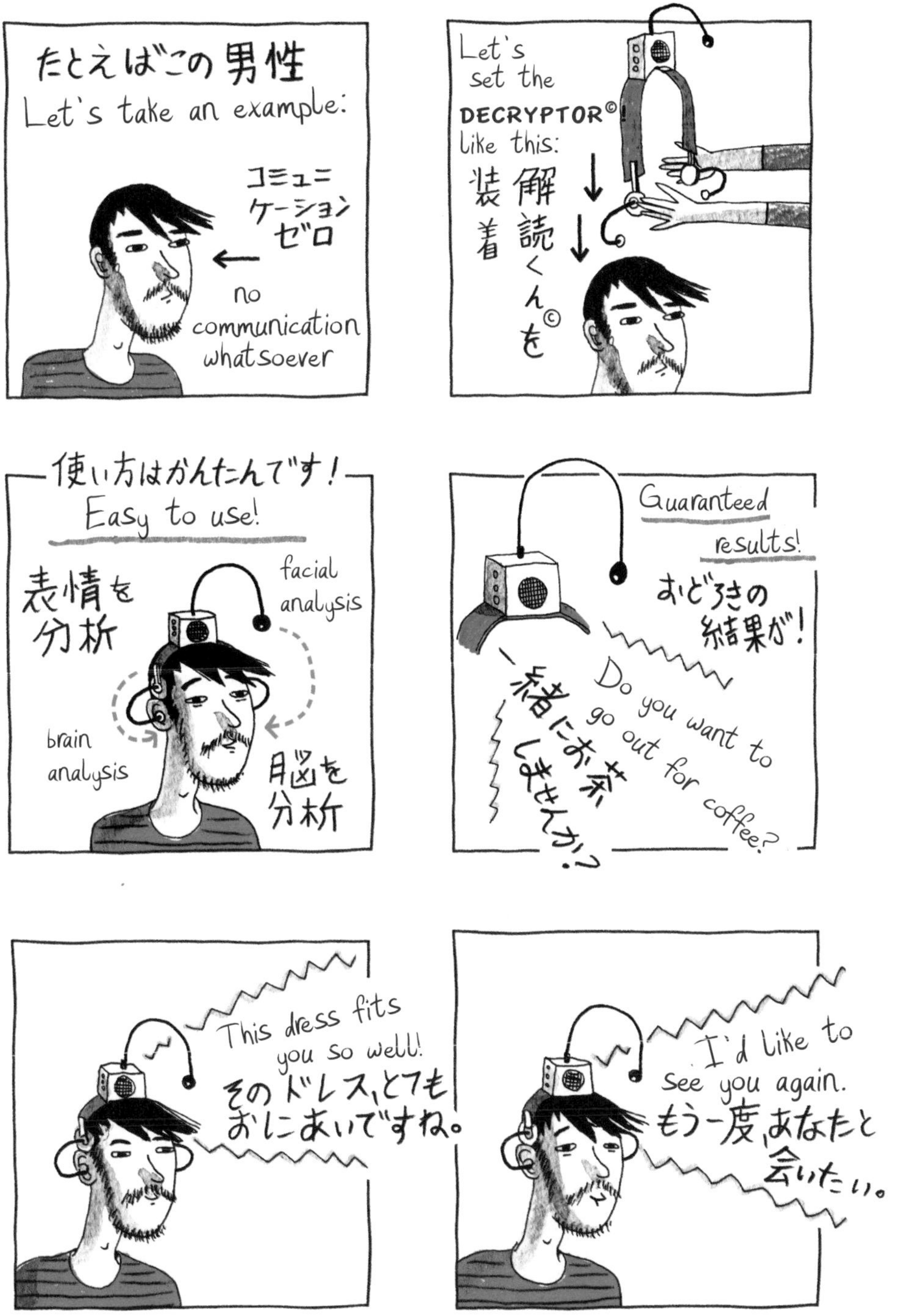
たとえばこの男性
Let's take an example:
コミュニケーションゼロ
no communication whatsoever
Let's set the DECRYPTOR© like this:
解読くん©を装着
使い方はかんたんです!
Easy to use!
表情を分析
facial analysis
brain analysis
脳を分析
Guaranteed results!
おどろきの結果が!
一緒にお茶しませんか!?
Do you want to go out for coffee?
This dress fits you so well!
そのドレス、とてもおにあいですね。
I'd like to see you again.
もう一度、あなたと会いたい。

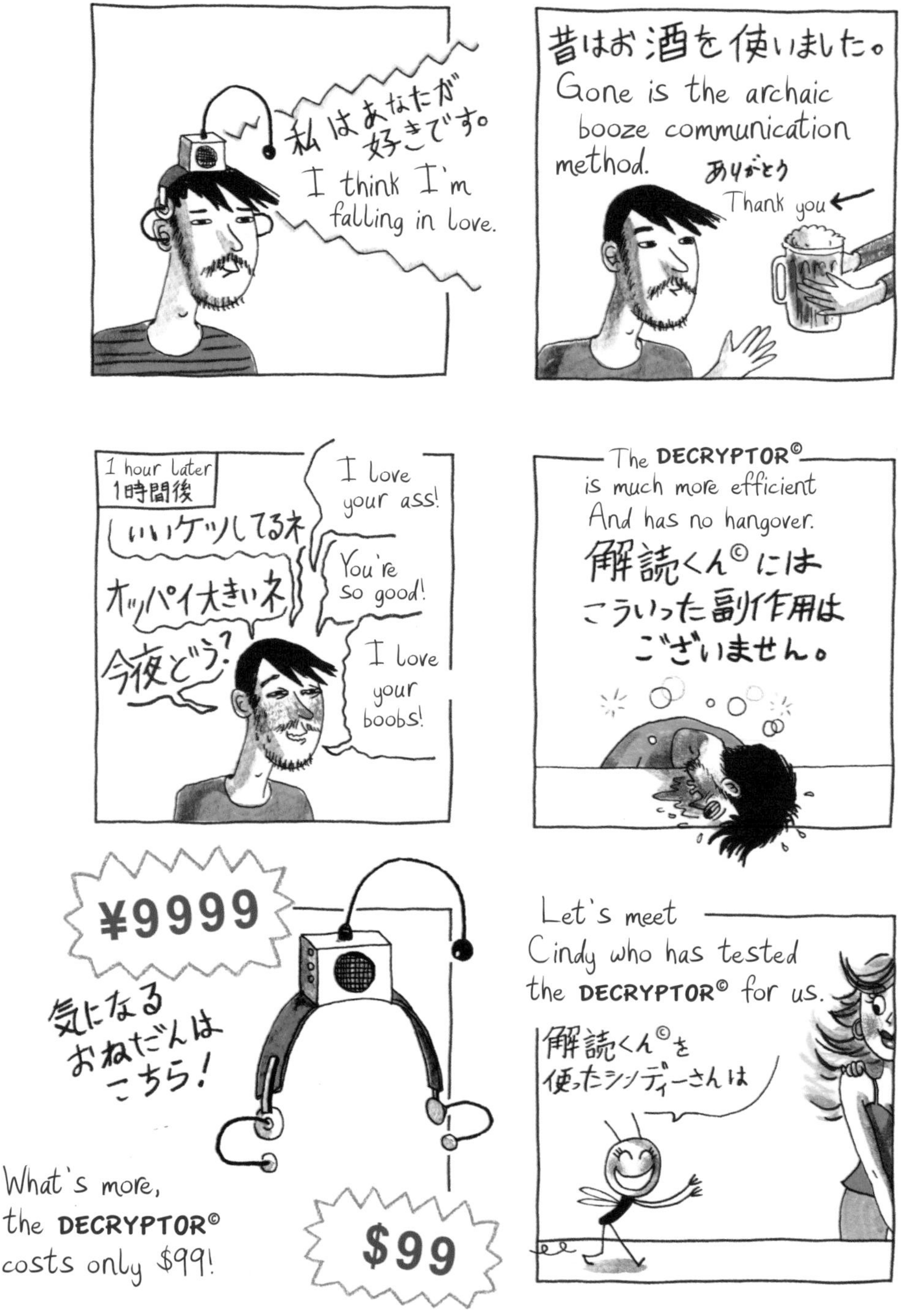
私はあなたが好きです。
I think I'm falling in love.
昔はお酒を使いました。
Gone is the archaic booze communication method.
ありがとう
Thank you
1 hour later
1時間後
いいケツしてるネ
I love your ass!
オッパイ大きいネ
You're so good!
今夜どう?
I love your boobs!
The DECRYPTOR© is much more efficient And has no hangover.
解読くん©にはこういった副作用はございません。
¥9999
気になるおねだんはこちら!
What's more, the DECRYPTOR© costs only $99!
$99
Let's meet Cindy who has tested the DECRYPTOR© for us.
解読くん©を使ったシンディーさんは

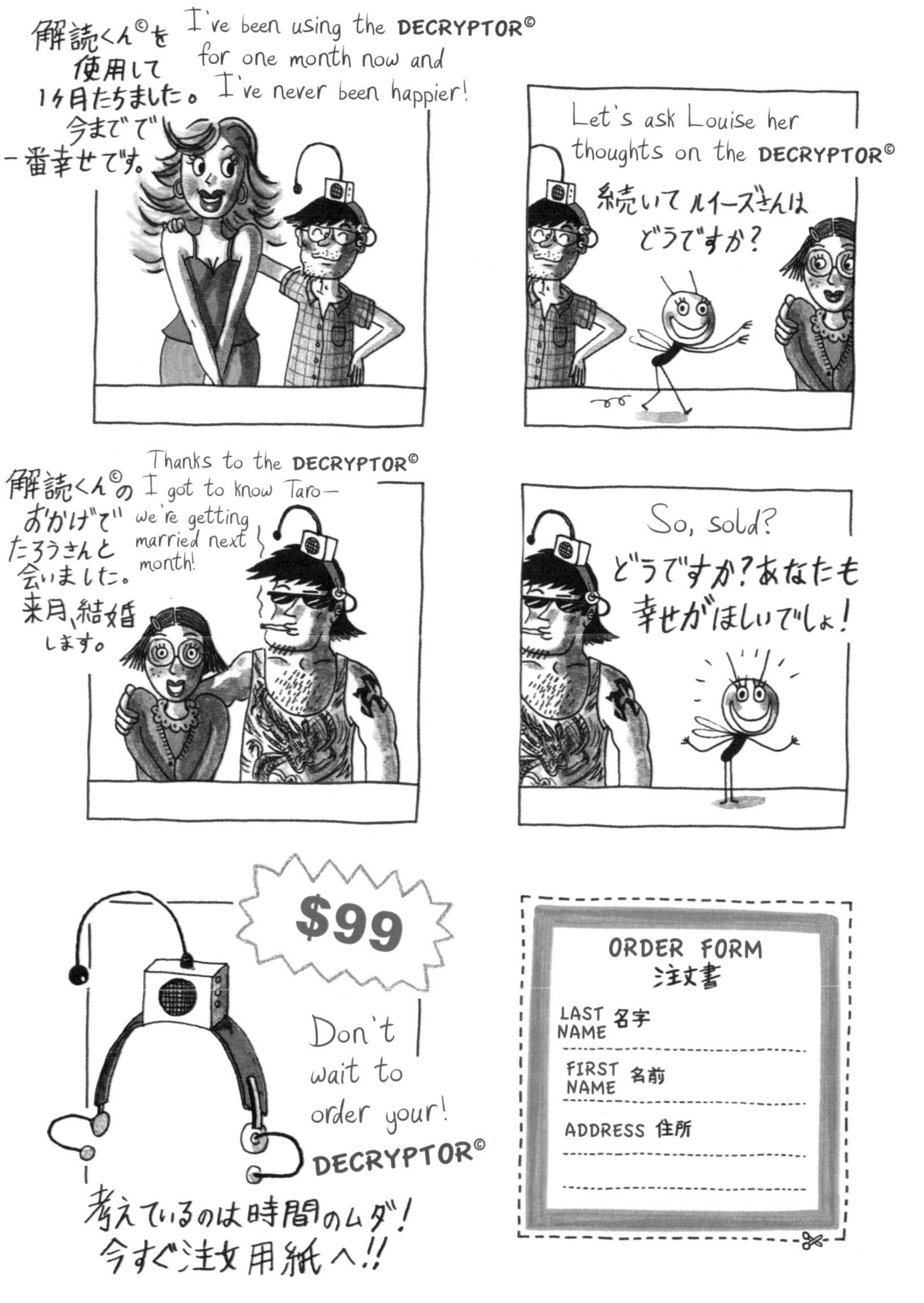

解読くん©を使用して1ヶ月たちました。今までで一番幸せです。
I've been using the DECRYPTOR© for one month now and I've never been happier!
Let's ask Louise her thoughts on the DECRYPTOR©
続いてルイーズさんはどうですか？
解読くん©のおかげでたろうさんと会いました。来月、結婚します。
Thanks to the DECRYPTOR© I got to know Taro—
we're getting married next month!
So, sold?
どうですか？あなたも幸せがほしいでしょ！
$99
Don't wait to order your! DECRYPTOR©
考えているのは時間のムダ！今すぐ注文用紙へ!!
ORDER FORM
注文書
LAST NAME 名字
FIRST NAME 名前
ADDRESS 住所

電車で見かける女性 Women on the Train

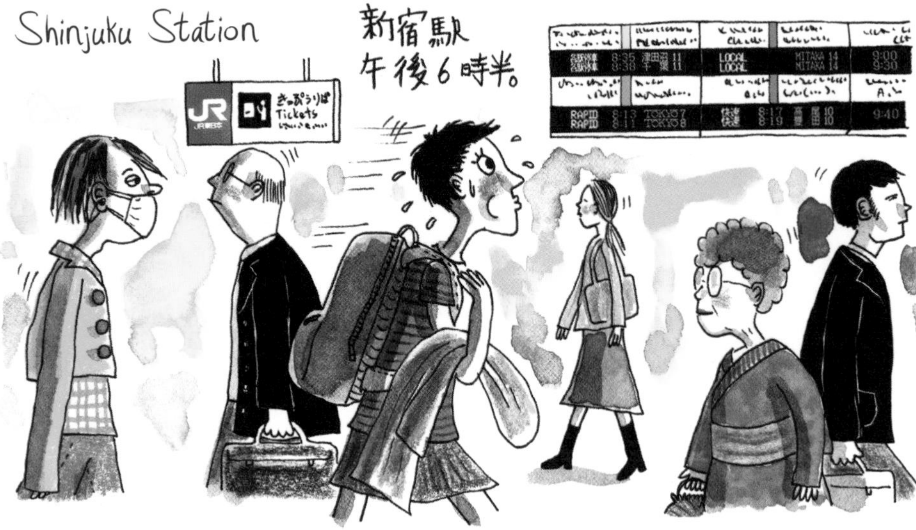
Shinjuku Station
新宿駅
午後6時半。
JR
きっぷうりば
Tickets

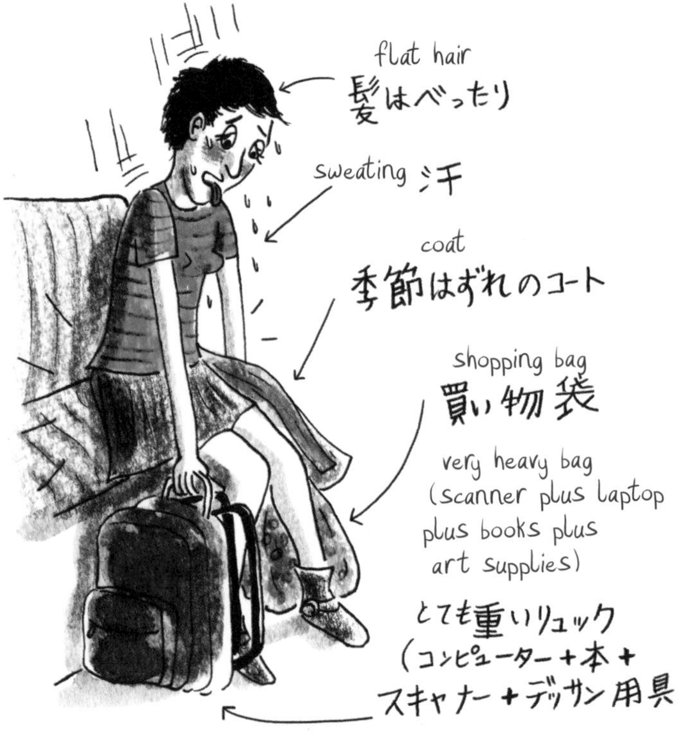
flat hair
髪はぺったり
sweating 汗
coat
季節はずれのコート
shopping bag
買い物袋
very heavy bag
(scanner plus laptop
plus books plus
art supplies)
とても重いリュック
(コンピューター+本+
スキャナー+デッサン用具

At the end of a full day giving animation classes here, a French class there, going to a job meeting somewhere else, then racing home for dinner, I am pooped.

今日もとてもいそがしいです。アニメのレッスンはあっち、フランス語のレッスンはこっち、仕事の面接はそっち。夕ごはんの時間に間に合わせるために帰るとちゅうです。今、本当につかれています。

私とぜんぜんちがう日本人女性たちのスタイル!

Whereas I am in this state, Japanese women on the train look like this:

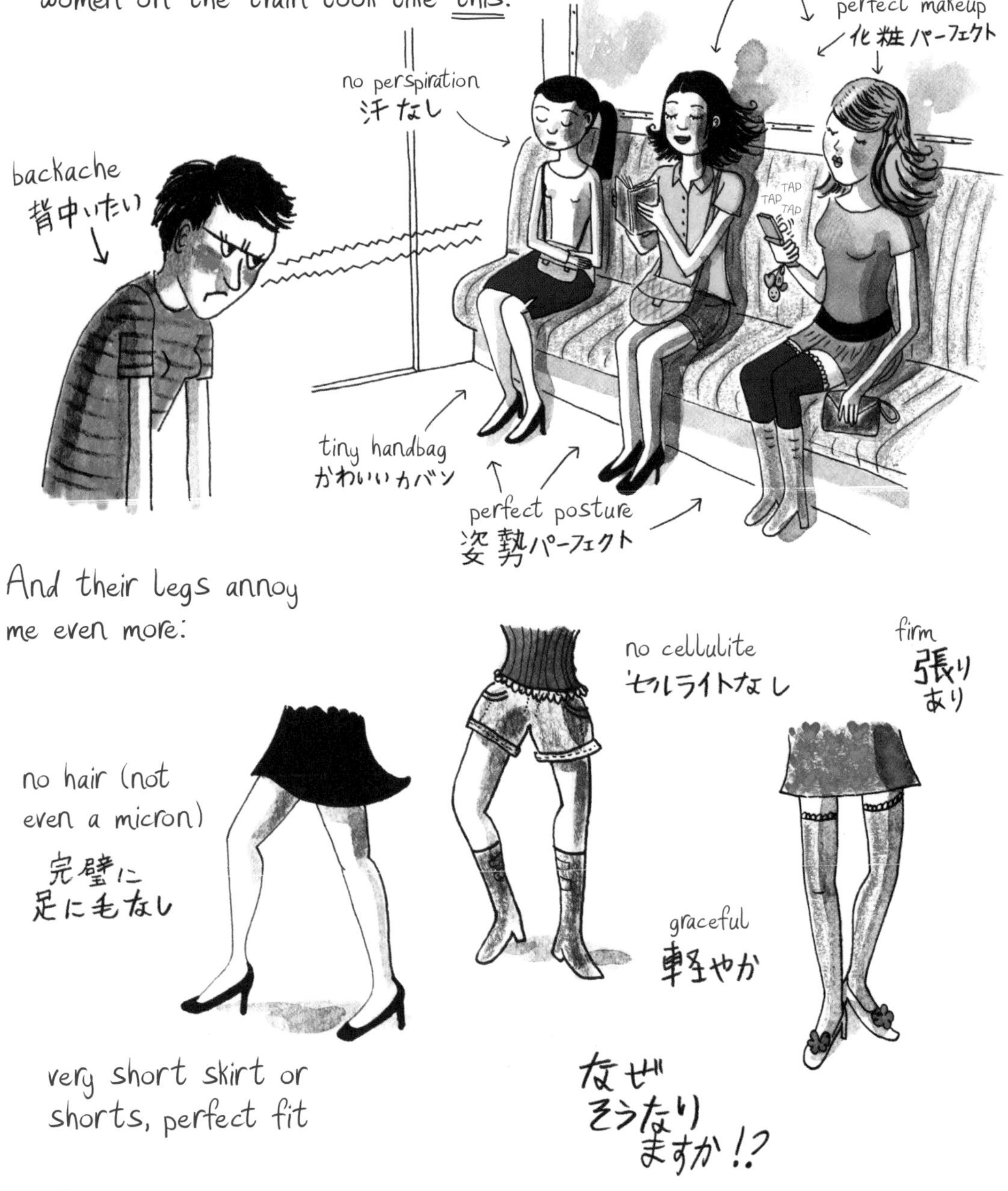
perfect hair
髪パーフェクト
perfect makeup
化粧パーフェクト
no perspiration
汗なし
backache
背中いたい
TAP TAP TAP
tiny handbag
かわいいカバン
perfect posture
姿勢パーフェクト
And their legs annoy me even more:
no cellulite
セルライトなし
firm
張りあり
no hair (not even a micron)
完璧に足に毛なし
graceful
軽やか
very short skirt or shorts, perfect fit
なぜそうなりますか!?

I Like
好き

I like watching the TV show "24" in Japanese.

日本語で話すドラマ「24」を見るのが好き。

"Moshi moshi"
もしもし...

I like the feeling you get at the end of an autumn afternoon.

秋の夕暮れ前のふんいきが好き。

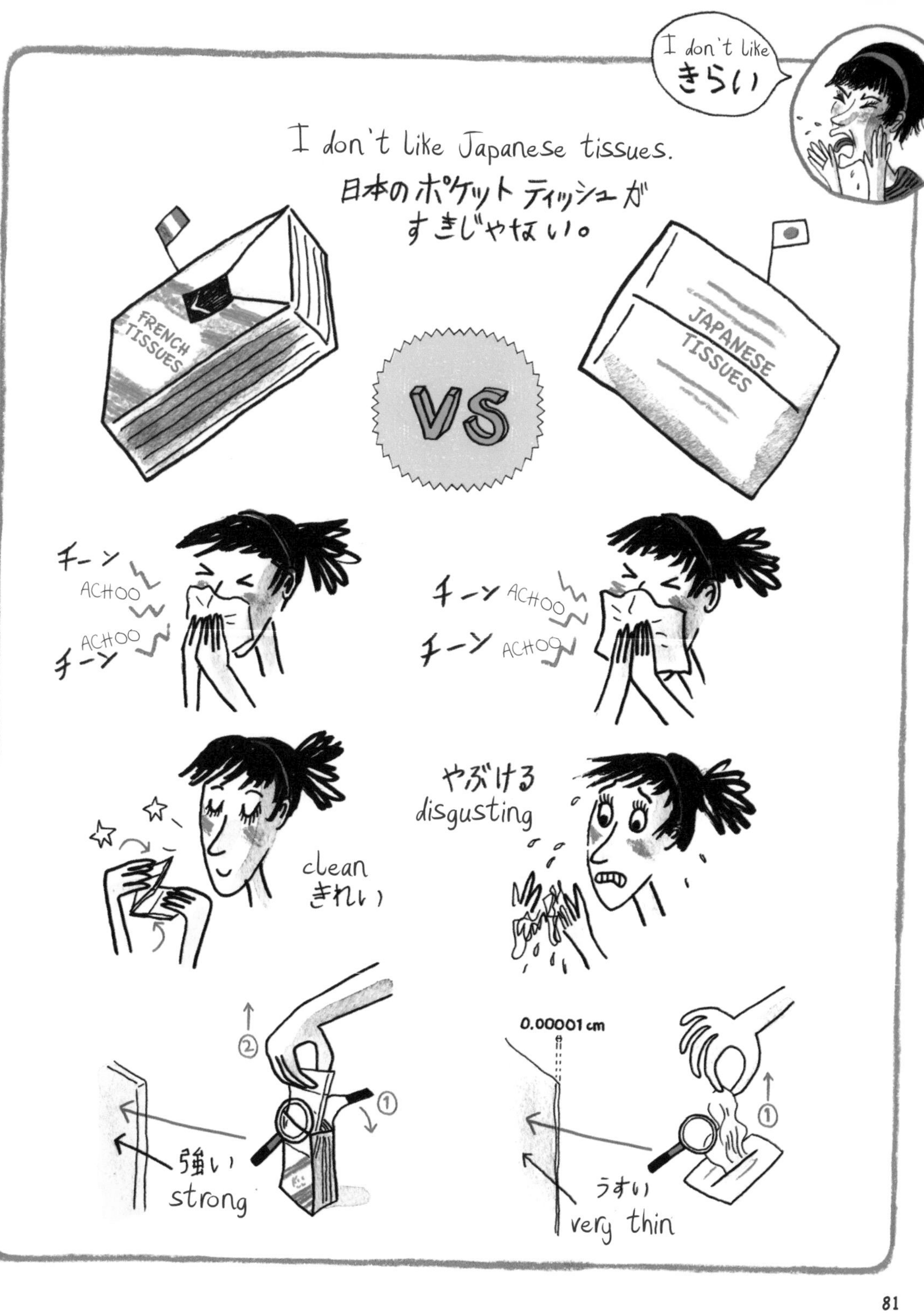
I don't like
きらい
I don't like Japanese tissues.
日本のポケットティッシュが
すきじゃない。
FRENCH TISSUES
VS
JAPANESE TISSUES
チーン
ACHOO
ACHOO
チーン
チーン ACHOO
チーン ACHOO
clean
きれい
やぶける
disgusting
②
①
強い
strong
0.00001 cm
①
うすい
very thin

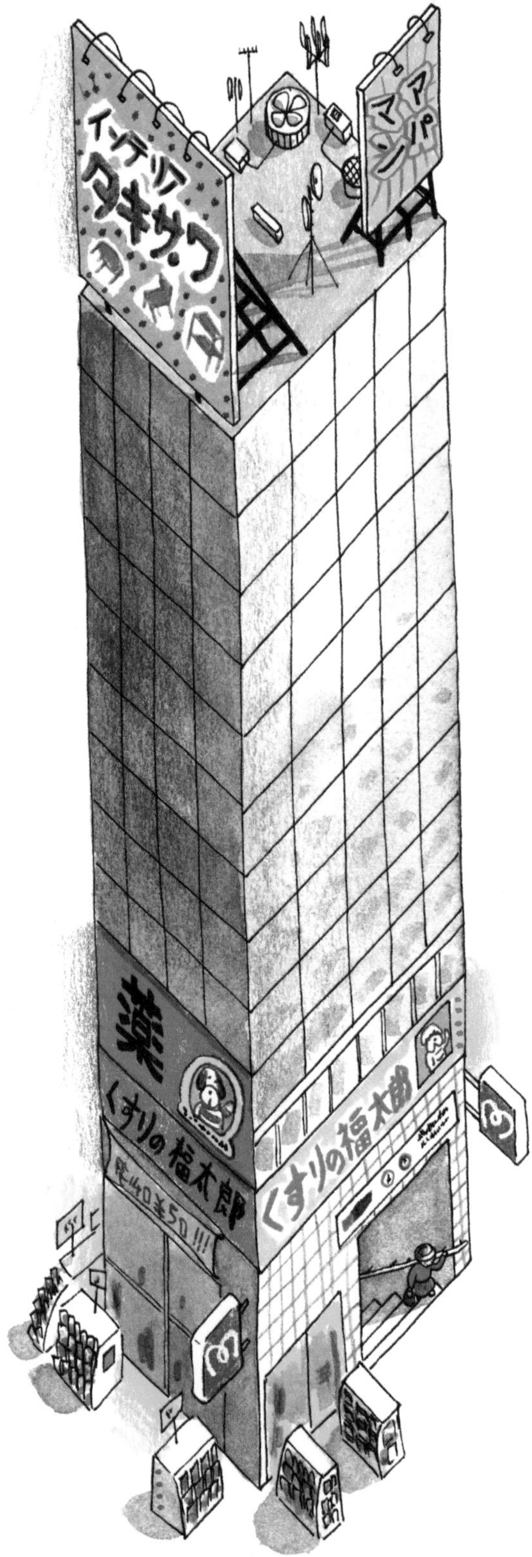
インテリア
タキザワ
アパマン
薬
くすりの福太郎
くすりの福太郎
くすりの福太郎

Living in
Meguro
目黒

Meguro 目黒

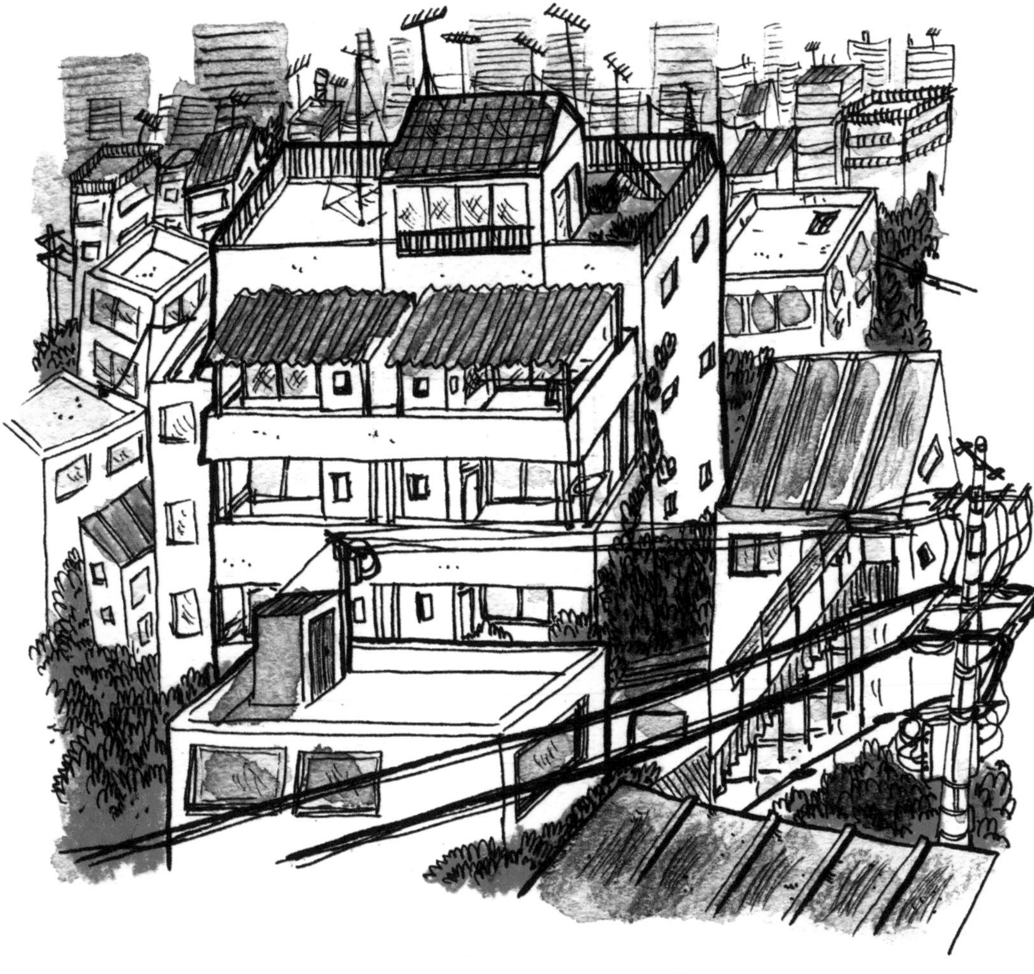

I've been in Japan for 18 months already and I still can't speak Japanese. So I break the piggy bank and register for Japanese classes. The school is in Shibuya, far from Tsuruse... But wait, I'm in luck! A spot opens up in a two-person shared rental in Meguro, right next to Shibuya!

日本で1年半。
まだ日本語を話せません。
決心して貯金を切りくずし、
渋谷にある日本語学校へ
行きます。ちょうどいいタイミングで、
目黒(渋谷に近い)の2人暮らし
シェアハウスに空きがあります。

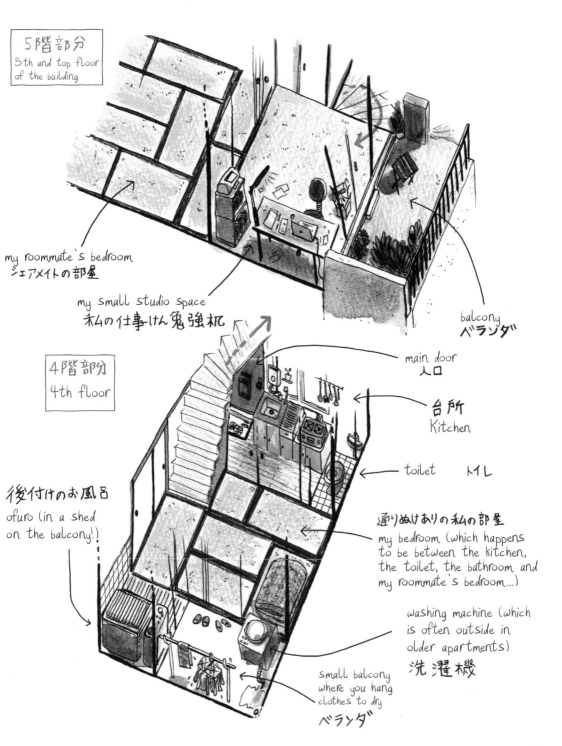

5階部分
5th and top floor
of the building

my roommate's bedroom
シェアメイトの部屋

my small studio space
私の仕事けん兎強机

balcony
ベランダ

4階部分
4th floor

main door
入口

台所
Kitchen

toilet　トイレ

後付けのお風呂
ofuro (in a shed
on the balcony!)

通りぬけありの私の部屋
my bedroom (which happens
to be between the kitchen,
the toilet, the bathroom and
my roommate's bedroom...)

washing machine (which
is often outside in
older apartments)
洗濯機

small balcony
where you hang
clothes to dry
ベランダ

85

70
70s
Condo Kit
年代
アパート
セット
70

This building dates from the early 70s, which is very old for Japan.

The following nine points confirm that I am indeed living in an old Japanese condo:

これから あげる
9つの ポイントで、
日本の 古い アパートの
スタイル が 分がります。

POINT 1

Metal entrance door (resembling a bunker door) with an integrated mailbox.

鉄製のドアに
鉄製の郵便受ケ

POINT 2

玄関の ちょっと
した あがリロ

As in most indoor spaces in Japan (and even in some restaurants and medical offices), you take off your shoes before going in.

In old condos, there's always a difference in level between inside and outside. This is not always the case in the newer places.

It makes cleaning up easier!

Tatami mats are always the same size.

70 in (177.8 cm)

35 in (88.9 cm)

畳のある部屋

tatami placement examples

POiNT 3
Except for the kitchen, the whole apartment has tatami flooring.

POiNT 4
カンカンカン風呂 (追いだき可)

No built-in system to heat the ofuro. You have to turn the thingy in order to activate the other thingy).

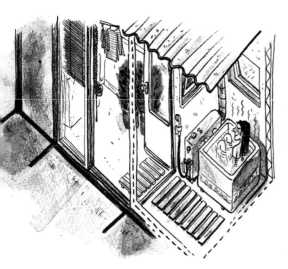

Crazy! When this apartment was first built there was no bath, because in those days people used to go to the public baths (sento).

"No problem, let's just install one on the balcony!" said the owner to himself... And that's why the ofuro is out here, in an add-on shed.

後付けのお風呂
このアパートは最初、
お風呂なしで建てられます。
が時代の変化もあり
今はベランダで入浴します。

ウォシュレット

POINT 5

All-ceramic 70s style toilet with a tiny washbasin where you can wash your hands in the water that's refilling the cistern. Very convenient—I don't know why they only have them in Japan.

POINT 6

State-of-the-art kitchen ventilation.

このタイプの
換気扇

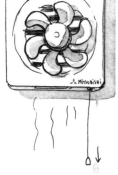

POINT 7

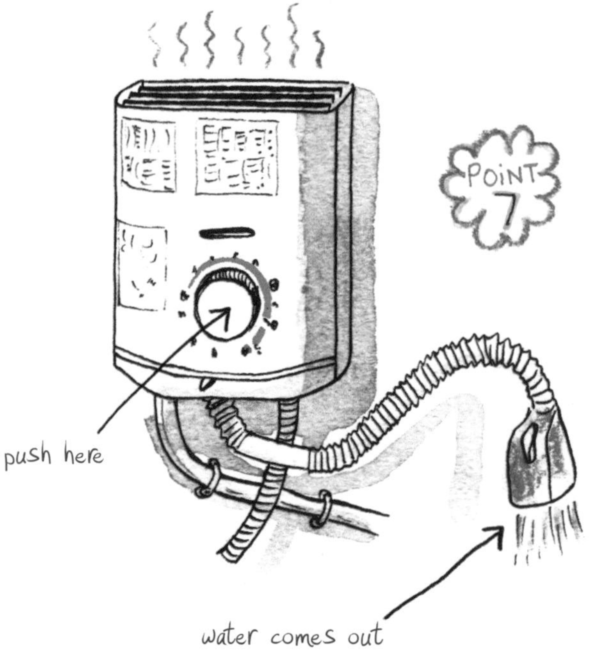

push here

water comes out

給湯器
The kitchen sink water heater, an add-on after the building was finished.

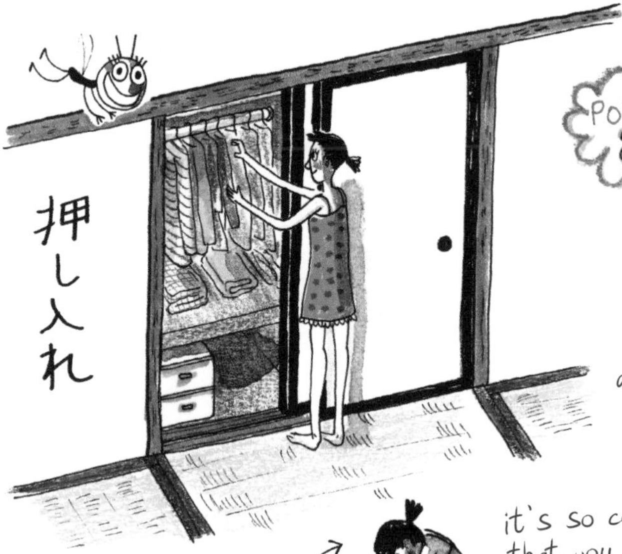
押し入れ

POINT 8

The apartment has built-in cupboards called oshiire. Normally you put your futon (traditional mattress), kake-buton (comforter) and makura (pillow) inside. But I don't have a lot of room, so I put all my stuff in there.

In apartments with tatami, you lay out your futon at night...

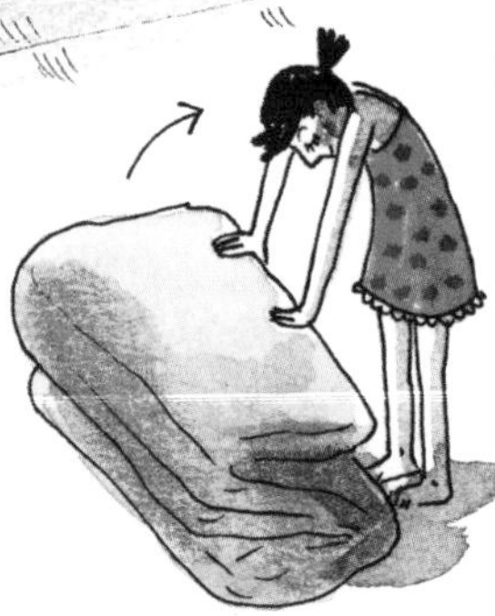

it's so comfortable that you sleep like a baby.

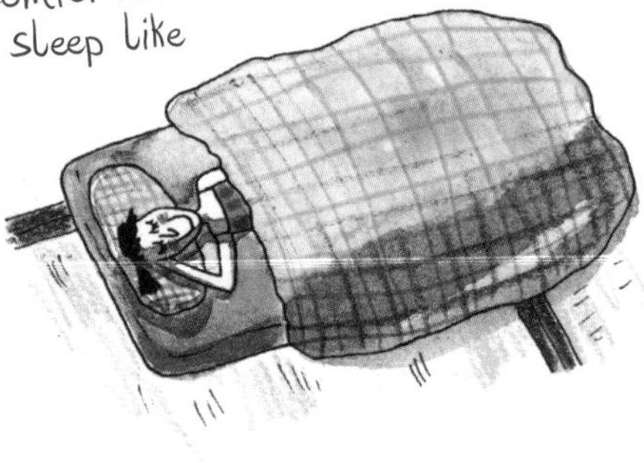

POINT 9

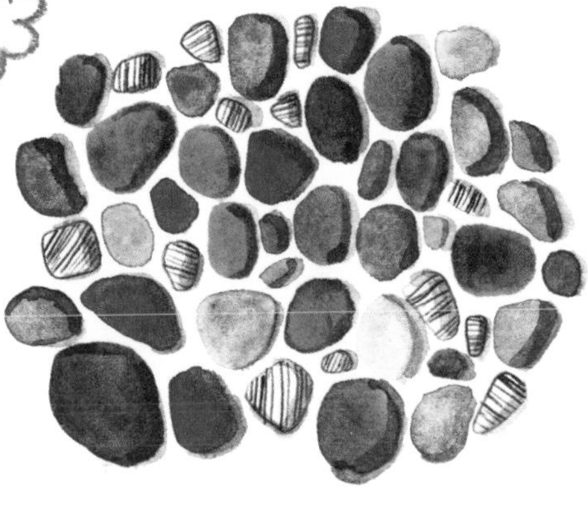

Pretty floor tiles in the bathroom that look like pebbles in a river.
お風呂とトイレの床にこの タイプのタイル

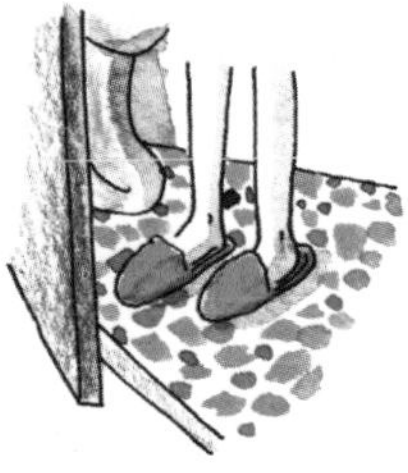

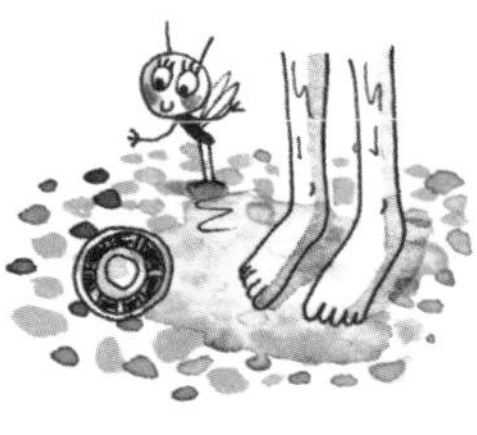

I highly recommend the Edo-Tokyo Museum (Ryogoku Station, 600 yen). This museum reconstructs all of Tokyo's history with life-size dioramas among other things. In the "70s Tokyo Apartment Architecture" exhibit, I thought I was in my home!

Japanese Language School 日本語の学校

毎日、自転車で日本語の
学校へ行く日々です。

Every day I go to Japanese
school on my little bike.

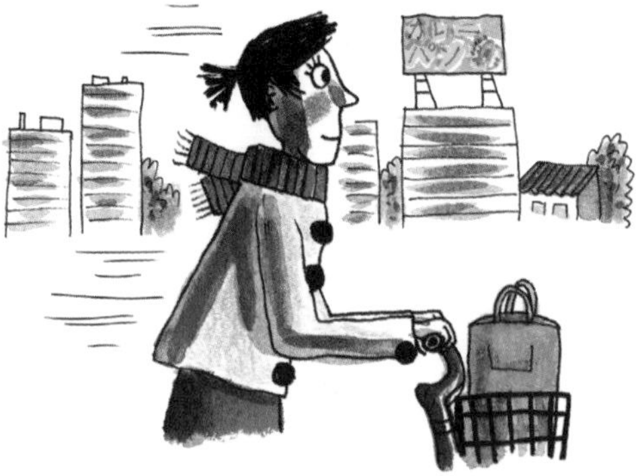

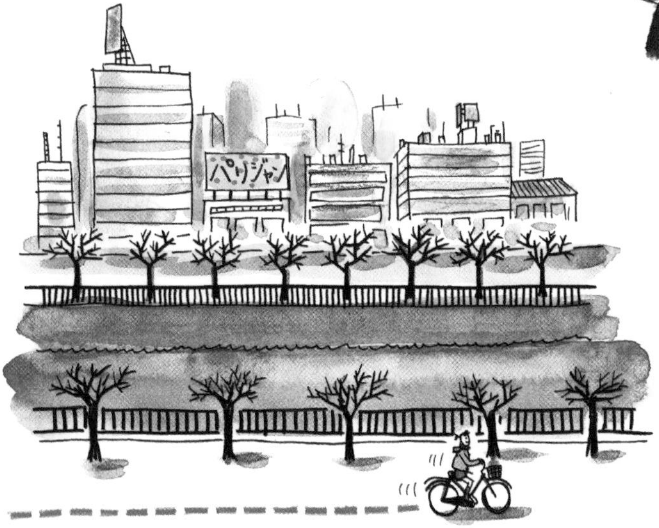
パリジャン

目黒川沿いが
通学路です。

I ride along the
Meguro River from Meguro
to Nakameguro...

西郷山公園
を越えます。

then I go through
Saigoyama Park...

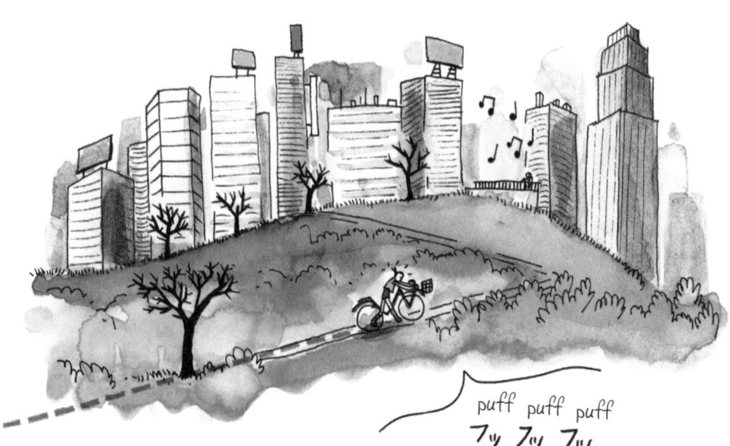
puff puff puff
フッ フッ フッ

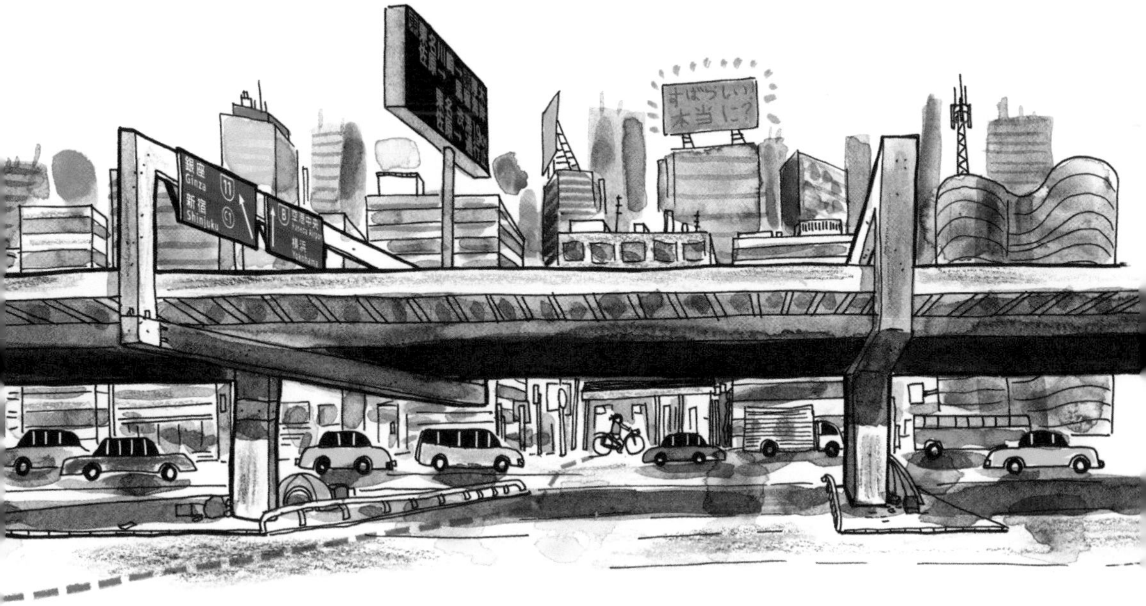

すばらしい!
本当に?
銀座
Ginza
新宿
Shinjuku

国道246に着いたら
学校はすぐそこです。

in order to end up on Highway 246
street underneath and highway above).

A few more yards and I'm at the
chool, where I park my bike.

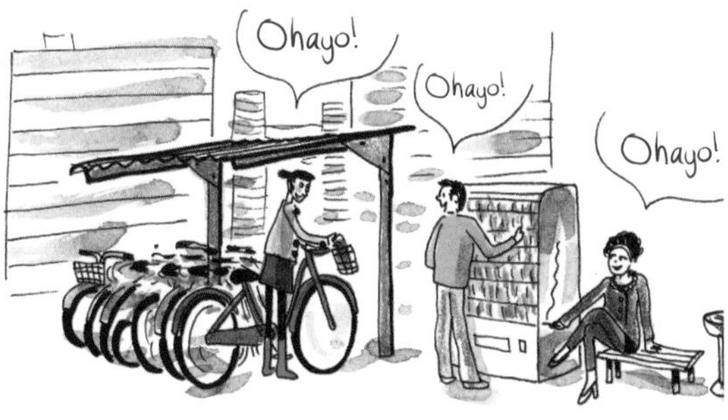

Ohayo!
Ohayo!
Ohayo!

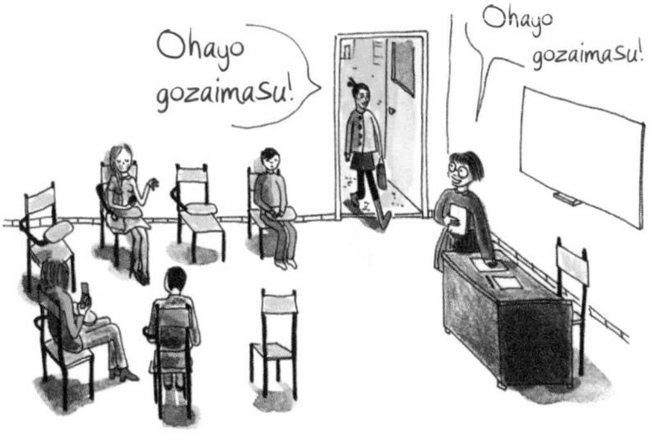

Ohayo gozaimasu!
Ohayo gozaimasu!

今日も一日がんばりましょう!

Come on, let's begin a full day
of studying Japanese!

私のクラスメイト… In my language classroom, there are…

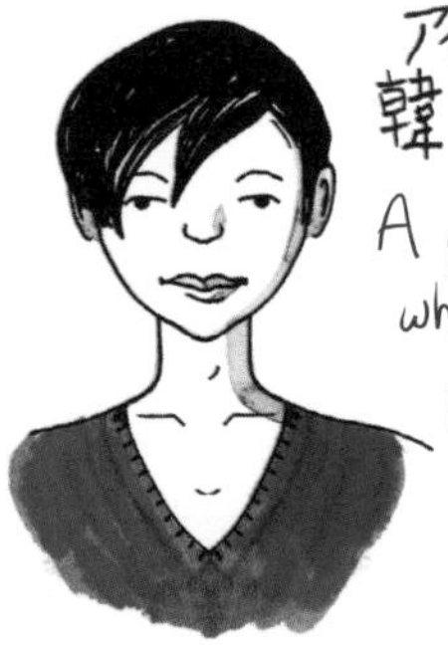

アイドルヘアーの韓国人。

A young Korean guy who always has a perfect hairdo.

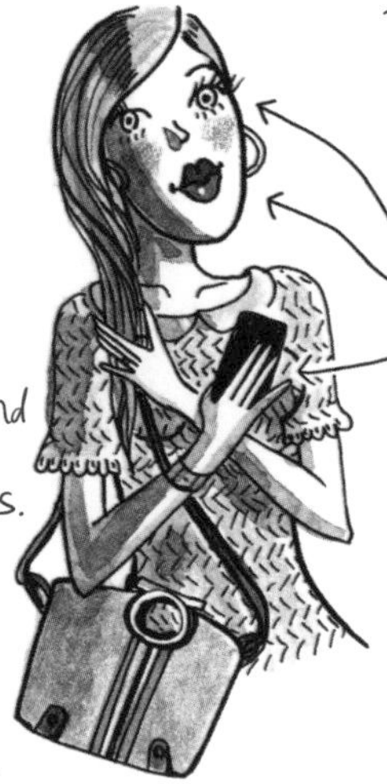

A hyper-rich Shanghainese who arrives everyday by taxi from her 5-star hotel.

上海出身スーパーメガリッチの女性。

I think her dad's best friend is a plastic surgeon

彼女のお父さんの友だちは、整形外科医かな？

毎日、六本木の5つ星ホテルからタクシーで来る。

Today, it's a Gucci bag and a Dolce & Gabbana dress.

今日はグッチのカバンとドルチェ＆ガッバーナの服。

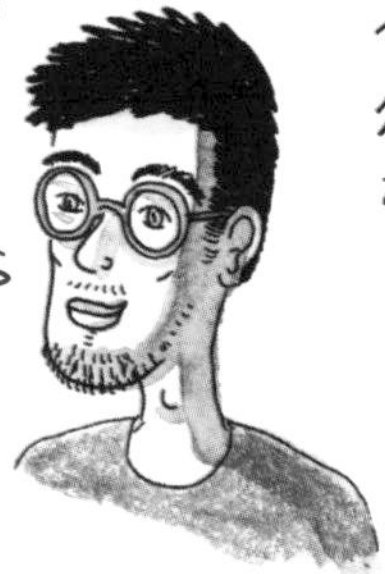

美大に行きたい台湾人。

A Taiwanese guy who plans on going to art school.

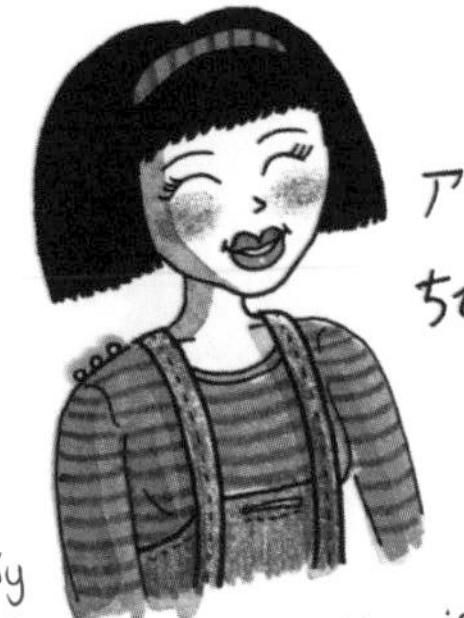

アラレちゃん＋ちびまるこちゃんの台湾人。

A super cute Taiwanese girl who's a mix between Punky Brewster and Amélie Poulain, the girl from the French movie.

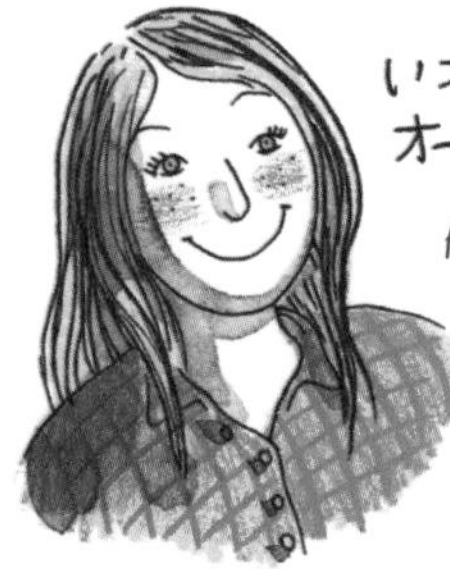

いつも笑顔のオーストラリア人。

An Australian girl, always smiling.

もちろん日本語の授業で先生は、日本語だけで説明します。

Of course, the classes are taught only in Japanese.

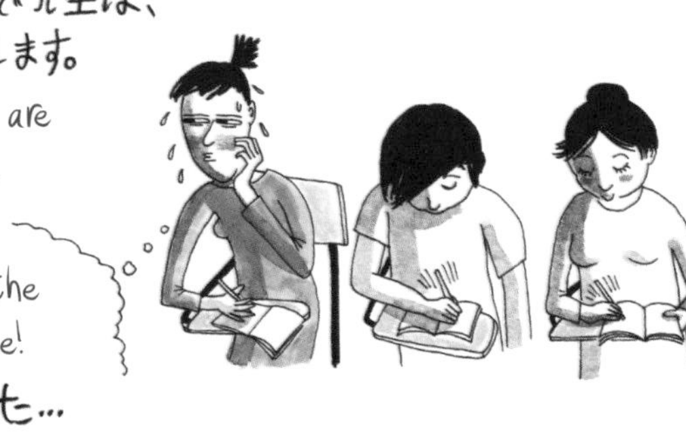

OK, I've already forgotten the meaning of the first sentence!

オッケ〜文の始めもわすれちゃった…

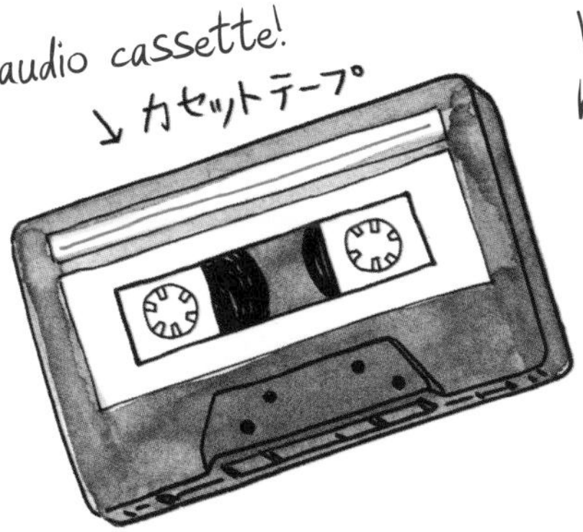
audio cassette!
カセットテープ

We practice pronunciation and grammar with high-tech materials.

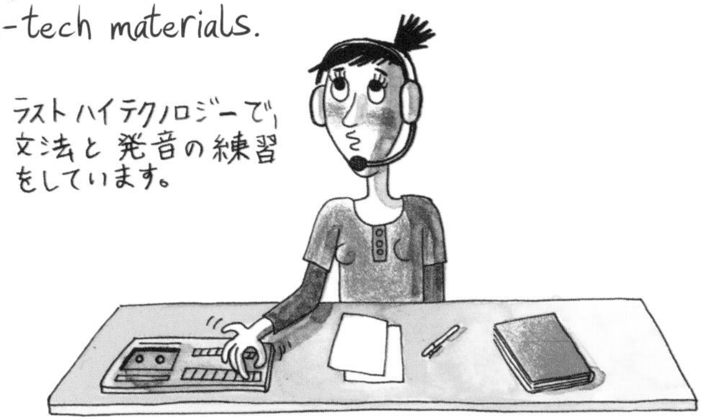
ラストハイテクノロジーで、
文法と発音の練習
をしています。

Kyo wa nan nichi desu ka?
Hai, Julie-san!

Then I'm picked by the school's sexiest teacher.

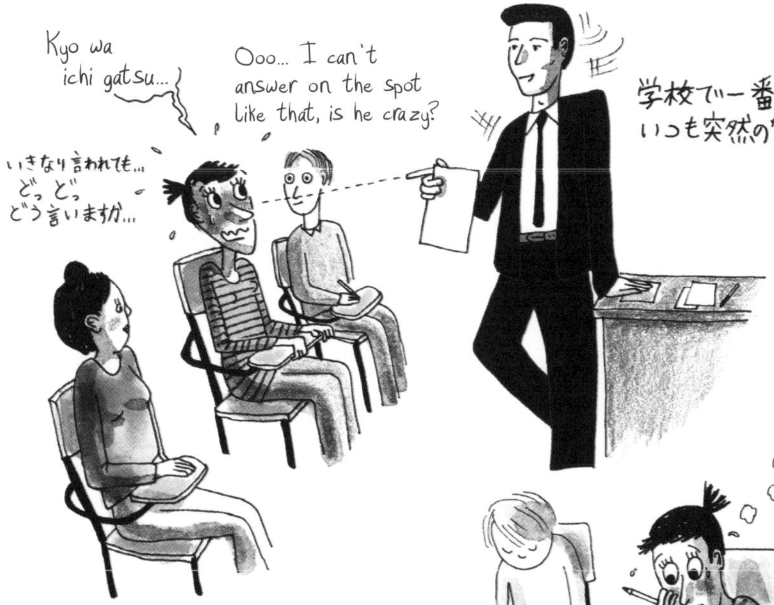
Kyo wa ichi gatsu...
Ooo... I can't answer on the spot like that, is he crazy?
いきなり言われても...
どっどっ
どう言いますか...

学校で一番かこいい先生は
いつも突然の質問でぼんやりできません。

So, ok, the character that looks like a guy blinking I think is aruku but what does it mean?

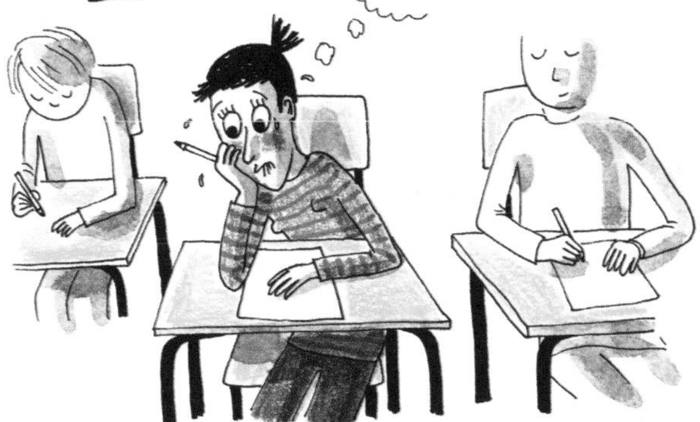

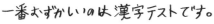

一番むずかしいのは漢字テストです。

The toughest are the <u>kanji</u> tests (Chinese characters that make up a good portion of the Japanese language. Each character has several meanings and possible pronunciations).

But day after day of study finally pays off, so much so that the other day, at Ebisu Station...

日々勉強します。
少しずつ日本語が分かるようになってきます。

恵比寿駅で...

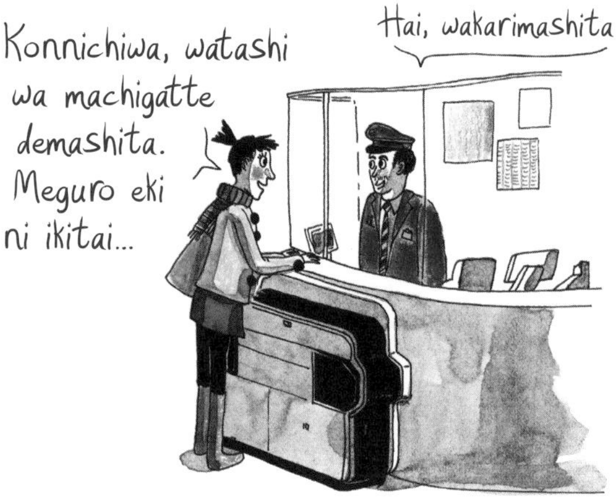
Konnichiwa, watashi wa machigatte demashita. Meguro eki ni ikitai...
Hai, wakarimashita...

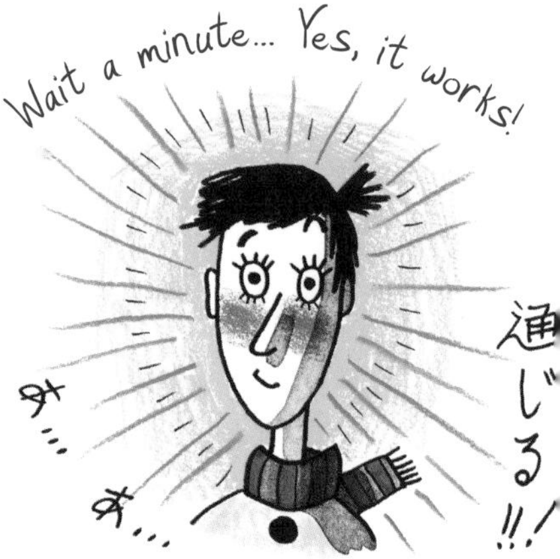
Wait a minute... Yes, it works!
あ...
あ...
通じる!!!

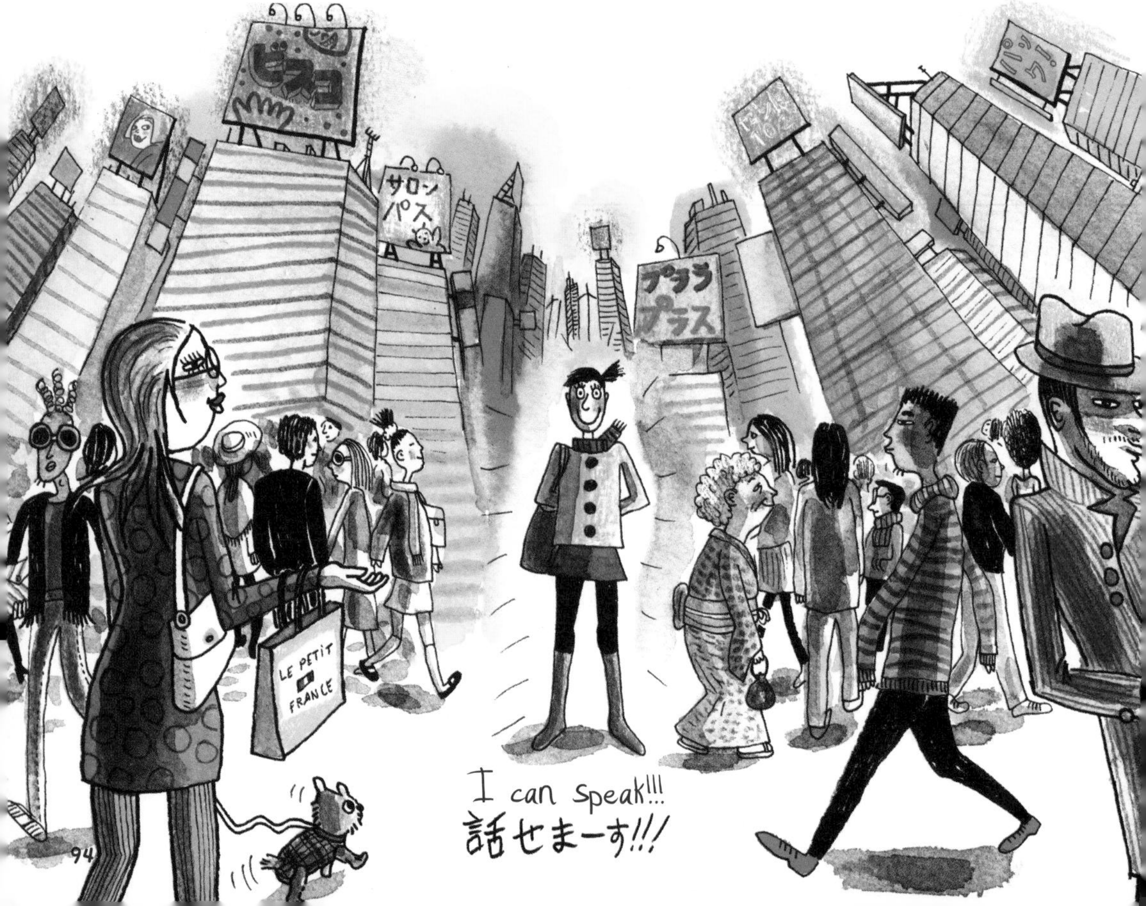
ピスコ
サロンパス
プララプラス
LE PETIT FRANCE
I can speak!!!
話せまーす!!!

The ATM

In Japan, ATMs are everywhere. It's a good thing I've made strides, because the Japanese number system can be hard to grasp at first.

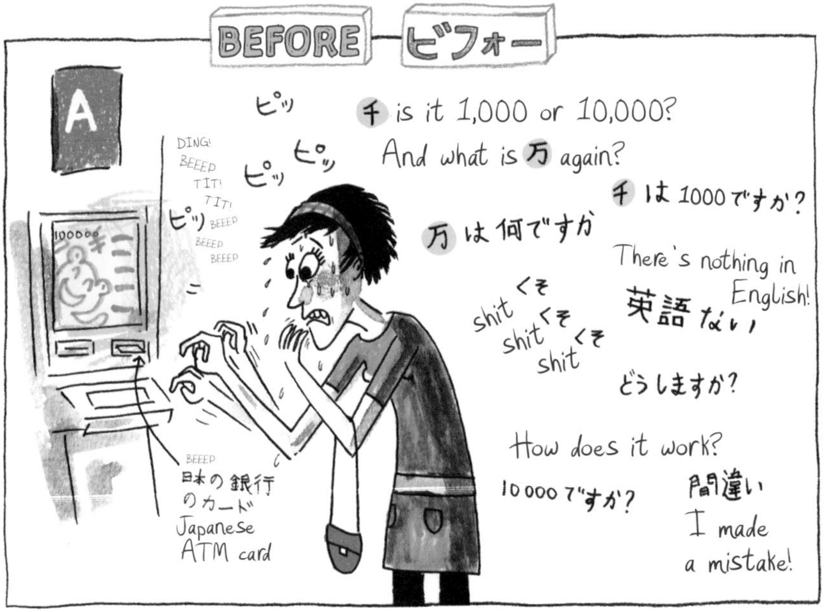
BEFORE ビフォー
A
ピッ
ピッ ピッ
DING!
BEEEP
TIT!
TIT!
ピッ BEEEP
BEEEP
BEEEP
千 is it 1,000 or 10,000?
And what is 万 again?
千は1000ですか？
万は何ですか
There's nothing in English!
英語ない
shit くそ
shit くそ
shit くそ
どうしますか？
How does it work?
10000ですか？
間違い
I made a mistake!
BEEEP
日本の銀行のカード
Japanese ATM card

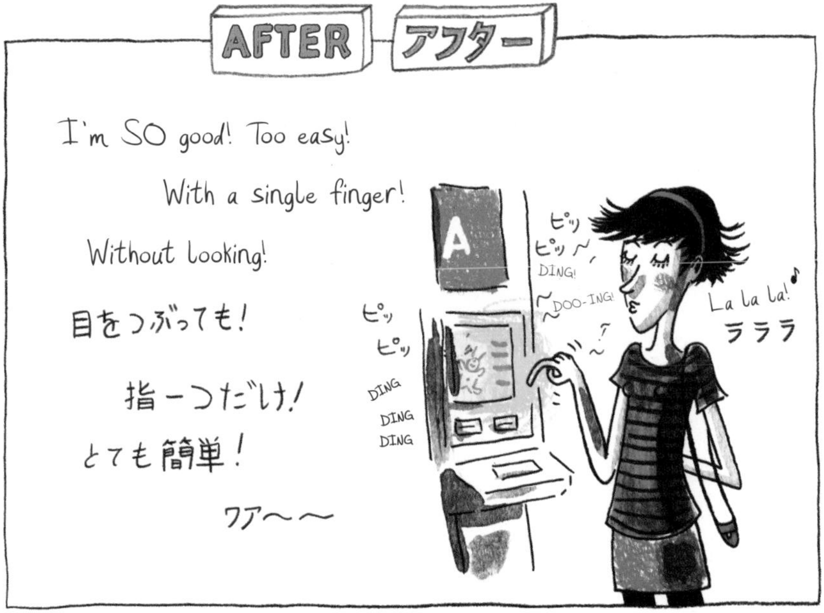
AFTER アフター
I'm SO good! Too easy!
With a single finger!
Without looking!
目をつぶっても！
指一つだけ！
とても簡単！
ワア〜〜
A
ピッ
ピッ〜
DING!
〜DOO-ING!
ピッ
ピッ
DING
DING
DING
La la la!
ラララ

The Police 警官

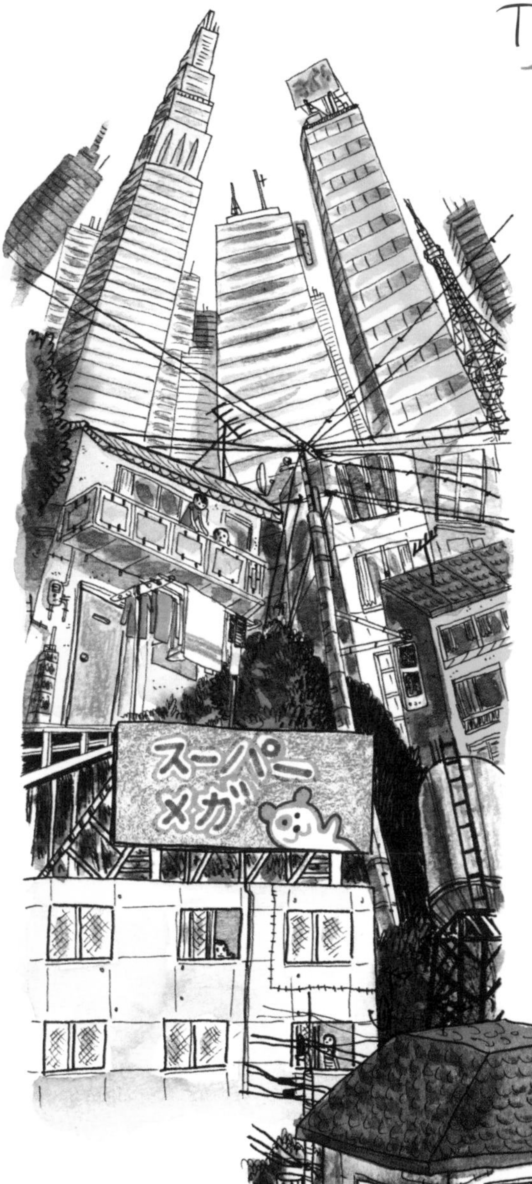

スーパー
メガ

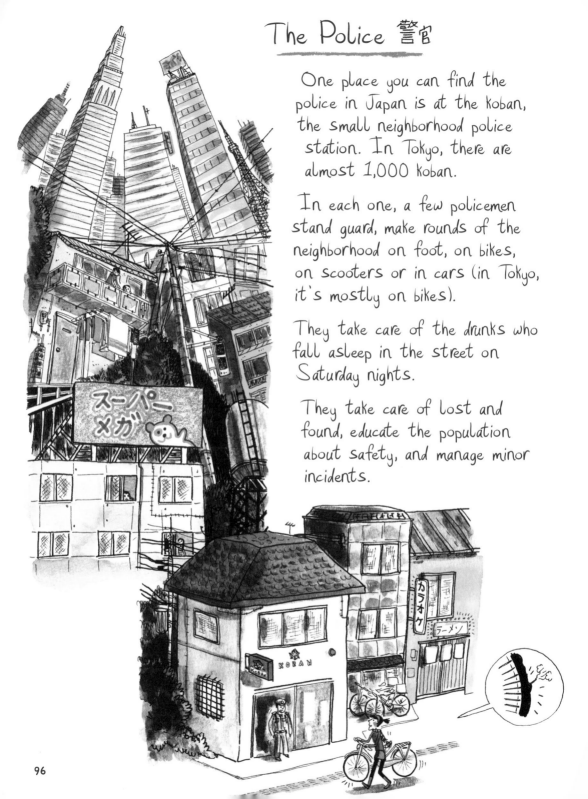

One place you can find the police in Japan is at the koban, the small neighborhood police station. In Tokyo, there are almost 1,000 koban.

In each one, a few policemen stand guard, make rounds of the neighborhood on foot, on bikes, on scooters or in cars (in Tokyo, it's mostly on bikes).

They take care of the drunks who fall asleep in the street on Saturday nights.

They take care of lost and found, educate the population about safety, and manage minor incidents.

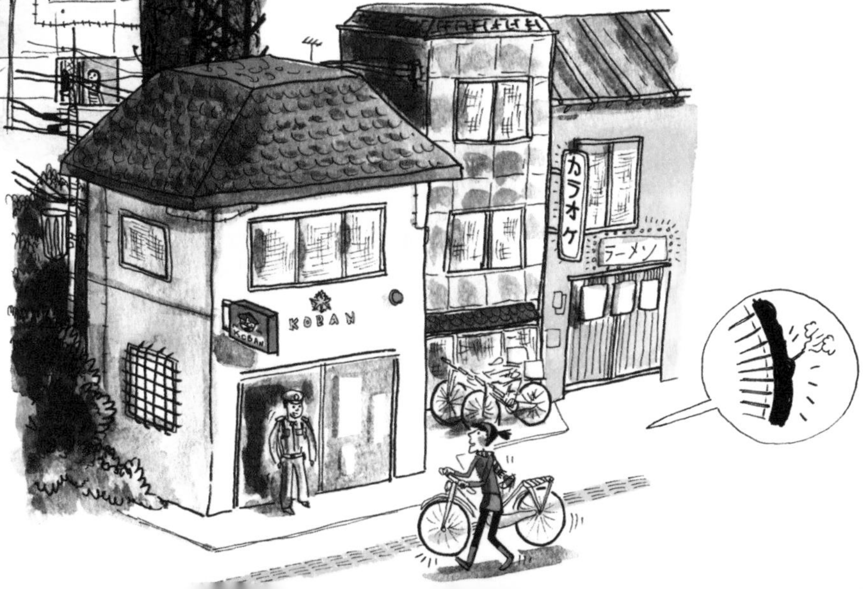

KOBAN
カラオケ
ラーメン

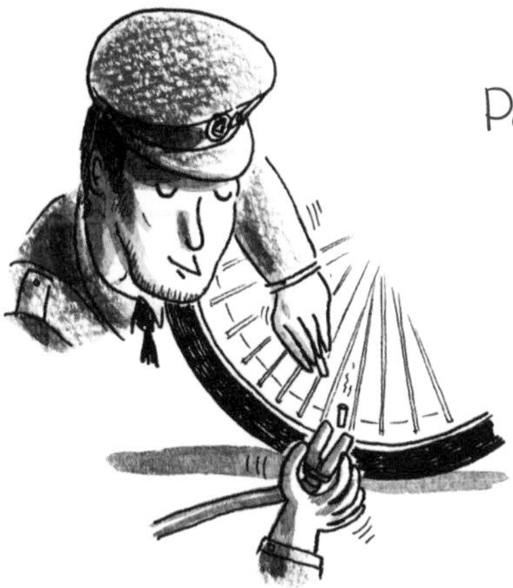

Policemen also inflate flat bike tires.

優しい警官。
私の自転車に空気を入れてくれます。

They look like old Cuban singers and show you the way when you're lost.

ブエナビスタ・ソシアルクラブの人みたいな警官。

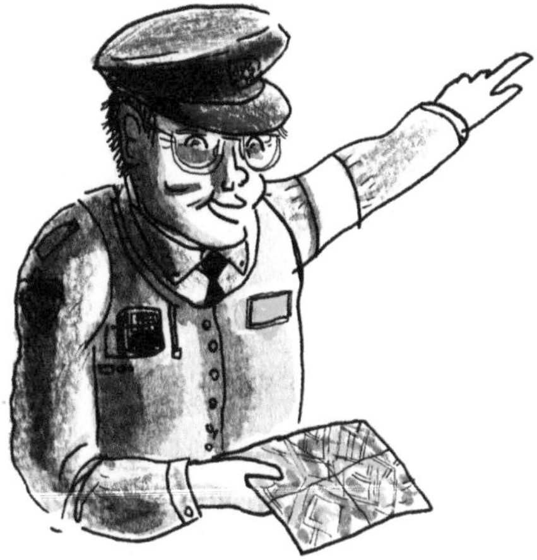

And the cherry on the cake—the police car apologizes!

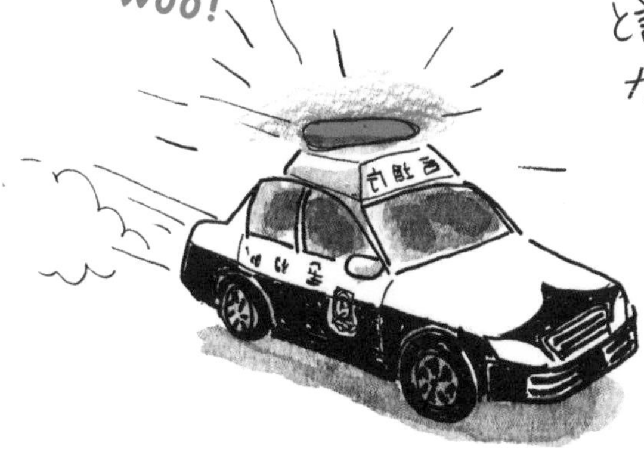
Sorry!
Excuse us!
Wee woo wee woo
wee woo!
We're turning right... thank you!
Sorry!

曲がる時「すみません、曲がります。」と言う警察はかくじつに日本だけです。

The Tohoku Earthquake 地震

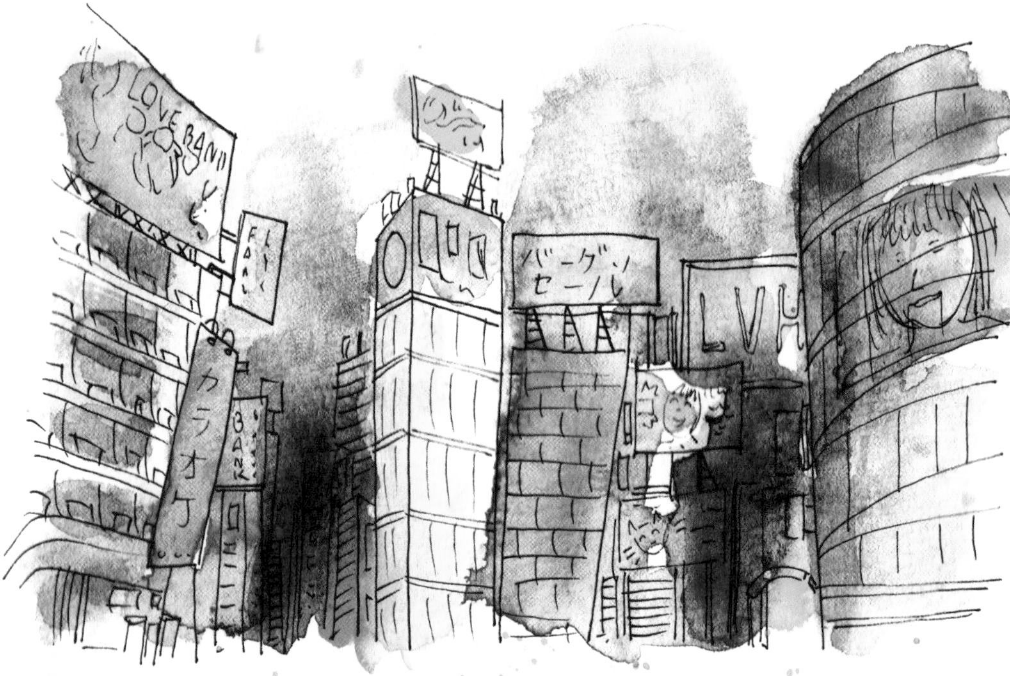

カラオケ
BANK
バーゲン
セール
LVH

Shibuya, March 11, 2011

2011年3月11日金曜日渋谷

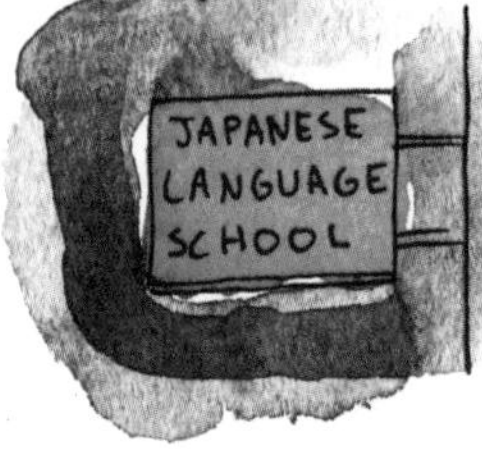

JAPANESE
LANGUAGE
SCHOOL

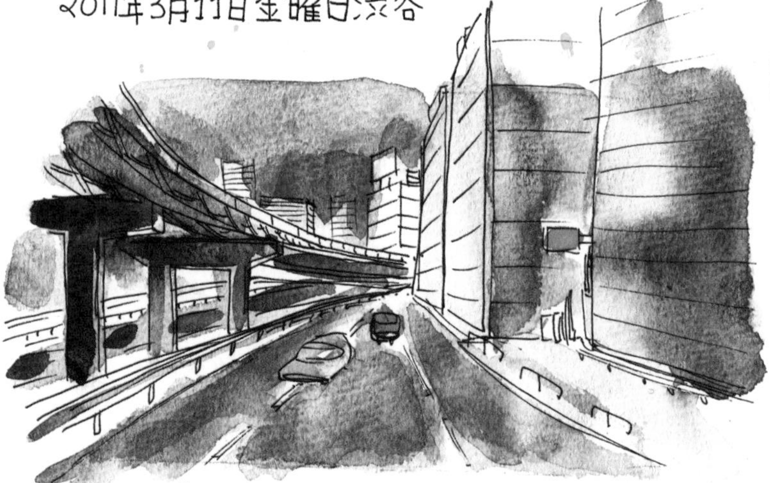

I'm at my Japanese class.

日本語学校で授業です。

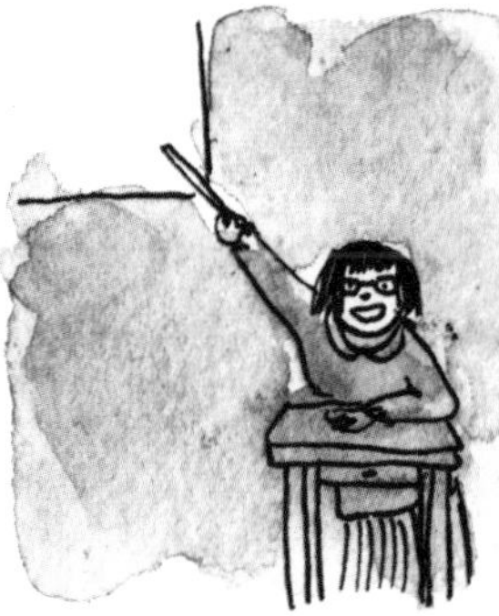

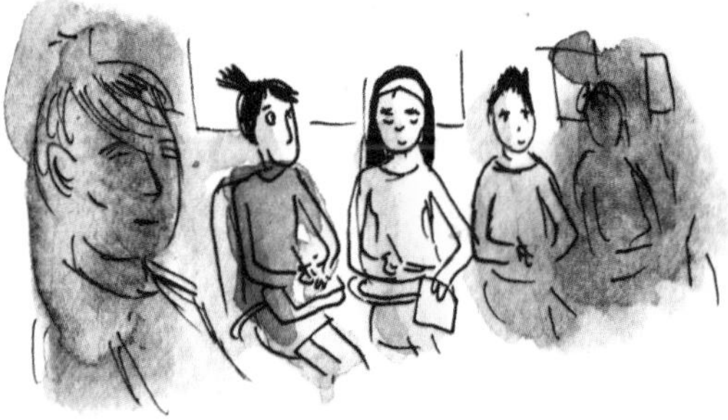

It's 2:46 pm when the ground starts shaking.
午後2時46分最初の地震があります。

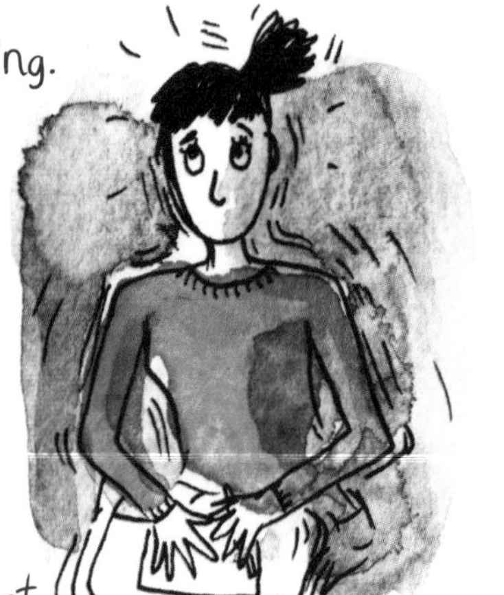

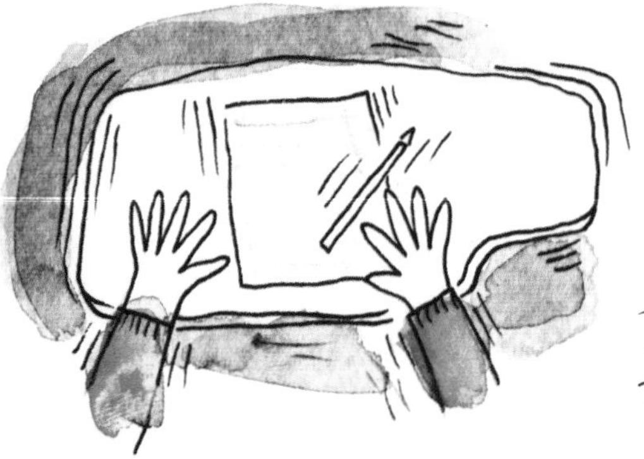

It's not
the first time
I've felt an earthquake in Japan.

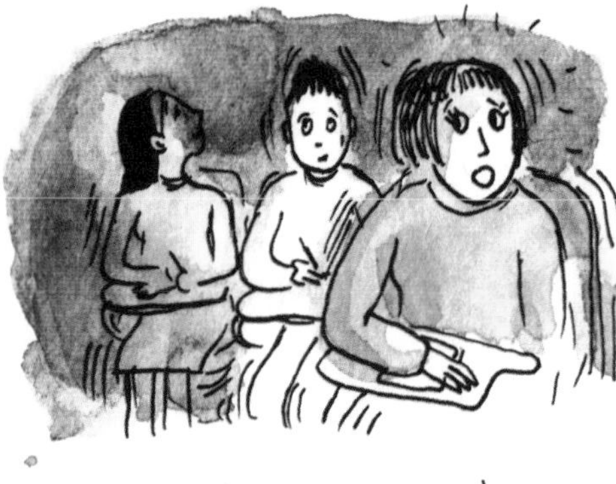

but...

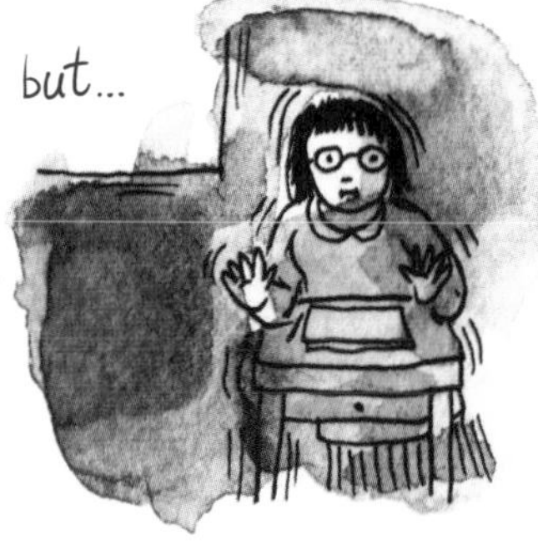

日本に住んでから
地震の経験はありますが...

this shaking...
今までにない...

とても強い揺れです。

is particularly long.

Everyone gathers.

みんな中庭に集まります。

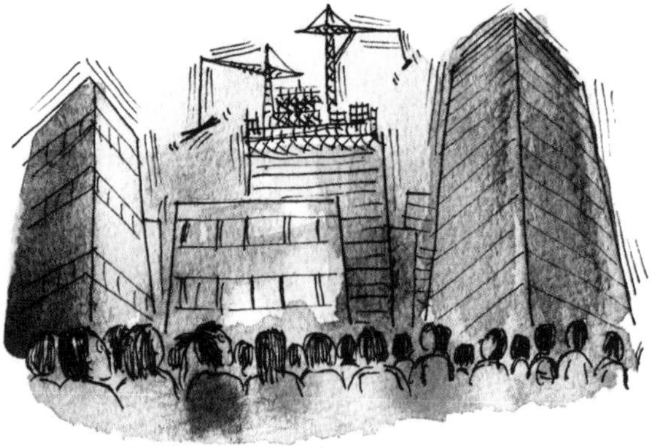

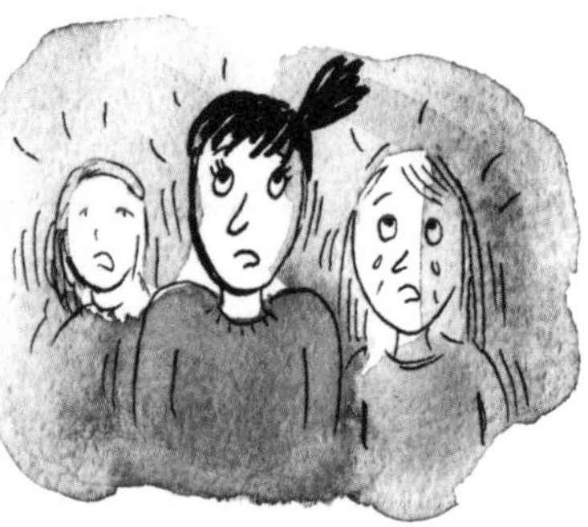

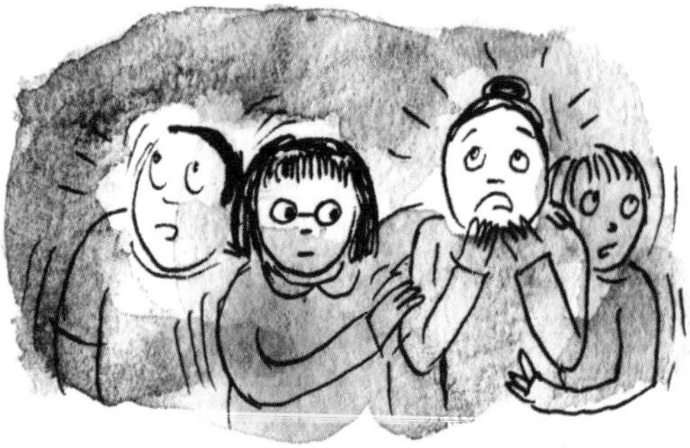

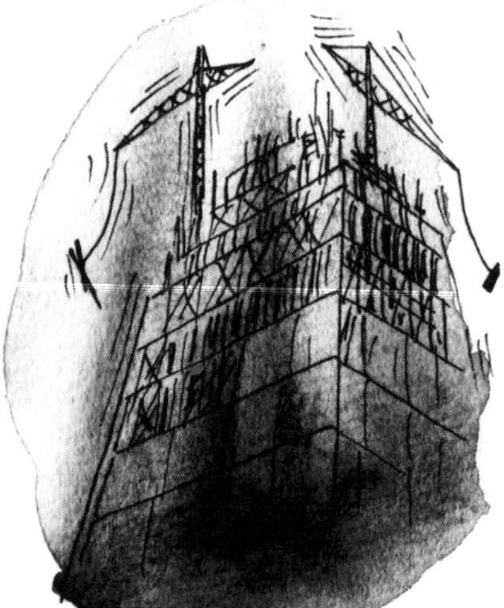

At the Japanese school, only the teachers and the office staff are used to earthquakes.

学校で日本人は少なく、
先生とスタッフだけです。
地震を理解しているのは
彼らだけです。

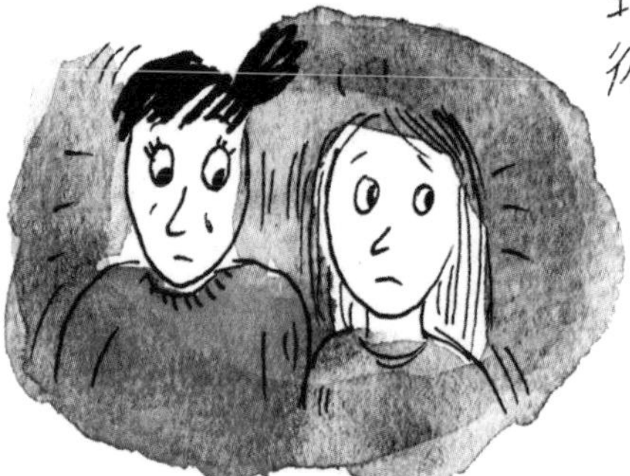

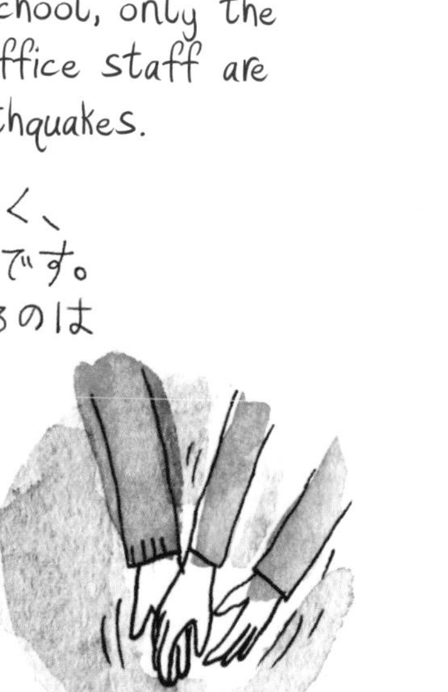

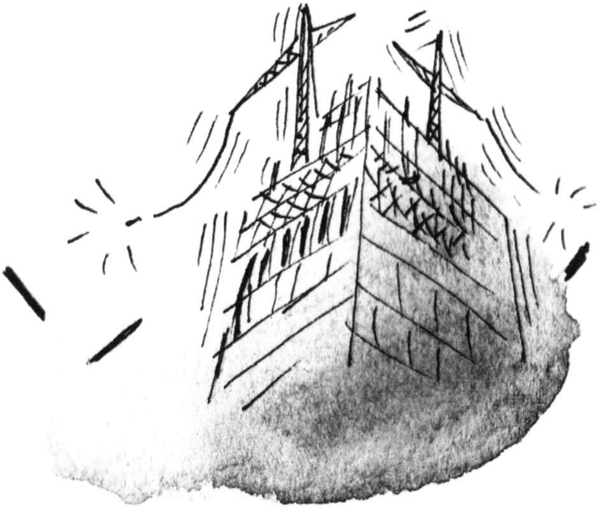

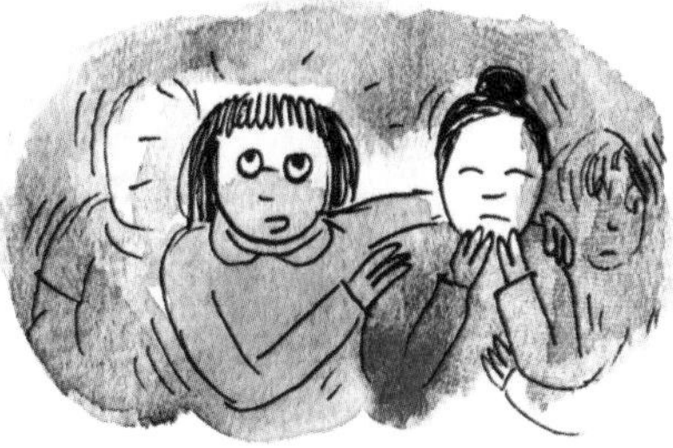

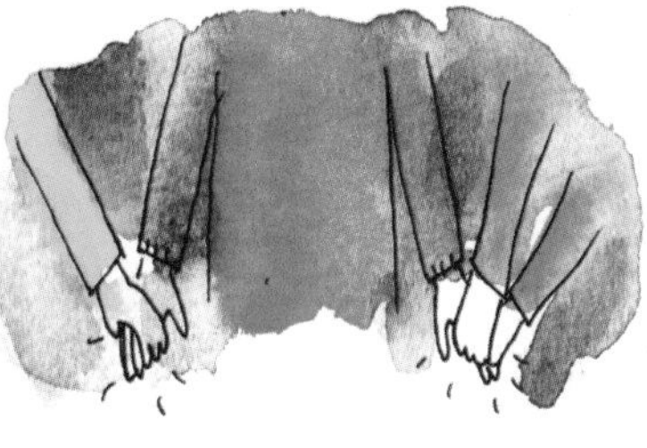

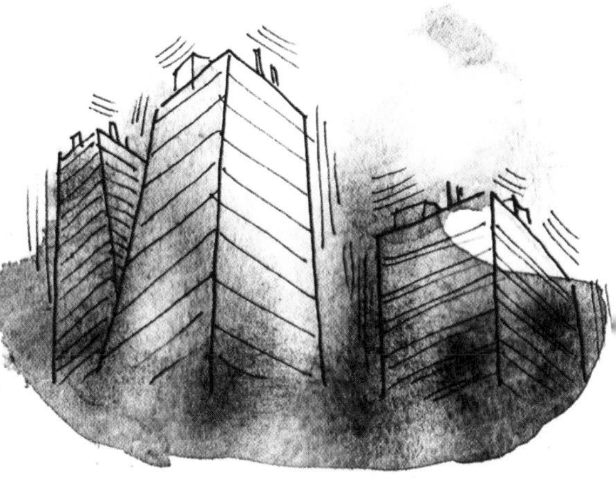

とても長い６分間。

The ground shakes for six long minutes.

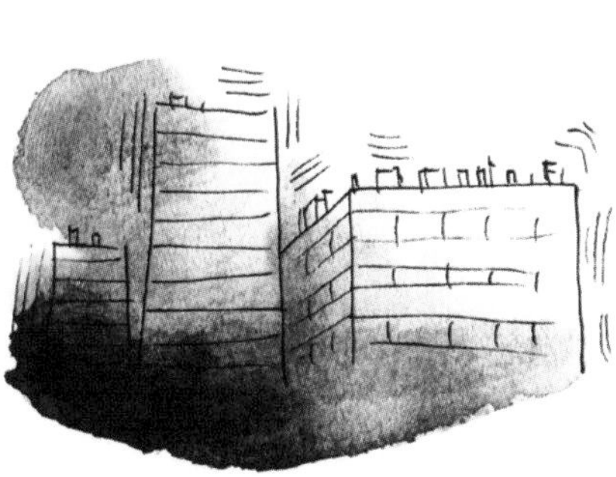

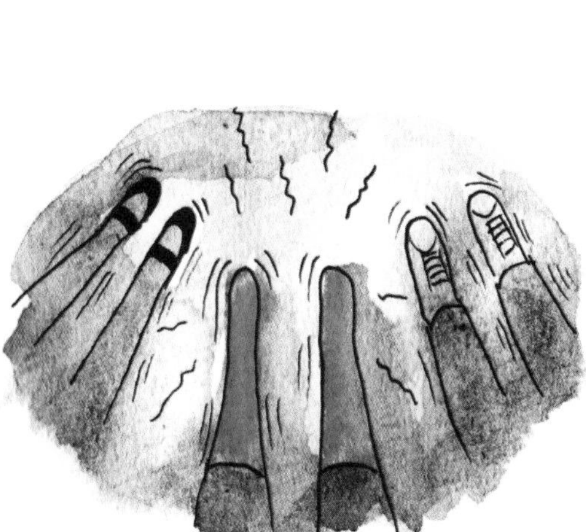

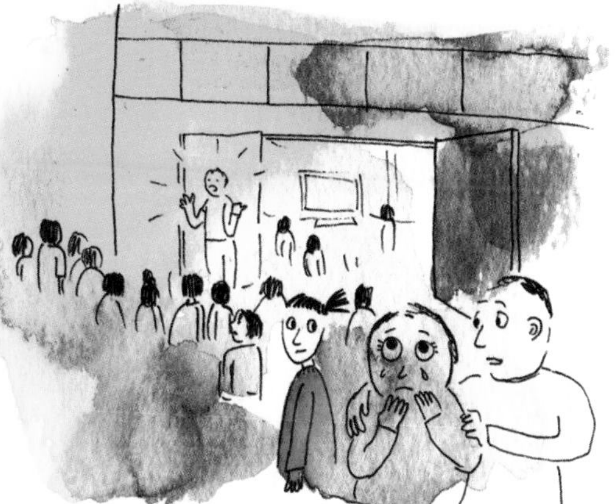

Look at this! On the news they say that in Miyagi the earthquake was a Shindo 7*! And Shindo 5+ for Tokyo!

「来て見て！ニュースで
宮城震度7 福島で6強と
いっているよ！東京は震度5強。

It is now 2:56 pm and a tsunami alert has been issued for the north-east Pacific coast.

午後2時56分。
大津波警報が出ます。

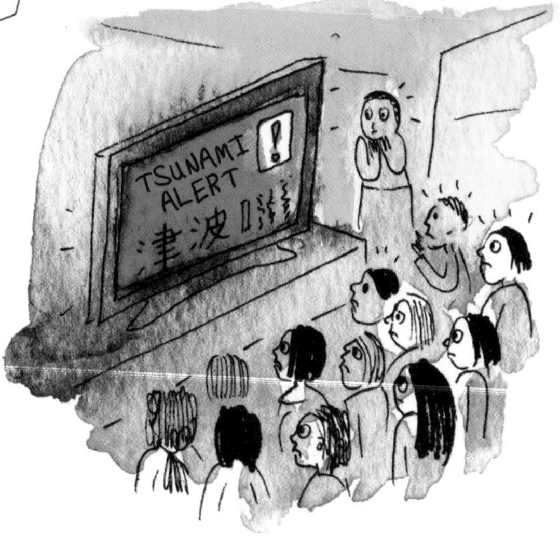
TSUNAMI ALERT
津波

Get out! Get out!

「出て！ 出て！」

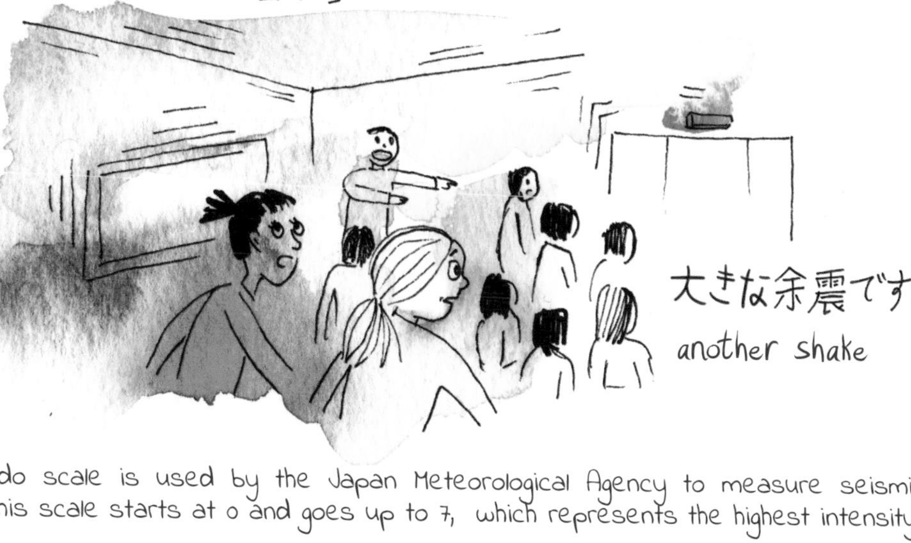
大きな余震です
another shake

* The Shindo scale is used by the Japan Meteorological Agency to measure seismic intensity. This scale starts at 0 and goes up to 7, which represents the highest intensity.

The school director tells everyone to go home— there won't be any more classes today.

家に帰って下さいと 校長先生が言います。

公共交通機関が ストップしたため、私と友達は 歩いて帰ります。

Public transport has stopped. I suggest to my friends that we walk to my place.

The main road Yamate Dori, normally not so crowded, is chock-full of people today.

山手通りを
たくさんの人が
歩いています。
見た事がない
光景です。

家に着いてガスをチェック。

As soon as I get home, I check the gas and pick up the stuff that has fallen onto the floor.

地震で落ちた物を
なおします。

The mobile phone network is still down.

In France, it's morning. I send my parents an email to let them know I'm okay.

インターネットのメールで
フランスの家族にメールを
送ります。
携帯は圏外のまま。

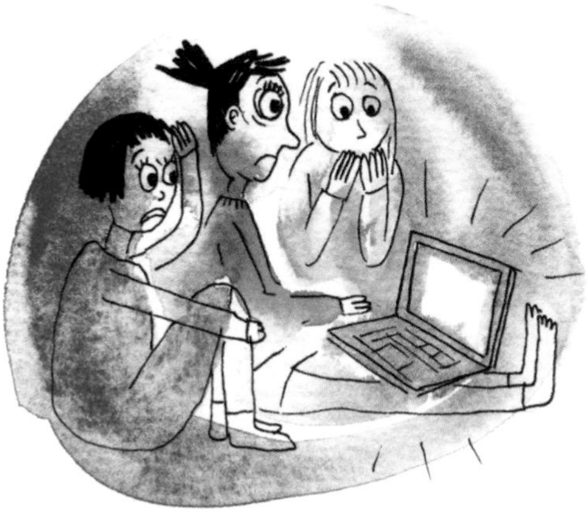

インターネットでライブのニュースを見ます。

Then we watch the news on the Internet.

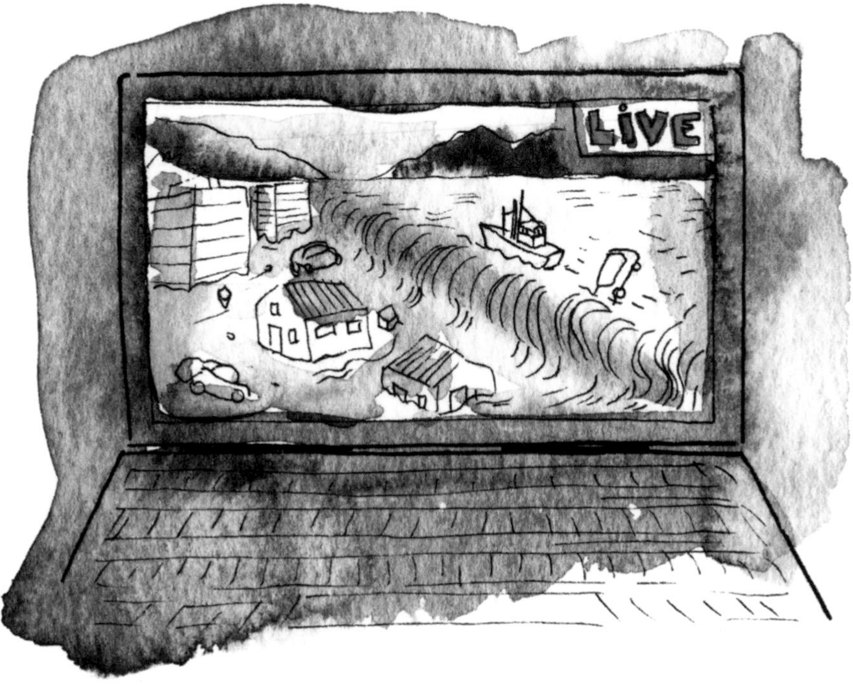
LIVE

「また大きな余震だ！出ましょう!!」 An aftershock! Quick! Let's get out!

What should we do? None of us wants to be alone.

どうしたらいい。私達、外国人だから...

"We should go where the Japanese are—they'll know what to do." We decide to go to a bar in Nakameguro.

「日本人が いる 所へ 行こう！」 中目黒の カフェ に 行きます。 「携帯に電波 もどった！」

"The network is back up!"

My friends manage to get in touch with their partners and they leave me to go meet them. As for me, I go meet a friend in Ebisu.

私は日本人の友達と恵比寿で会います。

なので、友達はそれぞれ 彼氏に会いに行きます。

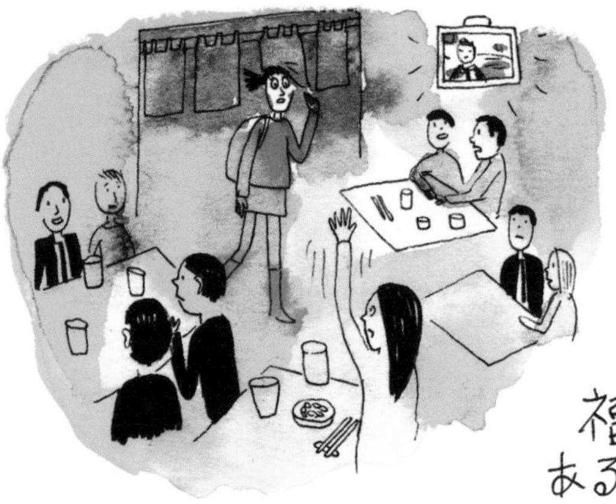

"Julie, I'm here!"
「あっ！ジュリここです！」

They say there's a radioactive leak at the Fukushima nuclear power plant!

福島で放射能もれがあるらしいです。

原発のまわりでは6000人が避難します。

I spend the night at my friend's, watching the news. Six thousand people living near the power plant are evacuated.

友達の家に泊まります。

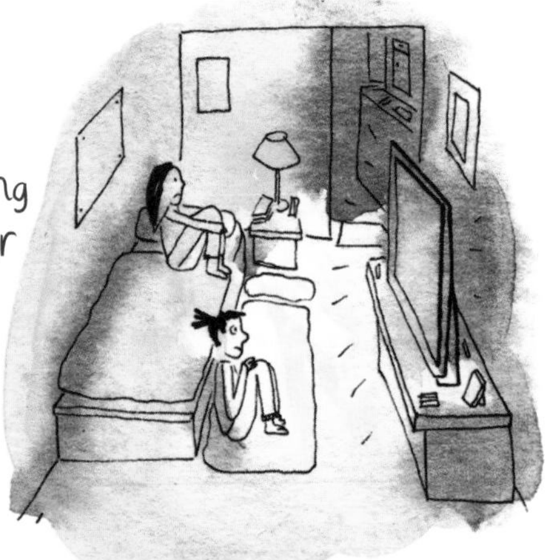

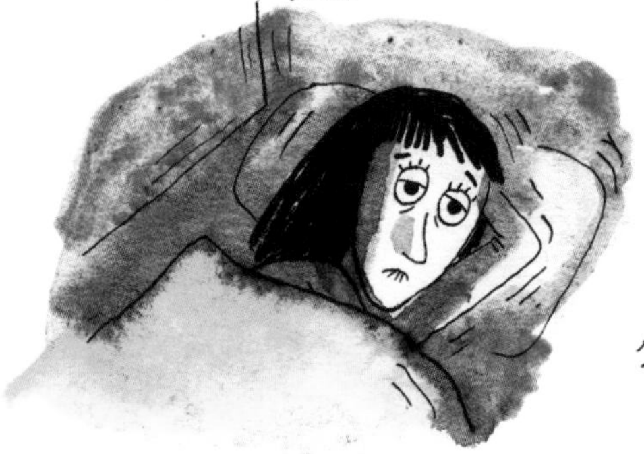

At 4:28 am, there's an exceptionally strong aftershock.

午前4時28分また大きな余震があります。

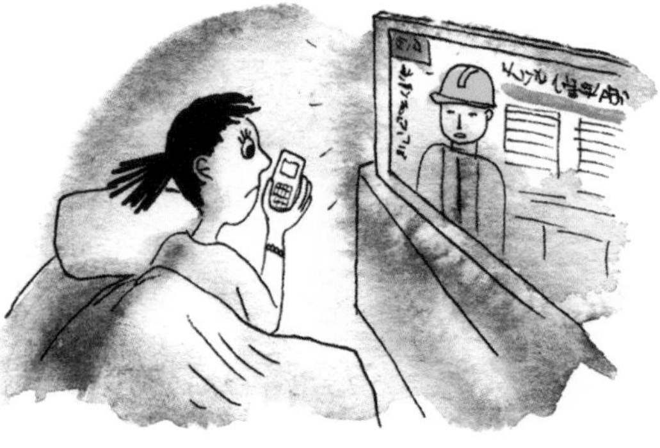

The morning news says that a cooling problem has been detected at the plant.

朝のニュースでは原発に問題があると言っています。

お水はボトル3本まで3　3 bottles maximum per person

empty

Before going home, I stop by the supermarket.

私の家にり帰る前に
スーパーへよります。

You're leaving for Hong Kong now?! You think it's unsafe because of the nuclear plant!

on the phone with a German friend

東京のドイツ人の友達との電話
「今から香港に行くの!?本当に放射能が
東京まで…」

The recommendation from the embassy is contradictory— they advise leaving Japan but also say the risk isn't that high.

フランス大使館から「日本を出て下さい。
でも大丈夫です。」と言う
予盾したメッセージ。

日本人の友達カップルの家に泊まります。
次の日、私は無神論者だけど
近くの神社にお参りします。

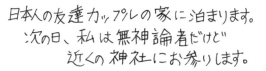

I spend the night at the house of a couple of Japanese friends. I'm an atheist, but the next morning, I can't stop myself from going to the shrine next to my place.

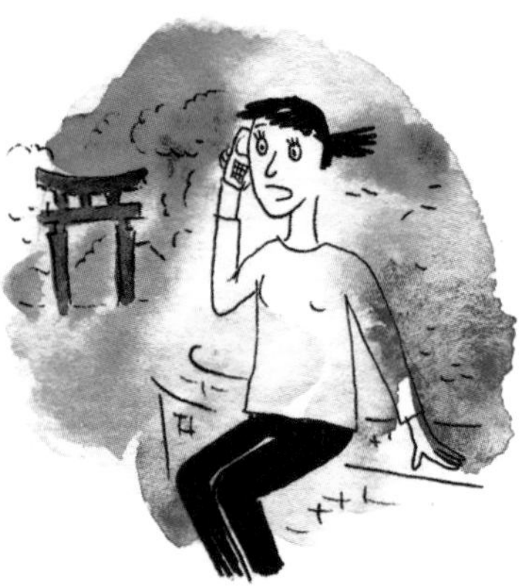

東京のフランス人の友達との電話
「今日まで横浜の会社にいたの…
今、あなたの家…
そうだね。私も日本をはなれたくない…
沖縄…一緒に…もうチケット買った…」

"So you've been stuck in Yokohama since yesterday? Oh, now you're home... Me neither, I don't wanna leave Japan... To Okinawa? You already have tickets?"

今から友達と沖縄に行くので、
私の家族は安心します。

I set off to meet a French friend and go to Okinawa with her. My family is relieved.

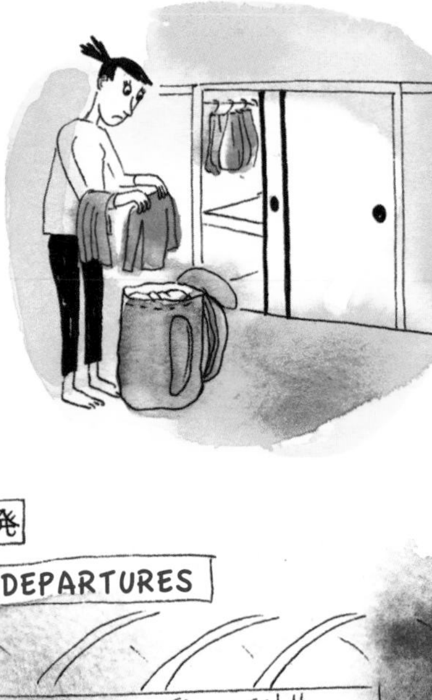

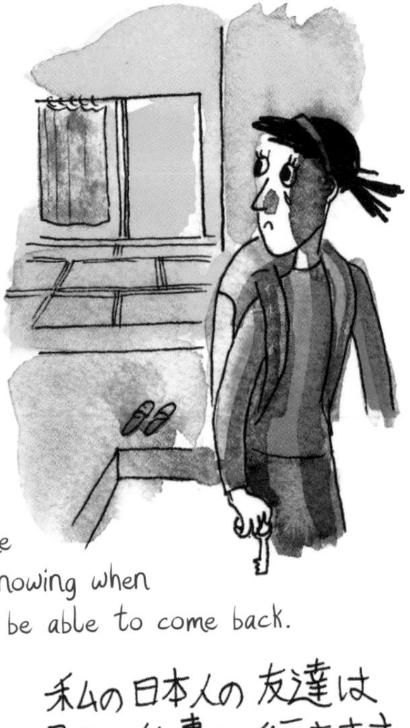

ここにまた
帰れるかな…

I leave my home without knowing when I'll be able to come back.

出発

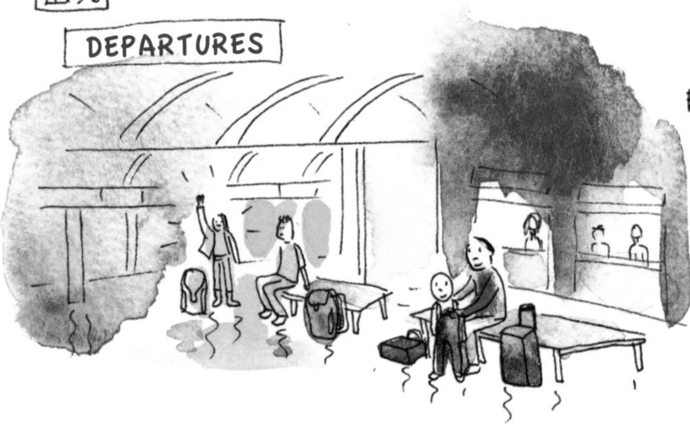
DEPARTURES

私の日本人の友達は
明日、仕事に行きます。
とても後ろめたいです。

I feel so guilty—my Japanese friends go back to work tomorrow...

I've been to Okinawa before, but on vacation.

This time, I don't even know if I'll go back to Tokyo.

東京から遠くはなれた所へ
行きます。
帰りが分からないまま。

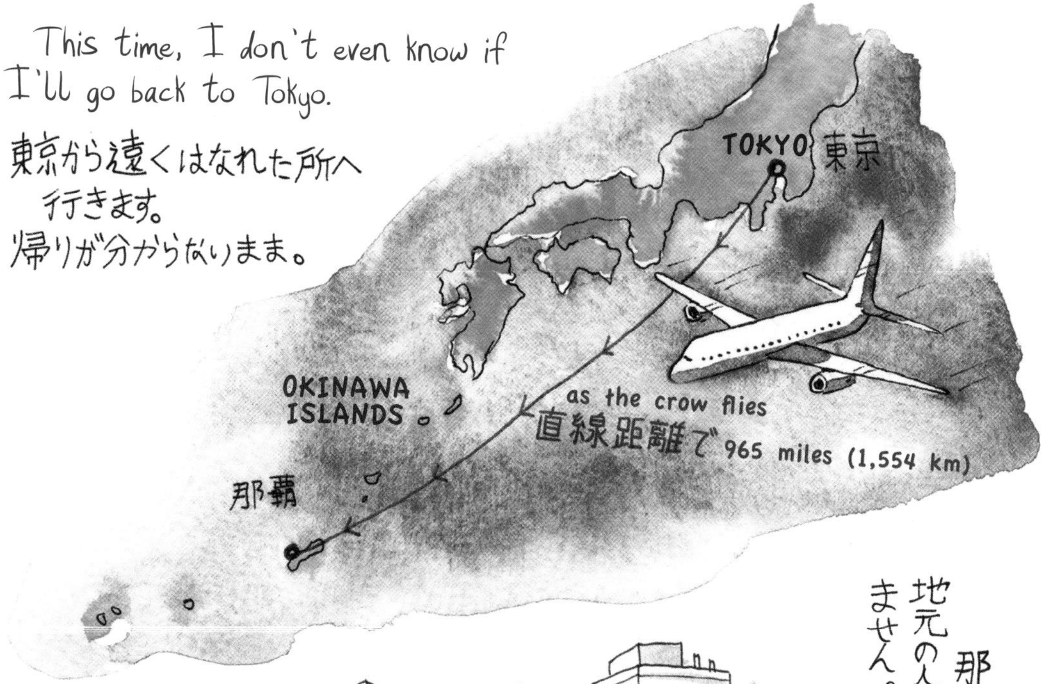
TOKYO 東京
OKINAWA ISLANDS
as the crow flies
直線距離で 965 miles (1,554 km)
那覇

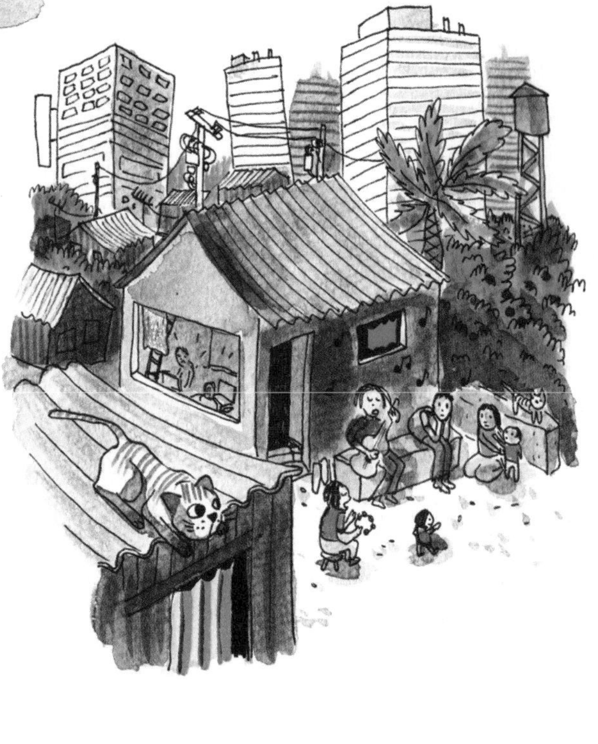

那覇の安いゲストハウスにいます。
地元の人からは事の重大さを感じられません。私達が考えすぎなのかな…

We find a cheap place to stay in a guest house in Naha, the capital. The residents don't seem to realize the gravity of the situation. Or is it us who are blowing this out of proportion?

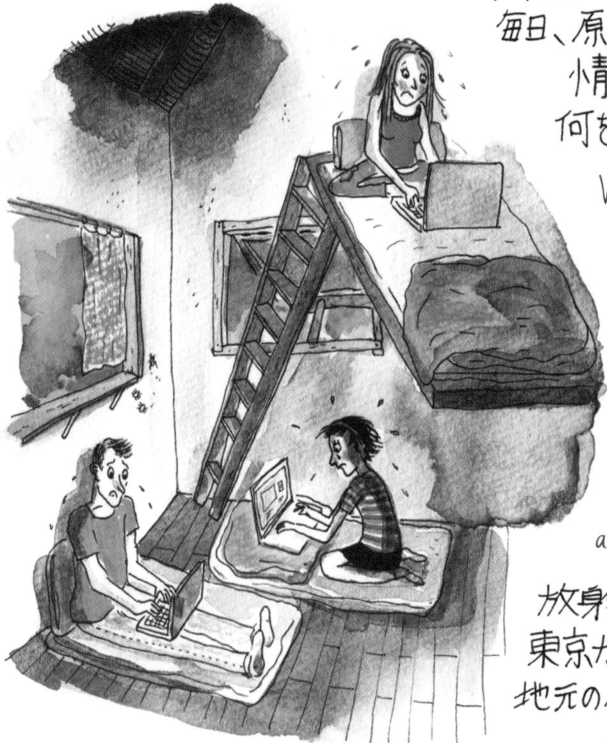

ゲストハウスに来た外国人たちは
毎日、原発のニュースをチェックします。
情報がさくそうしているので、
何を信じたらいいか分かりません。

With another French friend the three of us spend our time glued to our computers, waiting for news about the Fukushima nuclear plant.

It's a period of huge uncertainty since all the news is contradictory. What are we to believe?

放射能を避けるため、
東京から日本人の家族が来ます。
地元の人は事の重大さが分かります。

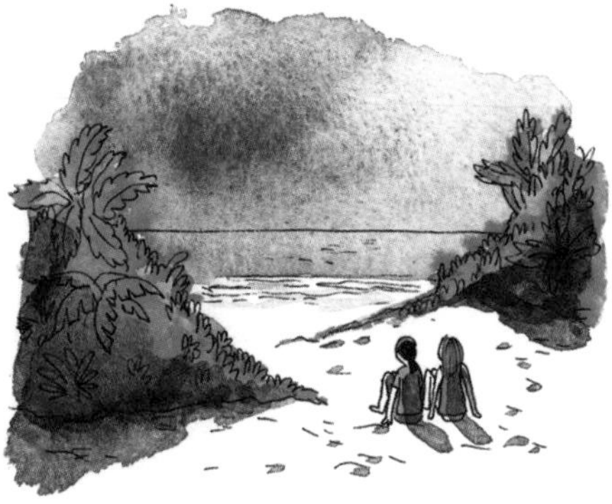

The local residents become less indifferent as Japanese families start arriving to escape the risk of radiation.

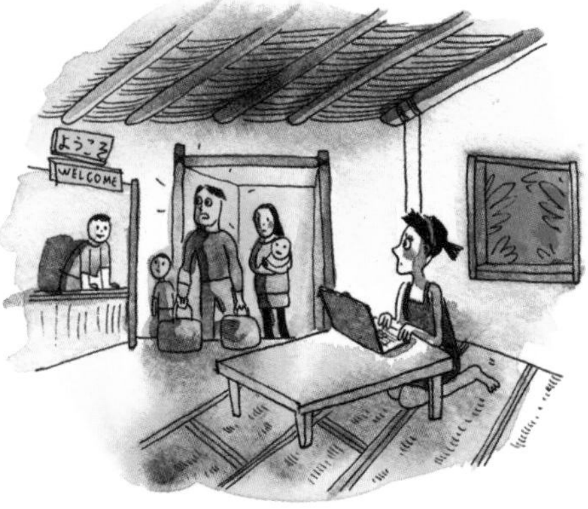
ようこそ
WELCOME

We visit the Okinawa countryside. It's gorgeous but our hearts aren't really into sightseeing.

沖縄の自然を見に行きます。
バカンスが感じられません。

At the Churaumi Aquarium

美ら海水族館へ

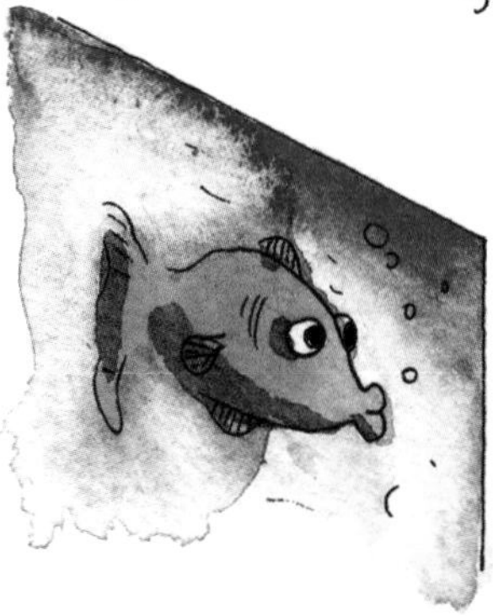

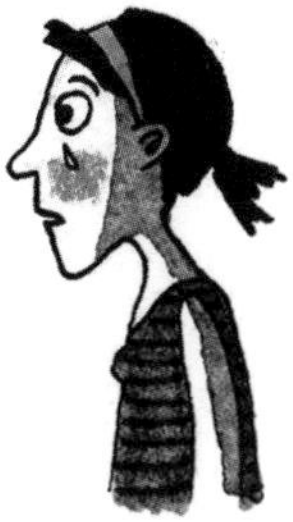

原子力発電は見かけは良さそうだけど、大災害を引きおこすので、一番良くないエネルギーだよね。指導者達は何回、同じまちがいをくり返したら、人間味のある再生可能エネルギーなどに投資を考えるのかな。

Nuclear energy seems like a great idea, but in fact it's really shitty, right? How many catastrophes and scandals before decision makers roll up their sleeves and seriously invest in renewables?

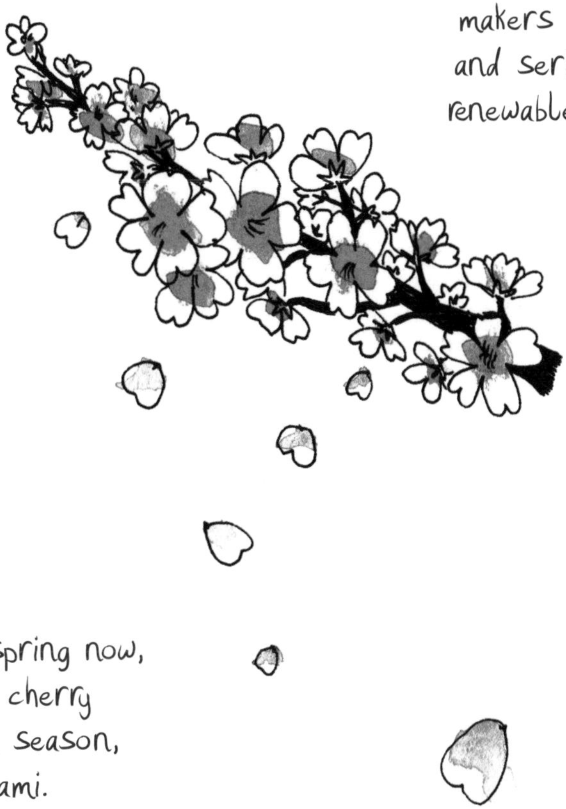

20日間沖縄にいた後で東京に戻ります。

After 20 days in Okinawa, we go back to Tokyo.

お花見の季節です。

It's spring now, bringing cherry blossom season, and ohanami.

Back Home 家に帰ります

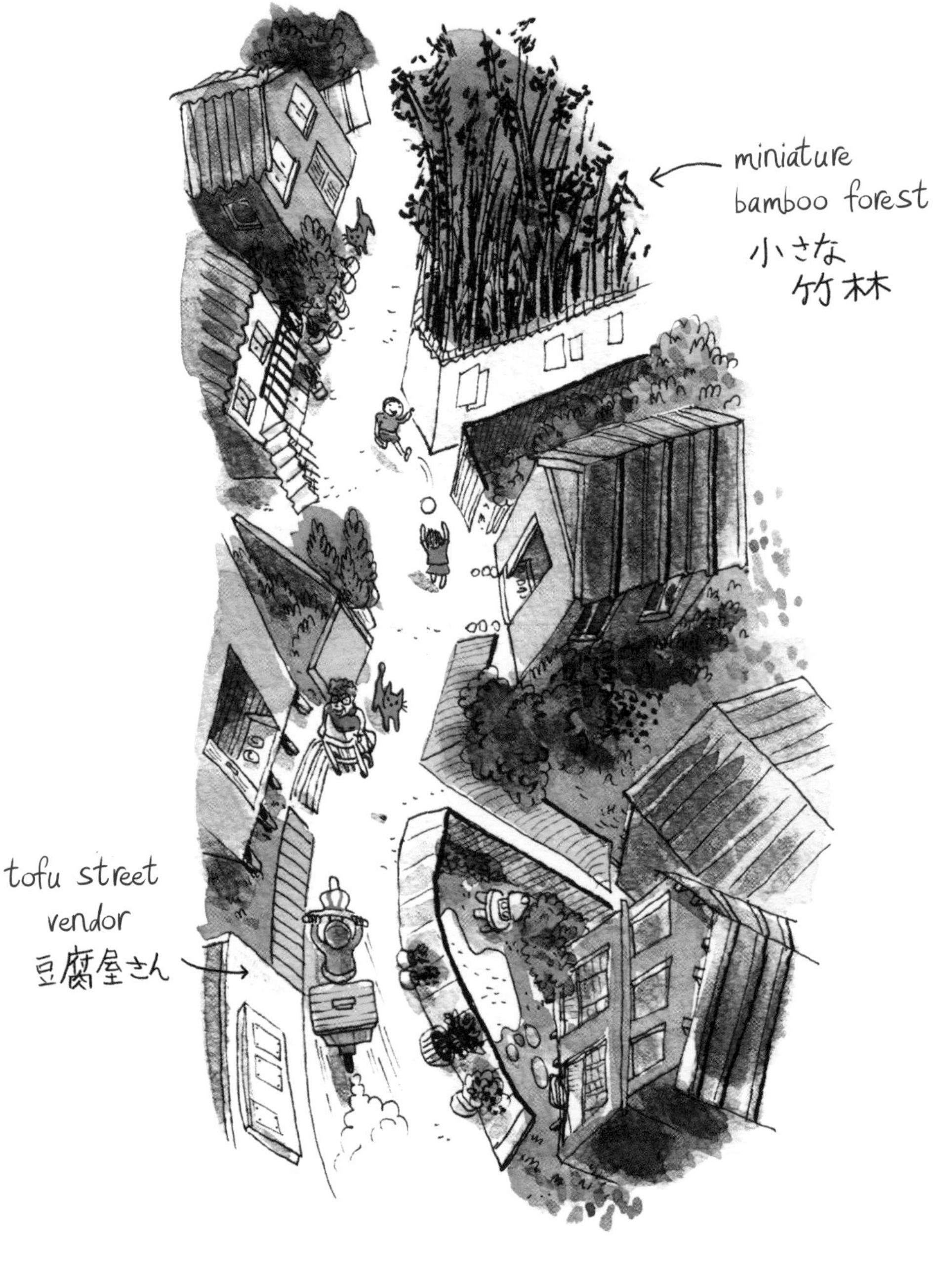
miniature
bamboo forest
小さな
竹林
tofu street
vendor
豆腐屋さん

ココビ
azaleas

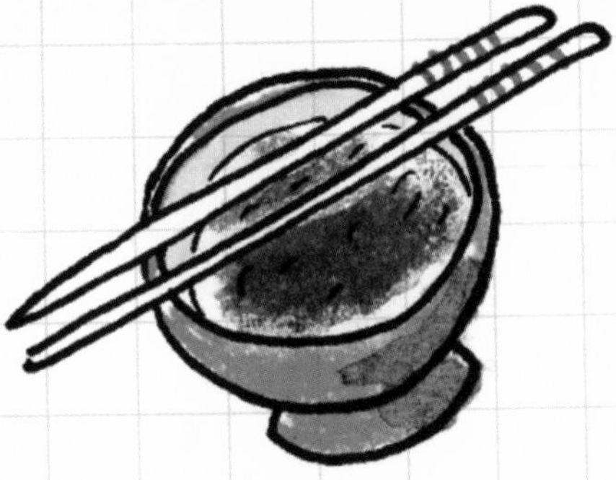

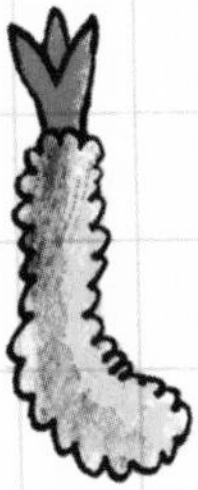

JAPANESE FOODS I LOVE

私のとても好きな日本食

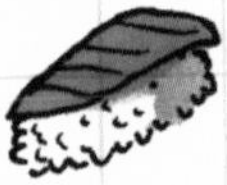

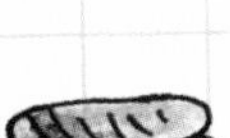

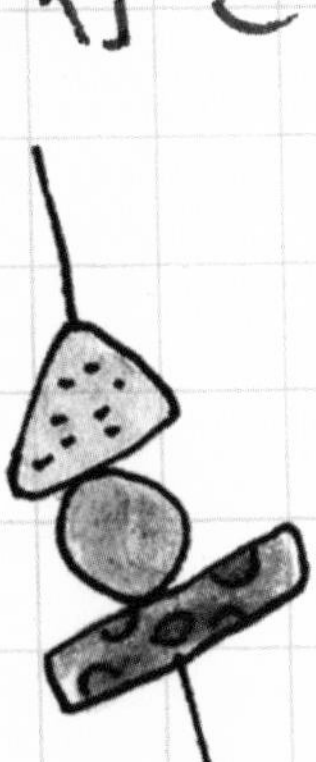

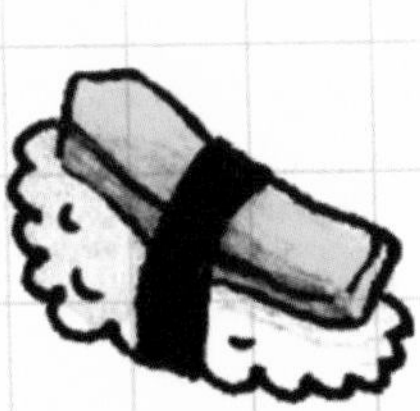

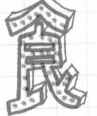

I love natto
納豆が好き

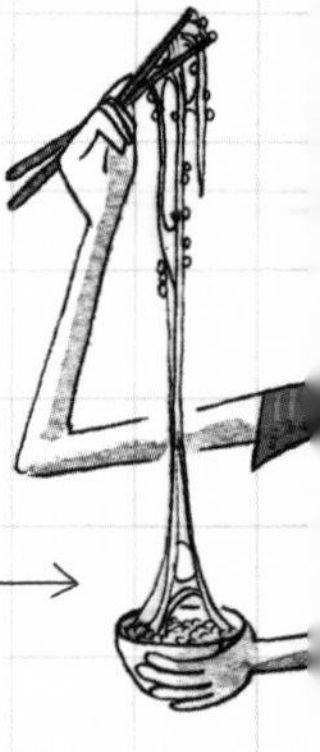

Natto is a traditional Japanese dish made of fermented soybeans. It's often served at breakfast, with a side of white rice.

To me, it smells like strong French Roquefort cheese, with a texture—how shall I put it?—between snot and glue. But natto is very healthy and is among those foods that help the Japanese live their famously long lives.

Mariko, the mom. →

私は今でこそ納豆を好きになったけど、日本人も少なからずそうである様に最初はまったくダメ！鶴瀬に住んでいた時、日本の、本当の家庭料理を理解しはじめます。マリコお母さんのおかげです。

Now I like natto, but at first, like most non-Japanese, I hated it! It was when I lived in Tsuruse that I started to really understand Japanese cooking, thanks to Mariko's skills.

117

Japanese Food: The Basics

とりあえず：日本食の味の基礎

These are the basic ingredients used in Japanese cooking:

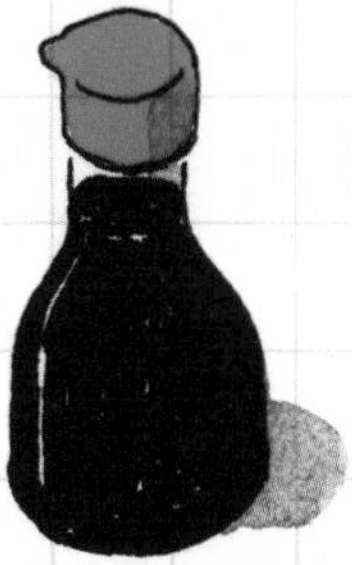

醤油

SHOYU

soy sauce

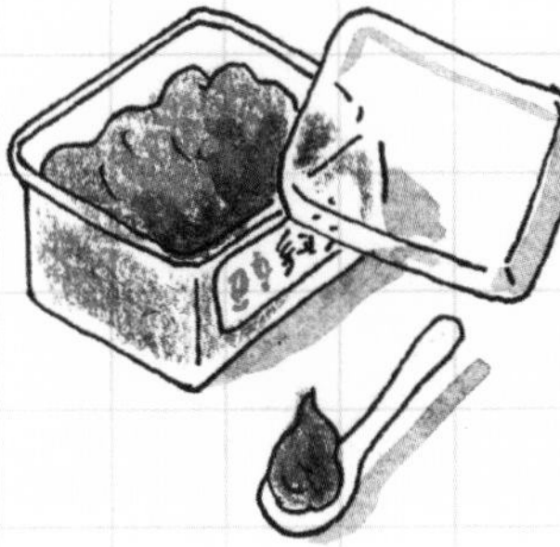

MISO みそ

A fermented paste made from soybeans, with either rice or barley, salt, water and a fermenting agent.

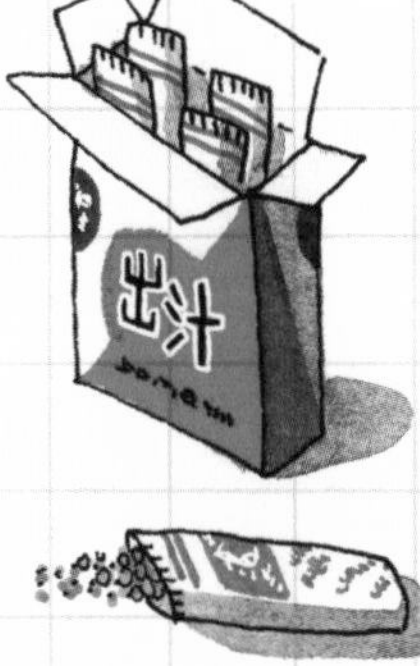
出汁

出汁

DASHI (in powder form)

soup stock

grain of rice →

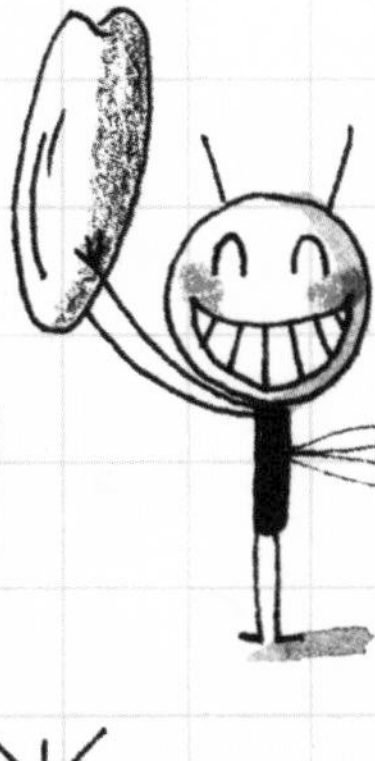

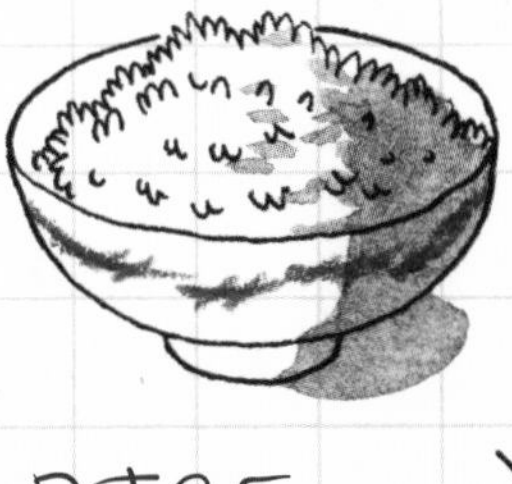

RICE 米

だしの材料
Dashi can be made from these ingredients:

NIBOSHI

small dried sardines

KOMBU

dried seaweed

煮干し

It looks like a piece of wood.

木に似てる

鰹節

KATSUOBUSHI

dried bonito (tuna)

grater specifically designed for dried bonito

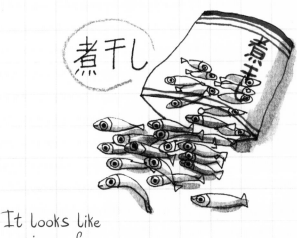

dried bonito shavings

私のとても好きな日本食は：

My favorite Japanese dishes

ONIGIRI (rice ball)

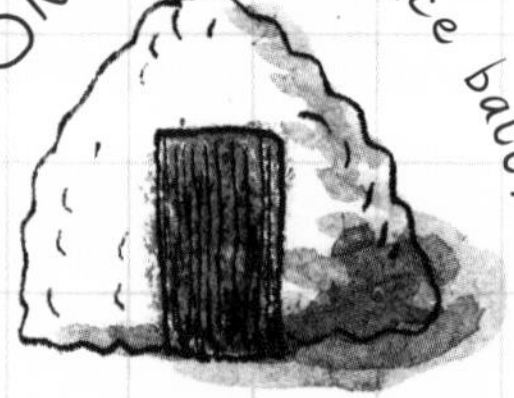

おにぎり

TAKOYAKI (savory dough ball with bits of octopus)

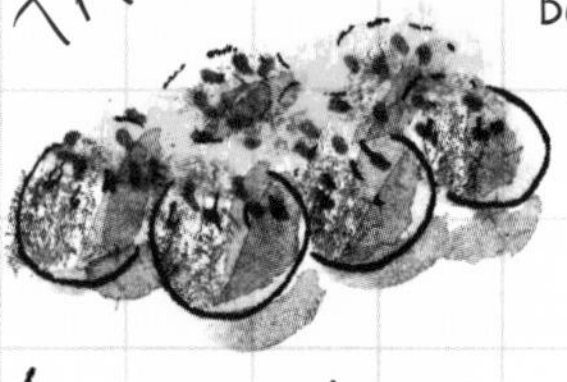

たこ焼き

GYUDON (beef rice bowl)

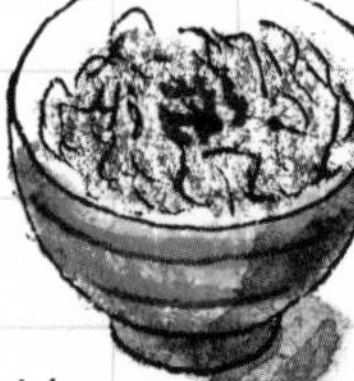

牛丼

サンドイッチ
SANDWICHES

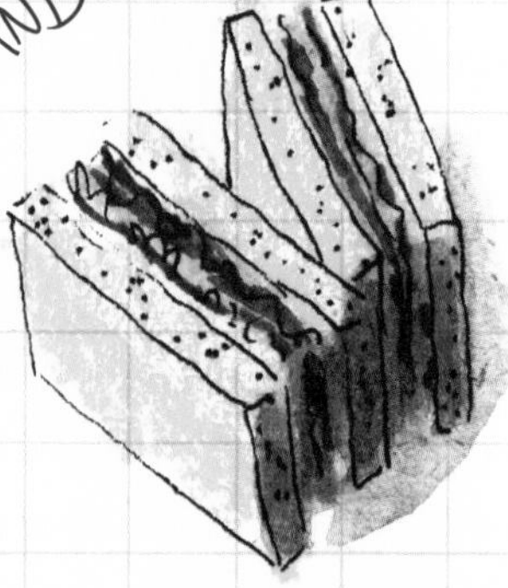

TONKATSU (breaded pork cutlet)

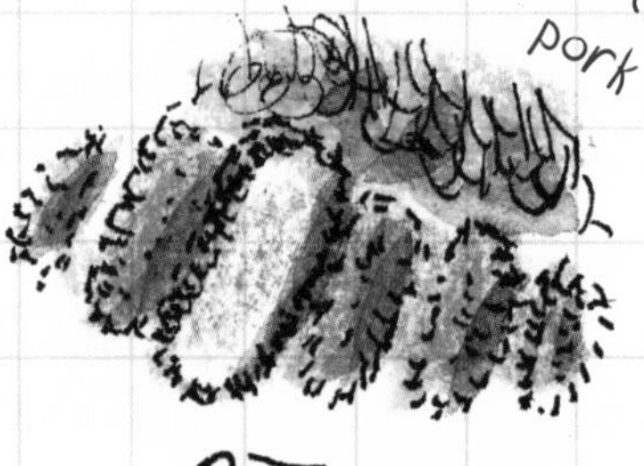

豚カツ

KATSUKARE (fried pork cutlet with curry sauce)

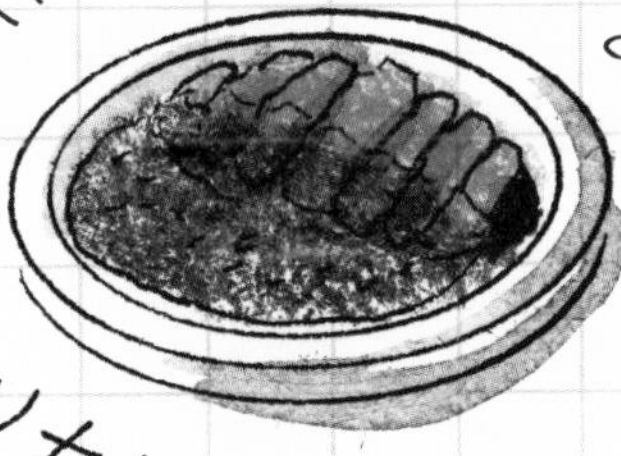

カツカレー

UNAGI DON (grilled eel with rice)

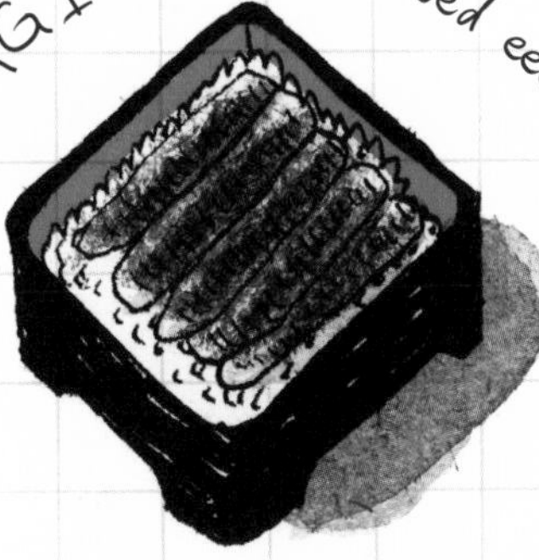

鰻重

RAMEN

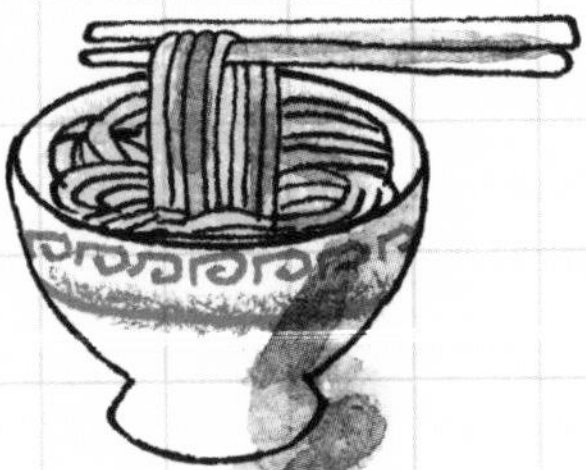

There are dozens of versions, with broths based on salt, miso, soy sauce, pork, etc.

ラーメン

(miso soup)
MISO SHIRU

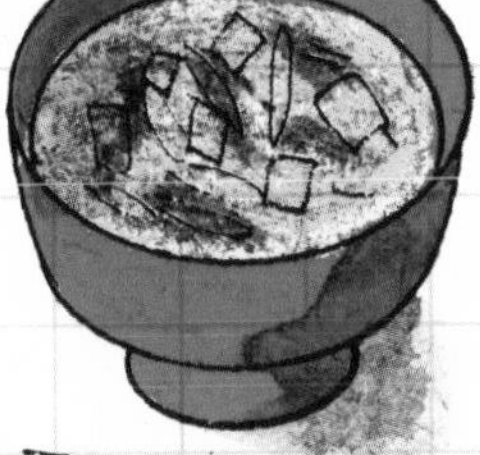

みそ汁

KAKE UDON (thick wheat noodles in a hot broth)

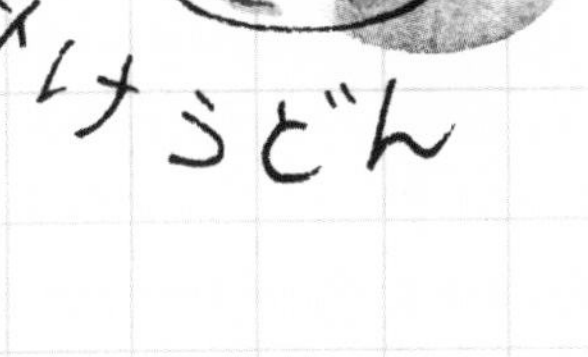

掛けうどん

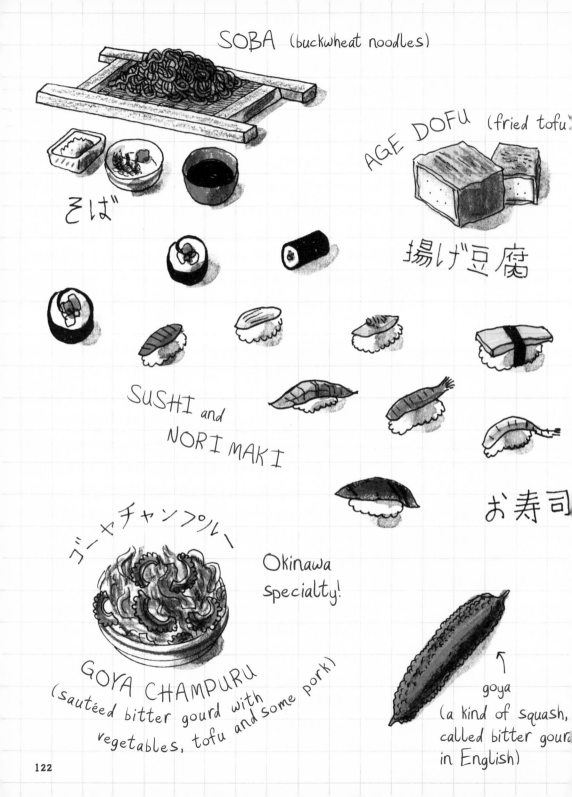

SOBA (buckwheat noodles)

そば"

AGE DOFU (fried tofu)

揚げ豆腐

SUSHI and NORI MAKI

お寿司

ゴーヤチャンプルー

GOYA CHAMPURU
(sautéed bitter gourd with vegetables, tofu and some pork)

Okinawa specialty!

↑
goya
(a kind of squash, called bitter gourd in English)

SOMEN

そうめん

(thin cold wheat noodles served mostly in summer)

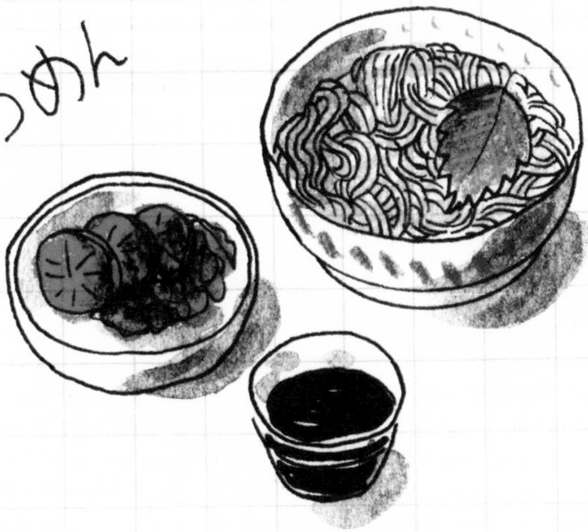

KITSUNE UDON

きつねうどん

(udon noodles with fried tofu on top)

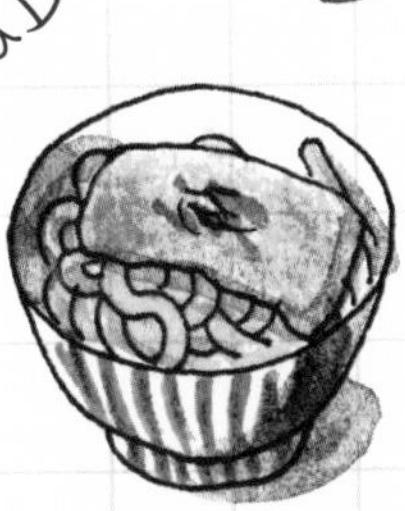

いです It's sweet!

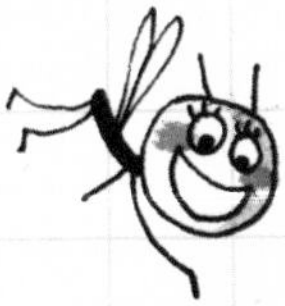

This one is sweet too!

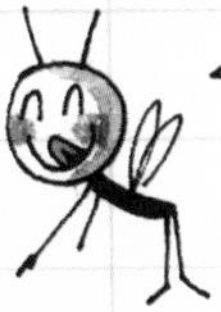

WARABI MOCHI

brown sugar syrup

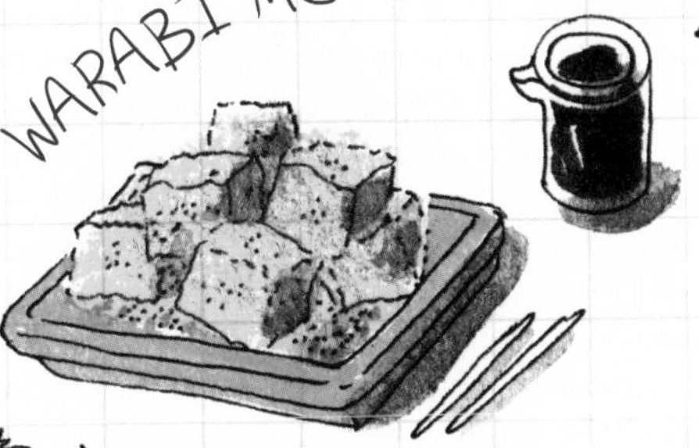

わらびもち

Jelly-like squares made from fern starch and sprinkled with kinako, a type of sweet, soybean flour.

八橋

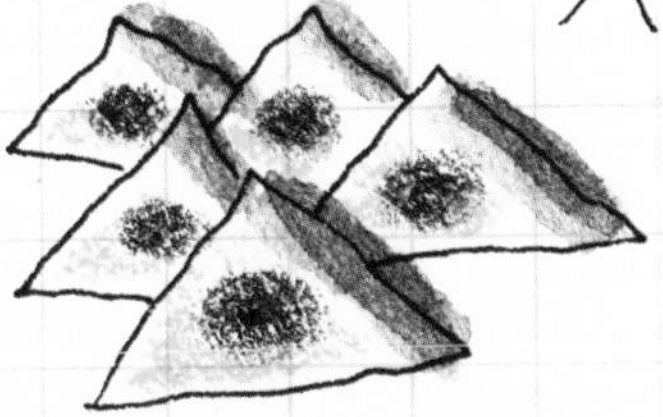

YATSUHASHI

Kind of ravioli that can be stuffed with cinnamon, red bean paste, jam or other fillings...

日本の 朝ごはん Japanese Breakfast

In France, traditionally, breakfast is <u>sweet</u>, not savory. It's one of the rare countries to have this tradition. But I've always liked eating savory things in the morning. What I hate is eating the same stuff over and over again. The great thing about Japan is that you can eat anything you like in the morning and nobody will make fun of you!

フランスの朝ごはんは甘いものだけです。この習慣は世界でもフランスだけだと思います。

私はフランス人だけど、昔から朝ごはんに色々なものを食べています。
まわりの人は皆、「朝からそれを食べるの?」といってしかめ面をします。

よかったです。日本では朝から何でも食べられます。誰も何もいいません。

SMALL SALAD サラダ

梅干 UMEBOSHI — Kind of salted, sour plums—they're invigorating in the morning!

TRADITIONAL BREAKFAST

GRILLED SALMON サーモン

JAPANESE OMELET — cooked in a square frying pan, with soy sauce, etc.

ひじき HIJIKI SEAWEED

rice bowl

塩こんぶ SALTED KOMBU SEAWEED FLAKES

miso soup みそ汁

納豆

the famous NATTO

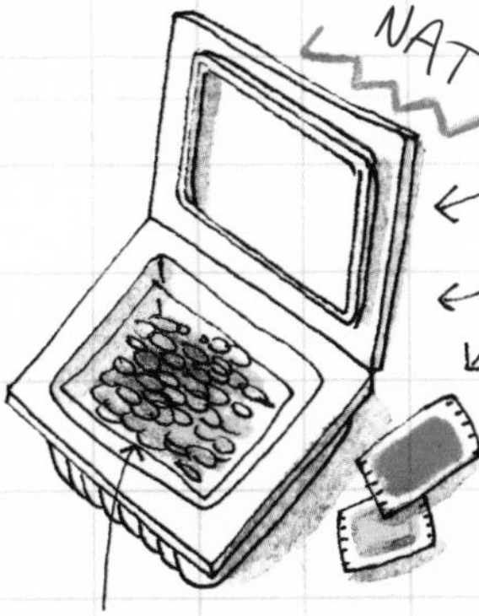

It's sold like this in stores, with packets of sauce.

plastic film delicately placed

納豆食べ方

small pieces of PUMPKIN

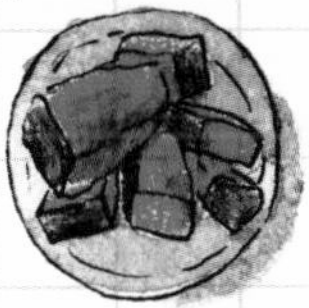

かぼちゃの煮付け

HOW TO EAT NATTO:

① You mix the sauces with chopsticks inside the container.

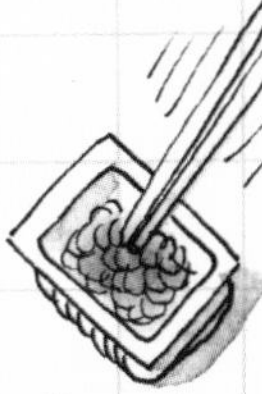

② You pour over your rice.

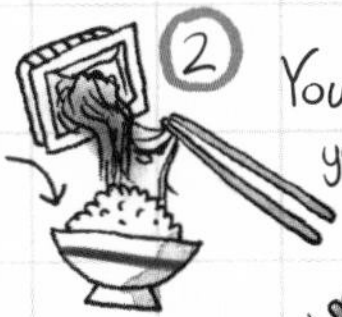

③ You try to eat it.

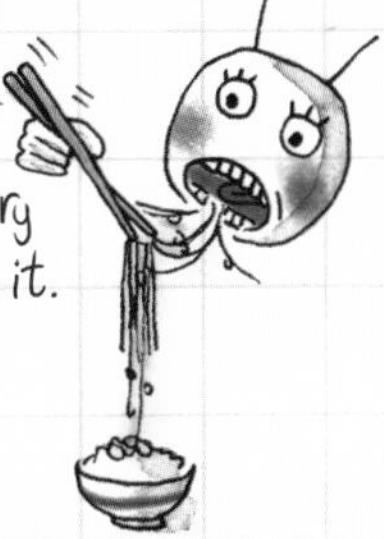

秋田名物

AKITA SPECIALTY

いぶりがっこ

IBURIGAKKO

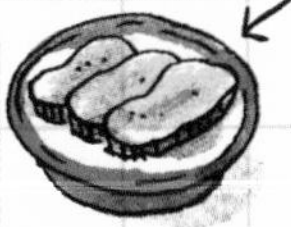

kind of marinated and smoked radish!

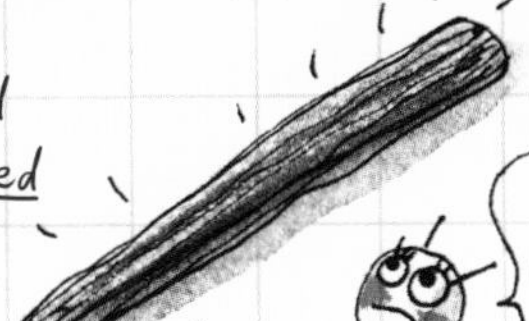

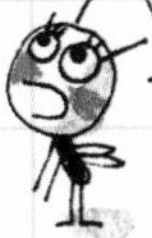

It looks like a piece of wood

APPLES

リンゴ

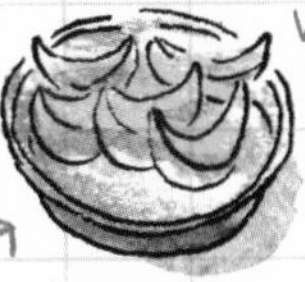

In Japan, fruit is often served cut in pieces and artfully arranged on a plate.

天ぷら

my favorite TEMPURA (delicate fritters)

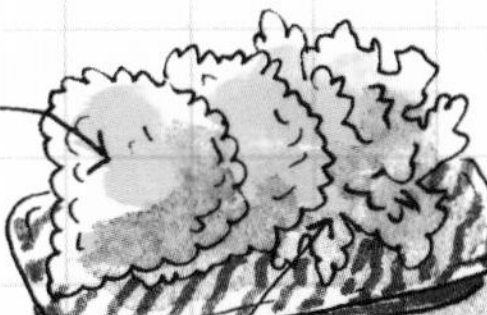

shiso leaf

maitake mushroom

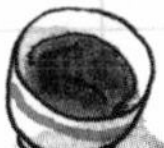

Apples are the specialty of Aomori, in the north.

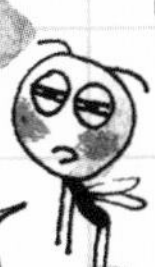

天ぷらの絵は難しいです…
Tempura is hard to draw!

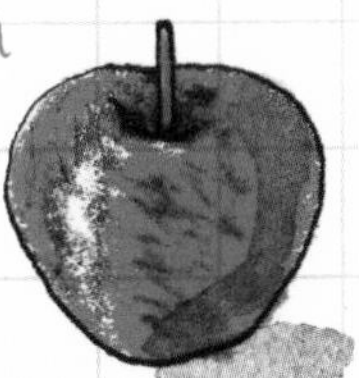

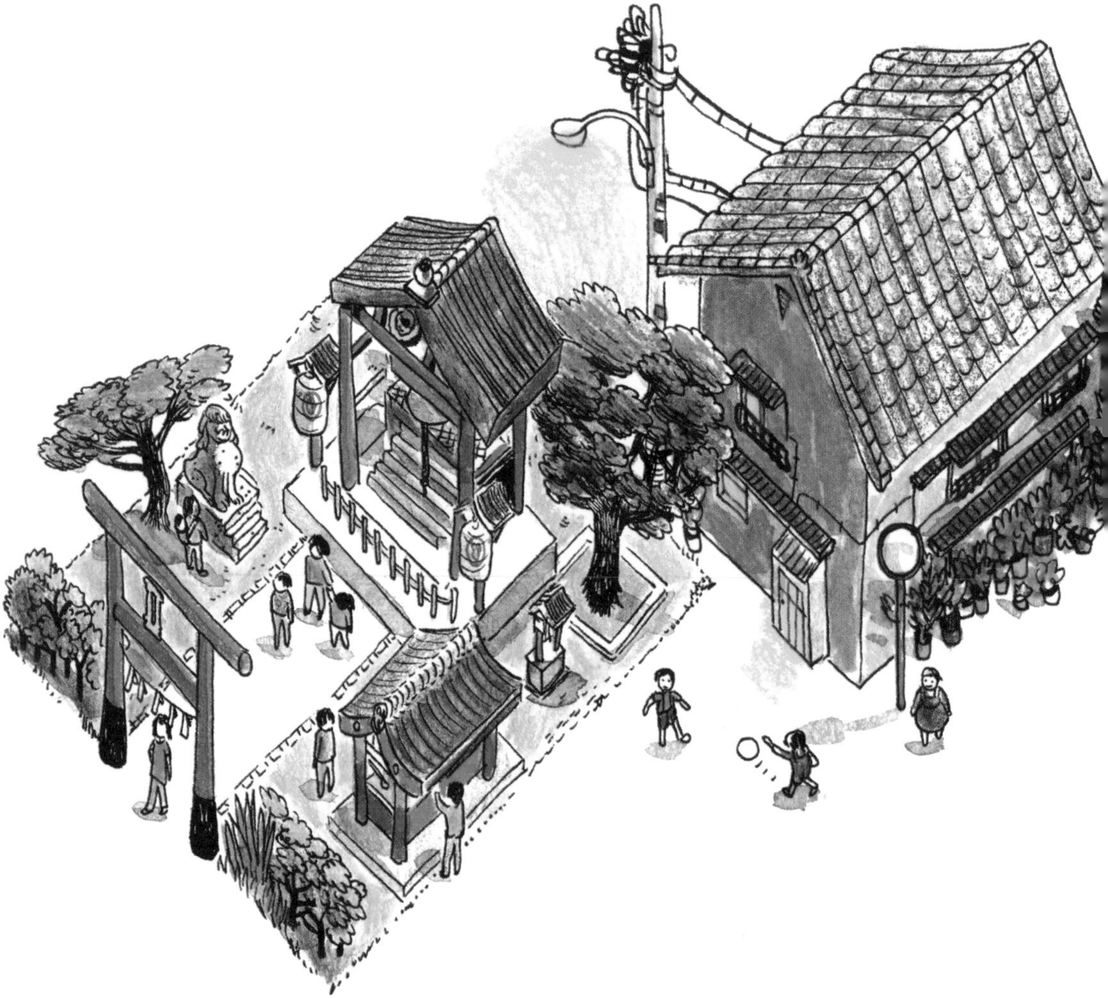

Living in

Himonya

碑文谷

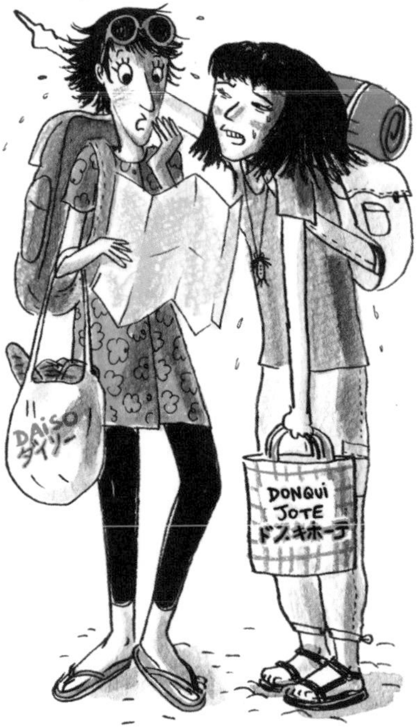
DAISO
ダイソー
DONQUI
JOTE
ドンキホーテ

My Homey Home in Himonya
碑文谷と言う私の休息地

After the earthquake, many
French families leave Japan.
There are no more drawing classes
I was giving to French kids or
the workshops I held at the
French School, so I'm almost
completely out of work.

Since my Japanese language
lessons have also ended, I'm
thinking of going back to France...

地震のあとで たくさんの
フランス人は 日本を
はなれます。
フランス人の 子供むけ
絵画 教室の キャンセル。
東京国際フランス学園での
ワークショップの キャンセル。
なので、私の仕事はなくなります。
私の日本語学校も 終わります。
フランスに帰らなきゃと思いますが…

But I apply for a full-time graphic designer position and... I get it! So I'm going to be in Japan a while longer. I decide to treat myself to living alone after years of having roommates.

運よくグラフィックデザイナーとして、会社で働く事が出来ます。もうちょっと日本にいれます。

これまで約10年以上、シェアメイトがいた私の人生。決断します。これからはひとり暮らしです。

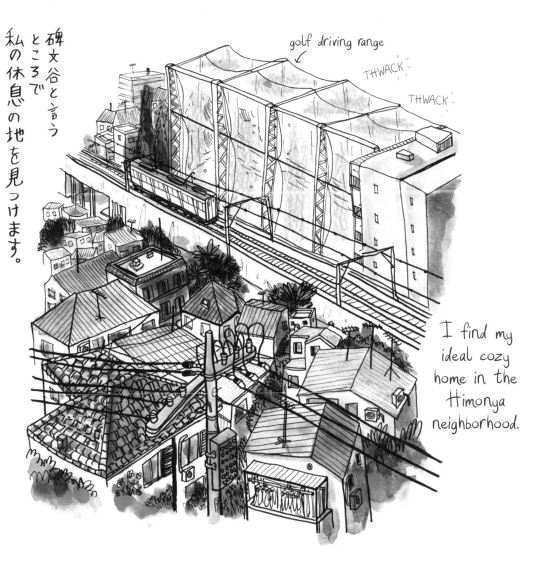

碑文谷と言うところで私の休息の地を見つけます。

golf driving range

THWACK

THWACK

I find my ideal cozy home in the Himonya neighborhood.

Again I'm living in a 70s apartment, with all the characteristic features.

また住むのは、70年代アパートセットです。

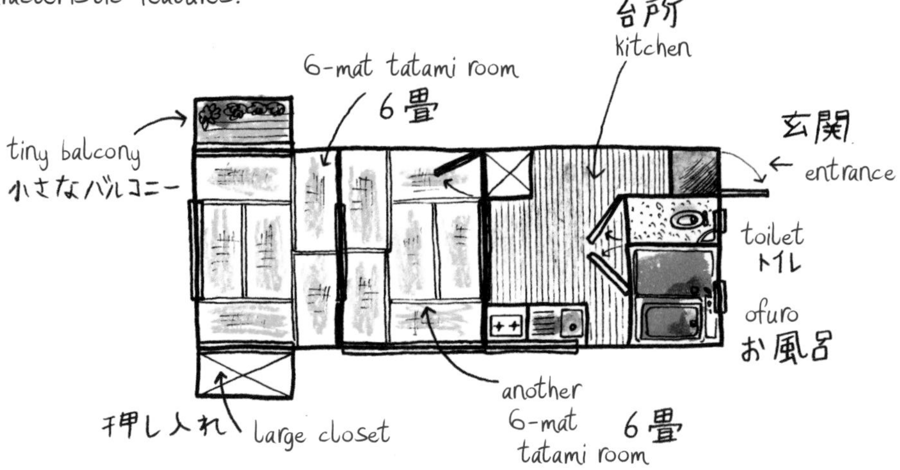
台所
kitchen
6-mat tatami room
6畳
tiny balcony
小さなバルコニー
玄関
entrance
toilet
トイレ
ofuro
お風呂
押し入れ
large closet
another 6-mat tatami room
6畳

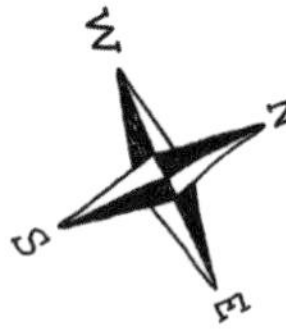

私(フランス人たち)は、東京といえば高層ビルが立ち並ぶ、映画「ブレード・ランナー」のイメージがどうしても強いですが、ここ碑文谷もまた東京なんですね。

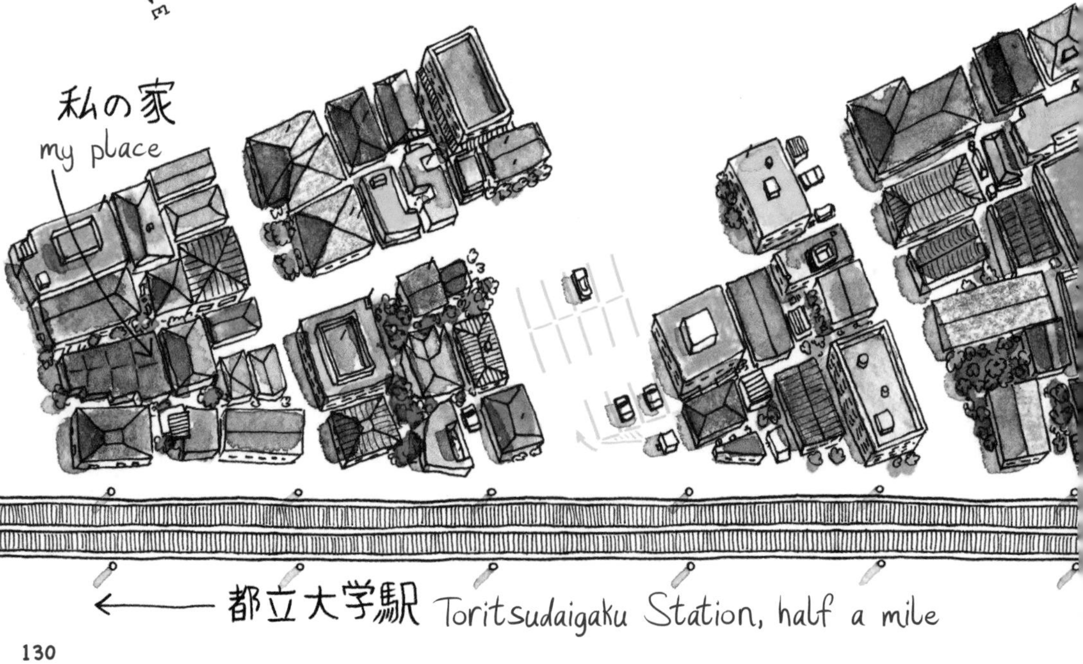
私の家
my place
← 都立大学駅 Toritsudaigaku Station, half a mile

With housing units made of tatami, thin partitions and rooms all slotted together, Japanese apartment blocks are like Lego buildings!

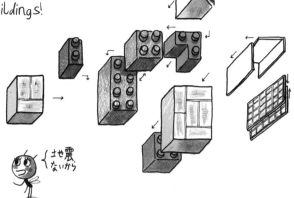

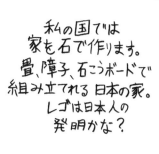

私の国では
家を石で作ります。
畳、障子、石こうボードで
組み立てれる 日本の家。
レゴは日本人の
発明かな？

{ 地震
ないから

My neighborhood, like many in Tokyo, has the feel of a village with its narrow alleys, plants growing here and there, its cats...

It's all thanks to a law that radically modifies the perception of urban space—in Japan, every car owner has to have a designated parking space. Go ahead and imagine your own city without all those cars along the sidewalks!

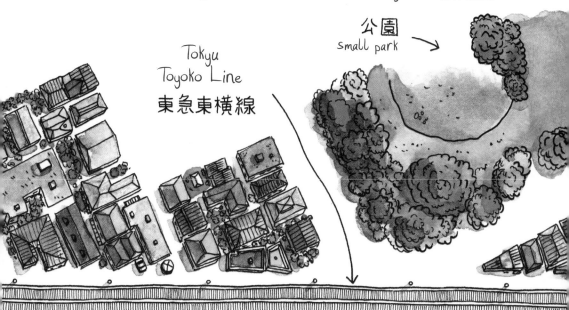

公園
small park

Tokyu
Toyoko Line
東急東横線

Gakugei Daigaku Station, half a mile   学芸大学駅 ⟶

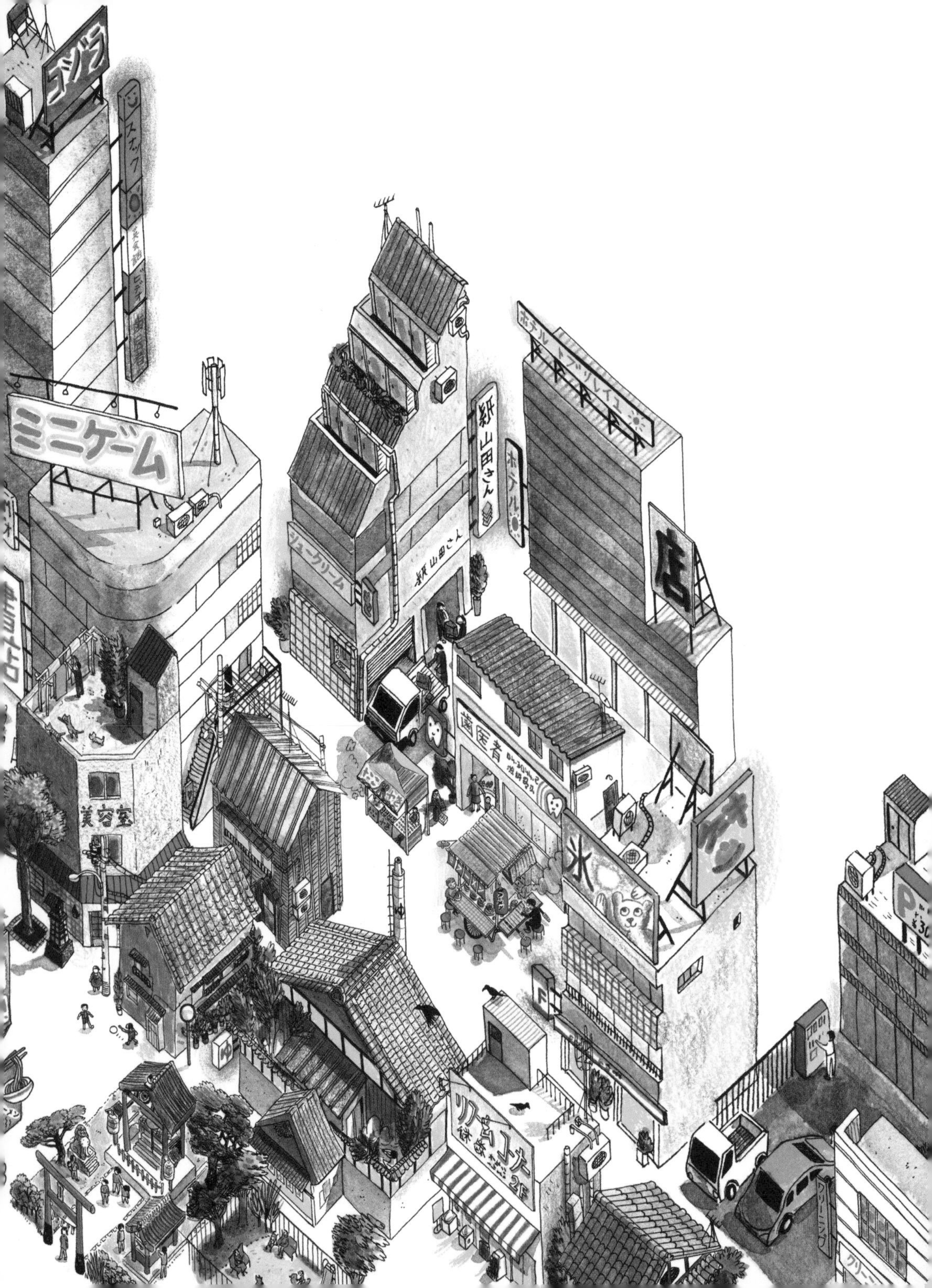
ゴジラ
スナック
ミニゲーム
紙山田さん
ホテル
シュークリーム
紙山田さん
店
歯医者
氷
美容室
2F
クリーニング

Japanese Trains 日本の電車

I've become a proper Tokyoite, working from 10 to 7, five days a week, for a tiny salary.

I take public transportation at rush hour every morning and every evening.

A **PASMO** transit pass is super convenient. You load it once and you can go through the ticket gates (well, actually there are no gates since almost nobody cheats, it's just an open entrance).

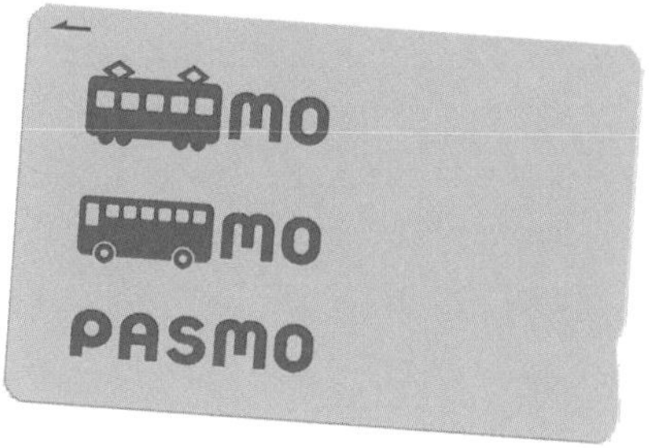
mo
mo
PASMO

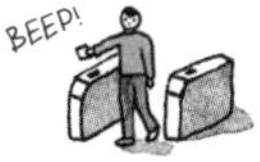
BEEP!

Public transportation is synonymous with horror for people who've never set foot in Japan—station guards who shove people into train cars, people packed like sardines, from morning till night.

With these passes, you can even buy stuff at vending machines or kombini*.

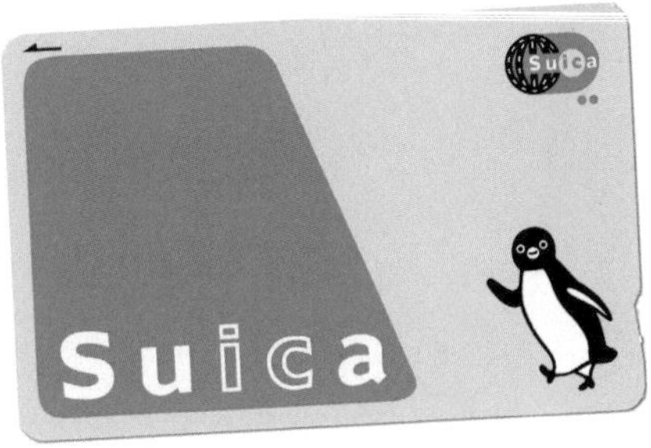
Suica
Suica

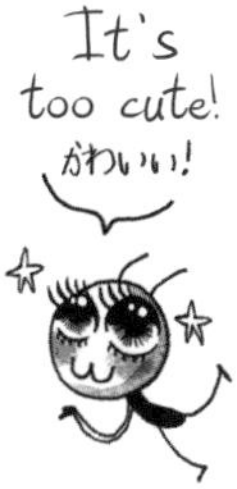
It's too cute!
かわいい!

私は東京で会社員です。
一週間に5日、10時から19時まで働きます。
通勤には公共交通機関を利用します。
日本に来た事がない人にとって、公共交通機関は
いつも混雑してせわしないイメージがあると思います。
もちろんラッシュアワーは本当に大変です。が…

* Kombini are 24/7 corner convenience stores where you can do anything from buying food to paying your gas bill.

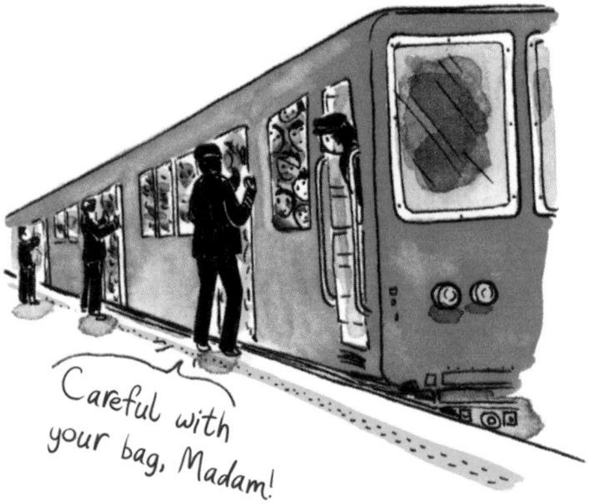
Careful with your bag, Madam!

It's true that at rush hour, and even more so on certain lines such as the Tozai line, the cars are packed. But it's well managed.

日本人の段取りのよさに
外国人は驚きます。
プラットホームにいるスタッフの
サービスの質！

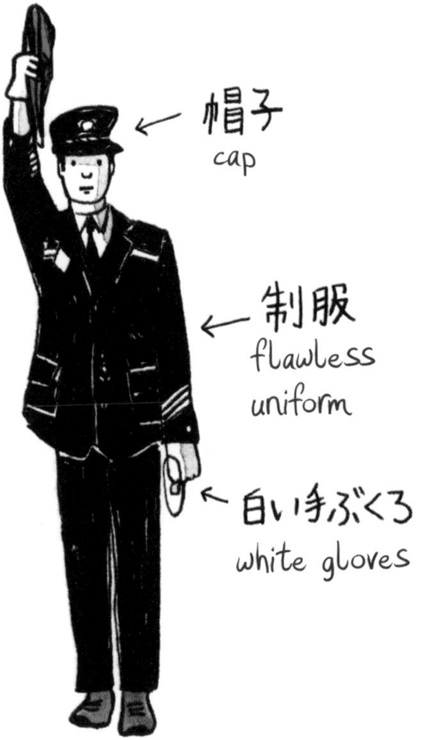
帽子
cap
制服
flawless uniform
白い手ぶくろ
white gloves

station guard

There are guards at each door to help people get out, get in and to check that the doors close properly.

People wait in line!

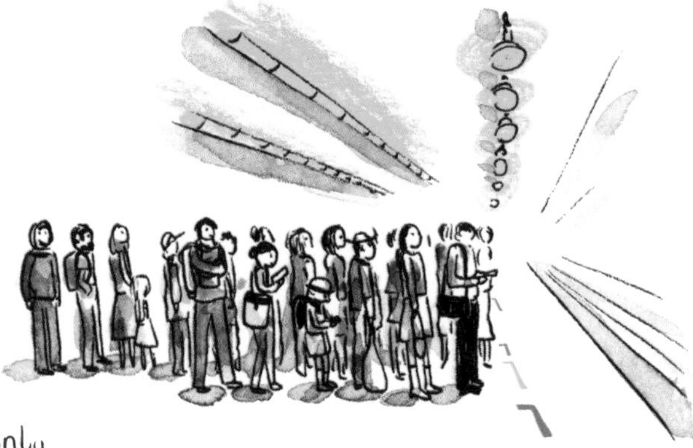

There are platform markings to tell people where to wait for a particular train.

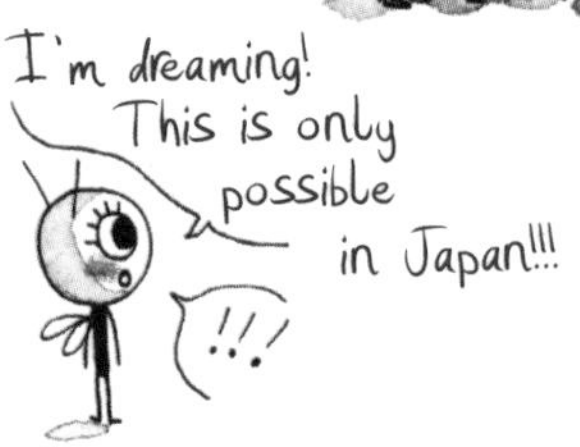
I'm dreaming! This is only possible in Japan!!!
!!!

日付
1 2 3 4 5 6 7 8 9 10 11 12 13 14 15
遅延時分
~15分
~30分
~45分
~60分
遅延証明書
表記のとおり、電車が遅れましたことを証明いたします。お急ぎのところ大変ご迷惑をおかけいたしました。
東京急行電鉄株式会社
※当社ホームページで遅延証明書を印刷できます。http://www.tokyu.co.jp/
遅延時分
~90分
~119分
120分以上
16 17 18 19 20 21 22 23 24 25 26 27 28 29 30 31

おなかに赤ちゃんがいます

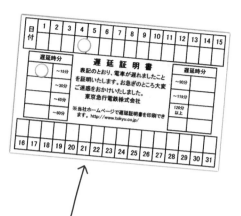

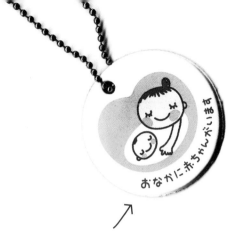

When there's a delay (very rare), the transit employees issue a certificate you can give to your boss, or your teacher, etc.

Small tag (given by the transit system to attach to your bag when you're pregnant so people will give you their seat).

People really do sleep heavily! Some even dream!

日本では電車の中で
深いねむりが出来ます。

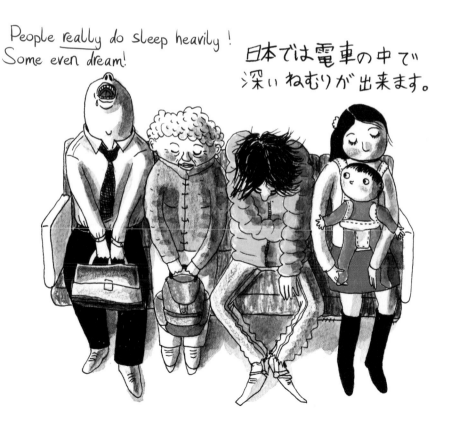

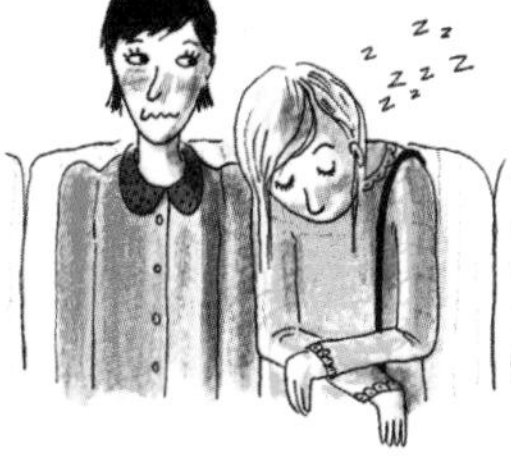

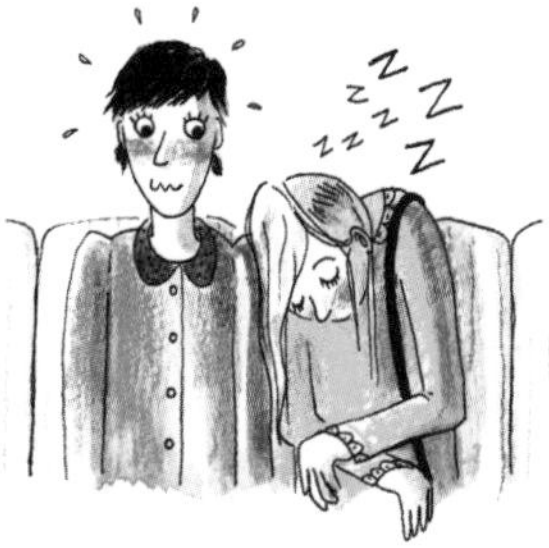

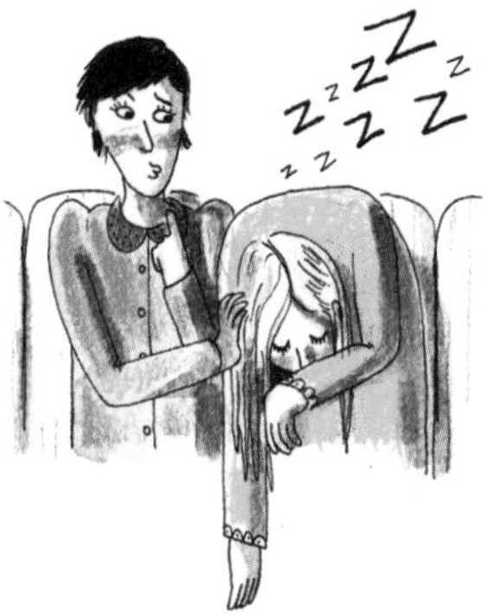

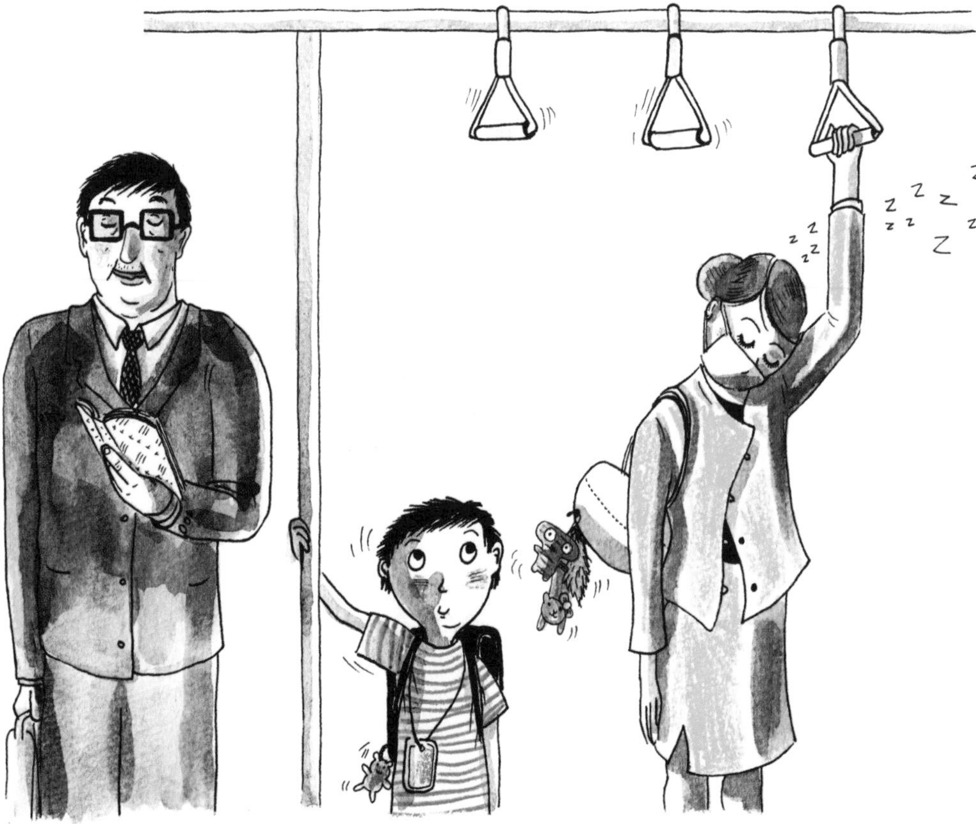

車内でおりがみのレッスン
impromptu origami lesson

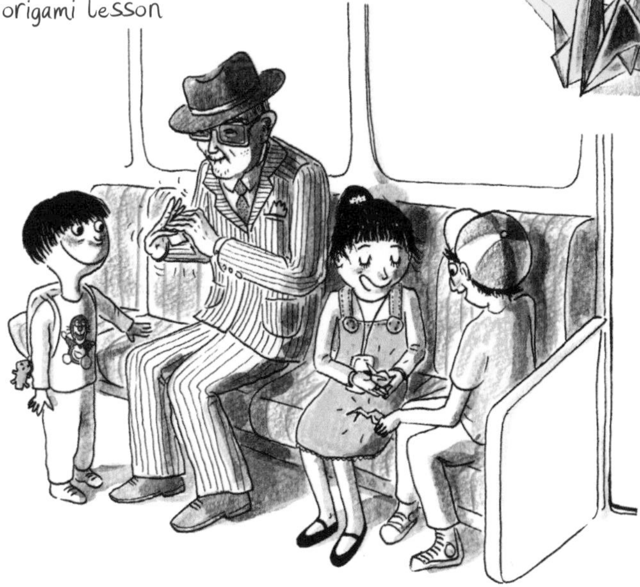

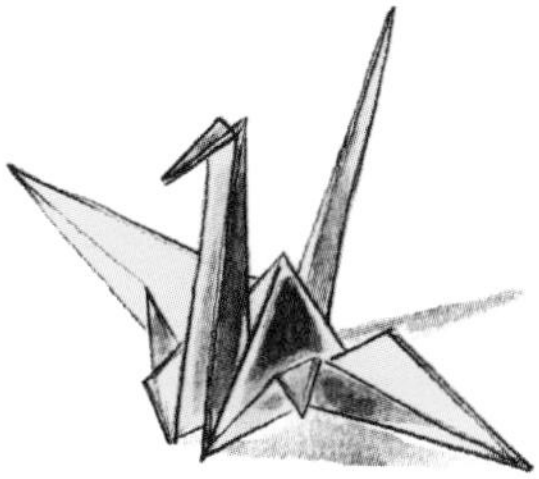

MASKS

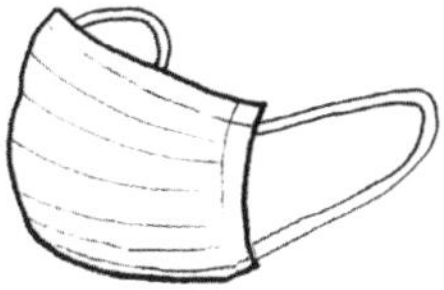

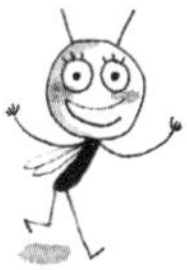

Hello! Many Japanese wear protective masks, even when there isn't a pandemic.

The Japanese don't wear masks to protect against pollution, as popular belief would have it. Tokyo air is no more polluted than that of other big cities, in fact the air is actually rather pleasant near the bay. The Japanese mostly wear masks when they're sick in order to avoid contaminating other people. Allergy sufferers wear them to protect themselves against pollen.

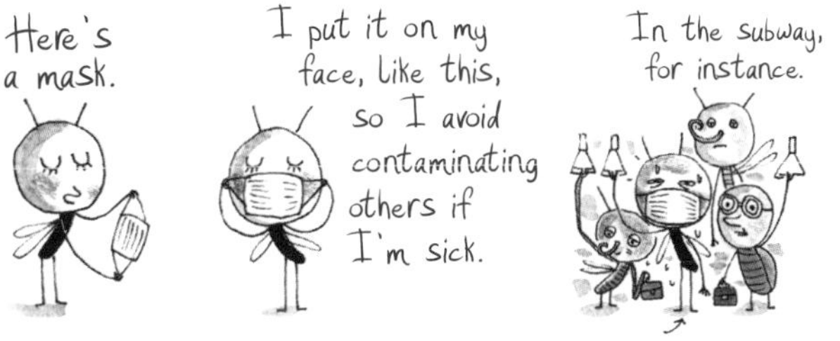
Here's a mask.
I put it on my face, like this, so I avoid contaminating others if I'm sick.
In the subway, for instance.

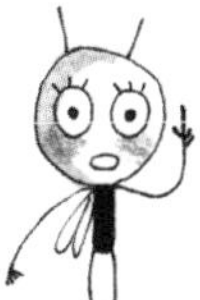

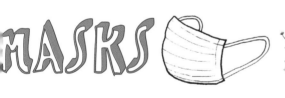

You can play bingo on the train.
車内でビンゴ遊び

BINGO!

スマートフォンする人！
Smartphone users!

①② ③ ④ BINGO! ねるん！
Sleepers!

① ② ③ ④ BINGO! ルイ・ヴィトン！
Louis Vuitton bags!

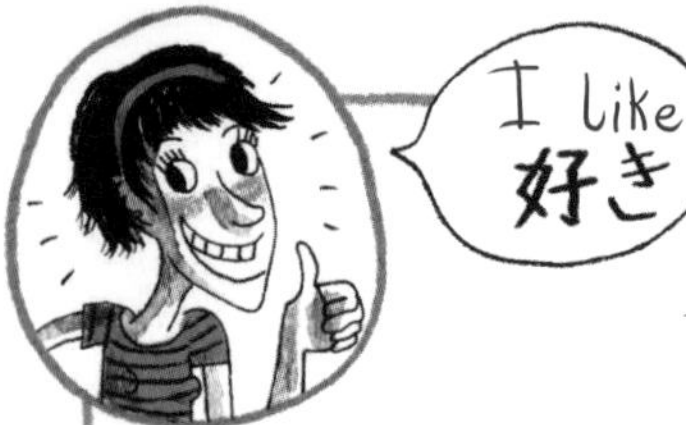
I like
好き

I like getting a care package from my family.

家族からのおくり物が大好きです。

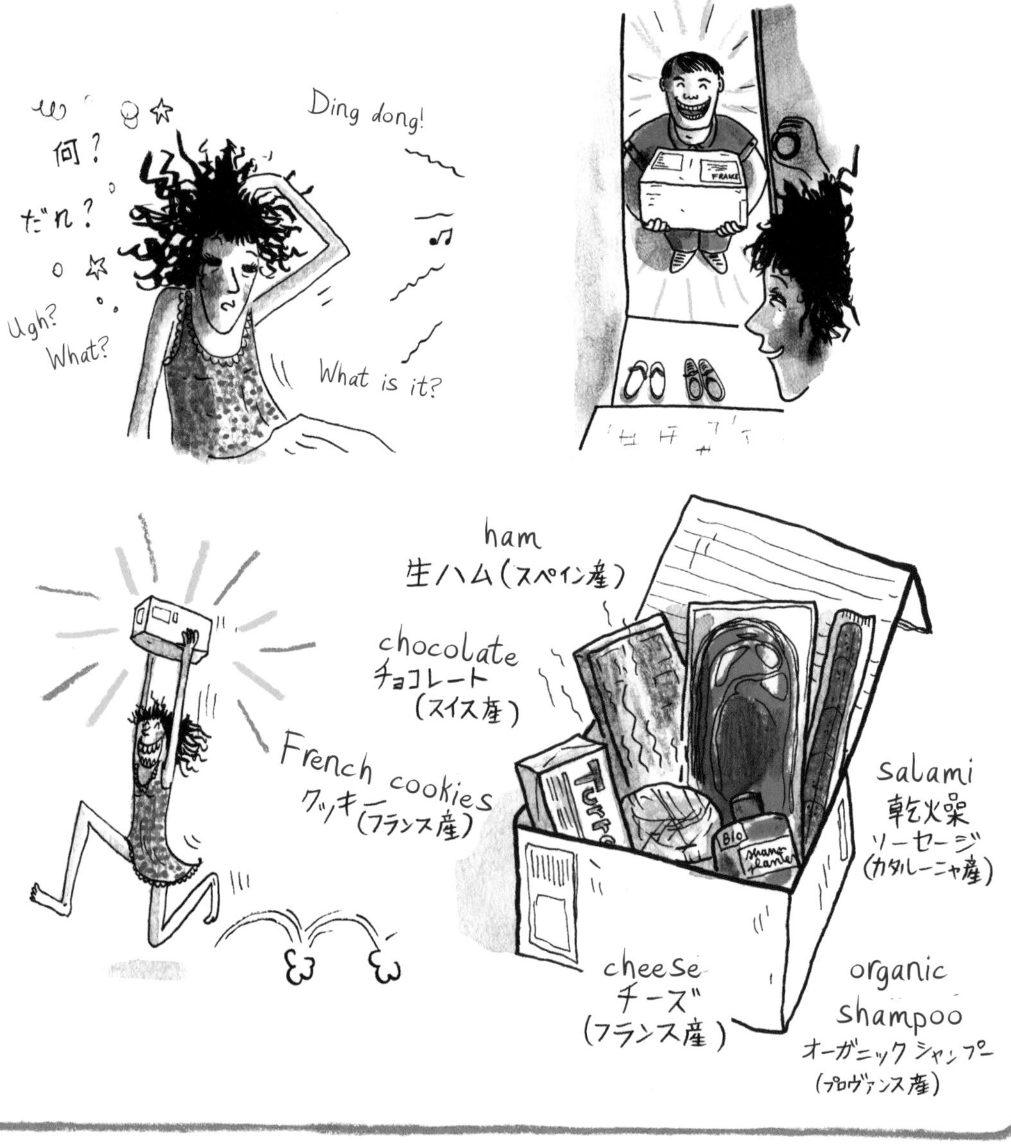
何？
だれ？
Ugh?
What?
Ding dong!
What is it?
FRANCE
ham
生ハム（スペイン産）
chocolate
チョコレート
（スイス産）
French cookies
クッキー（フランス産）
salami
乾燥
ソーセージ
（カタルーニャ産）
cheese
チーズ
（フランス産）
organic
shampoo
オーガニック シャンプー
（プロヴァンス産）

I don't like
きらい

I don't like aftershocks. 余震がきらいです。

東京はぜんぜんだいじょうぶ！
Everything is fiiiiine in Tokyo!!!

my mom and dad
on Skype
SKYPEでわたしの
母と父

I don't like the trucks that collect bulky trash and drive very slowly through the neighborhood on Sunday mornings, speakers blaring.

休日の朝早くから近所をまわる廃品回収車がきらいです。

テレビ…
TV SETS! 冷蔵庫…
FRIDGES!
COMPUTERS!
コンピュータ…

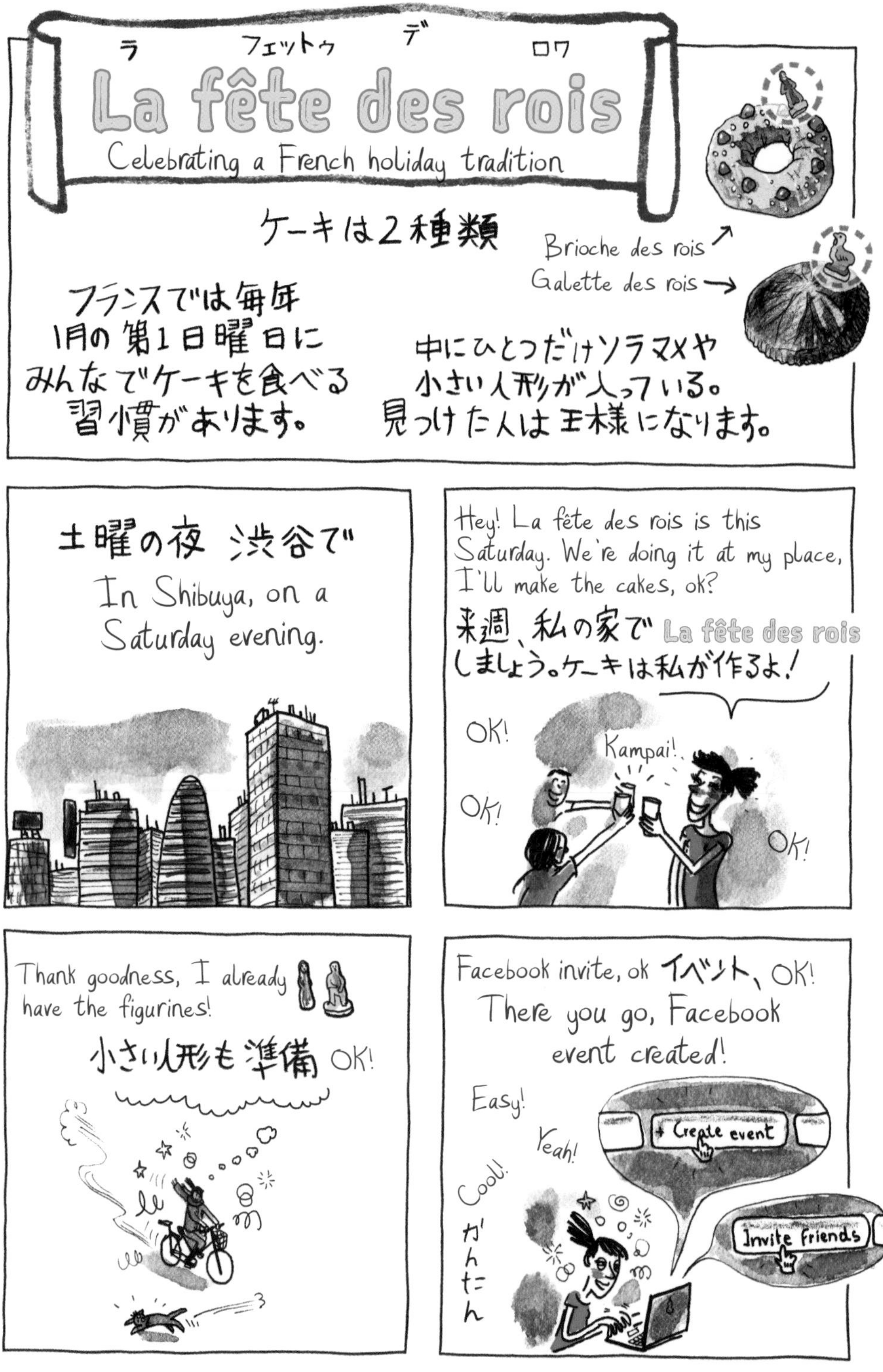

ラ　フェットゥ　デ　ロワ
La fête des rois
Celebrating a French holiday tradition
ケーキは2種類
Brioche des rois
Galette des rois
フランスでは毎年
1月の第1日曜日に
みんなでケーキを食べる
習慣があります。
中にひとつだけソラマメや
小さい人形が入っている。
見つけた人は王様になります。
土曜の夜　渋谷で
In Shibuya, on a Saturday evening.
Hey! La fête des rois is this Saturday. We're doing it at my place, I'll make the cakes, ok?
来週、私の家で La fête des rois しましょう。ケーキは私が作るよ!
OK!
Kampai!
OK!
OK!
Thank goodness, I already have the figurines!
小さい人形も準備 OK!
Facebook invite, ok イベント、OK!
There you go, Facebook event created!
Easy!
Yeah!
Cool!
かんたん
+ Create event
Invite friends

Good Advice
いい助言

今日の助言
Today's Advice

Never use Facebook when you're drunk!

よっぱらいの時 FACEBOOK を 使わないでね！

朝 In the morning

← bedhead
朝のかみ

participants (34)
参加 (34)

Jolm Bch.
Mouhikh.
REPain

participants
参加 (34)

Céline Zaba

WOW... I can't wait to taste your homemade galettes!

あなたのガレットを食べたい！

like · comment

Michel Dupont

You're baking your own cakes? So cool!

自分でガレットを作るの？
楽しそう！

shit

So I really have to bake those cakes, huh?

本当に？
ケーキを
作らなければ
なりません...

shit

shit

shit

COME ON, YOU CAN DO IT!

がんばります

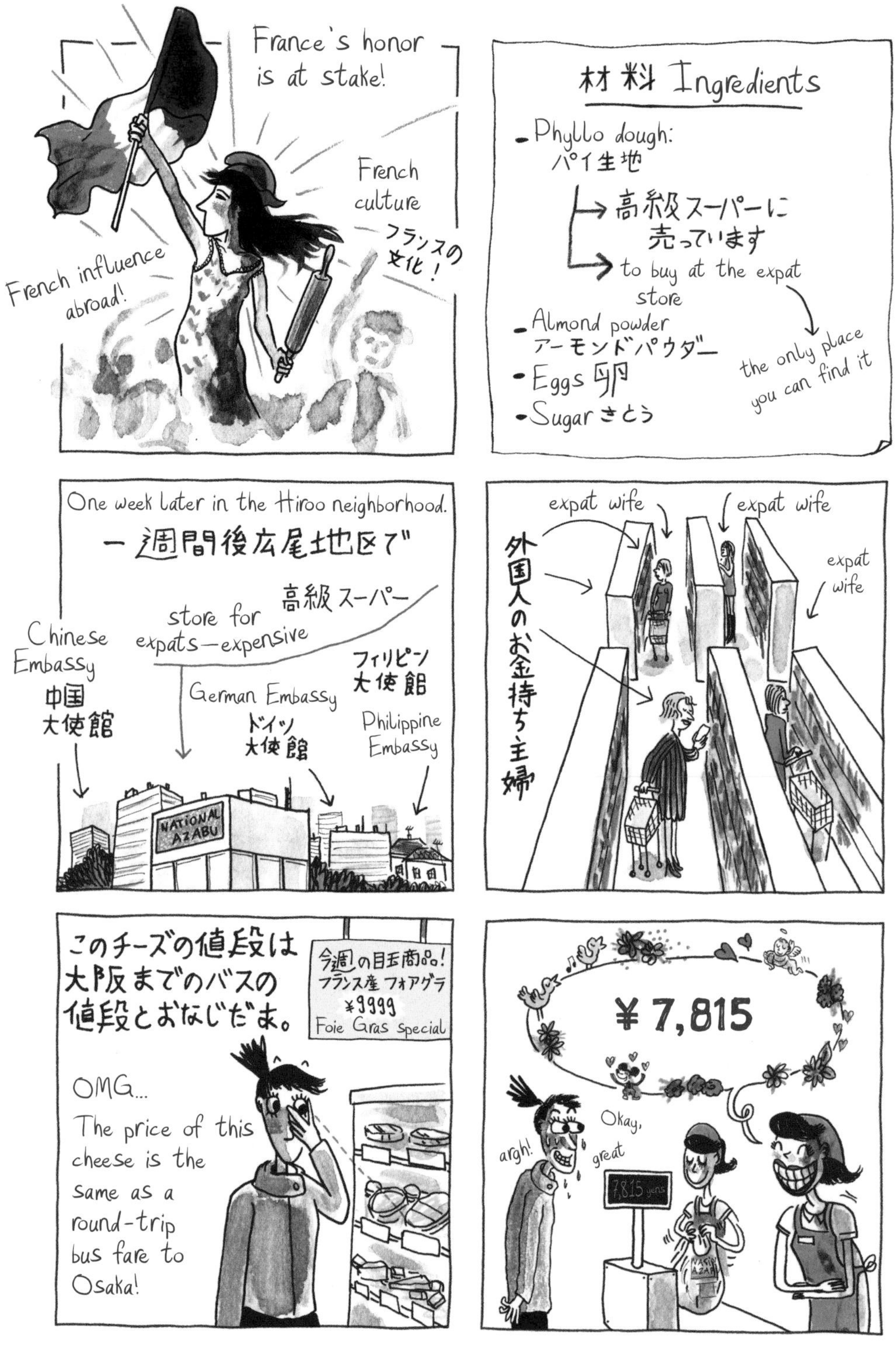
France's honor is at stake!
French culture
フランスの文化！
French influence abroad!
材料 Ingredients
Phyllo dough:
パイ生地
高級スーパーに売っています
to buy at the expat store
the only place you can find it
Almond powder
アーモンドパウダー
Eggs 卵
Sugar さとう
One week later in the Hiroo neighborhood.
一週間後広尾地区で
高級スーパー
store for expats—expensive
Chinese Embassy
中国大使館
German Embassy
ドイツ大使館
フィリピン大使館
Philippine Embassy
NATIONAL AZABU
expat wife
expat wife
expat wife
外国人のお金持ち主婦
このチーズの値段は大阪までのバスの値段とおなじだま。
今週の目玉商品！
フランス産 フォアグラ
¥9999
Foie Gras special
OMG...
The price of this cheese is the same as a round-trip bus fare to Osaka!
¥7,815
argh!
Okay, great
7,815 yens

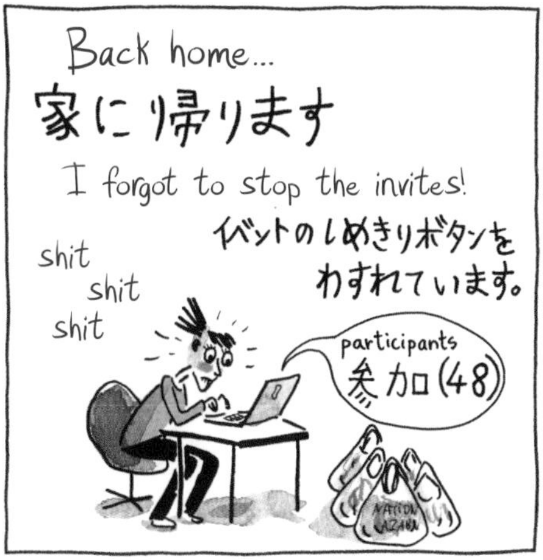
Back home...
家に帰ります
I forgot to stop the invites!
イベントのしめきりボタンをわすれています。
shit
shit
shit
participants
参加(48)

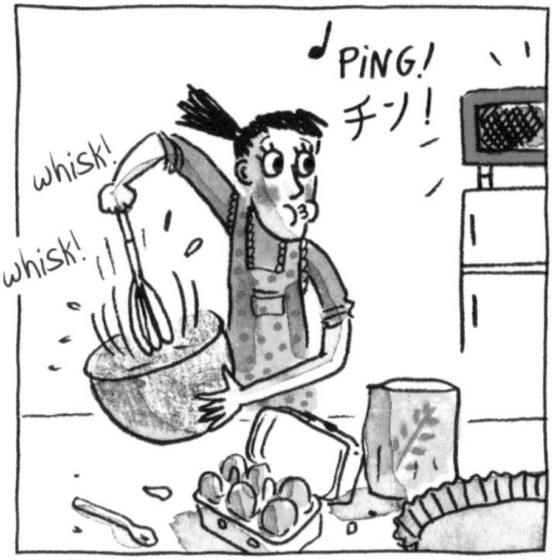
PING!
チン!
whisk!
whisk!

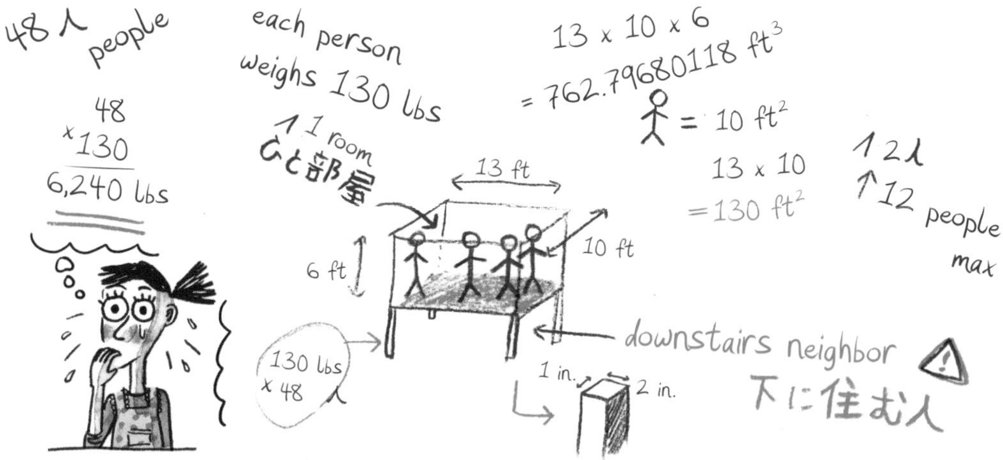
48人 people
48
x130
6,240 lbs
each person
weighs 130 lbs
1 room
ひと部屋
13 ft
6 ft
10 ft
130 lbs
x 48 人
1 in.
2 in.
13 x 10 x 6
= 762.79680118 ft³
= 10 ft²
13 x 10
=130 ft²
12人
12 people
max
downstairs neighbor
下に住む人

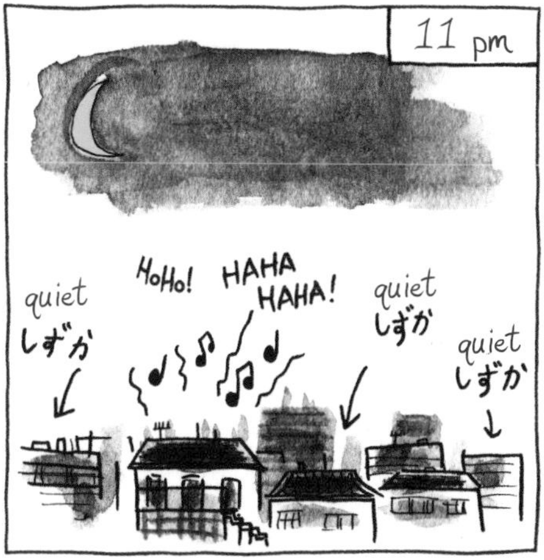
11 pm
quiet
しずか
HoHo!
HAHA
HAHA!
quiet
しずか
quiet
しずか

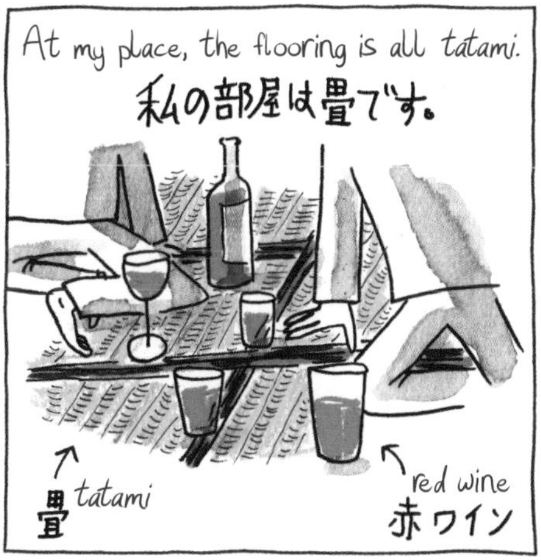
At my place, the flooring is all tatami.
私の部屋は畳です。
畳 tatami
red wine
赤ワイン

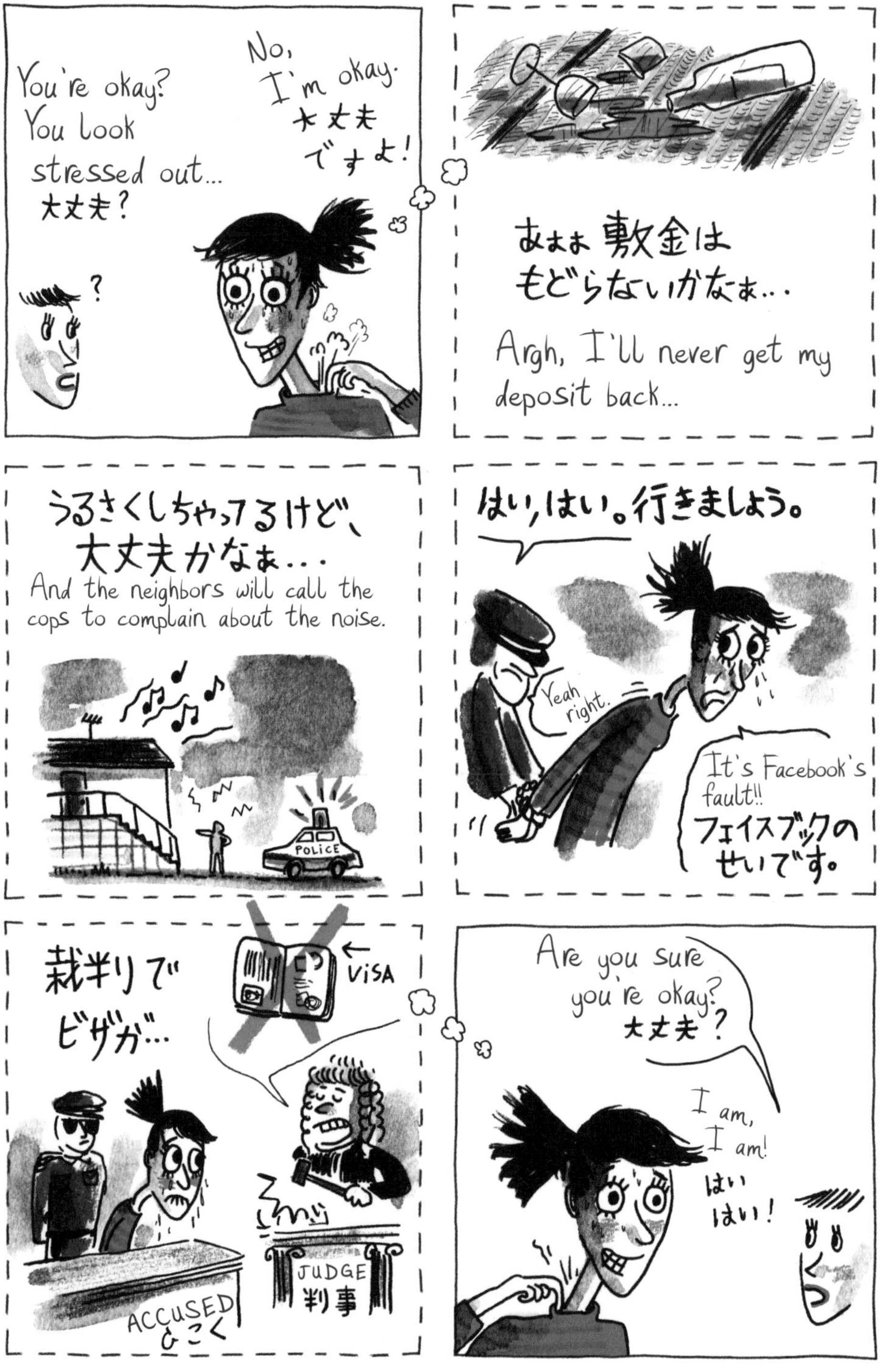

You're okay? You look stressed out... 大丈夫？
No, I'm okay. 大丈夫ですよ！
?
あぁぁ 敷金はもどらないかなぁ...
Argh, I'll never get my deposit back...
うるさくしちゃってるけど、大丈夫かなぁ...
And the neighbors will call the cops to complain about the noise.
POLICE
はい、はい。行きましょう。
Yeah right.
It's Facebook's fault!! フェイスブックのせいです。
裁判でビザが...
VISA
JUDGE 判事
ACCUSED ひこく
Are you sure you're okay? 大丈夫？
I am, I am! はいはい！

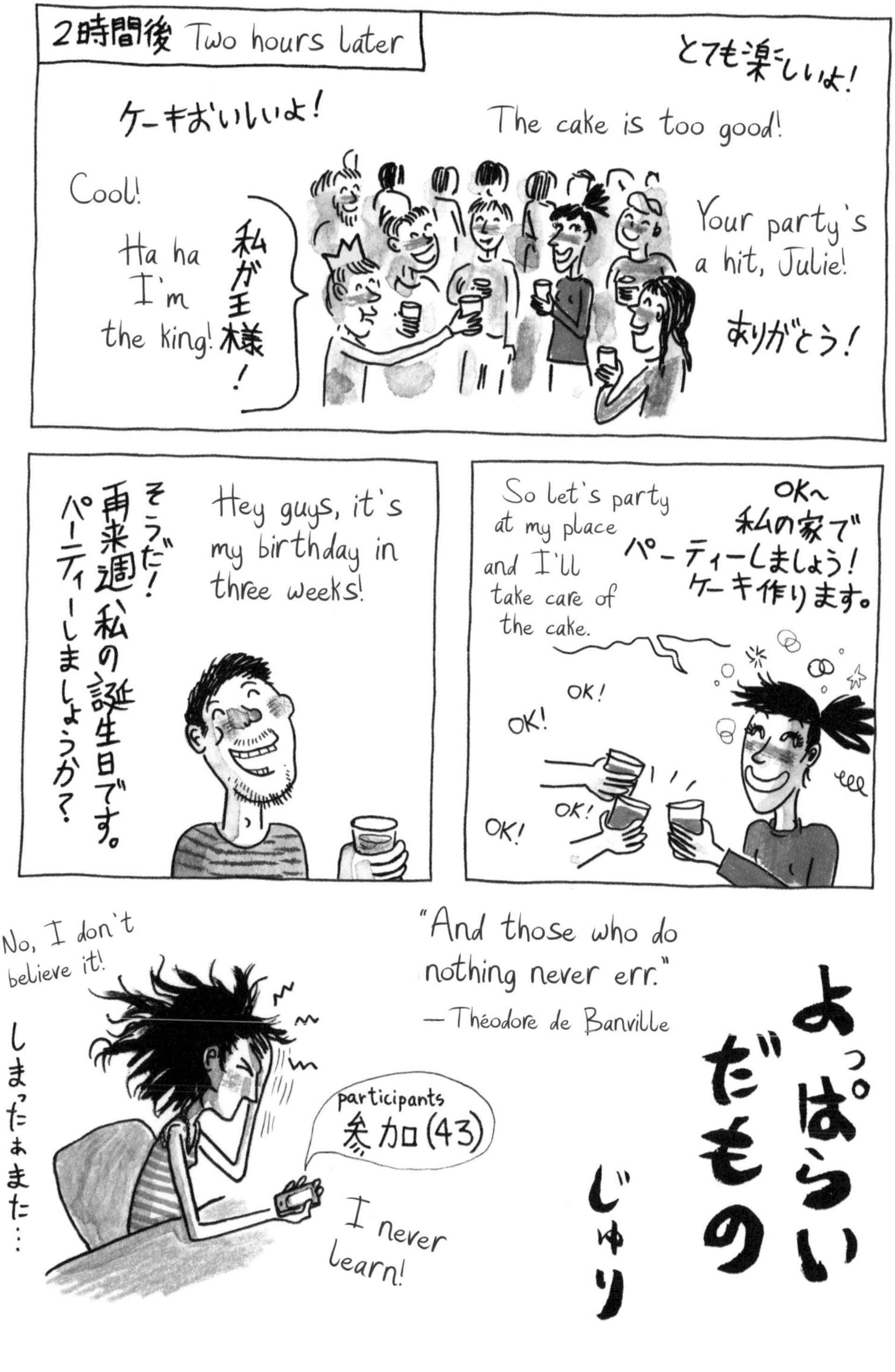
2時間後 Two hours later
とても楽しいよ!
ケーキおいしいよ!
The cake is too good!
Cool!
Ha ha I'm the king!
私が王様!
Your party's a hit, Julie!
ありがとう!
そうだ! 再来週私の誕生日です。パーティーしましょうか?
Hey guys, it's my birthday in three weeks!
So let's party at my place and I'll take care of the cake.
OK～ 私の家でパーティーしましょう! ケーキ作ります。
OK!
OK!
OK!
OK!
No, I don't believe it!
しまったぁまた…
participants
参加(43)
I never learn!
"And those who do nothing never err."
—Théodore de Banville
よっぱらいだもの
じゅり

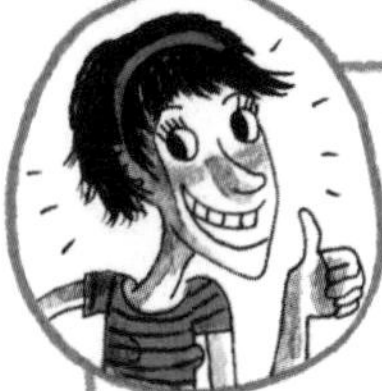

I like 好き

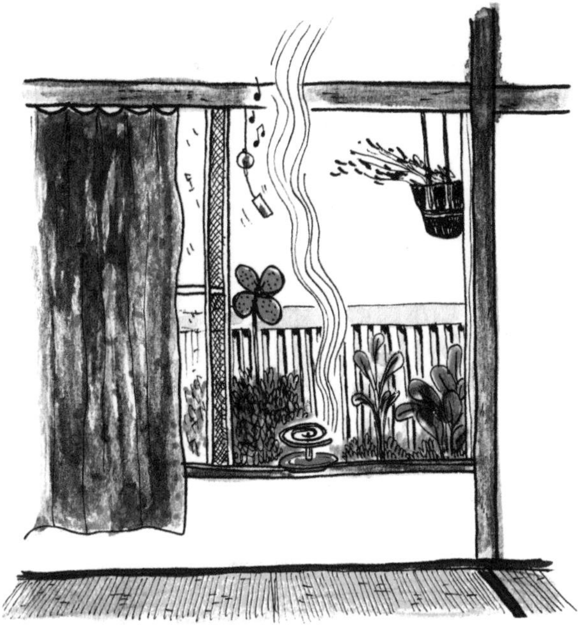

I like my tiny balcony.

私のミニテラスが好きです。

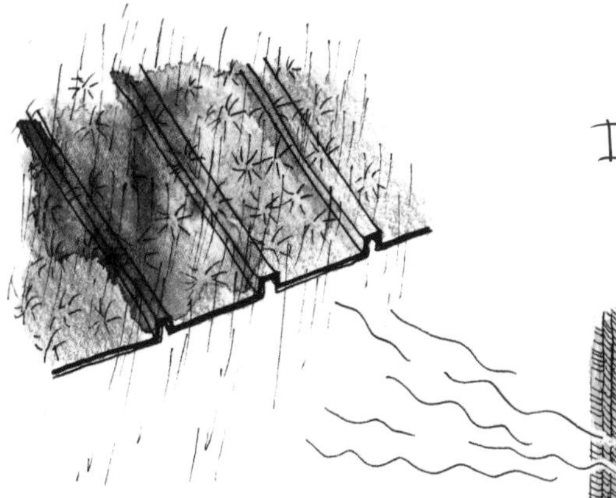

I like listening to the rain from my futon.

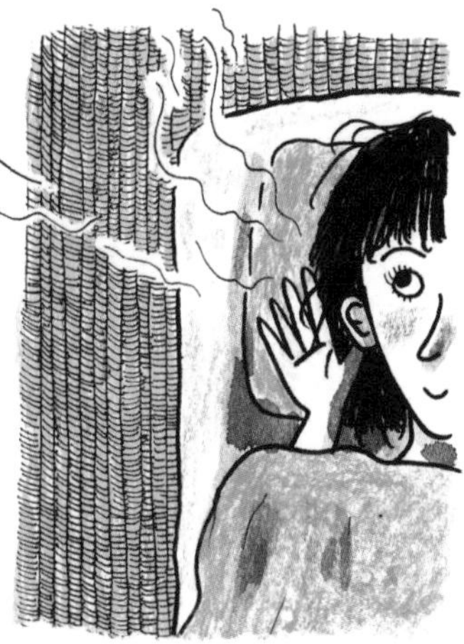

布団の中で雨の音を聞くのが好きです。

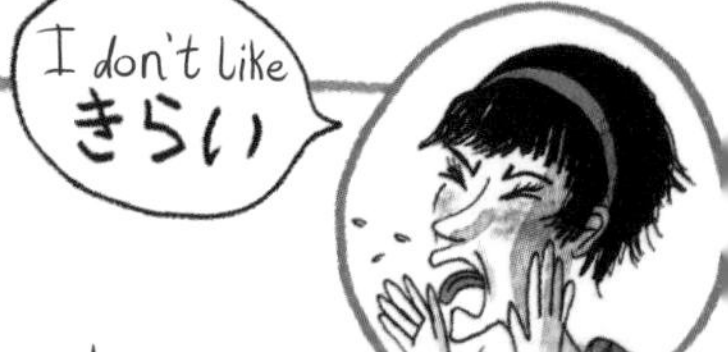
I don't like
きらい

I don't like being woken up by an earthquake.
地震で起こされるのがきらいです。

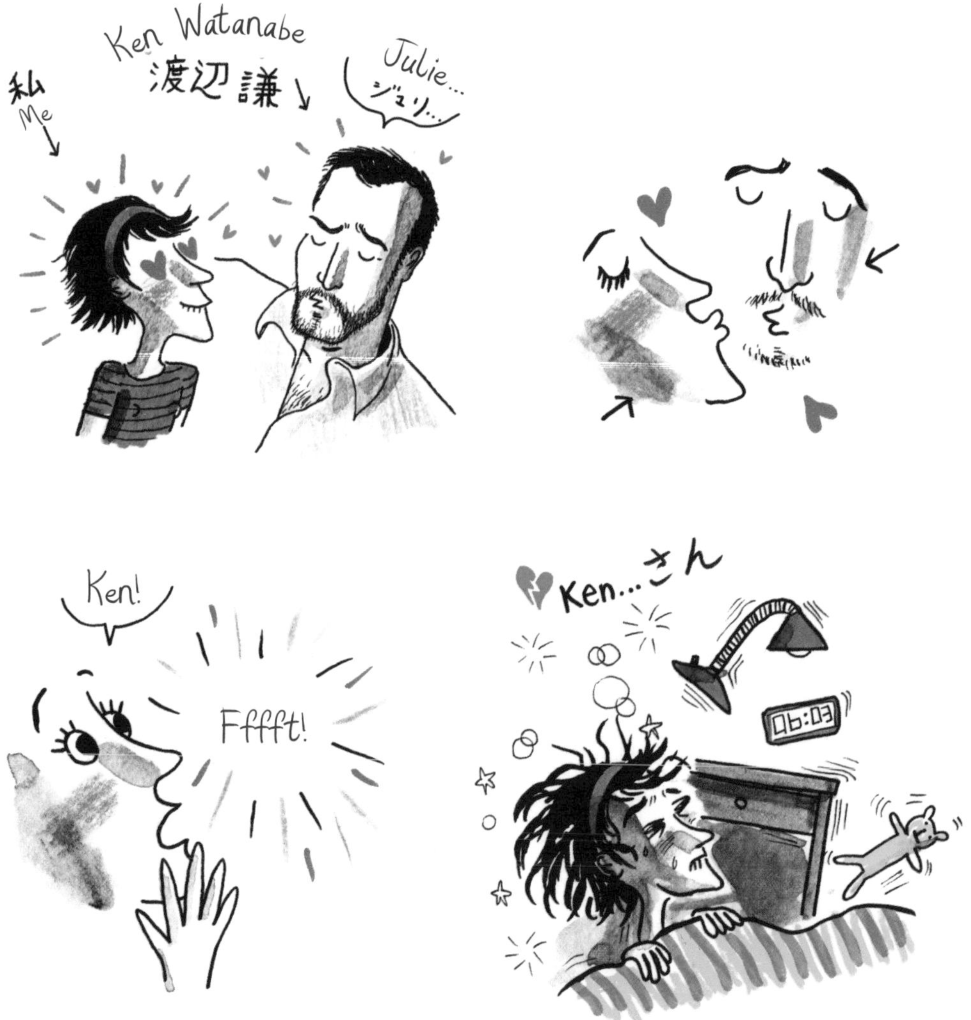
Ken Watanabe
渡辺謙
私
Me
Julie...
ジュリ...
Ken!
Fffft!
Ken...さん
06:03

山ガール Mountain Girl

友達とキャンプ場での音楽
フェスに行きます。
遅く到着した私達の場所は、
もちろんキャンプ場のはしっこです。

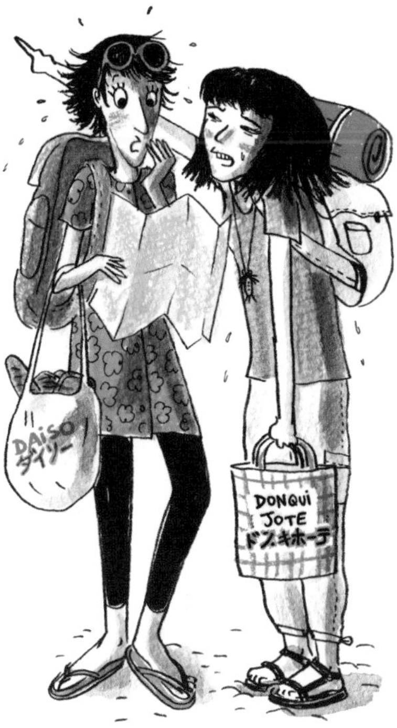
DAISO
ダイソー
DONQUI
JOTE
ドン・キホーテ

This weekend, I'm going to a music festival in the mountains with friends. We're staying at the campground they've set up for the festival goers. Of course, we're the last to arrive—everybody's already settled in.

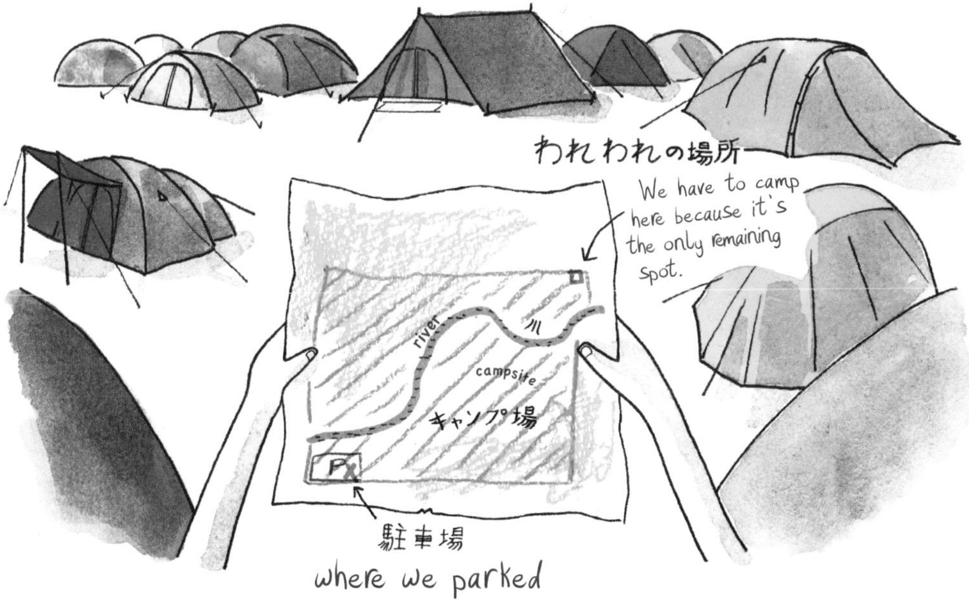
われわれの場所
We have to camp here because it's the only remaining spot.
river
川
campsite
キャンプ場
P
駐車場
where we parked

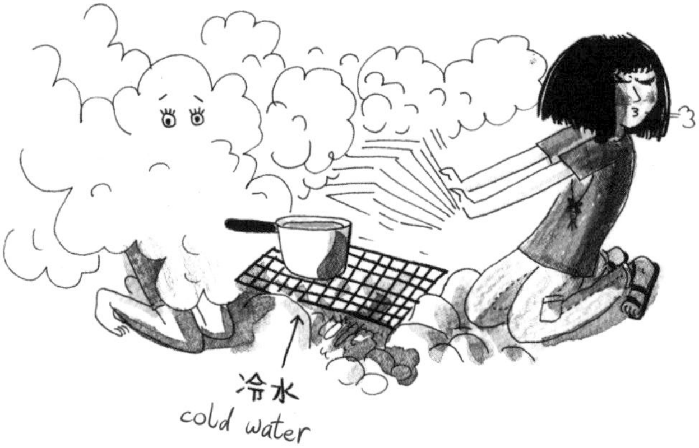
冷水
cold water

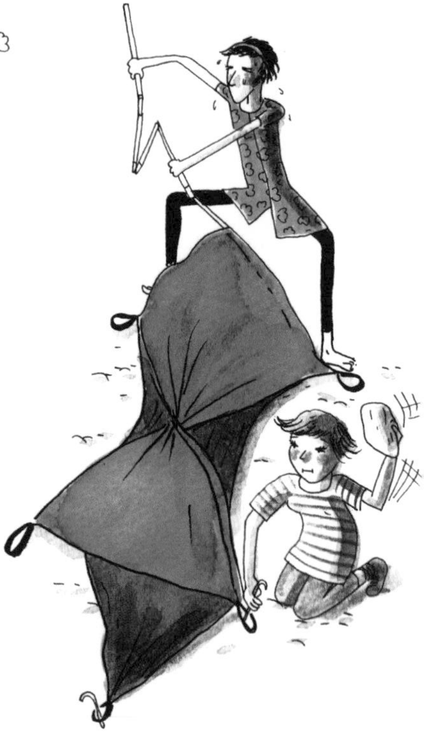

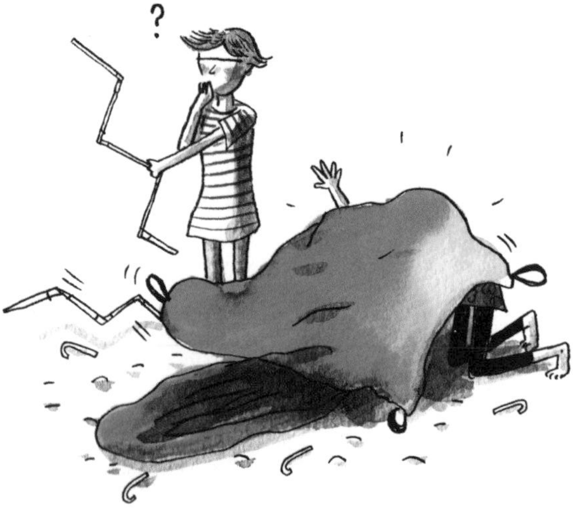

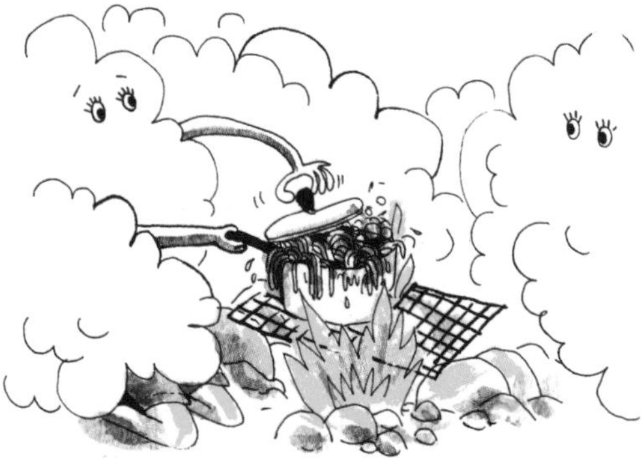

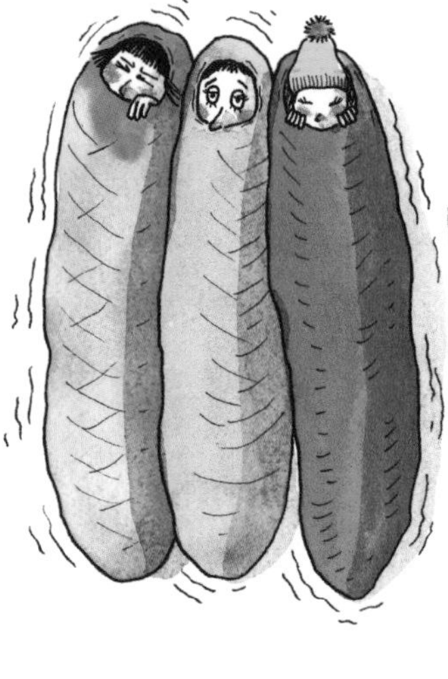

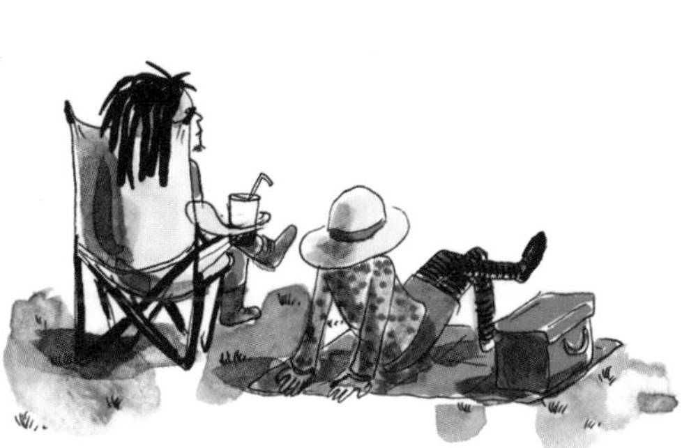

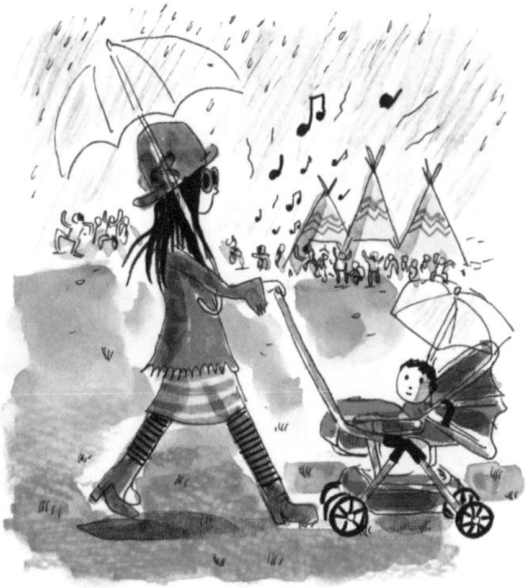

Everybody else is super prepared and equipped with expensive, high-end gear.

他のグループの食べ物や服は
スタイリッシュで
ハイクオリティーなキャンプ用具を使っています。
私達は正反対です。

Still, I doubt that a solar-powered *takoyaki** maker is indispensable.

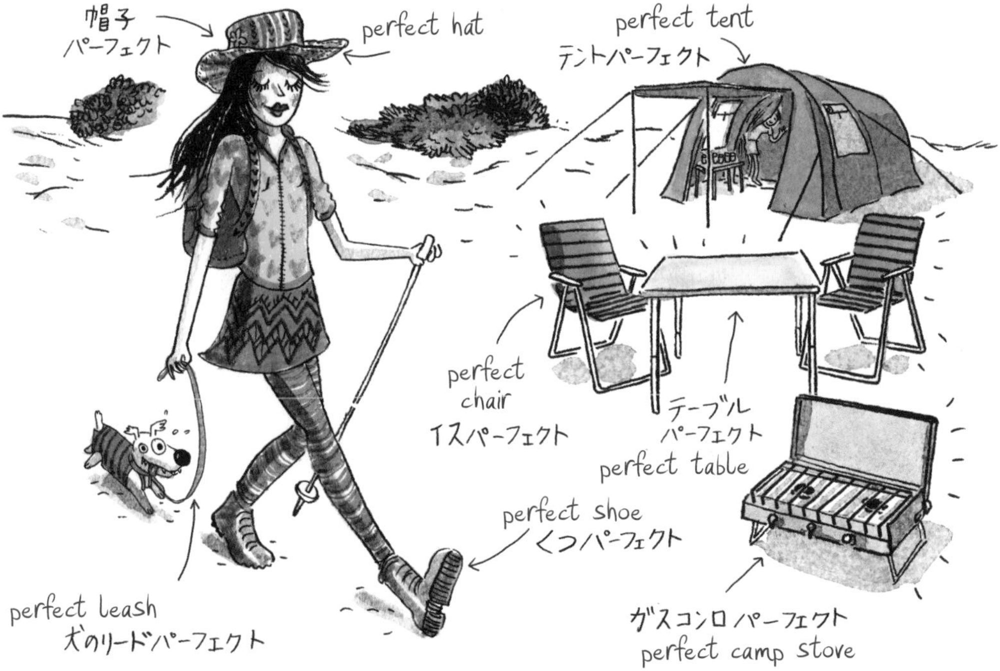

帽子
パーフェクト
perfect hat
perfect tent
テントパーフェクト
perfect
chair
イスパーフェクト
テーブル
パーフェクト
perfect table
perfect shoe
くつパーフェクト
perfect leash
犬のリードパーフェクト
ガスコンロパーフェクト
perfect camp store

* Takoyaki: "octopus balls" of dough filled with bits of chopped octopus and made in a special molded pan.

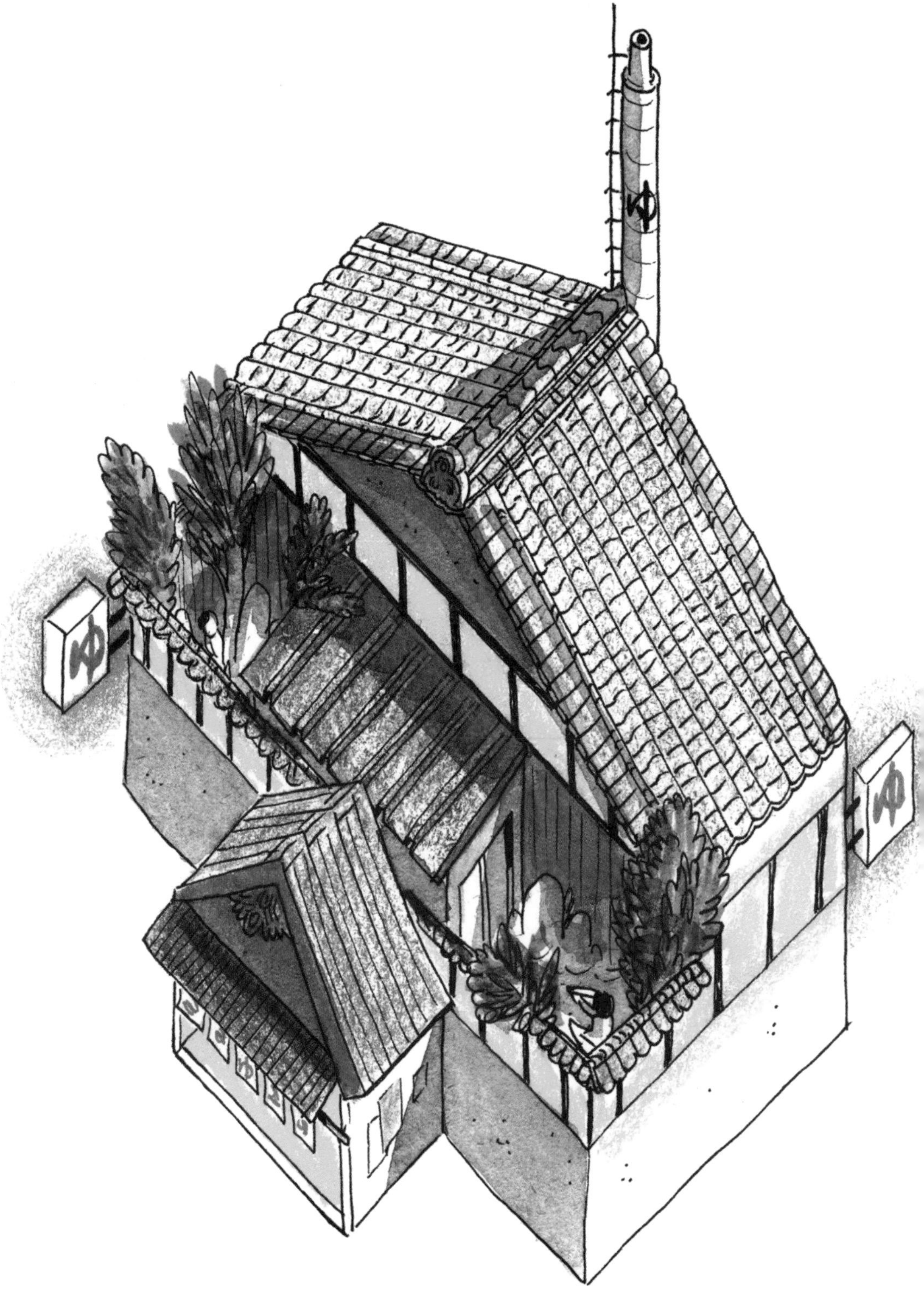
ゆ
ゆ
ゆ

Living in

Kiyosumi-Shirakawa

清澄白河

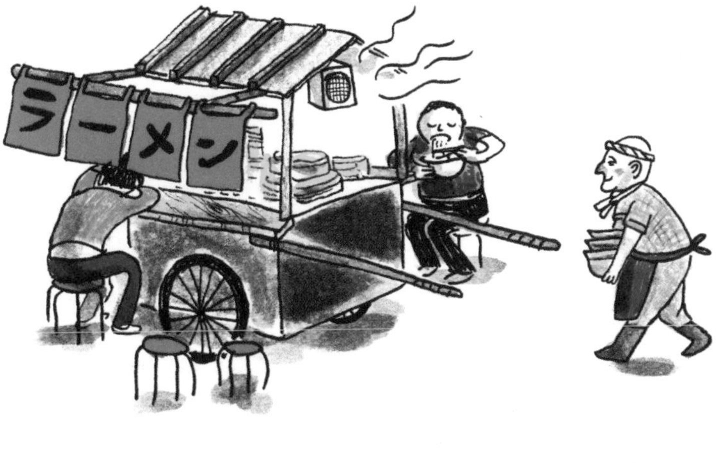

ラーメン

Tokyo Love Story 東京ラブストーリー

I quit my full-time job and go back to freelancing. I rent my apartment to a friend for two months and I go on a trip to Hong Kong.

会社員の仕事をやめ、
2ヶ月間、日本のアパートを
友達にお願いして、
香港に行きます。

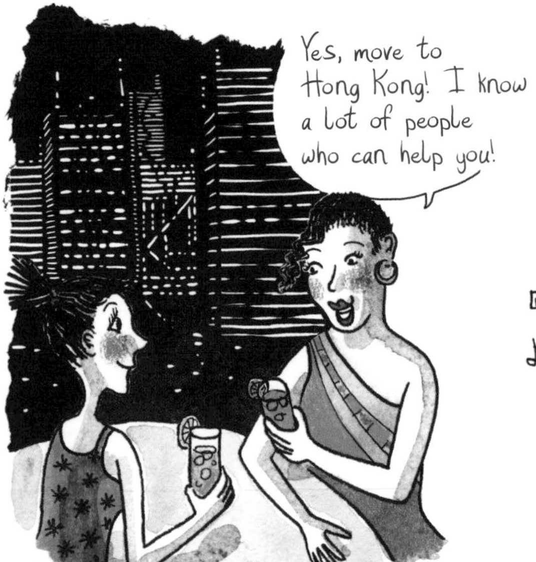
Yes, move to Hong Kong! I know a lot of people who can help you!

An American friend lives there and works as a "digital marketer." I'm not sure what it means exactly but it sure sounds classy!

香港に住むアメリカ人の友達は
『デジタルマーケティング』という仕事。
よく分からないけど、超クール な響き！

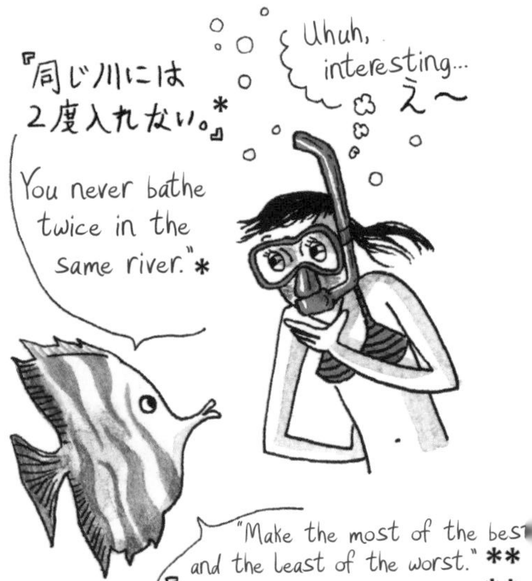
『同じ川には
2度入れない。*』
"You never bathe twice in the same river."*
Uhuh, interesting...
え〜

Then I spend several weeks in the Gili Islands near Bali, where I talk to philosopher fish.

そして数週間、インドネシアのギリ島で
哲学者の魚と話します。

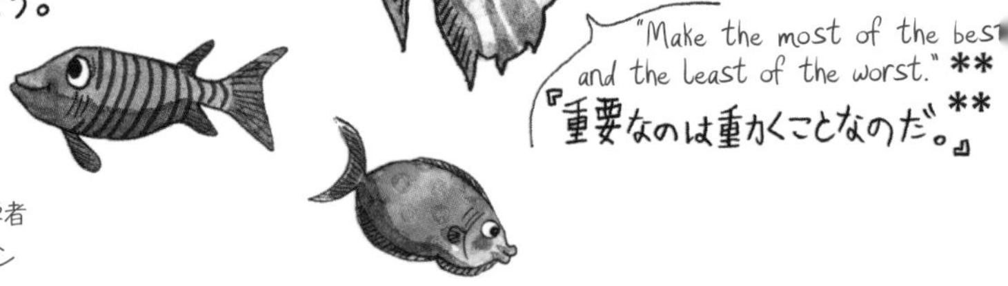
"Make the most of the best and the least of the worst."**
『重要なのは動くことなのだ。**』

* Heraclitus ** R. L. Stevenson

* ヘラクレイトス：古代ギリシアの哲学者

** ロバート・ルイス・スティーヴンソン

Upon my return to Tokyo, I decide I need a change of scene. I've made up my mind— I'm moving to Hong Kong!

バイバイ東京！
There you go! Got my ticket, here I come Hong Kong!

東京へもどって決断です。
香港に引っこしします。

I buy a one-way Tokyo to Hong Kong ticket.

片道チケットを買います。

I give three months' notice to my landlord, I arrange a shared rental in Hong Kong and I start selling my stuff.

まずアパートの退去手続き
（3ケ月前）をして、
香港のシェアハウスを
予約します。家財道具の
処分もしはじめます。

But... my well-prepared plan falls apart the day when ...

しかし…私の引っこし計画に暗雲がたれこめます。

a giant Hello Kitty invades Tokyo! キティちゃんが東京を襲う！

No, that was a joke. It was the day that Tokyo vegetation grew like crazy and the city found itself carpeted in forest within a few hours!

ははは。キティ襲撃はジョークで、
本当は植物が増殖し、更に
巨大化して東京を飲みこむ！

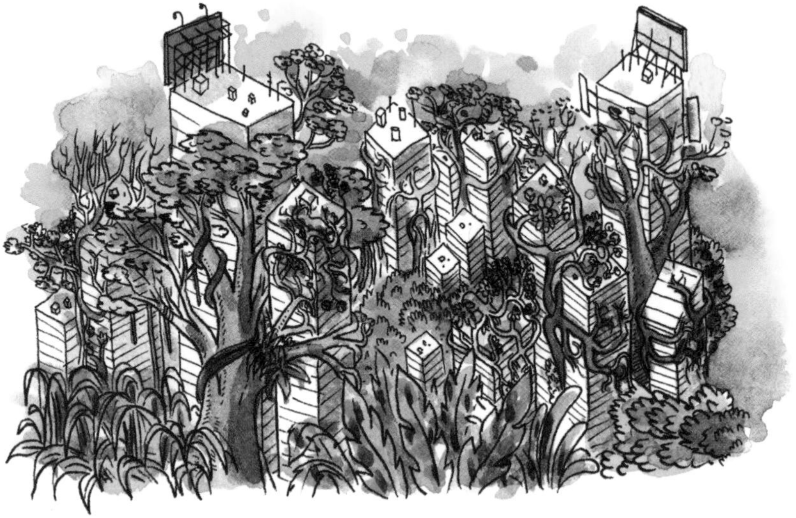

No, sorry, I joke too much. My plan to go live in Hong Kong got derailed the day that I ... meet Issei.

ははは。東京ジャングルはジョークで、
本当は イッセイ という人と出会う！

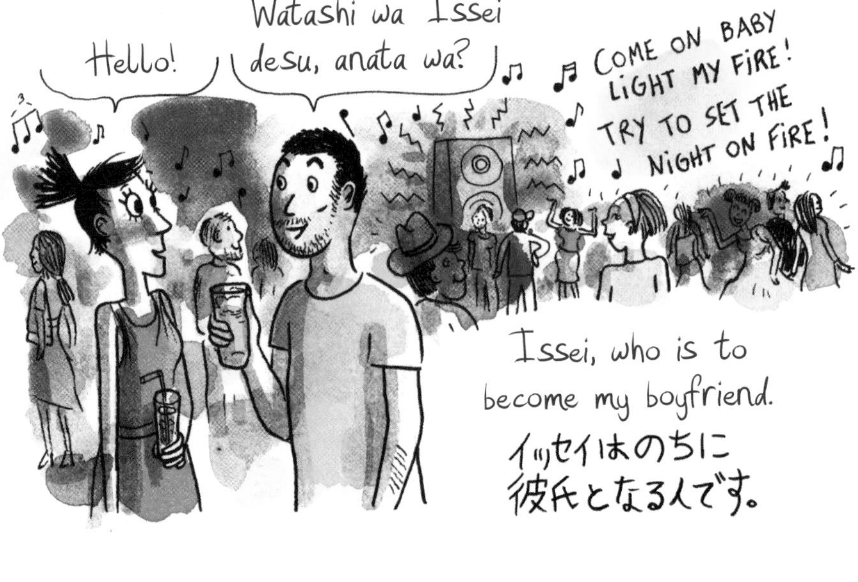
Hello!
Watashi wa Issei desu, anata wa?
COME ON BABY LIGHT MY FIRE! TRY TO SET THE NIGHT ON FIRE!

Issei, who is to become my boyfriend.

イッセイはのちに
彼氏となる人です。

So after three months of romance and enjoying every moment of my last weeks in Japan, here I am in Hong Kong. I look for work as planned, but frankly, I'm just not motivated, even less so when Issei turns up like Prince Charming looking for Cinderella.

のこり3ケ月のロマンス。
最後のひと時を楽しみながら
香港に着きます。
仕事を探す計画だったけど、
モチベーションが下がります。
その上、イッセイが私に会いに来ます。

Well, if you were tempted to come back to Japan, you could come live with me. I'm just saying.

えーと、もし あなたが…
東京に…り帰りたいなら…
私の家に…でもいいんじゃないかな…

shy guy in love ⟶

⟵ shy girl in love

Oh really?
そう？
本当に！

That's all it took for me to cancel my plans to settle in Hong Kong. Instead I follow my love back to Tokyo!

Hong Kong

Tokyo

私の香港移住計画を
急きょキャンセルし、
イッセイと東京へ帰ります。

Issei's place (to become _our_ place) is right next to
Kiyosumi-Shirakawa Station. It's an old Tokyo neighborhood,
not well known by tourists or other Westerners. This is
where our new life of love and romance will begin.

イッセイのアパート (のちに 私たちのアパートになる) は
清澄白河駅のすぐ近くにあります。ここは東京に古くからある街です。
観光客と日本に住む外国人にとってはあまり有名ではありません。

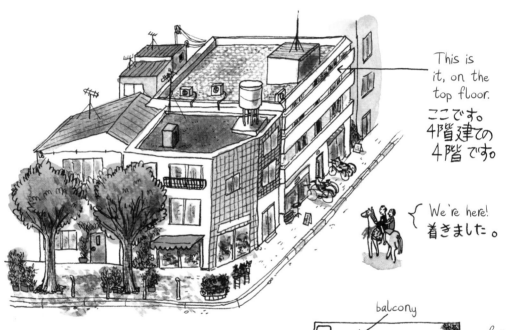

This is
it, on the
top floor.
ここです。
4階建ての
4階です。

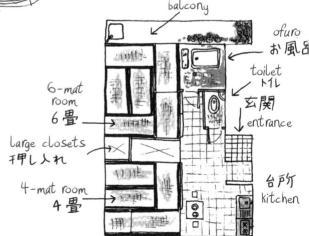

We're here!
着きました。

Another 70s-style
apartment! I'm an
expert now.

ここも70年代アパートのスタイル。
もう わかります。

balcony

ofuro
お風呂

toilet
トイレ

玄関
entrance

6-mat
room
6畳

large closets
押し入れ

4-mat room
4畳

台所
kitchen

Summer has arrived in Tokyo. We've put a camping table on the balcony. Lulled by the song of the semi, we enjoy sashimi bought this morning at the Tsukiji fish market, and a good white wine.

東京にまた夏がやって来ます。
バルコニーにキャンプテーブルを
おいて、朝、築地で買った
刺身を白ワインとともに味わいます。
蝉の唄を聞きながら。

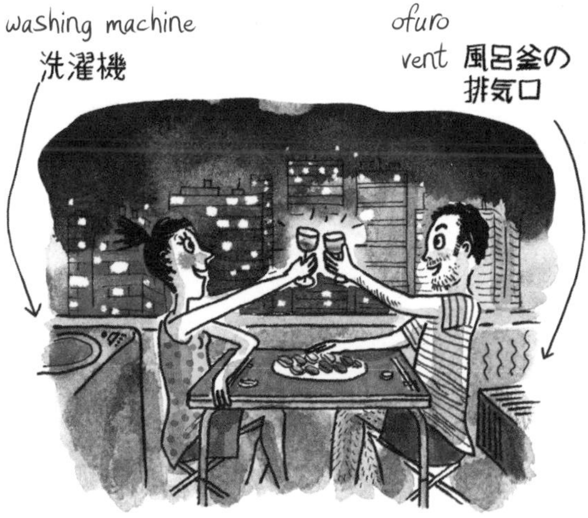
washing machine
洗濯機
ofuro vent
風呂釜の排気口

A new life begins!
新しい生活がはじまります。

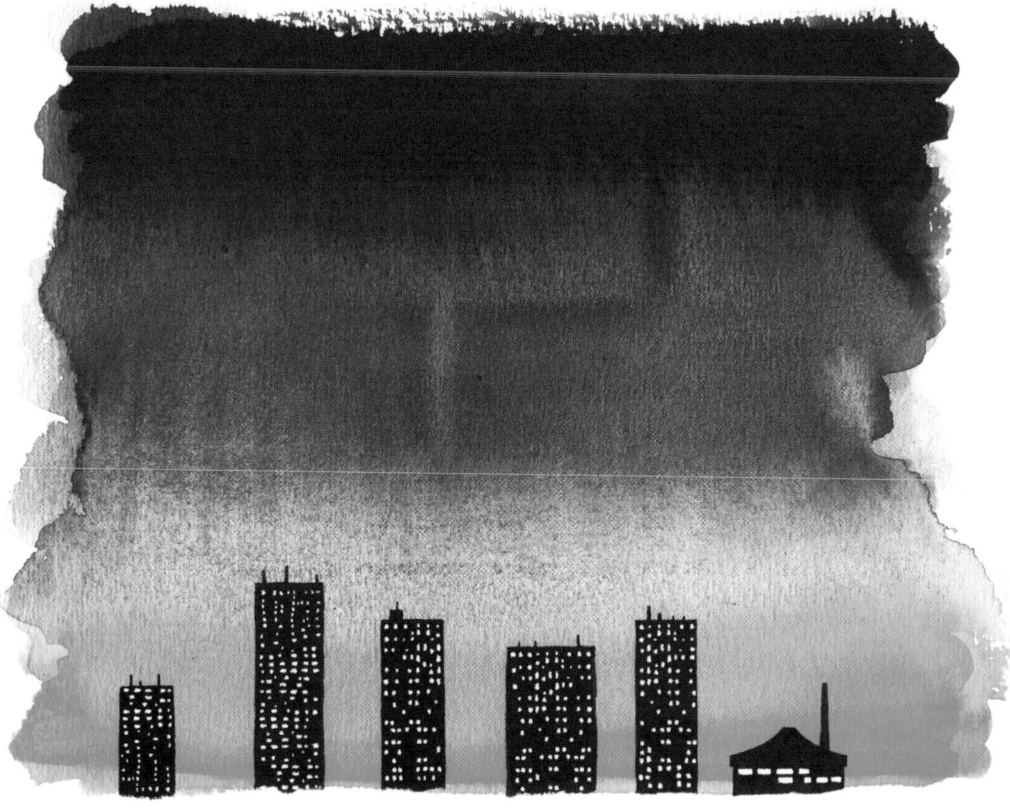

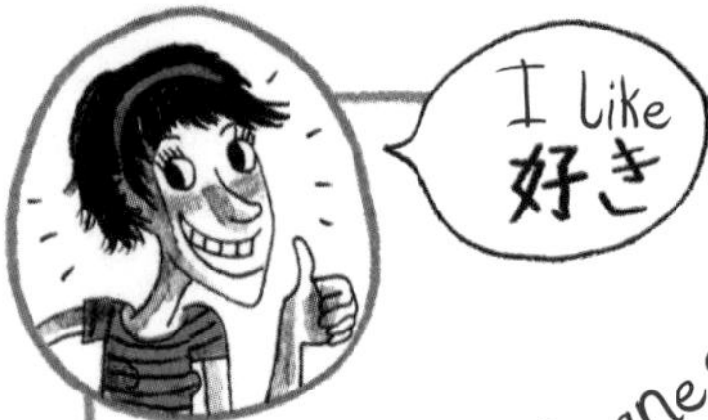
I like
好き

I like Japanese toilets!
ウォシュレット 大好きです!

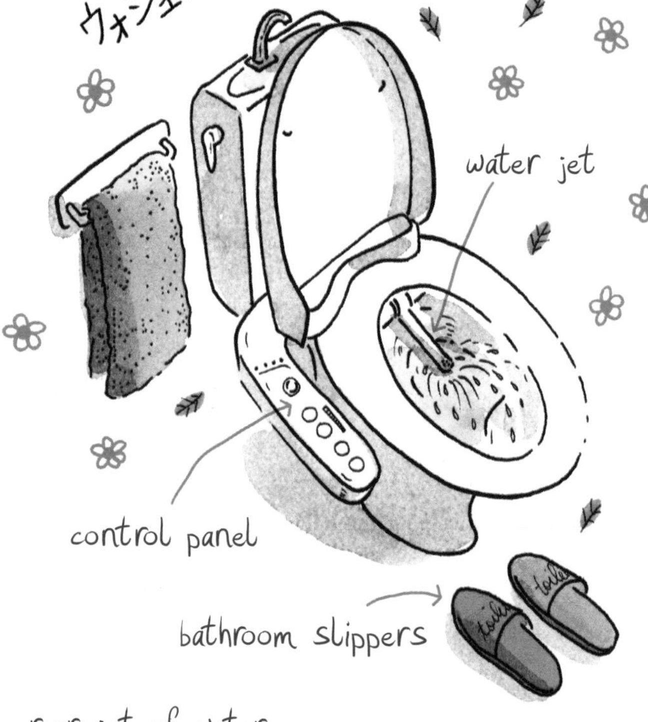
water jet
control panel
bathroom slippers

Very convenient feature:

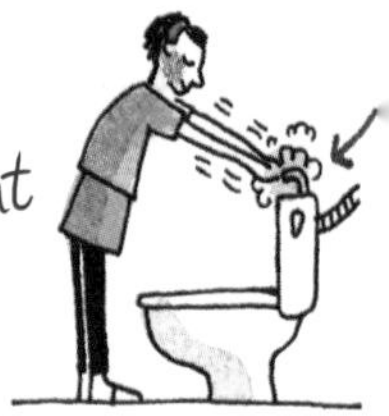

1. You flush. Water in the cistern is diverted to the bowl.
2. As the cistern fills up again the water goes through a tiny washbasin on top of the toilet! That way, you can wash your hands immediately, without wasting water.

Why does this system only exist in Japan?

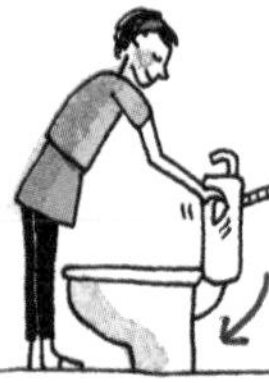

ウォシュレット のトイレは
日本だけです。

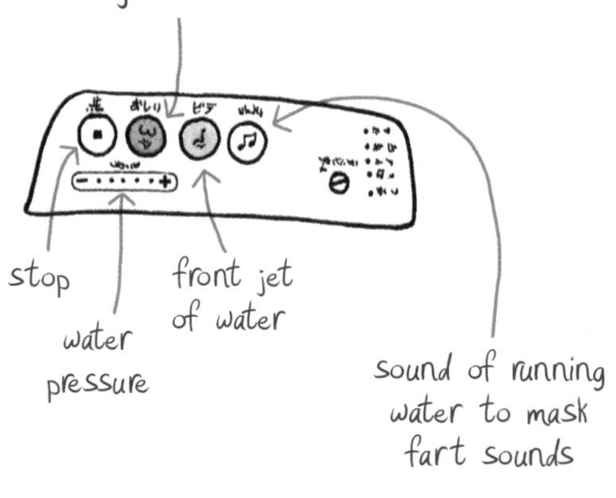
rear jet of water
stop
water pressure
front jet of water
sound of running water to mask fart sounds

There are toilets with other options: heated seat, bottom dryer, automated opening/closing of the lid, deodorizer, etc.

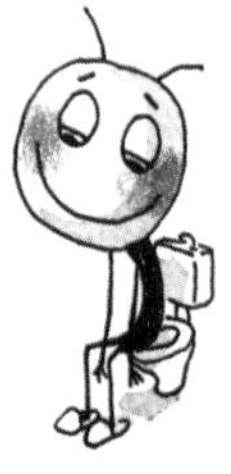

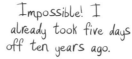

I don't like
きらい

Hey! I'm going to France for two weeks—do you wanna come with me?

2週間
フランスに
行くけど
一緒にどう？

Impossible! I already took five days off ten years ago.

できません。
10ヶ月前に
有休を
5日間、
取ったから。

I don't like the fact that the Japanese never use all their paid leave!

日本人の有休を
取らない事が
きらいです。

I have six days off: I'm going to visit Madrid, Barcelona, Paris and Strasbourg!

私は有休6日間で、
マドリード、バルセロナ、
パリ、ストラスブールに行きます。

どっ、どう
しますか！
たった6日間で。

How is that possible?

You French are individualists and not productive.

あなたたちフランス人は、
個人主義で生産的
ではありませんから。

Noooooo!

First, France is among the most productive countries per hours worked. Second, when you're on vacation, your colleague takes care of your stuff, and when they're on vacation, you take care of their stuff—that's team spirit! Third, if you take a two-week break, you go back to work refreshed, so you're more productive than if you were overworked and stressed. And, you've had time to ask yourself about your place in this world and your purpose in life.

まず、フランスの1時間あたりの生産能力は先進国の中でも上位にあります。
次に、ある人が有給を取った時、同僚がその人の仕事をする。
これはグループスピリットだと思います。そして、二週間のまとまった休みの後では、
リフレッシュした頭で仕事に取り組めると思います。
過労とストレスでは、生産的な仕事が出来ないはずです。
ところで、あなたの人生とは何ですか？

Everyday Life in the Shitamachi
下町の生活

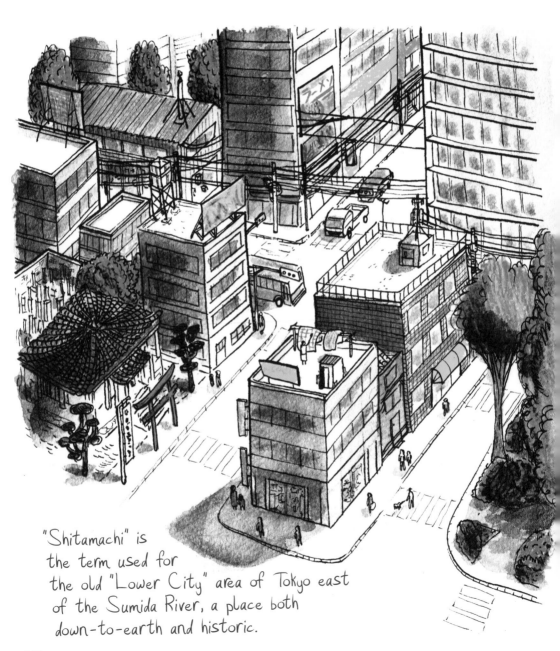

"Shitamachi" is the term used for the old "Lower City" area of Tokyo east of the Sumida River, a place both down-to-earth and historic.

Not far from our home is a dorm for sumo wrestlers. I often see them doing everyday things.

At the kombini

Low-key style →

丁髷
Chonmage is the official hairdo for sumo wrestlers—they have to keep this hairdo all the time!

髪賓付け油 →

← The hairdo stays in place with bintsuka-age, a special hair oil for osumo-san.

gangsta sweatshirt

ギャングスタデザインのパーカー

When they go by, you can smell the fragrant bintsuke-age.

At the laundromat
コインランドリー

近所には、相撲部屋があるので、力士をよく見かけます。

165

Shitamachi in Summer
夏

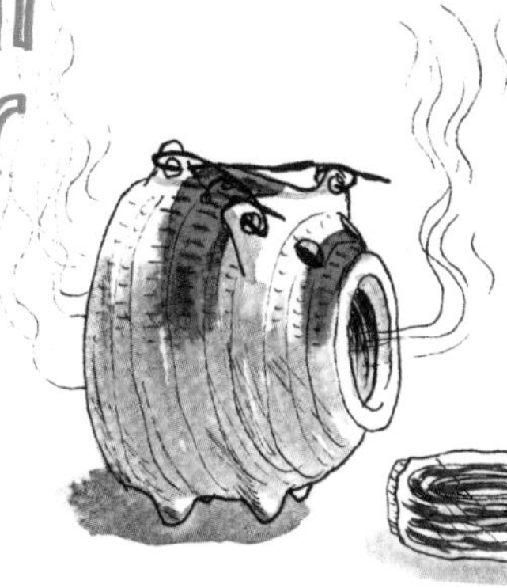

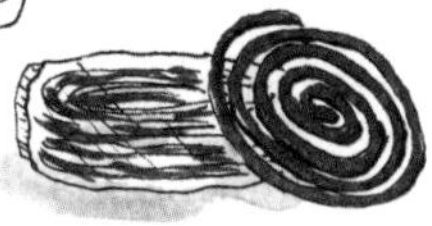

Katori senko are incense sticks in spiral form, used to repel mosquitoes.

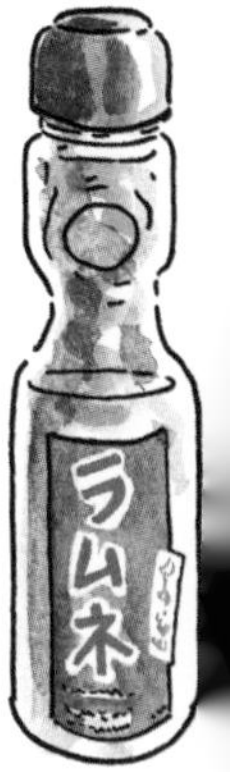
ラムネ

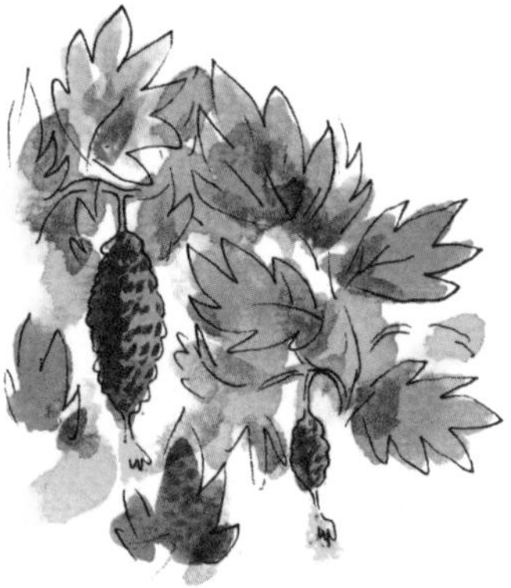

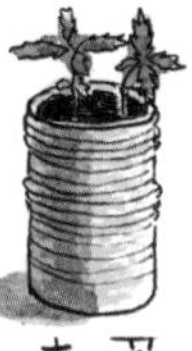

We're trying to grow goya.

ゴーヤーの芽

まっ茶
matcha (green tea powder)

あんこ
anko (red bean paste)

れん乳
condensed milk

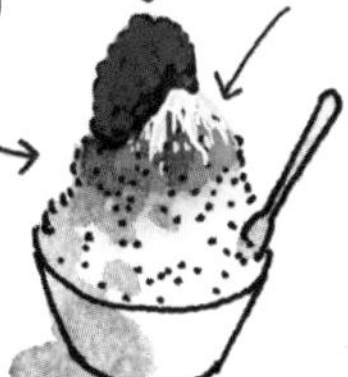

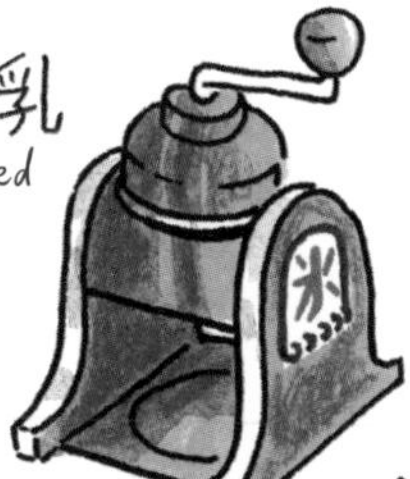
氷

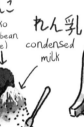

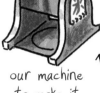

our machine to make it ourselves

私たちのかき氷機。

Kakigori is crushed ice you can top with syrup, condensed milk, anko (red bean) paste... Yummy, it's so simple and so good!

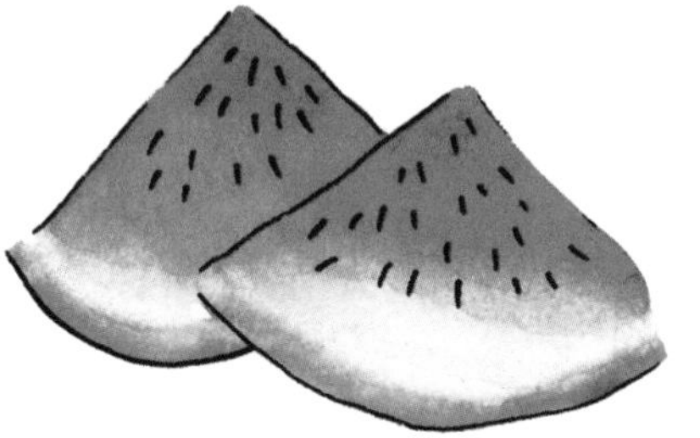

Every day the cat watches cars go by.

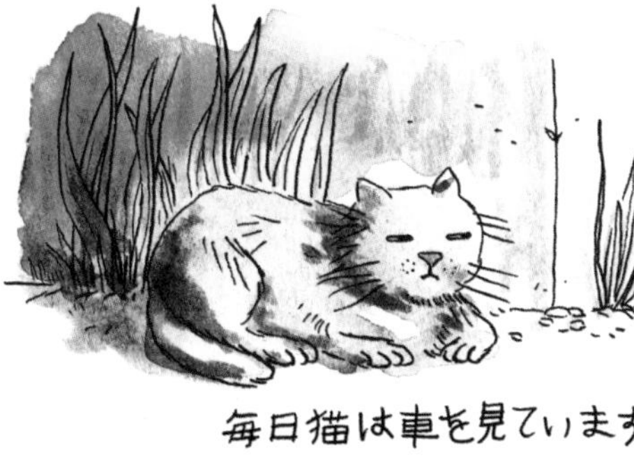

毎日猫は車を見ています。

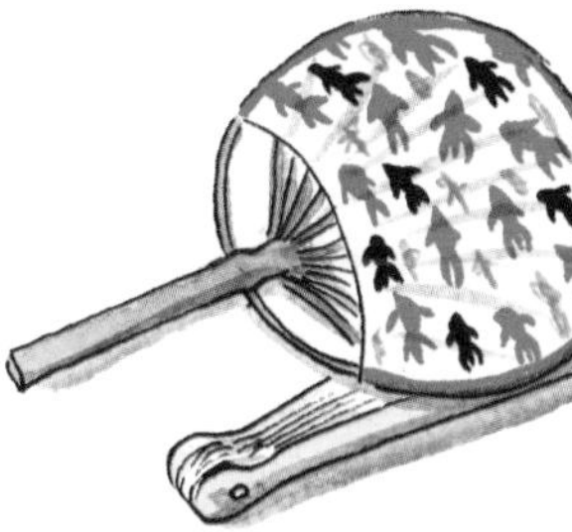

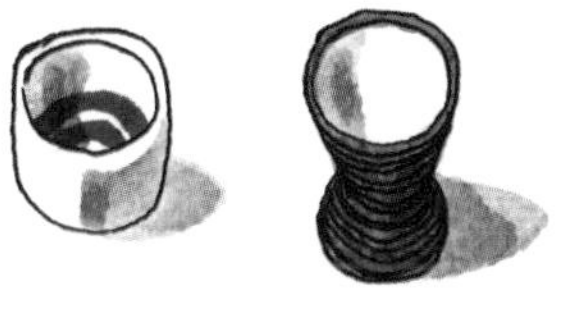

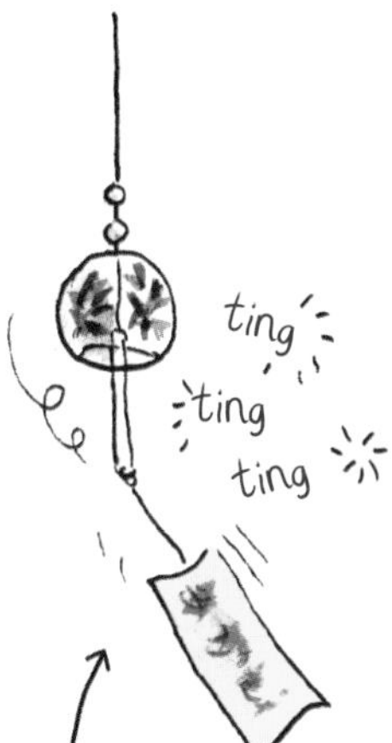
ting
ting
ting

Iconic summer item: fuurin (wind chime) that you hang up so it rings in the breeze.

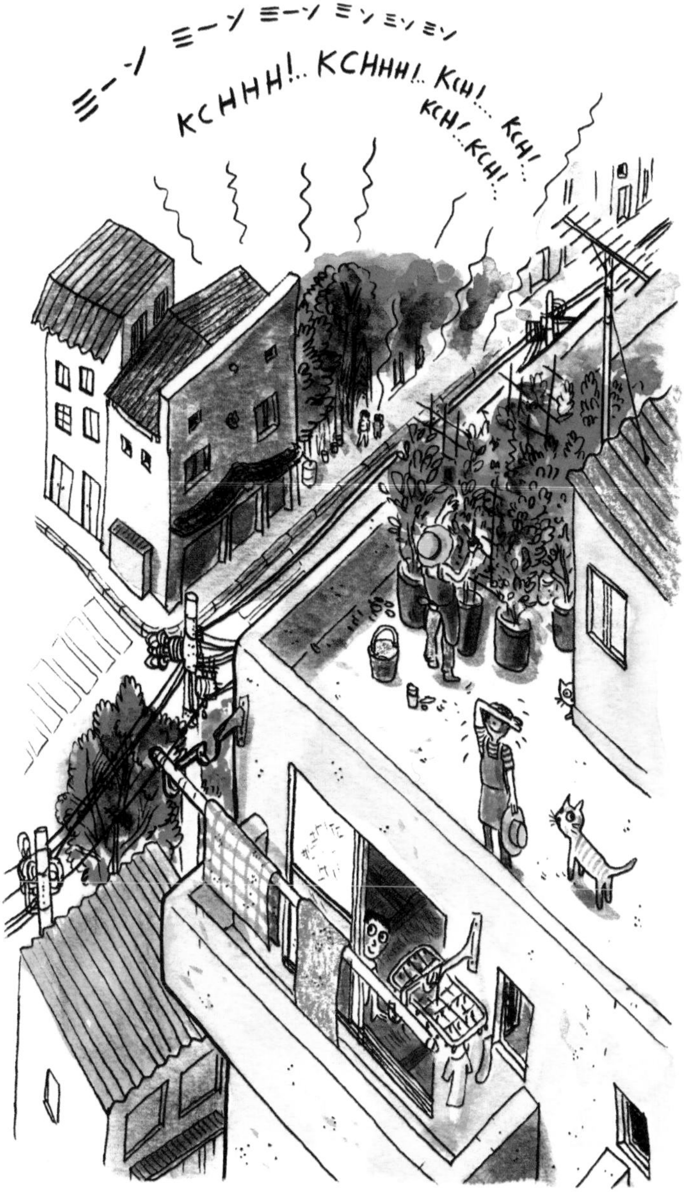
ミーン ミーン ミーン ミンミンミン
KCHHH!.. KCHHH!.. KCH!... KCH!..KCH!.. KCH!...

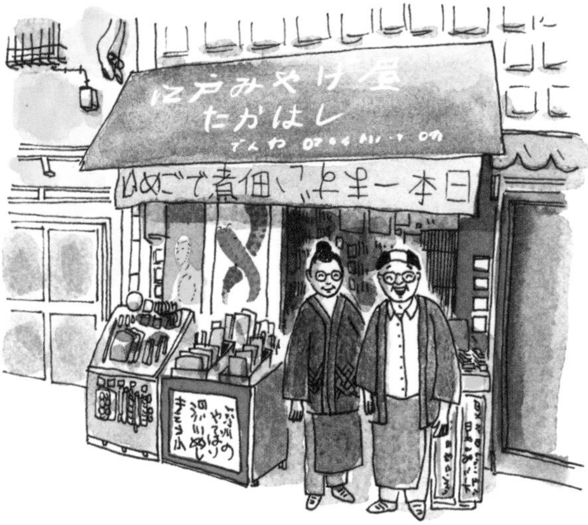
江戸みやげ屋
たかはし

Around our place, there's a small traditional souvenir shop owned by an adorable couple. You can buy Japanese candy, antique toys, local food specialties, maps, posters, calendars—a true Ali Baba's cave inside 130 square feet!

近くのお土産屋の
夫婦はいつも私に
声をかけてくれます。

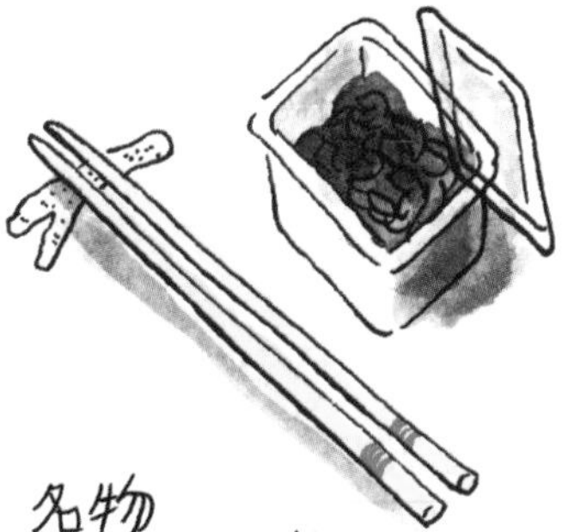

← clams cooked in soy sauce (local specialty)

名物
あさりの佃煮。

We live above a "teishoku" restaurant: they serve set meals like rice + soup + side, cafeteria style. It's very convenient when you're too lazy to cook.

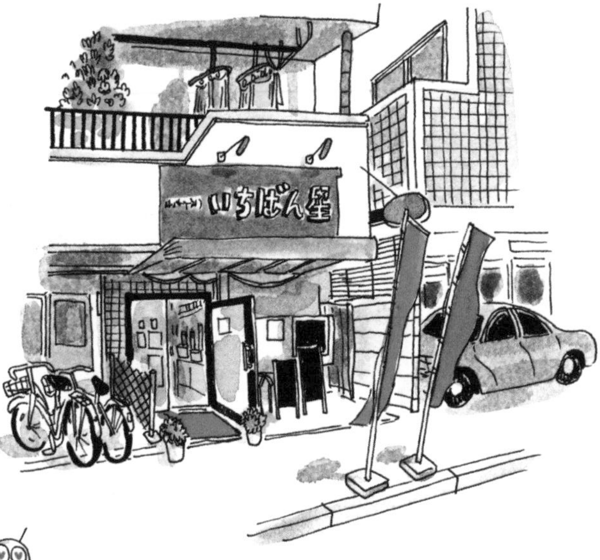
いちばん屋

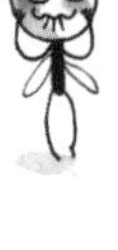

アパートの1階には洋食屋があります。
メンチカツとからあげのMix定食は絶品。

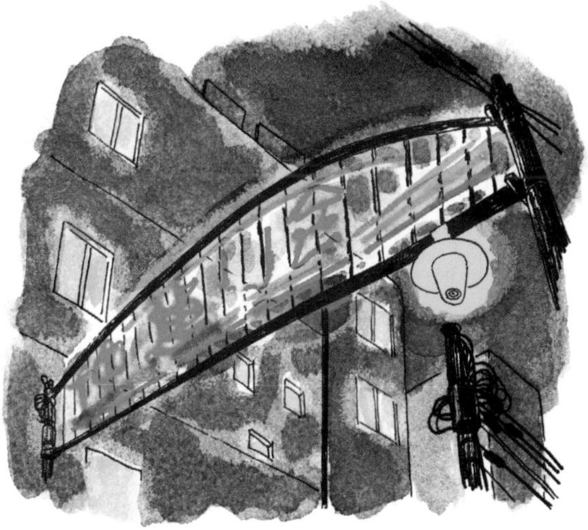

A sake masu. It's a square wooden cup.

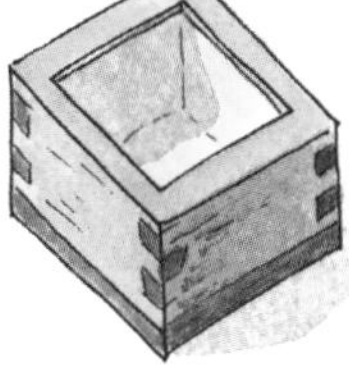

The word sake in Japanese means alcohol in general. Nihonshu is the Japanese word for what we call sake in the West. It has an alcohol content of around 15 percent.

a fall fish specialty: sanma

秋刀魚

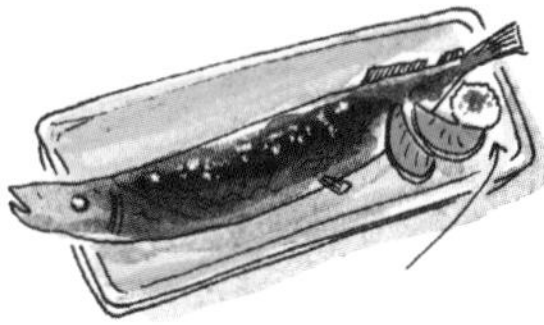

grated daikon radish

izakaya = a bar that also serves food)

There's a typical small neighborhood izakaya at the corner of our street.

コの字型の大衆居酒屋

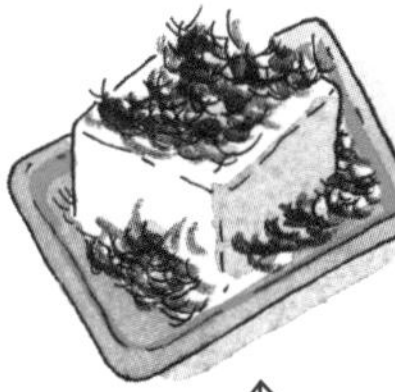

fresh tofu with katsuobushi (bonito flakes)

下町の息抜きスタイル。

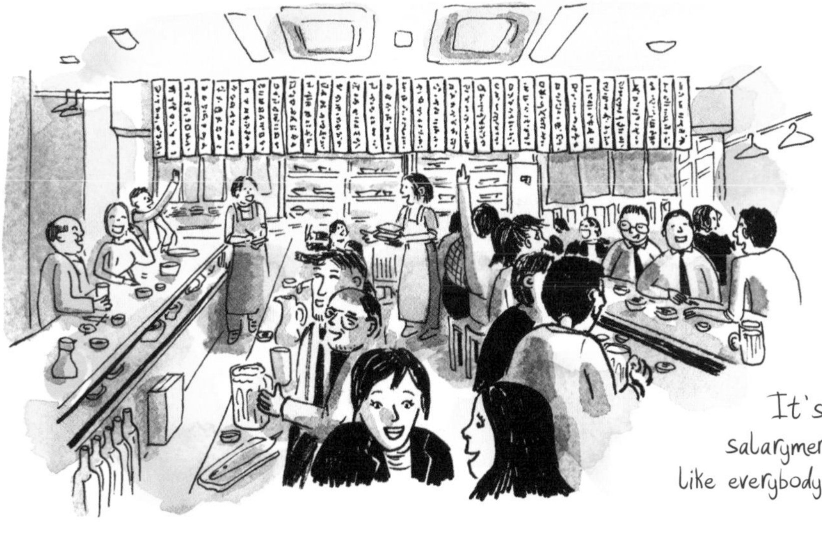

It's full of salarymen—it almost looks like everybody knows each other.

近所には親切なおじいさんのいる文房具屋や、

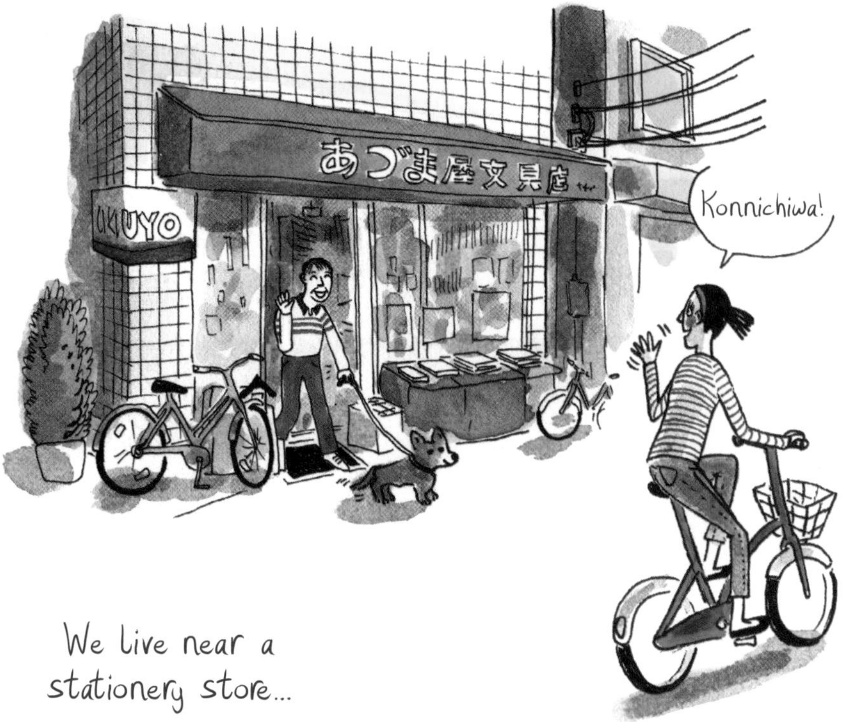
あづま屋文具店
Konnichiwa!

We live near a stationery store...

...And also near the MOT, the contemporary art museum, facing Kiba Park.

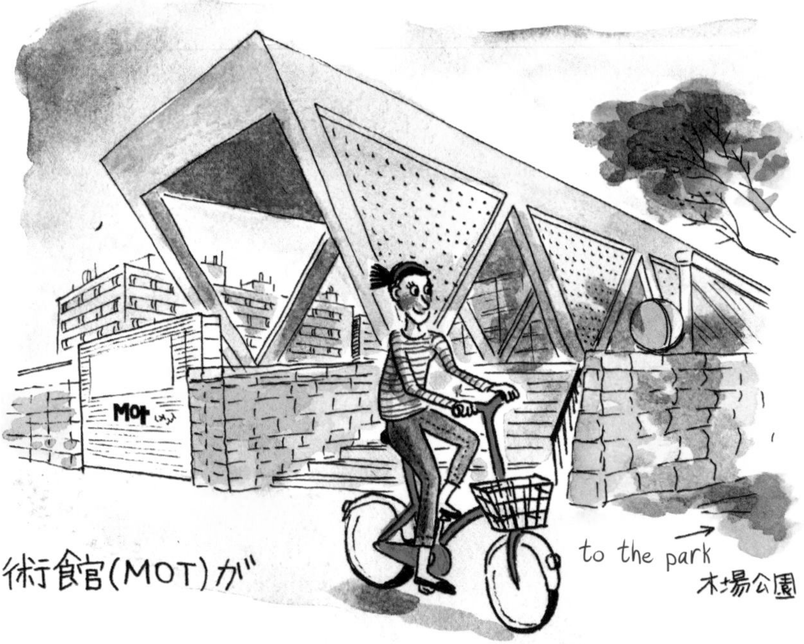
MOT
to the park
木場公園

木場公園、
東京現代美術館(MOT)が
あります。

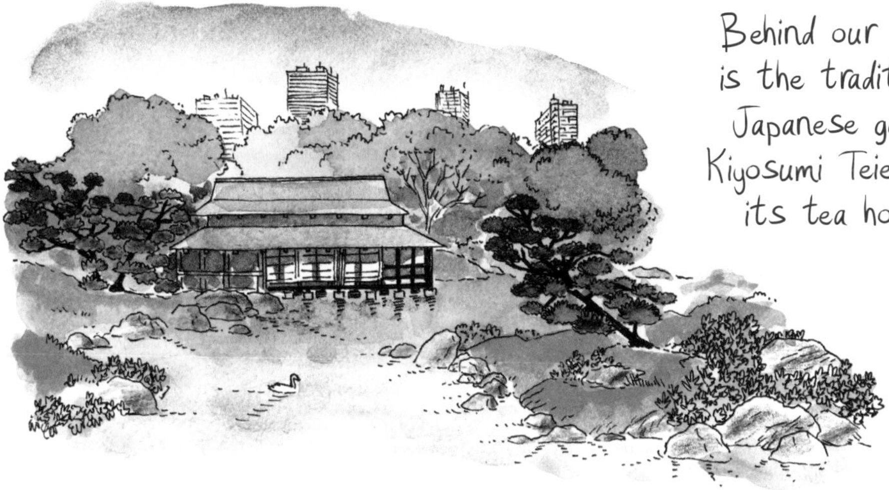

Behind our place is the traditional Japanese garden Kiyosumi Teien with its tea house.

It's an area full of canals and—naturally—many bridges.

近くの清澄庭園には
よくリフレッシュしに行きます。
この辺りでは沢山の
水路に様々な橋がかかっています。
水辺が好きな私にとって
とても気持ちがいい所です。

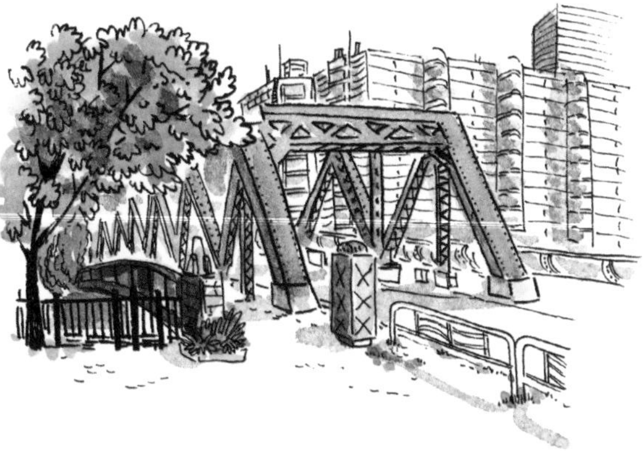

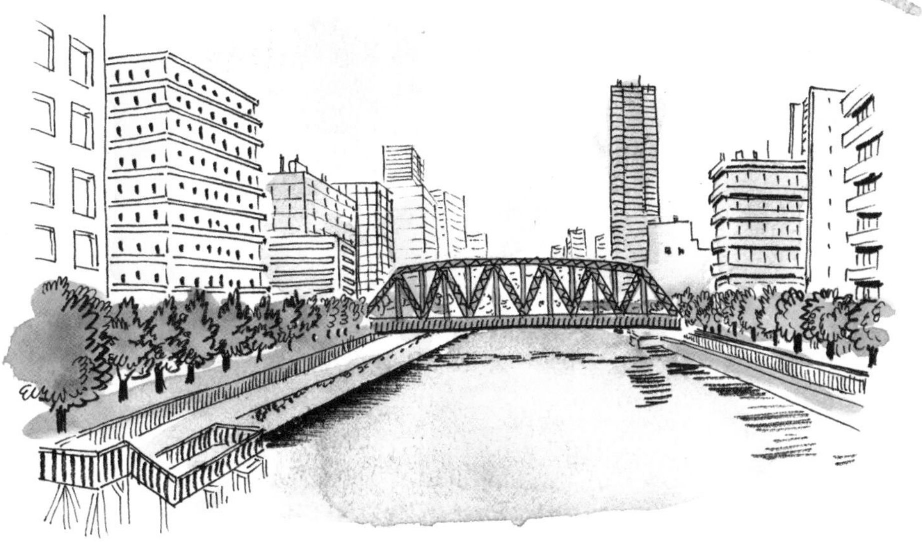

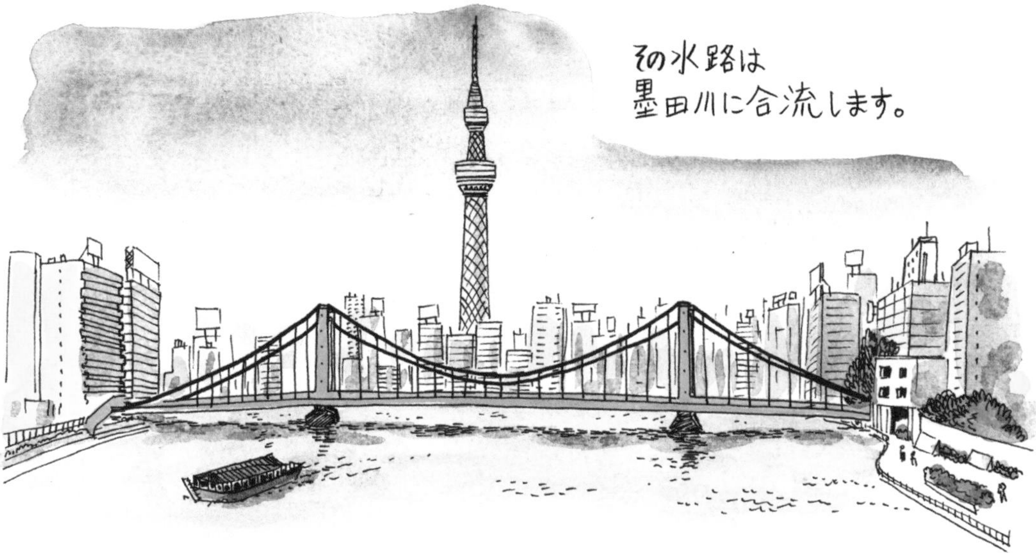
その水路は
墨田川に合流します。

All the canals flow into one of Tokyo's major rivers, the Sumida.

松尾芭蕉も住んでいた所です。
この界隈では彼の記念碑がよく
見られます。今は銅像の松尾芭蕉が
静かに墨田川の流れを眺めています。

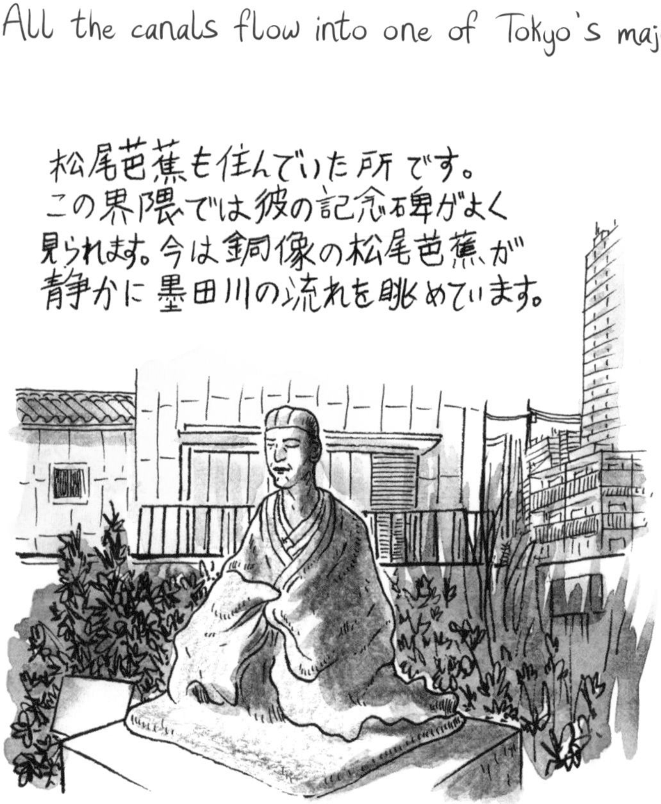

In 1860 the famous poet Basho came to live here.

On the banks of the river, a bronze statue represents him meditating. Everywhere in the neighborhood are monuments in his honor.

Konan コーナン

(The Hardware Store)

BZZZZZ

Right now... 今...

BWWWRRR

... I am making furniture (to store all the stuff that came with my invasion of Issei's apartment).

FRRRR
RFFRRR

私は家具を作っています。
(私の荷物がイッセイの
スペースを侵略しつつ
あるため)

So I go to Konan
(the hardware store,
not the Barbarian).

なので、「コーナン」に行きます。
(アニメのコナンではなく、
ホームセンターのコーナンです)

① Entrance 入口

② Garden
center
グリーン
コーナー

③ Food stall

たこ焼き、たい焼きのお店

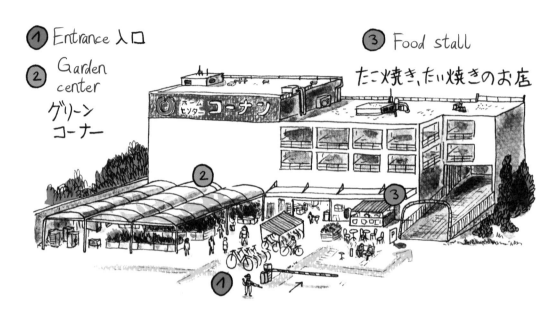

The old man at the entrance
looks like a character from
Buena Vista Social Club.

人口のおじさんは
ブエナビスタ・ソシアルクラブの
人みたい。

In the garden center, a xylophone arrangement of the soundtrack from Ponyo* plays all day long.

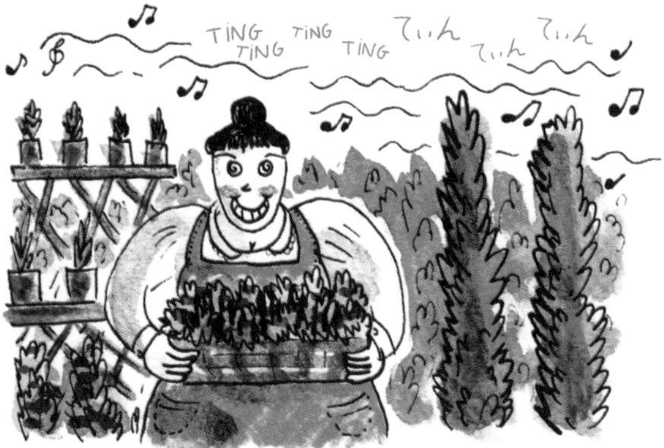
TING TING TING TING
てぃん てぃん てぃん

グリーンコーナーでは1日中
ポニョの木琴歌なし
バージョンがくり返し流れています。

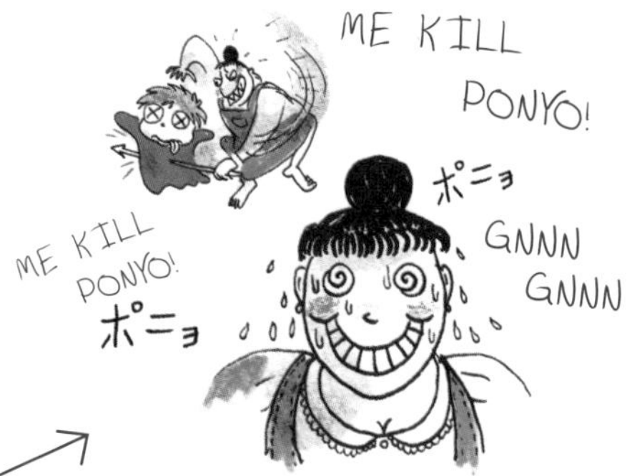
ME KILL PONYO!
ポニョ
GNNN GNNN
ME KILL PONYO!
ポニョ

6時間後のスタッフ。

a store clerk after six hours of continuous xylophone music

At the food stall, they sell freshly cooked takoyaki (octopus dumplings) and taiyaki (beanpaste waffles).

不思議です。いつもコーナンに
入る前におなかがすきます。

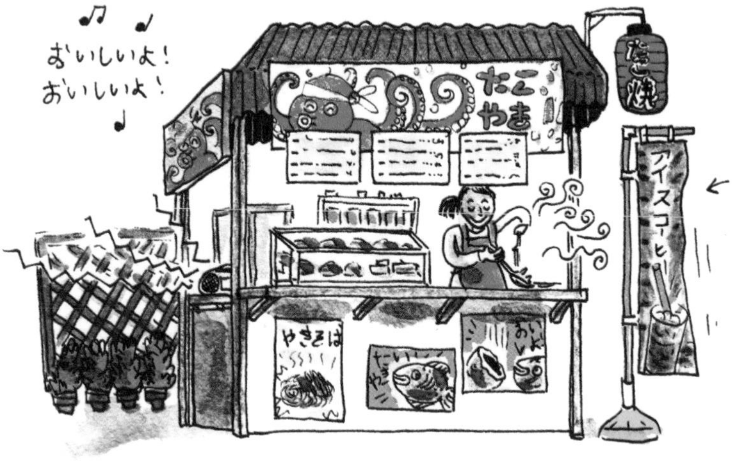
おいしいよ！
おいしいよ！
たこやき
たこ焼
アイスコーヒー
やきそば

* *Ponyo* is the animated movie that came out in 2008 from Studio Ghibli, written and directed by Hayao Miyazaki.

How to Impress People

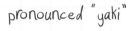 Japanese is fantastic

Here are several dish names that use the word "yaki" meaning "grilled."

pronounced "yaki"

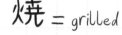 焼 = grilled

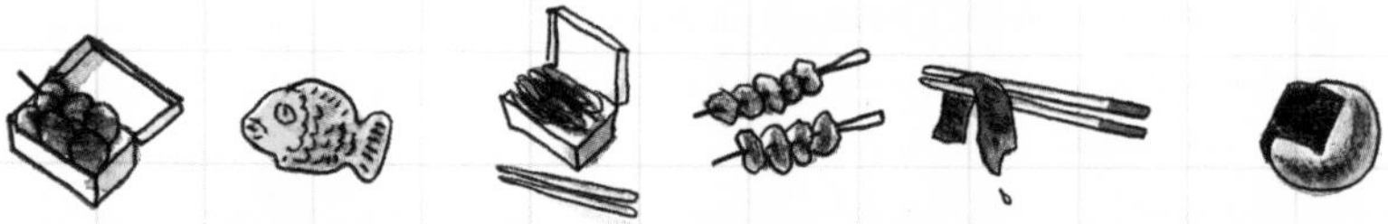

<u>Tako</u>(yaki) <u>Tai</u>(yaki) (Yaki)<u>soba</u> (Yaki)<u>tori</u> (Yaki)<u>niku</u>

↓ grilled octopus

↓ grilled bream

↓ grilled soba noodles

↓ grilled chicken

↓ grilled meat

<u>I</u>sobe ("next to the ocean") (yaki)

This is a metaphor since it describes a mochi (rice cake) grilled then wrapped in seaweed.

<u>Taiyaki</u> Kind of bream-shaped waffle.

<u>Takoyaki</u> octopus-stuffed balls

Inside...

toothpick for eating (a pain)
↓

On top:
- nori powder
- katsuobushi
- mayo
- takoyaki sauce

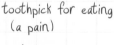

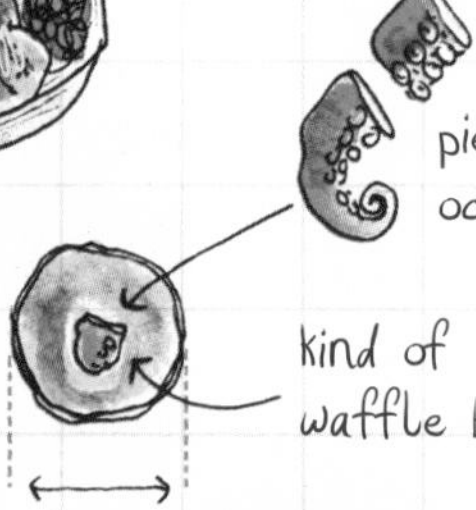

taiyaki waffle iron

... anko, sweet red bean paste. It's tasty but not as sweet as the cake fillings we're used to in the West.

CUTAWAY VIEW

piece of octopus

kind of waffle batter

1½ inches

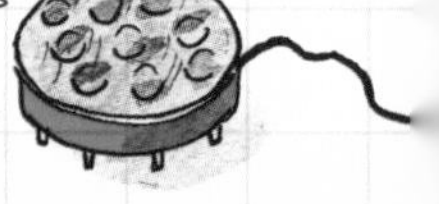

electric → takoyaki maker

Inside the Konan store, you can enjoy synthesizer arrangements of all the big hits. I like playing the game "name the band and the title."

店内では洋楽邦楽のヒット曲で、歌なしシンセサイザーバージョンが流れお客さんを楽しませてくれます。私の楽しみは「この曲は何ですか？」ゲームをする事です。

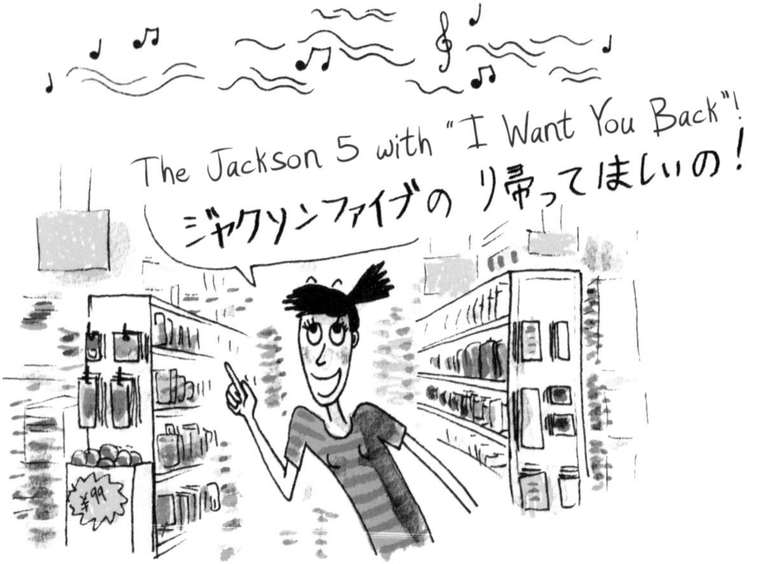

The Jackson 5 with "I Want You Back"!
ジャクソンファイブの帰ってほしいの！
¥99

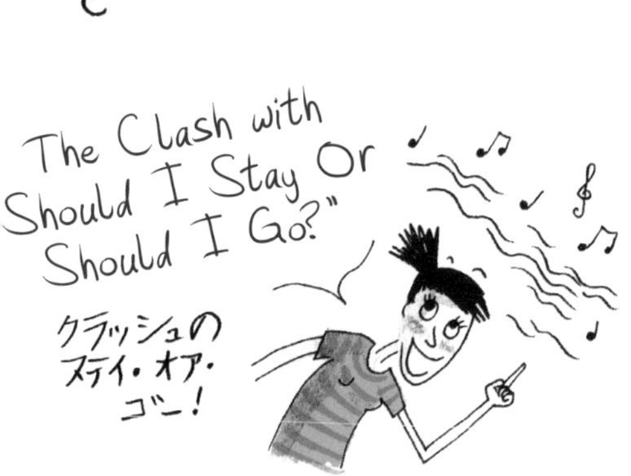

The Clash with "Should I Stay Or Should I Go?"
クラッシュのステイ・オア・ゴー！

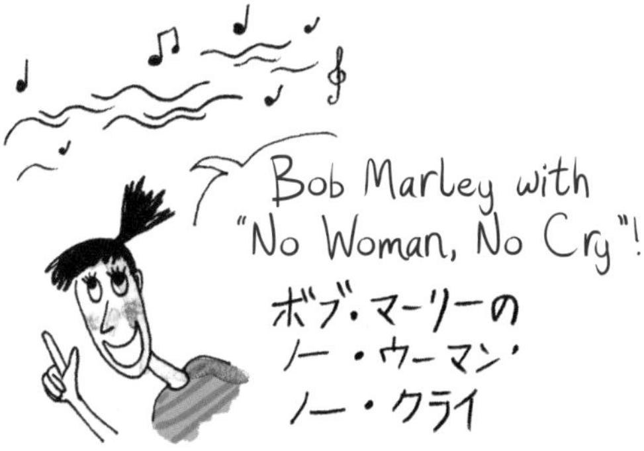

Bob Marley with "No Woman, No Cry"!
ボブ・マーリーのノー・ウーマン・ノー・クライ

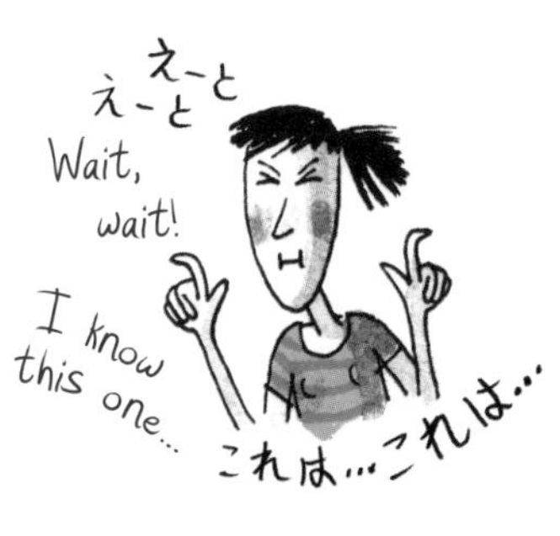

えーと えーと
Wait, wait!
I know this one...
これは…これは…

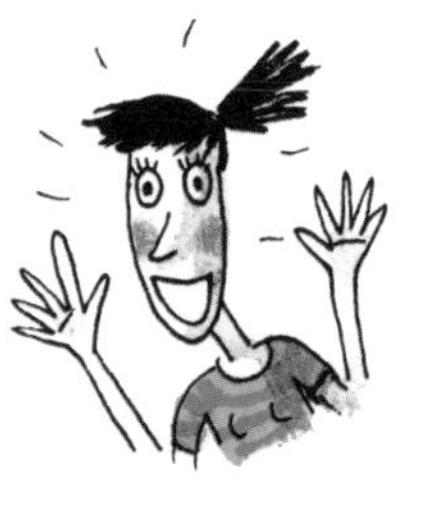

Yes! It's Elton John with "Your Song"!
あっ！エルトン・ジョンの僕の歌は君の歌！

Since I'm freelancing and job hunting I have time to go to Konan on weekdays.

It's pretty sparse except for:

They wear special hats to protect themselves from the sun. They look like a kind of elegant Robocop.

little old ladies

おばあさん

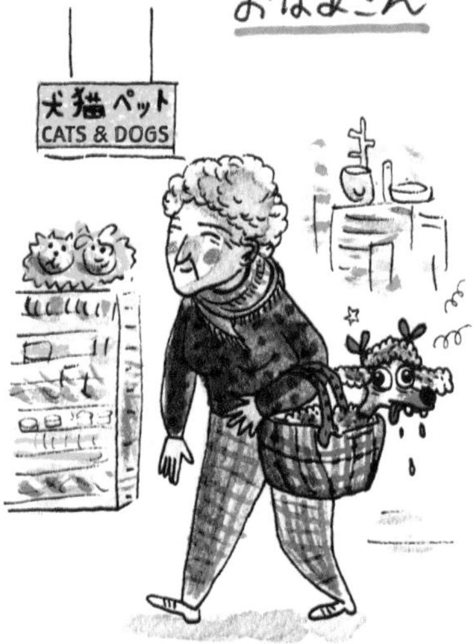

犬猫ペット
CATS & DOGS

homemakers...

主婦

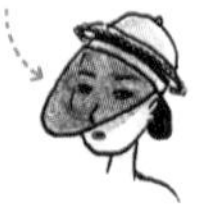

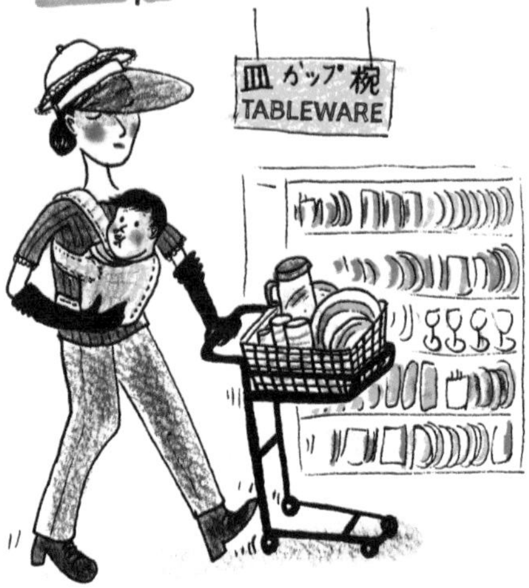

皿 カップ 椀
TABLEWARE

...and construction workers. 買物をする職人たち

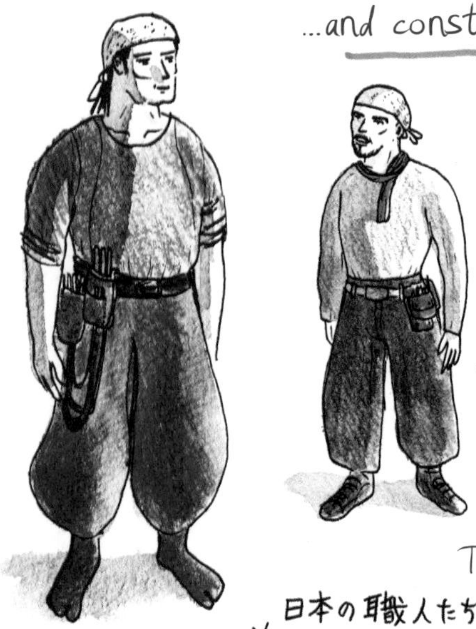

Construction workers or city gardeners wear outfits inspired by traditional Japanese clothes:

ニッカポッカスタイル

knickerbocker-style pants

たび スタイル

"tabi" style shoes

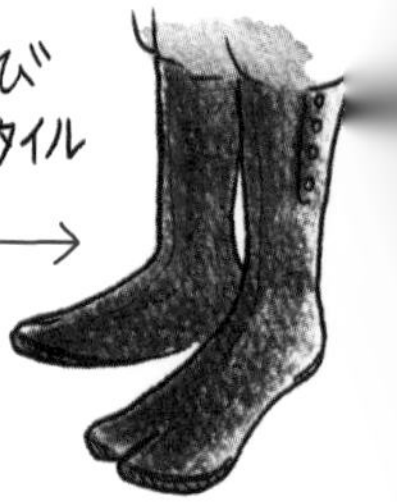

They look really cool.

日本の職人たちは、まるで伝統衣装を着ているみたいです。ここでも日本の風習を見かけます。

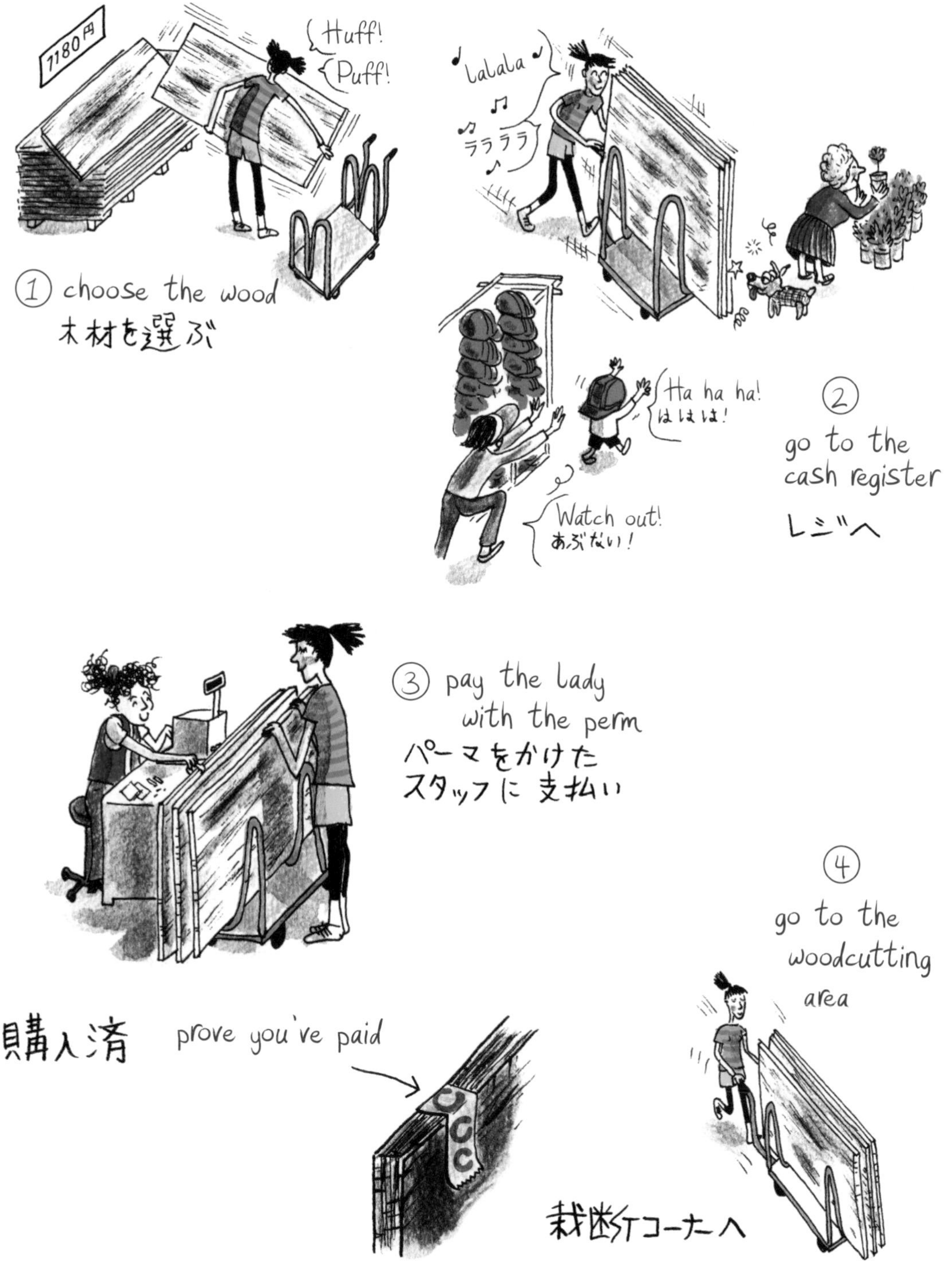
1180円
Huff!
Puff!
① choose the wood
木材を選ぶ
LaLaLa
ラララララ
Ha ha ha!
ははは!
Watch out!
あぶない!
② go to the cash register
レジへ
③ pay the lady with the perm
パーマをかけたスタッフに支払い
購入済
prove you've paid
④ go to the woodcutting area
裁断コーナーへ

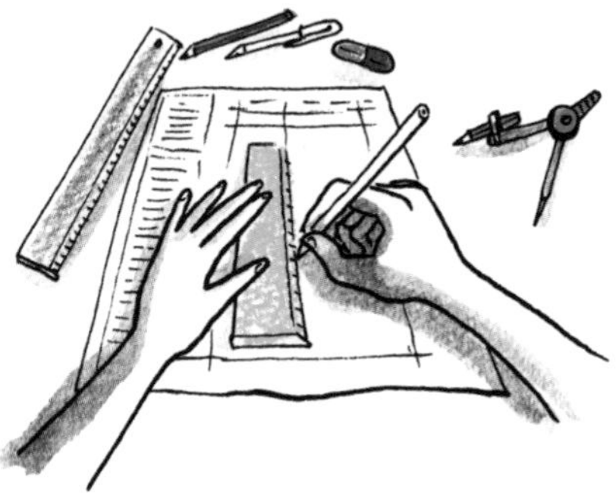

Then you have to draw the shape you want cut out, on special paper that they have. You can even borrow pens, pencils, erasers and rulers.

裁断コーナーにある筆記用具で平面図を書きます。
学校を思い出します。

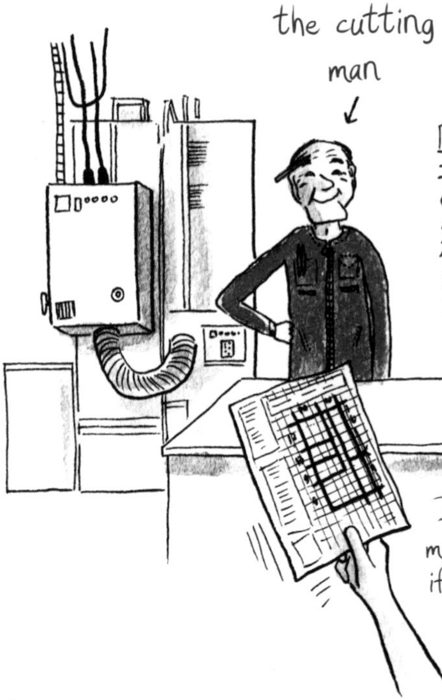

the cutting man
I give him my paper as if he was a teacher

スタッフは、図工の先生みたい。

Once the wood is cut, you can use saws, hammers, sandpaper, etc. free of charge.

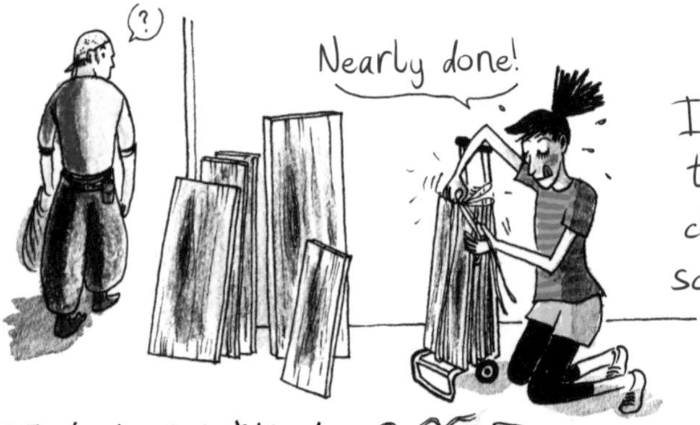

?
Nearly done!

It's like my technical drawing classes at school.

切った木材はきれいに束ね、キャリーカートにのせます。

I stack up all my planks on my cart and push them home.

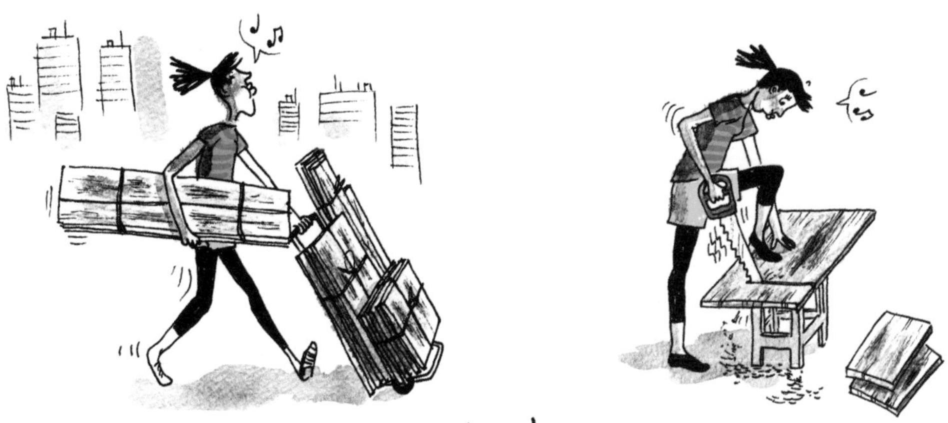

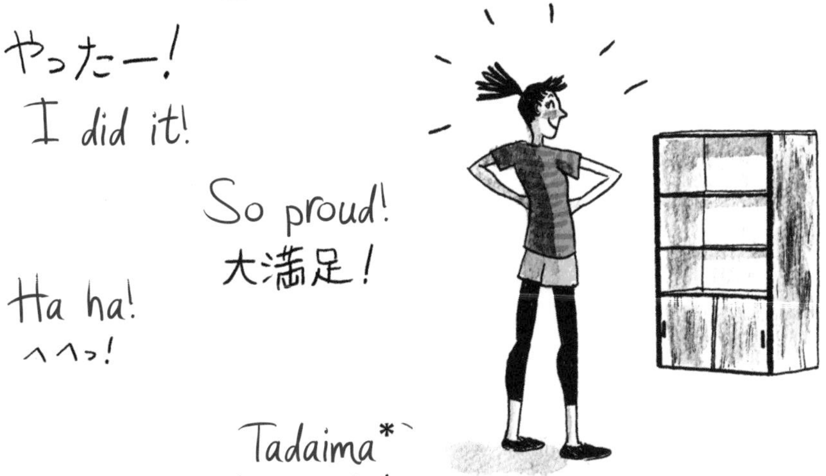

やったー!
I did it!
So proud!
大満足!
Ha ha!
へへっ!

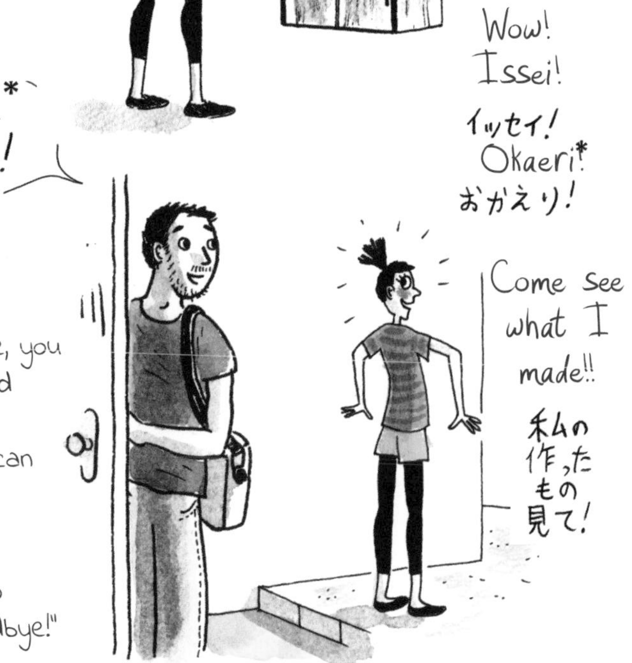

Tadaima*
ただいま!
Wow!
Issei!
イッセイ!
Okaeri!*
おかえり!
Come see what I made!!
私の作ったもの見て!

* **tadaima, okaeri, ittekimasu** and **itterasshai**

In Japan, when you come back home, you say "**Tadaima!**" (it can be translated as "I'm back!") to which you answer "**okaeri!**" or "**okaeri nasai!**" (which can be translated as "Glad you're back!")

When you leave the house, you say "**Ittekimasu!**" (meaning "I'm going!") to which you reply "**Itterasshai!** ("Goodbye!" "See you later!" "See you in a bit!")

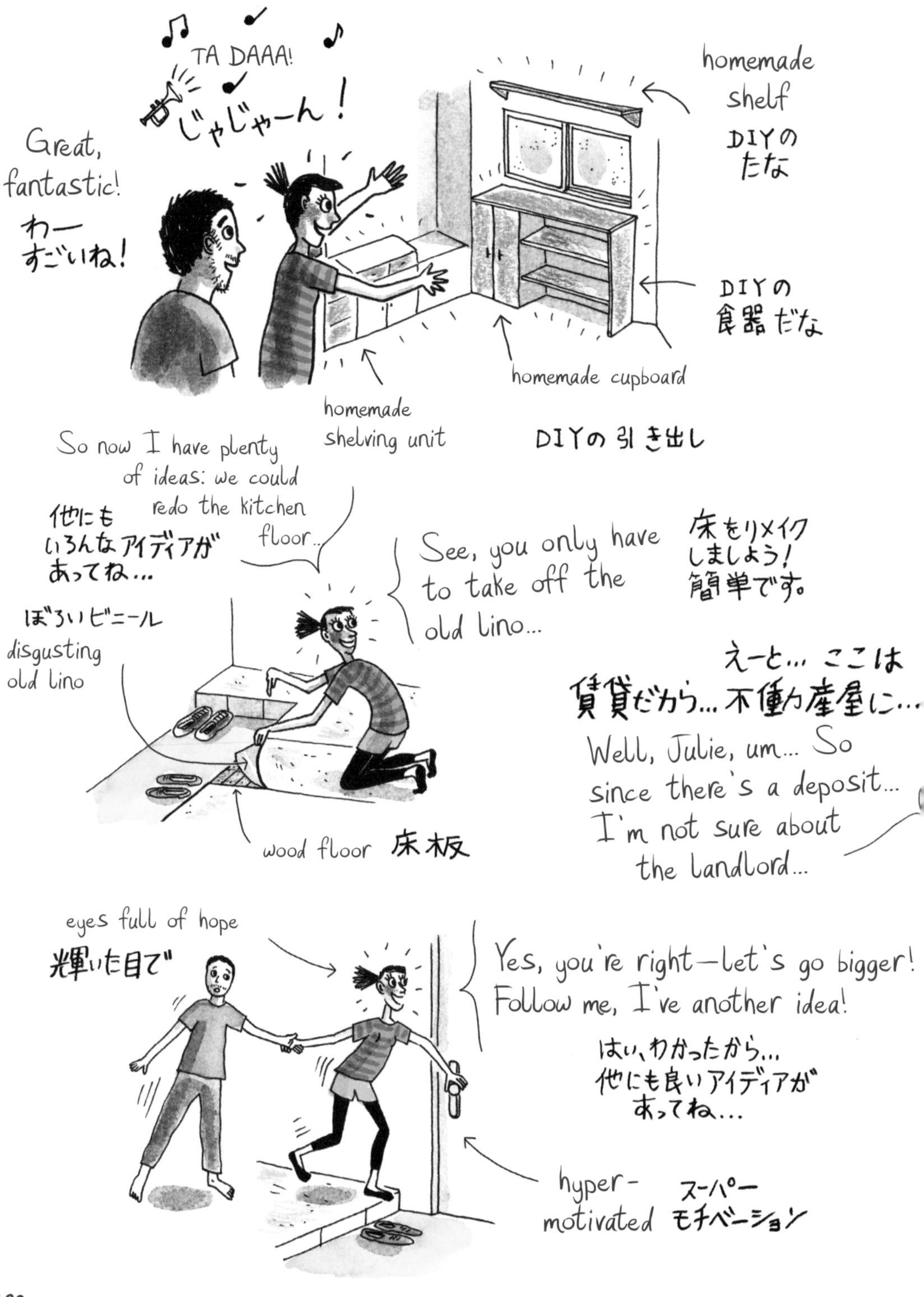
TA DAAA!
じゃじゃーん！
Great, fantastic!
わー すごいね！
homemade shelf
DIYのたな
DIYの食器だな
homemade cupboard
homemade shelving unit
DIYの引き出し
So now I have plenty of ideas: we could redo the kitchen floor...
他にもいろんなアイディアがあってね…
See, you only have to take off the old lino...
床をリメイクしましょう！簡単です。
ぼろいビニール
disgusting old lino
wood floor 床板
えーと… ここは賃貸だから… 不動産屋に…
Well, Julie, um... So since there's a deposit... I'm not sure about the landlord...
eyes full of hope
輝いた目で
Yes, you're right—let's go bigger! Follow me, I've another idea!
はい、わかったから… 他にも良いアイディアがあってね…
hyper-motivated スーパーモチベーション

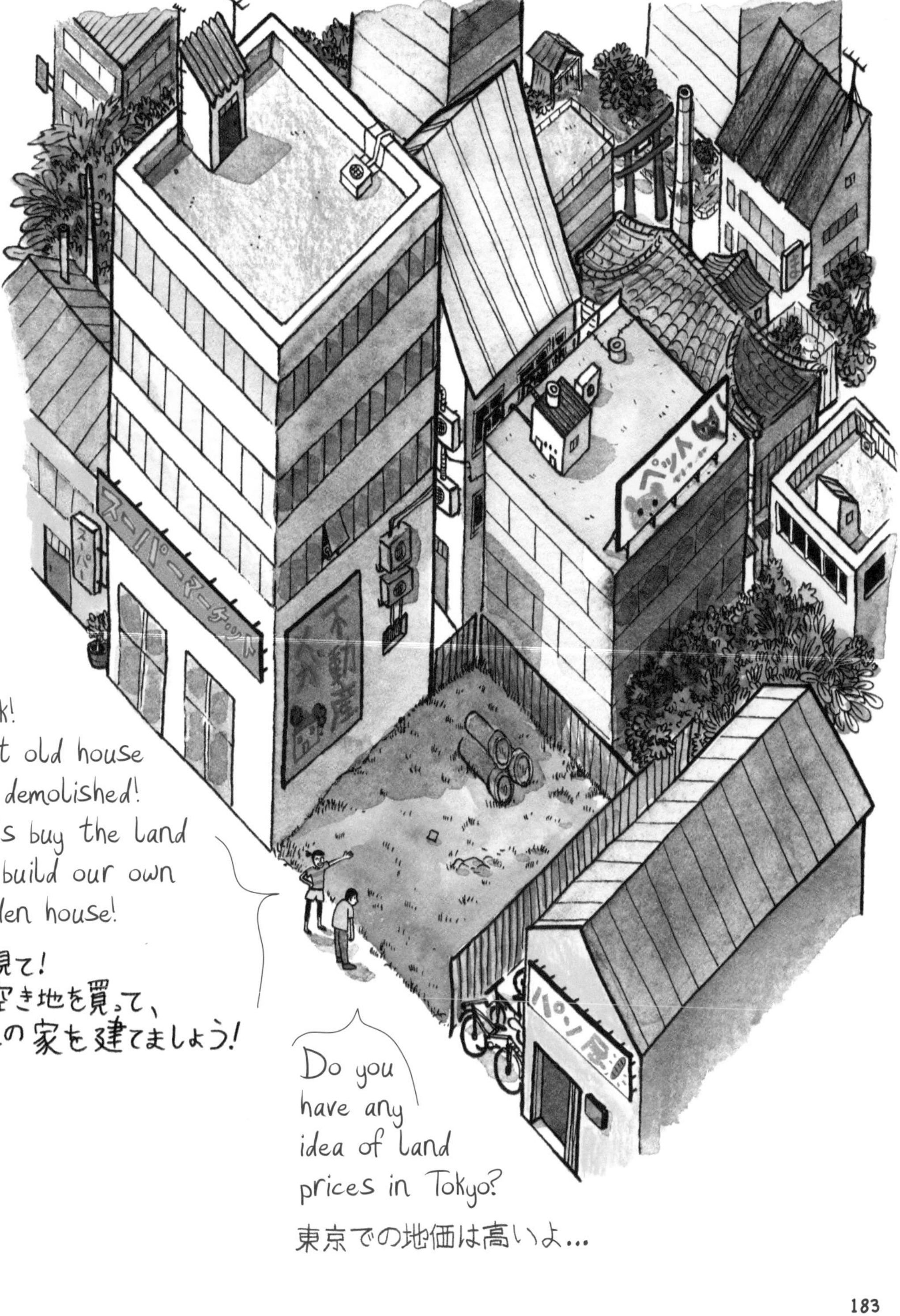
Look!
That old house
was demolished!
Let's buy the land
and build our own
wooden house!
ほら見て！
この空き地を買って、
木造の家を建てましょう！
Do you
have any
idea of land
prices in Tokyo?
東京での地価は高いよ…
不動産
パン屋

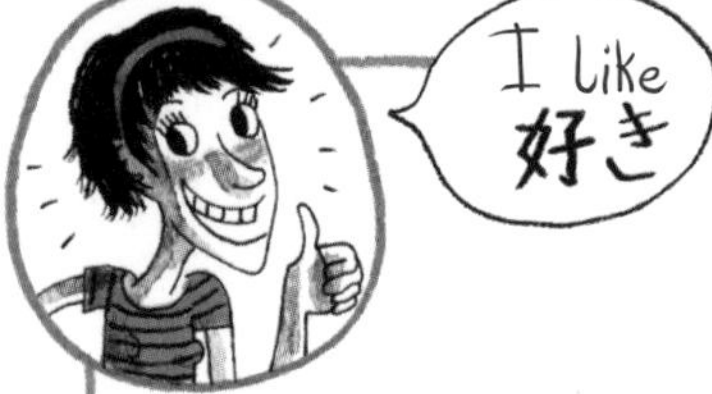
I like
好き

I like the street vendors and food trucks in my neighborhood.
いどう販売車が好きです。

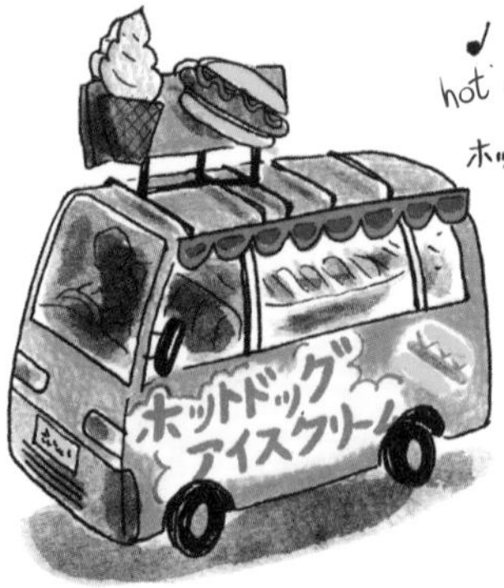
ホットドッグ
アイスクリーム

hot dogs, ice cream
ホットドッグ, ホットドッグ
アイスクリーム

the ice cream and hot dog vendor.
ホットドッグと アイスクリーム

the fruit and vegetable vendor

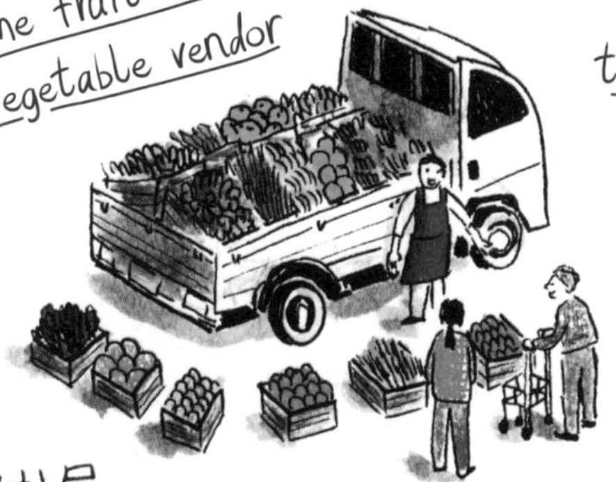

やお屋

The Third Man theme tune
映画「第三の男」の音楽

the baker
パン屋

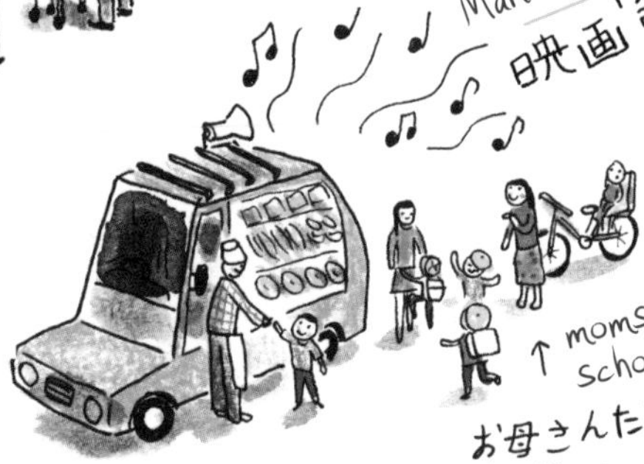

↑ moms after school
お母さんたち
学校の後で

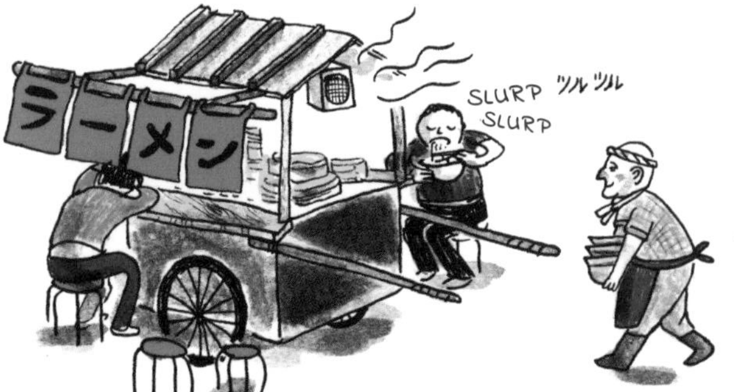
ラーメン
SLURP ツルツル
SLURP

the ramen vendor
ラーメン屋

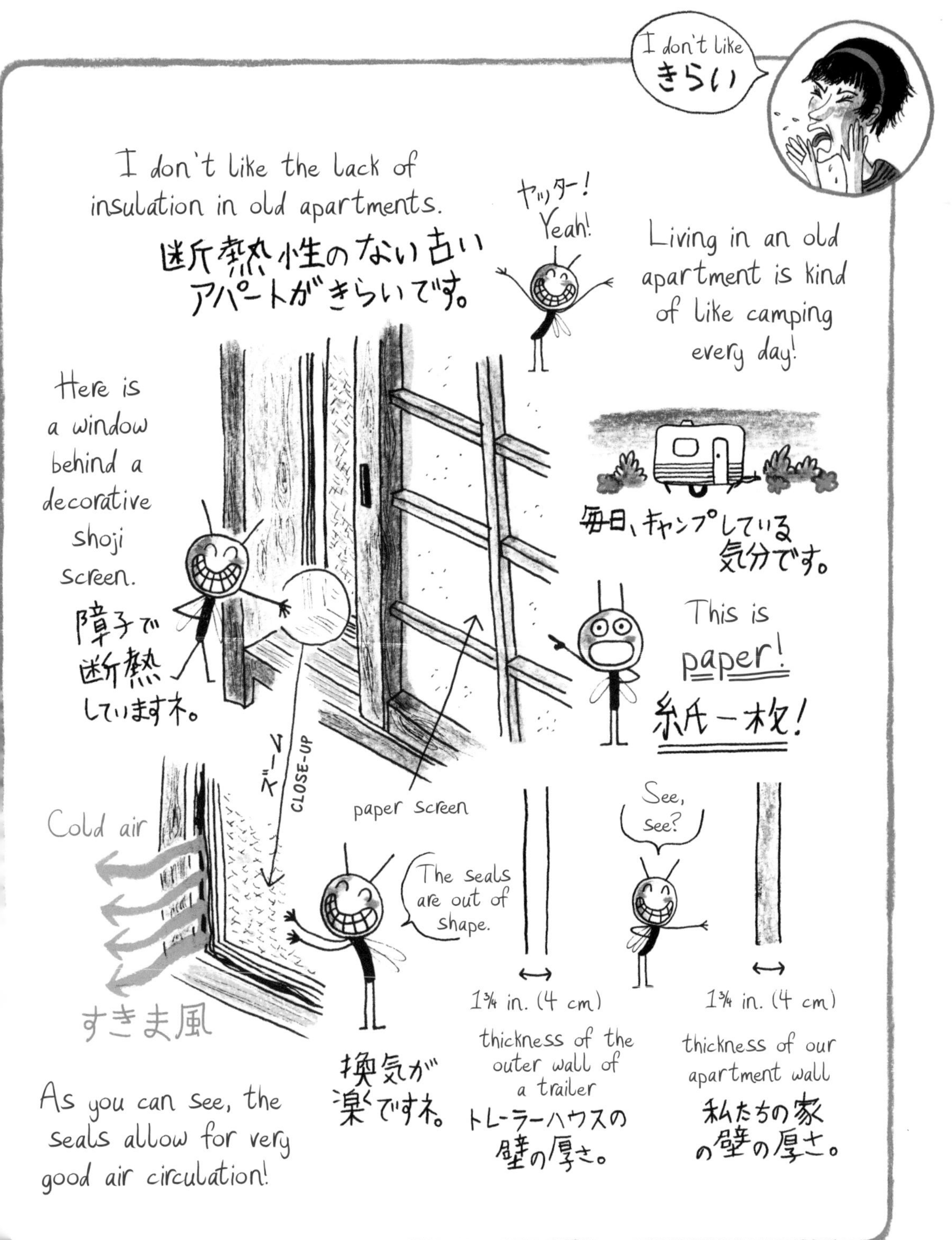
I don't like
きらい
I don't like the lack of insulation in old apartments.
断熱性のない古いアパートがきらいです。
ヤッター!
Yeah!
Living in an old apartment is kind of like camping every day!
毎日、キャンプしている気分です。
Here is a window behind a decorative shoji screen.
障子で断熱していますネ。
This is paper!
紙一枚!
ズーム
CLOSE-UP
paper screen
Cold air
すきま風
The seals are out of shape.
換気が楽ですネ。
As you can see, the seals allow for very good air circulation!
See, see?
1¾ in. (4 cm)
thickness of the outer wall of a trailer
トレーラーハウスの壁の厚さ。
1¾ in. (4 cm)
thickness of our apartment wall
私たちの家の壁の厚さ。

The Part-timer アルバイト

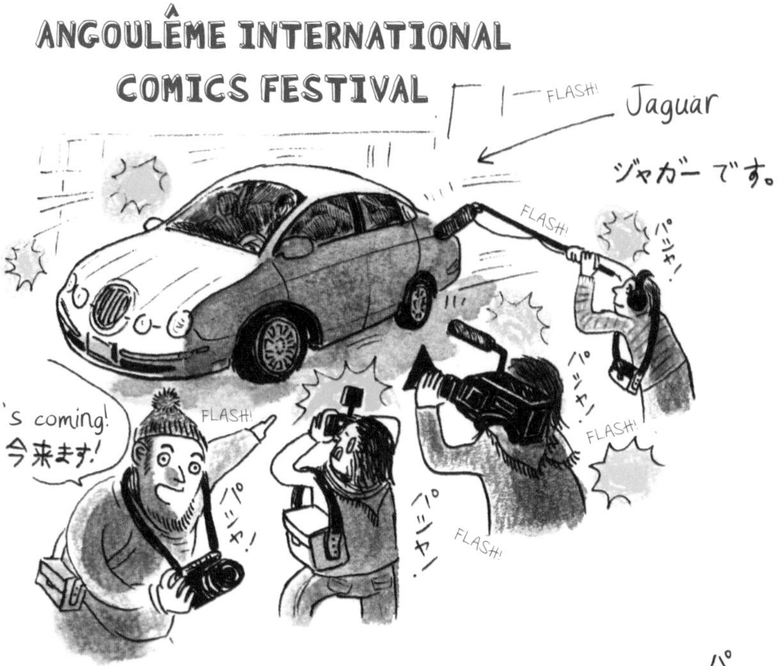

ANGOULÊME INTERNATIONAL COMICS FESTIVAL
FLASH!
Jaguar
ジャガーです。
FLASH!
パシャ!
She's coming!
今来ます!
FLASH!
パシャ!
FLASH!
パシャ!
パシャ!
FLASH!

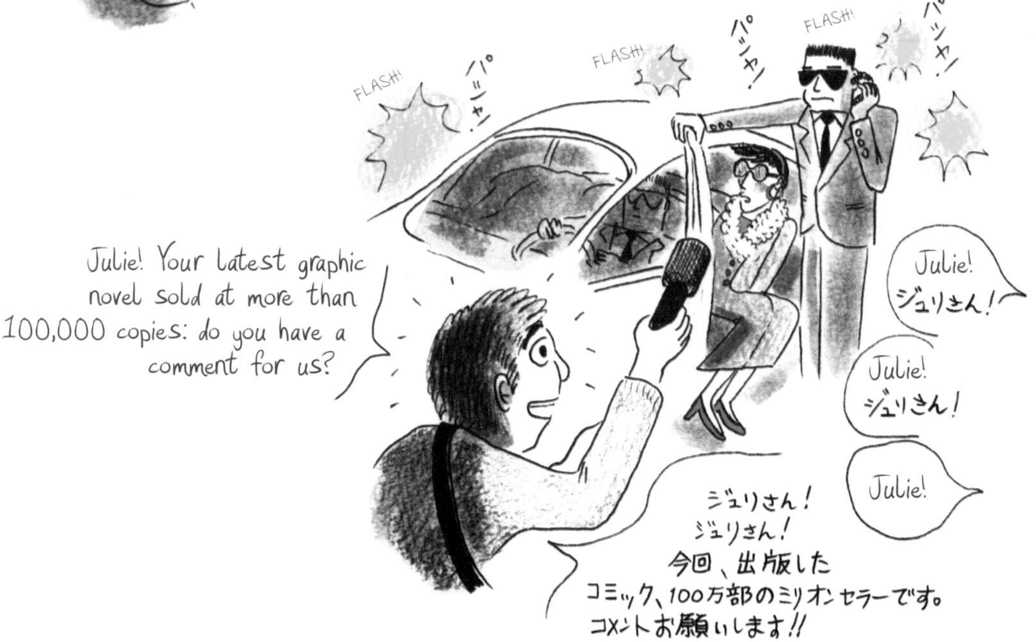

FLASH!
パシャ!
FLASH!
パシャ!
FLASH!
パシャ!
Julie! Your latest graphic novel sold at more than 100,000 copies: do you have a comment for us?
Julie!
ジュリさん!
Julie!
ジュリさん!
Julie!
ジュリさん!
ジュリさん!
今回、出版したコミック、100万部のミリオンセラーです。
コメントお願いします!!

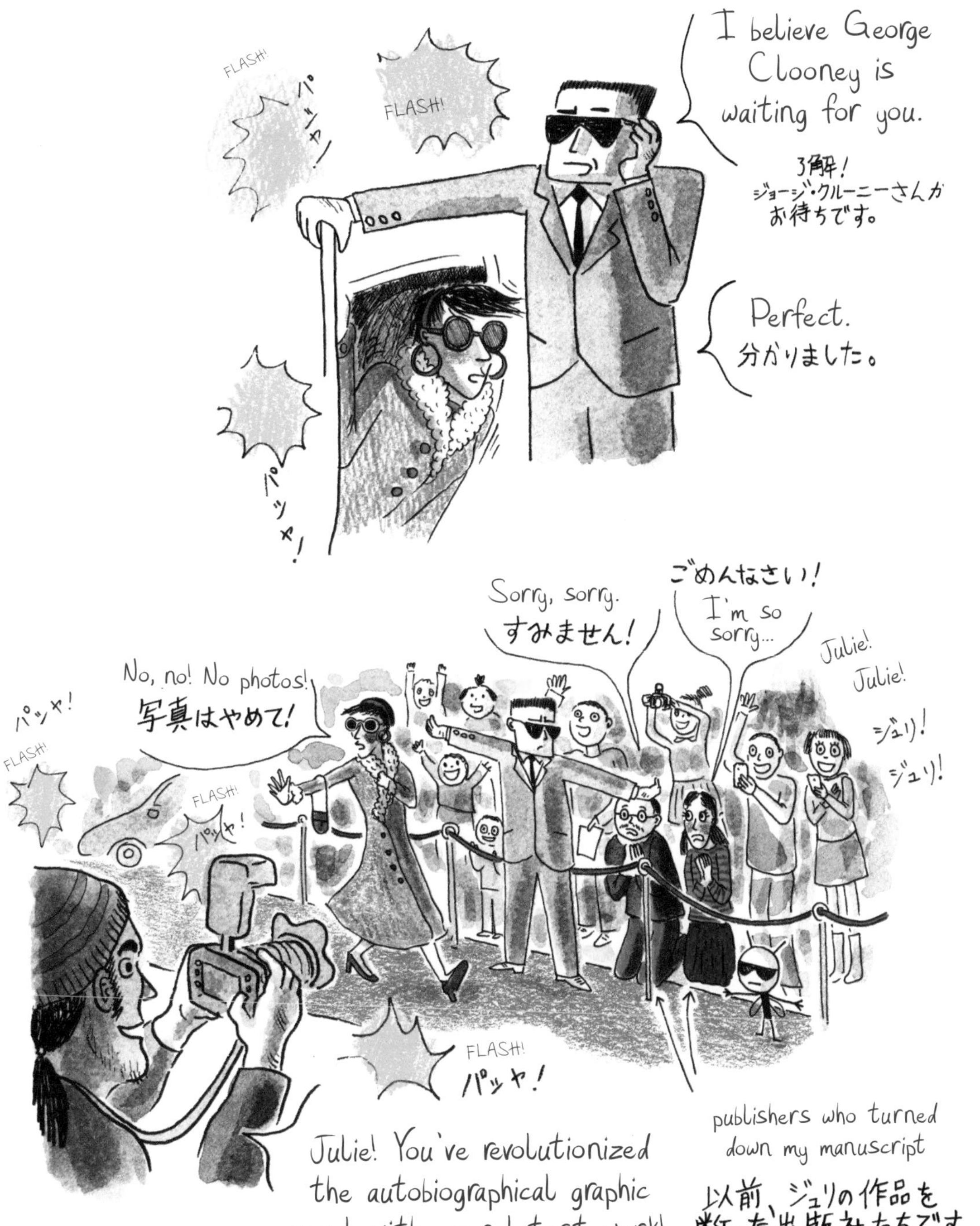
FLASH!
パシャ！
FLASH!
I believe George Clooney is waiting for you.
了解！ジョージ・クルーニーさんがお待ちです。
Perfect.
分かりました。
パシャ！
Sorry, sorry.
すみません！
ごめんなさい！
I'm so sorry...
Julie!
Julie!
ジュリ！
ジュリ！
No, no! No photos!
写真はやめて！
パシャ！
FLASH!
FLASH!
パシャ！
FLASH!
パシャ！
Julie! You've revolutionized the autobiographical graphic novel with your latest work! A comment please?!
publishers who turned down my manuscript
以前、ジュリの作品を断った出版社たちです。

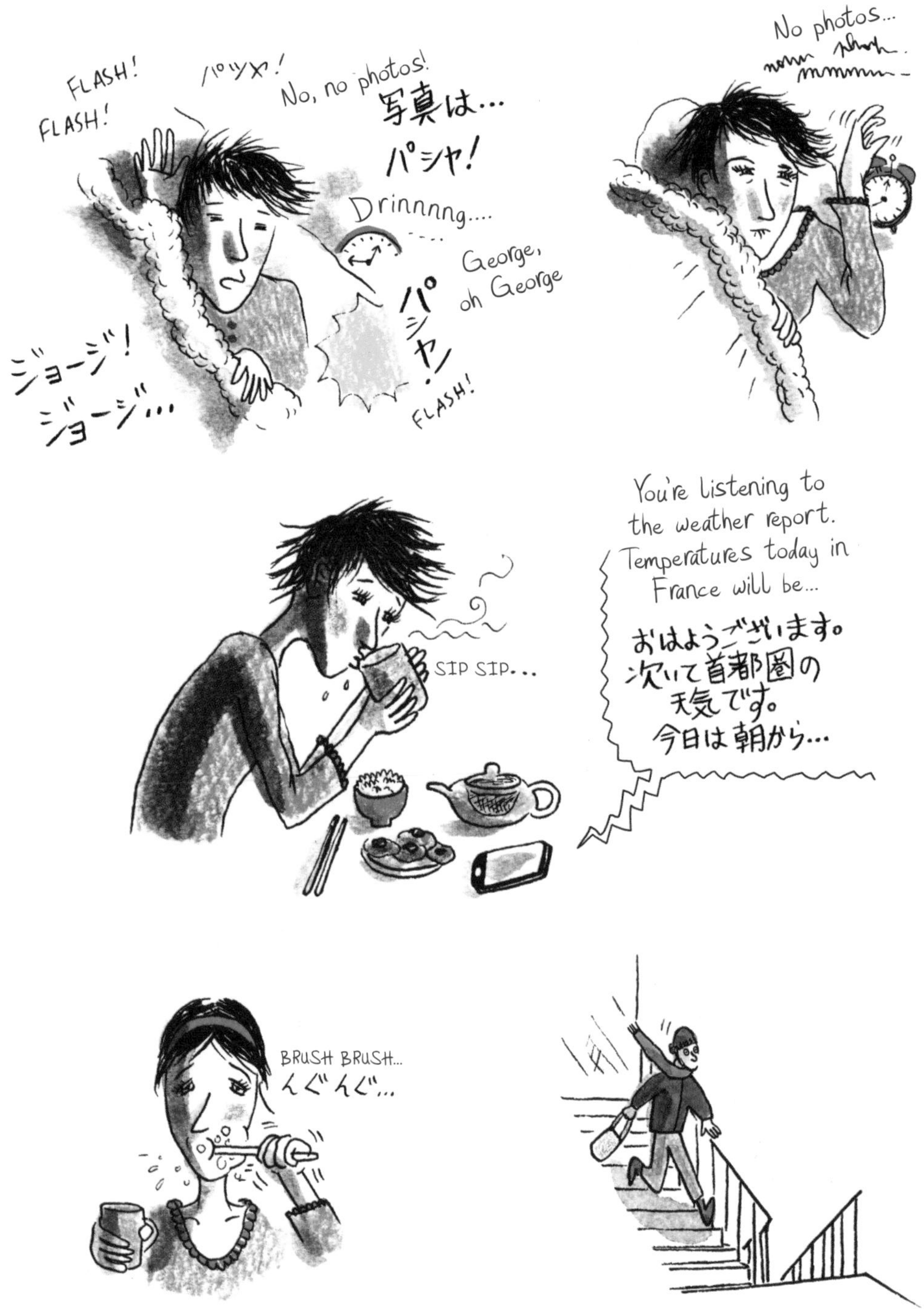
FLASH!
FLASH!
パツャ!
No, no photos!
写真は…
パシャ!
Drinnnng....
George, oh George
ジョージ!
ジョージ…
パシャ!
FLASH!
No photos...
You're listening to the weather report. Temperatures today in France will be...
おはようございます。
次いで首都圏の
天気です。
今日は朝から…
SIP SIP...
BRUSH BRUSH...
んぐんぐ…

Well no,
I'm not an
international
star and
George
Clooney is
not my chum.

ジョージ・クルーニーは私の友達ではありません。
有名スターでもありません。

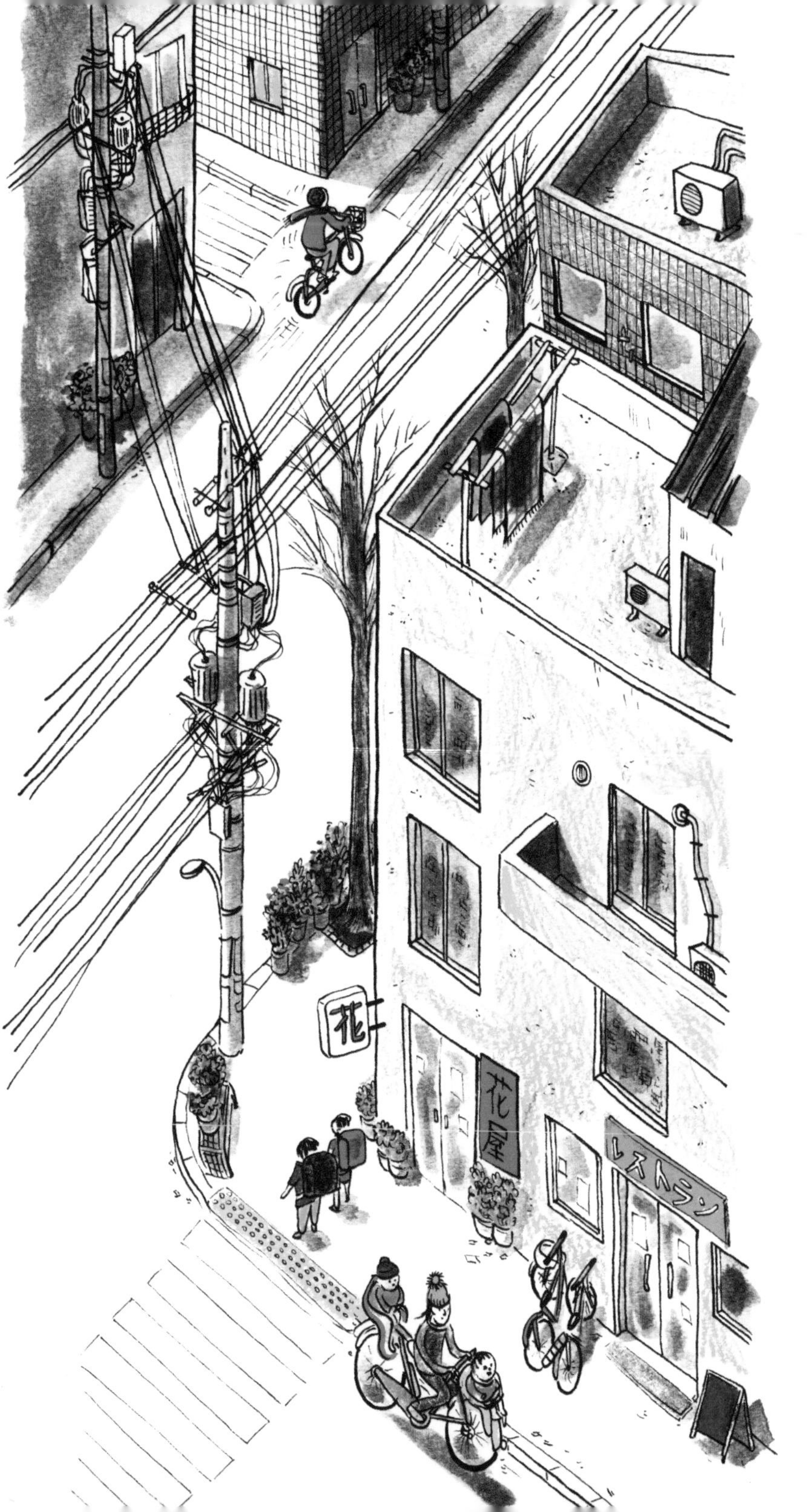

花
花屋
レストラン

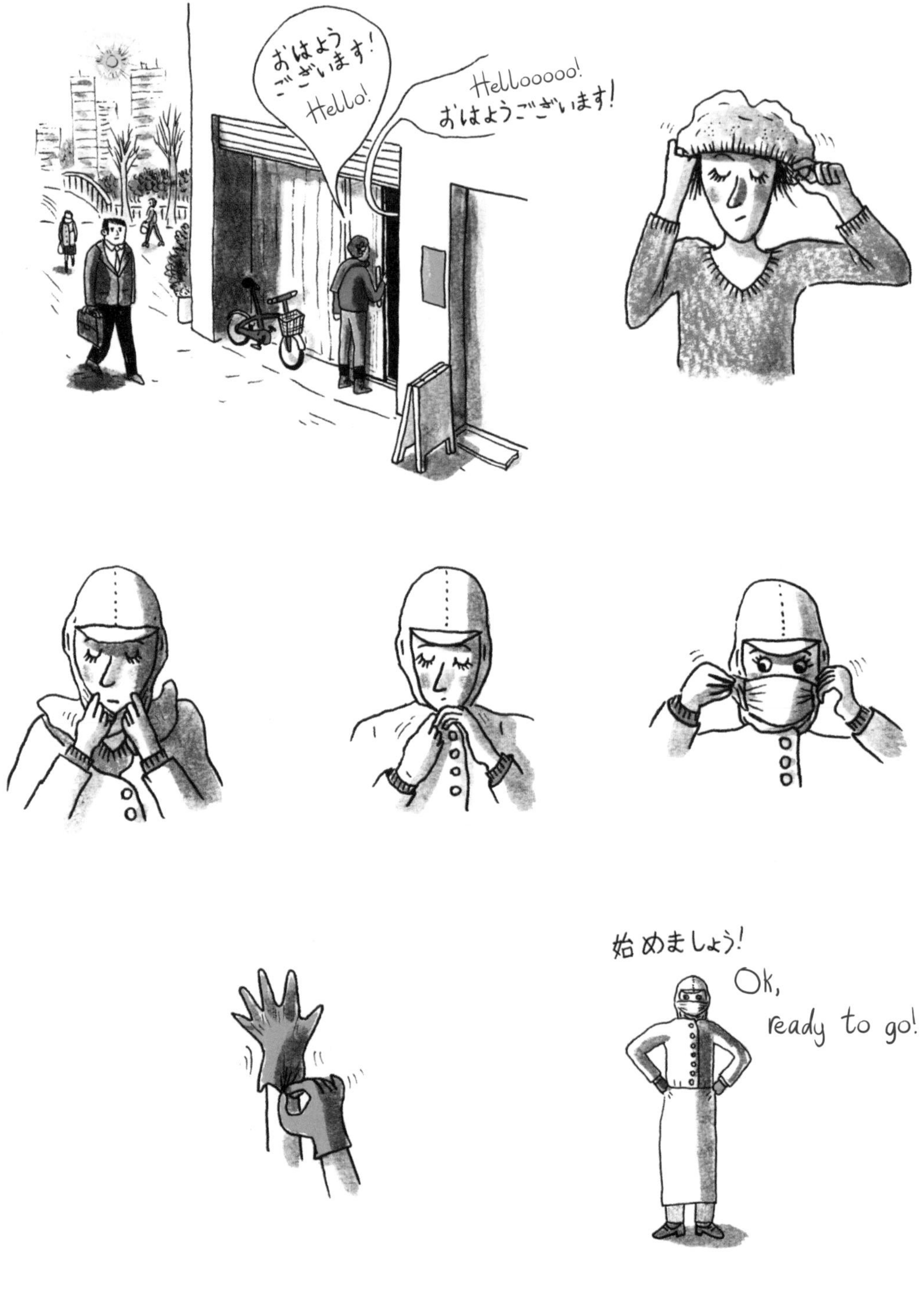
おはようございます!
Hello!
Hellooooo!
おはようございます!
始めましょう!
Ok,
ready to go!

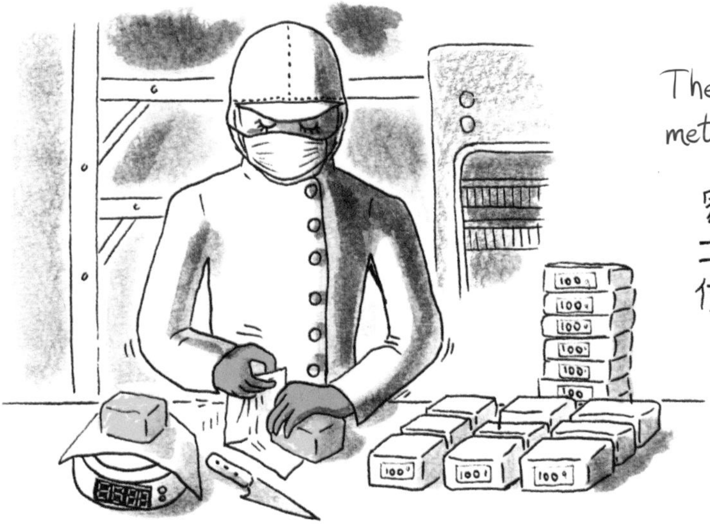

The truth is I make meth to pay my rent.

家賃の支払の為、
コカイン工場で
働きます。

Ha ha, no, just kidding. I'm really working part-time in a factory that makes French pastries.

は、は、は冗談です。
本当はフランスの
ケーキ屋の工場で
働きます。

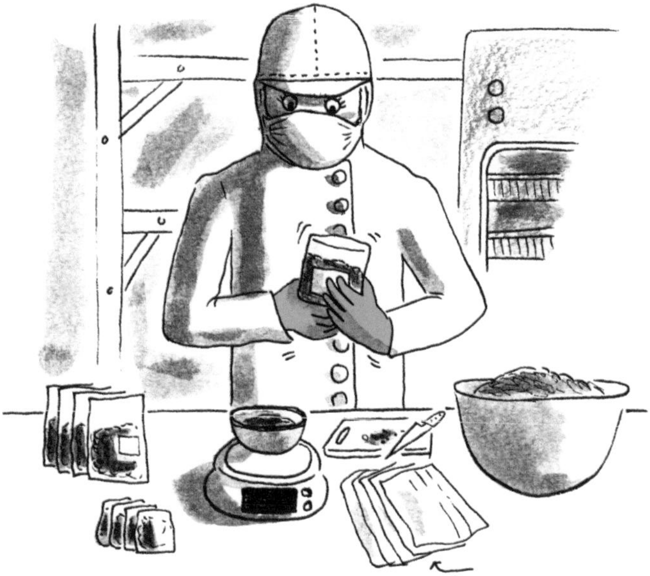
ビニール袋
plastic baggies

I'm beginning to think I'm watching too many American TV series.

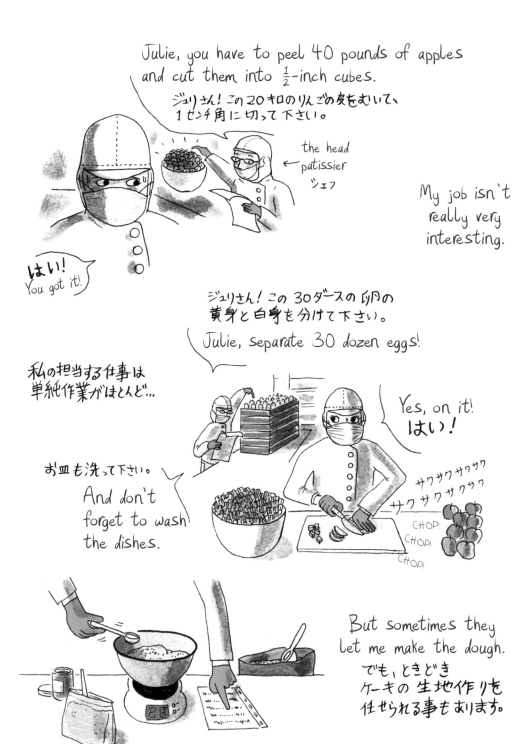

Julie, you have to peel 40 pounds of apples and cut them into $\frac{1}{2}$-inch cubes.

ジュリさん！この20キロのりんごの皮をむいて、1センチ角に切って下さい。

the head patissier
シェフ

My job isn't really very interesting.

はい！
You got it!

ジュリさん！この30ダースの卵の黄身と白身を分けて下さい。

Julie, separate 30 dozen eggs!

私の担当する仕事は単純作業がほとんど…

Yes, on it!
はい！

お皿も洗って下さい。

And don't forget to wash the dishes.

サクサクサクサク
サクサクサクサク

CHOP!
CHOP!
CHOP!

But sometimes they let me make the dough.

でも、ときどきケーキの生地作りを任せられる事もあります。

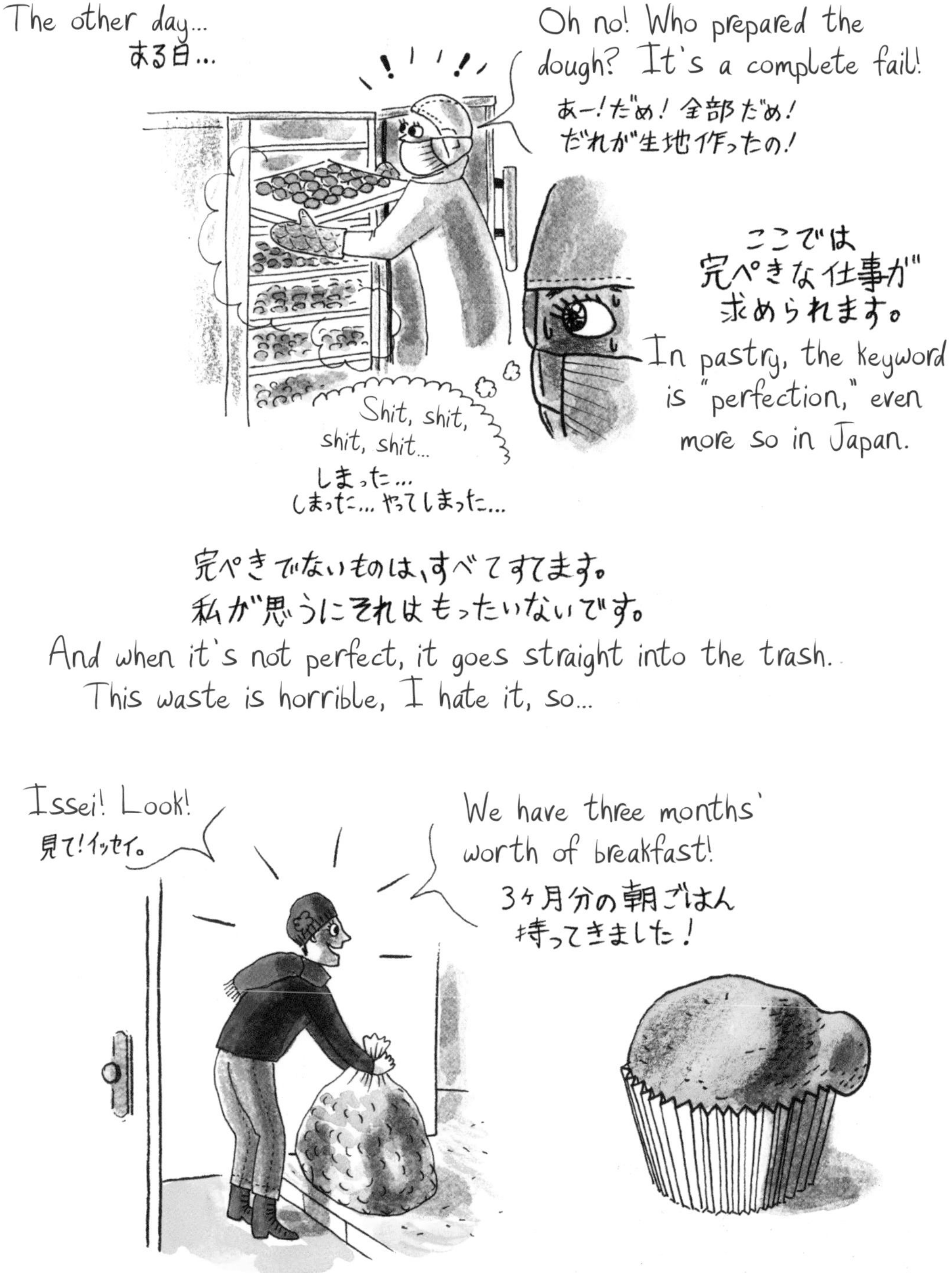
The other day...
ある日...
Oh no! Who prepared the dough? It's a complete fail!
あー!だめ!全部だめ!
だれが生地作ったの!
Shit, shit, shit, shit...
しまった...
しまった...やってしまった...
ここでは
完ぺきな仕事が
求められます。
In pastry, the keyword is "perfection," even more so in Japan.
完ぺきでないものは、すべてすてます。
私が思うにそれはもったいないです。
And when it's not perfect, it goes straight into the trash.
This waste is horrible, I hate it, so...
Issei! Look!
見て!イッセイ。
We have three months' worth of breakfast!
3ヶ月分の朝ごはん
持ってきました!

Epilogue エピローグ

Issei works nights. At first, it's not a problem. But thinking about the future and talking as a couple, we decide it would be better if he finds a job with physically less challenging hours.

イッセイは夜勤のある仕事をしています。
今は問題ないけど、私たちの未来を考えた時、
他の仕事があればもっと良い生活になるんじゃ
ないかと言う話になり、

イッセイはちがう道に
すすむ為、
勉強する事になります。

For Issei to find day work and honest wages means he needs new training.

So after long hours of discussion, we come up with a brilliant idea—go live in France for a couple of years, long enough for Issei to start learning French and go to university there.

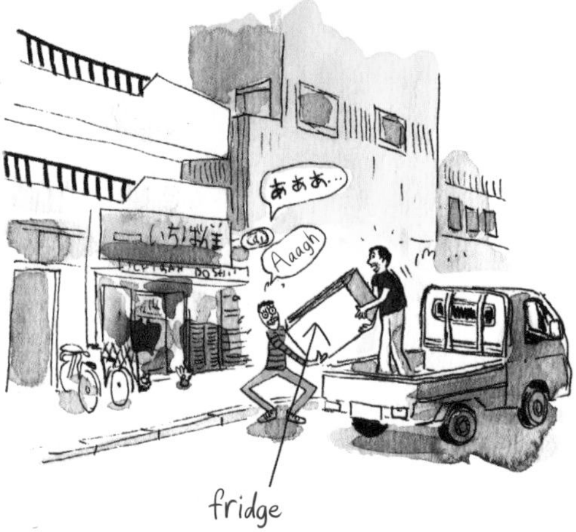
あああ…
Aaagh
fridge

議論の末、良い構想にたどり
着きます。2人で、
フランスへ行き、1,2年間住み、
その間、イッセイは大学で教育を受けます。
まずはフランス語の勉強からスタート。

First, we sell or give away all my stuff.
まず、私たちの荷物を処分します。

Ok, so the fridge goes to Marie's, the gas stove to Aki's, the table to Kimiko's, then the plants to Phil's, the washing machine to...

こうゆうルートです：
冷蔵庫はマリーその次ガス
コンロはアキ、その次テーブルはクミコ、
その次 観葉植物はフィル、その次洗濯機は…

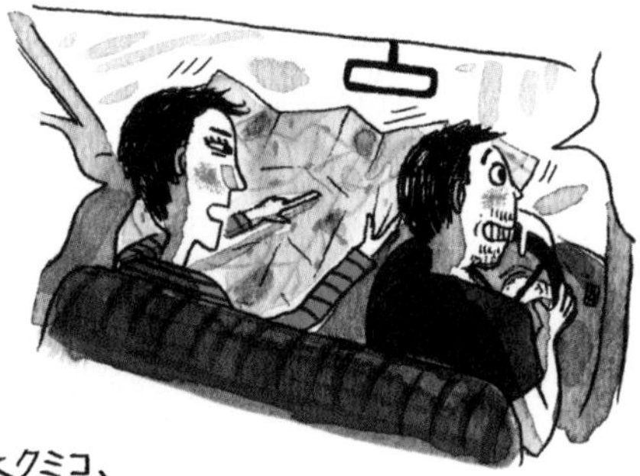

Hey, Julie, the map isn't see-through!

ちょっとージュリ！
地図で前が
見えないよ！!!

"FREE, HELP YOURSELF"
どうぞご自由に。

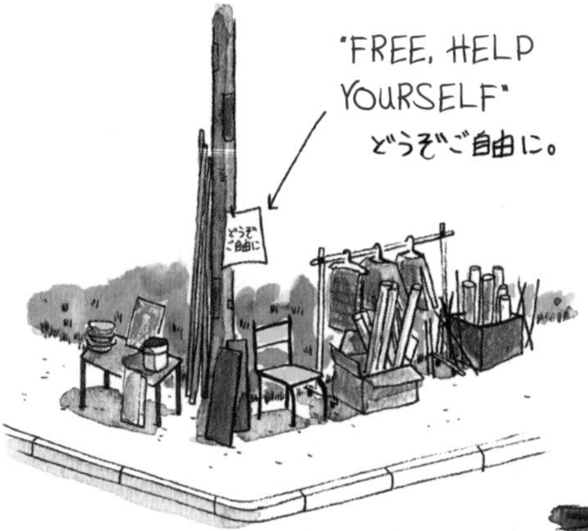
どうぞご自由に

Second, Issei quits his job.
次にイッセイは仕事を辞めます。

Third, we say goodbye to our apartment.
そして、思い出のある
私たちのアパートに
別れを告げます。

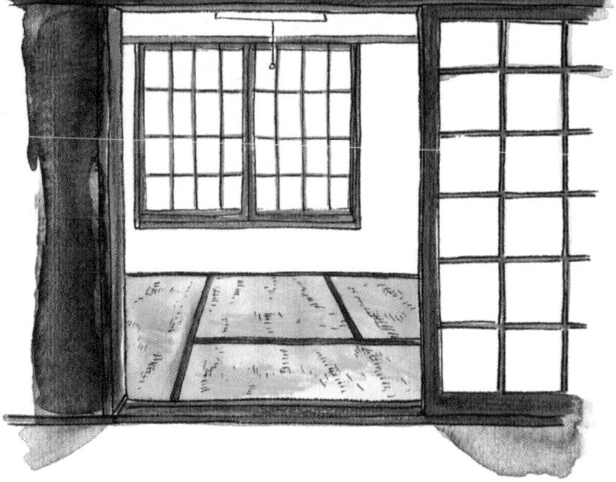

Before we fly away to France, we spend a week in Akita, at Issei's parents' place.

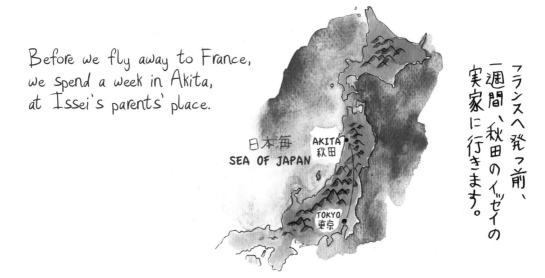

フランスへ発つ前、一週間、秋田のイッセイの実家に行きます。

日本海
SEA OF JAPAN

AKITA
秋田

TOKYO
東京

This is winter, in the far north of Japan.

冬の北国です。

We spend two blissful days in Tsuru no yu,
a beautiful and famous onsen deep in the mountains.

「鶴の湯」1泊。静かなひとときです。

Translation: 鶴 の 湯

TSURU → Japanese crane (bird)

YU → hot water

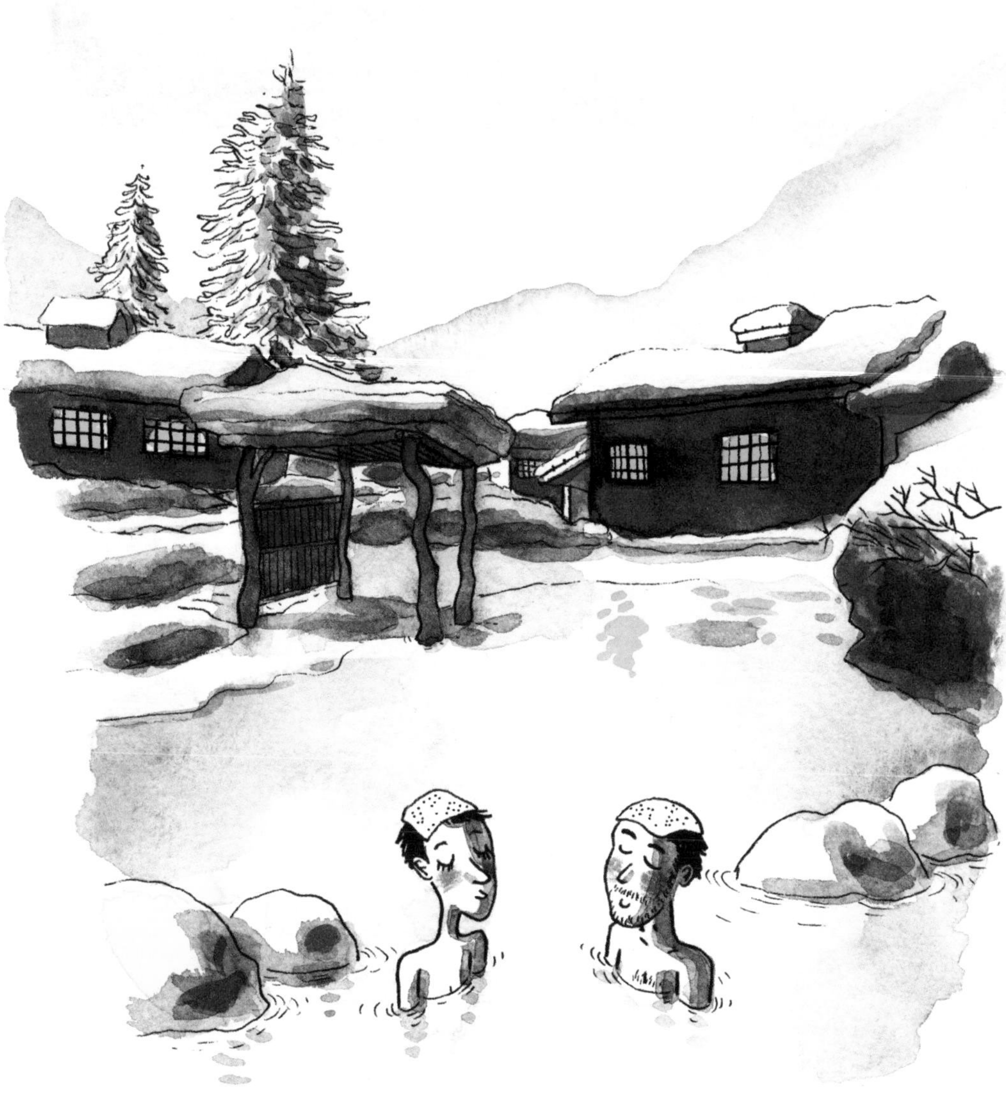

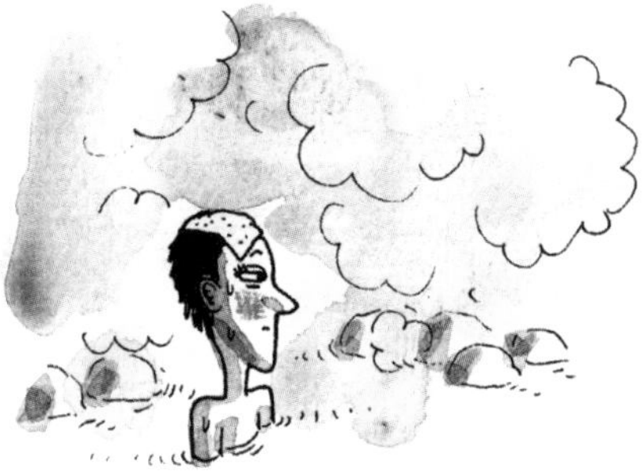

Wow... With all this steam,
I can't see a thing!
わぁ… ゆげで
ぜんぜん見えない!

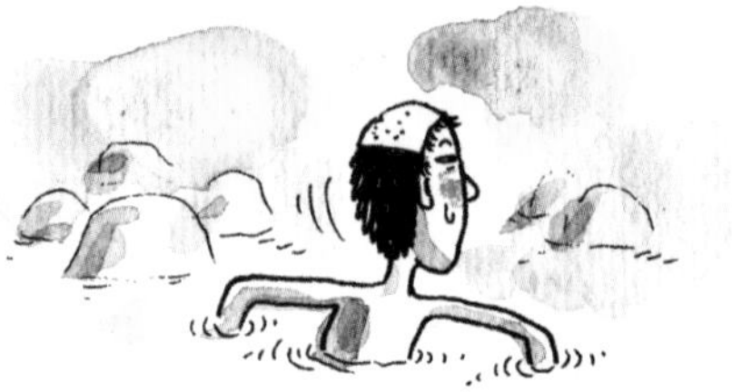

Where did Issei go?
イッセイは どこ行った…?

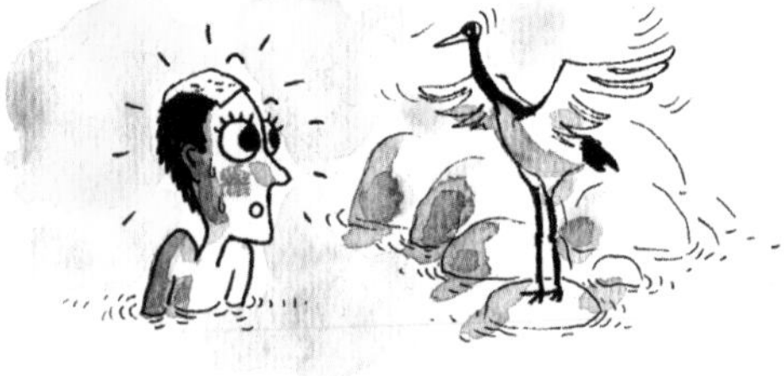

Oh! A Japanese crane!!
あっ! 鶴!!

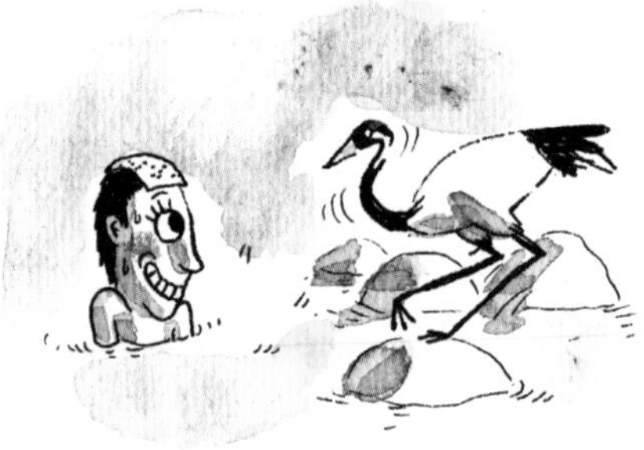

Well, hello! はっ どうも!

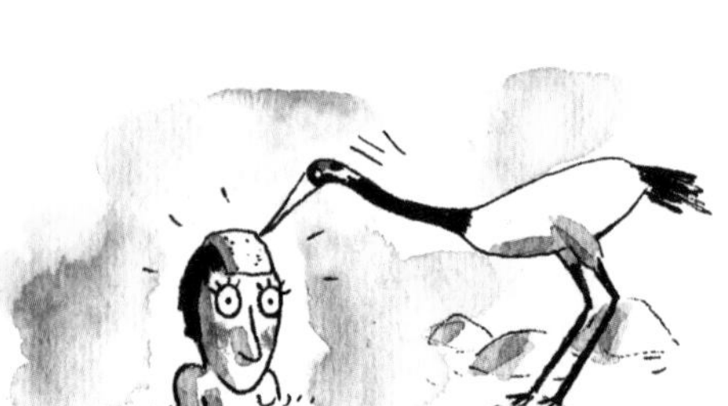

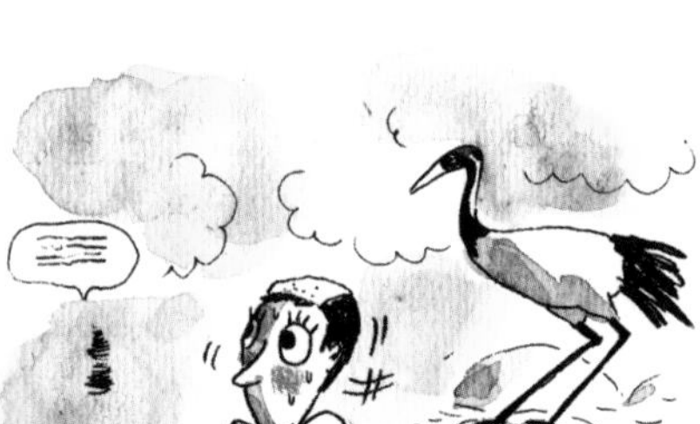

Crazy! It disappeared!

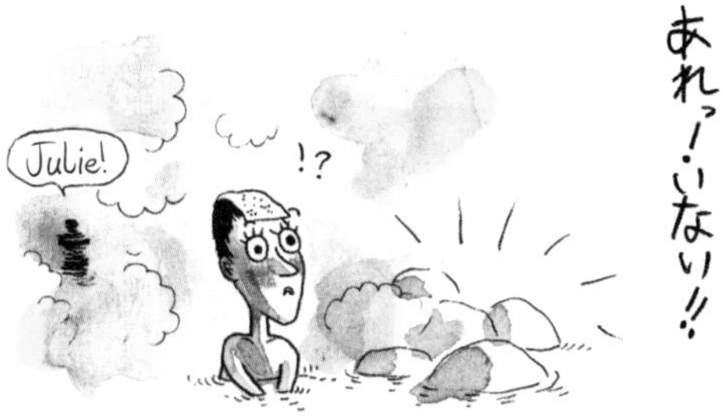
Julie!
!?
あれっ!いない!!

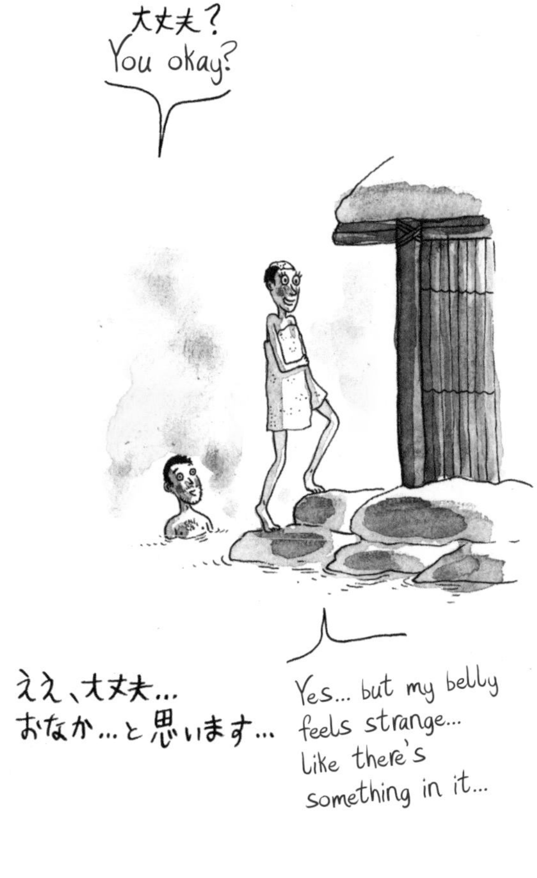
大丈夫?
You okay?
ええ、大丈夫...
おなか...と思います...
Yes... but my belly feels strange... Like there's something in it...

A few days later, we're on our way to France from Tokyo.

数日後、東京から
フランスに行きます。

ご心配なさらないで下さい。お預りのお荷物は、
アブダビ空港にて、自動的に
お乗り換便へと移されますので。

Don't worry, your luggage will be automatically transferred during your layover in Abu Dhabi.

Issei, make her sign a statement in her own blood.

血判状を
お願い
します。

Our whole life is contained in these bags.

私たちの人生
すべてが入ったバック。

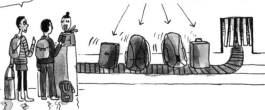

...Going through Abu Dhabi airport...

アブダビ空港にて…

MOLEX
YVAN SAINT
PIOR
PARFUMS
CHUNEL

高級じゃないテーブル

expensive and tasteless sandwich

コスパのよくないサンドイッチ

dirty table

Look! Its our bag!

あれだ！
私たちのバック！

Then, Charles-de-Gaulle

そしてシャルル・ド・ゴール空港。

But we can't grab it because of all the people hogging the space around the carousel.

そうだけど…1周目はむりだね。
それと、見て見てイッセイ。足元！
並らんで待つための
ラインがないでしょ！

We continue our journey on the Paris métro.*

次はパリの地下鉄。

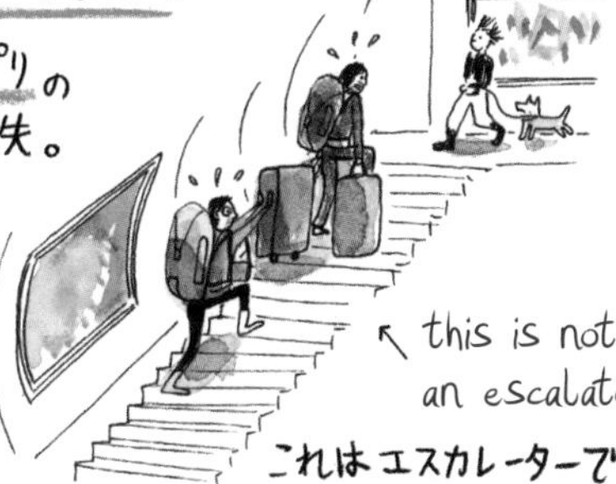

this is not an escalator

これはエスカレーターではありません。

I'm stuck! あいー！

Ouch! はさまれたー!!*

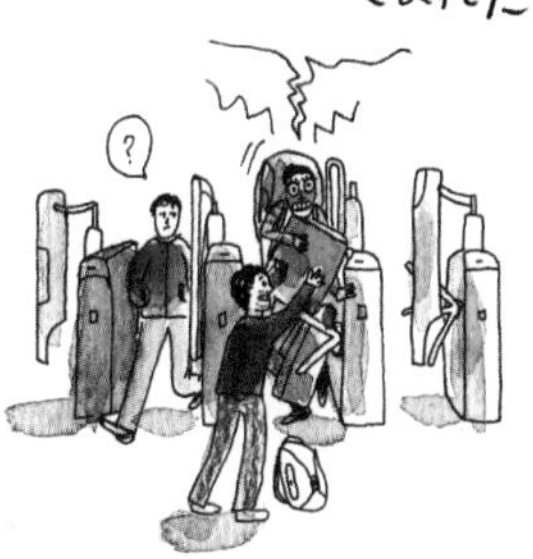

もしもし、あなた！
今電車の中です。
先生いわく、私の痔は…

Hello, dear? Yes, I'm on the train. Yes, the doctor said that my hemorrhoids are...

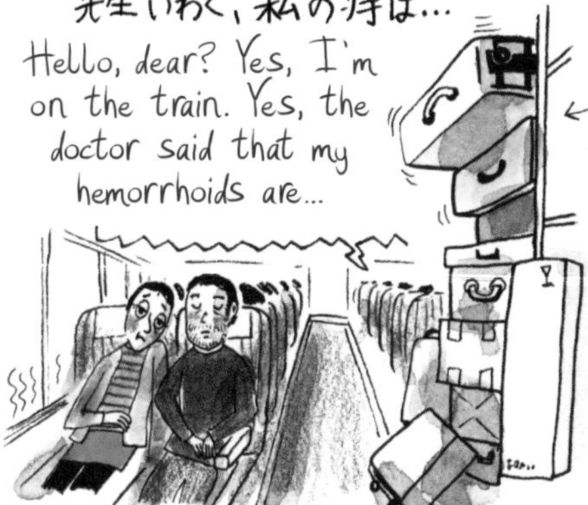

Then the TGV**... その次はTGV。**

This is not a "Compression" sculpture by César Baldaccini; this is the luggage space, as conceived by train designers who never travel by train.

まるでスーパーにある詰め放題袋の様な荷物置き場です。
きっと荷物置き場のデザイナーは、電車で旅をした事がないと思います。

We arrive at last at our new house in Saint-Nazaire-en-Roussillon, near Perpignan, in the south.

最後はペルピニャン市の近くのサン・ナゼール村の新生活する家にに着きます。

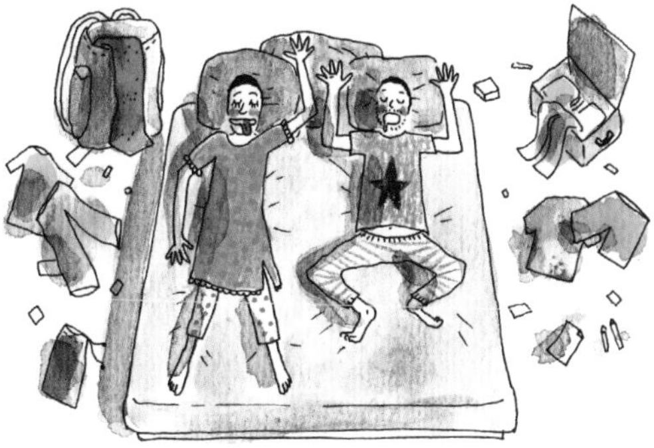

* パリの地下鉄の改札はトム・クルーズもびっくり！沢山の荷物を持っては、ミッション・インポッシブルです。

* very surprised by the Paris métro. Getting through it makes you feel like you're Tom Cruise in *Mission Impossible*.

** フランス版新幹線

** The French high-speed train.

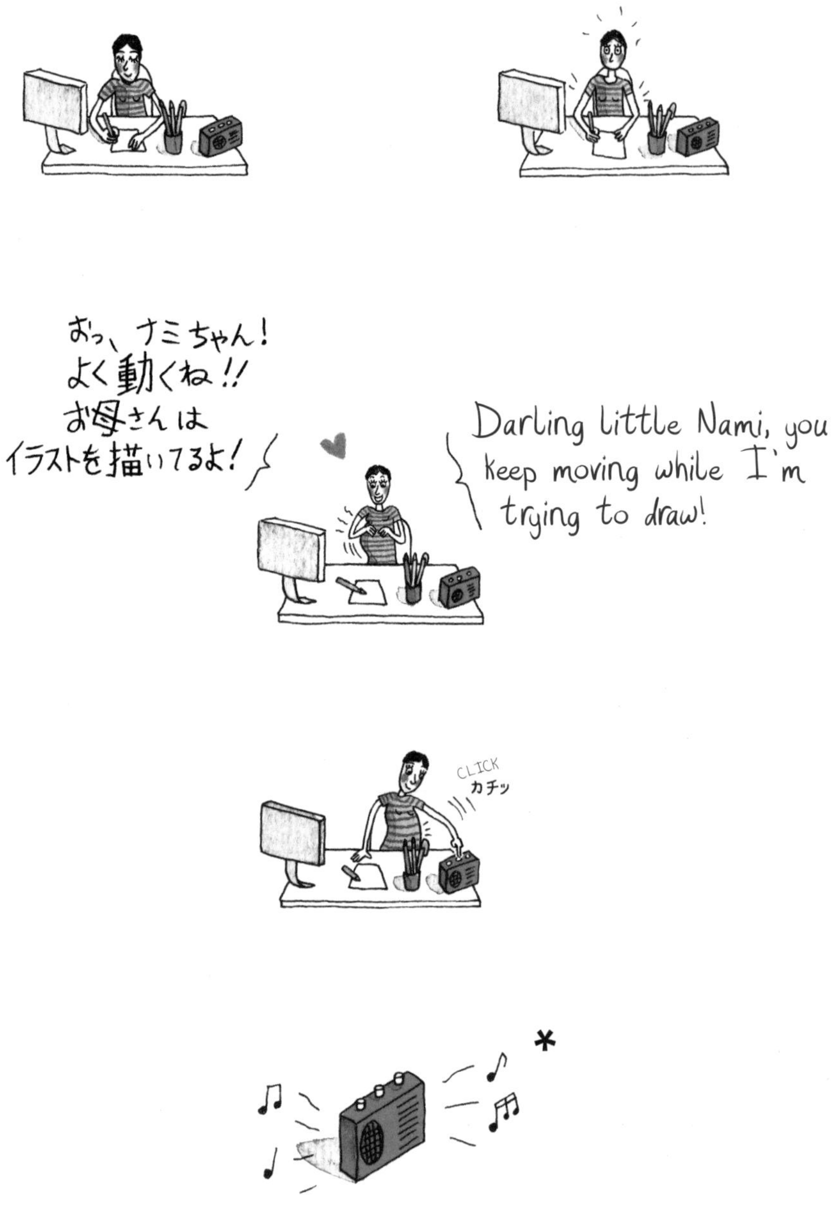
おっ、ナミちゃん！よく動くね！！お母さんはイラストを描いてるよ！
Darling little Nami, you keep moving while I'm trying to draw!
CLICK
カチッ
*

* スター・ウォーズ エピソード5／帝国の逆襲「反乱軍艦隊／エンドタイトル」ジョン・ウィリアムズ

* Soundtrack: "Finale" by John Williams from *Star Wars Episode V: The Empire Strikes Back*

Afterword

So Issei and I got married and our daughter Nami was born in 2016. After two years in France we decided to move back to Tokyo and a whole new chapter of our Tokyo Love Story began. But that will have to wait until my next book . . .

結婚して、娘のなみちゃんは2016年に生まれました。
フランスに2年間住んでいてから、東京に戻って、
新しい冒険が始まりました！

Japanese stories not yet told
まだまだある日本の話

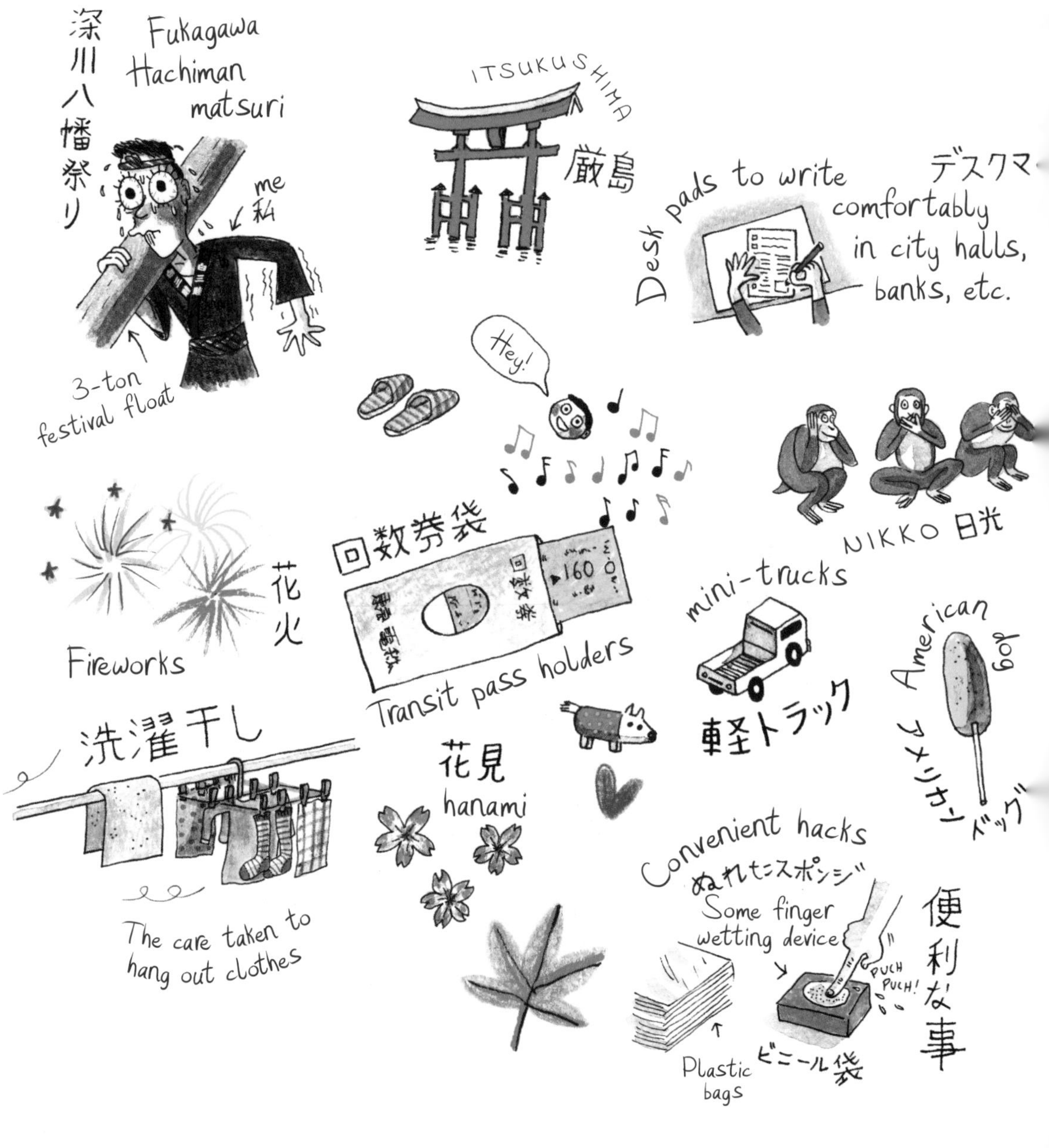

深川八幡祭り
Fukagawa Hachiman matsuri
me
私
3-ton festival float
ITSUKUSHIMA
厳島
Desk pads to write comfortably in city halls, banks, etc.
デスクマ
Hey!
NIKKO 日光
Fireworks
花火
回数券袋
▶160
Transit pass holders
mini-trucks
軽トラック
American dog
アメリカンドッグ
洗濯干し
The care taken to hang out clothes
花見
hanami
Convenient hacks
ぬれたスポンジ
Some finger wetting device
PUCH PUCH!
便利な事
Plastic bags
ビニール袋

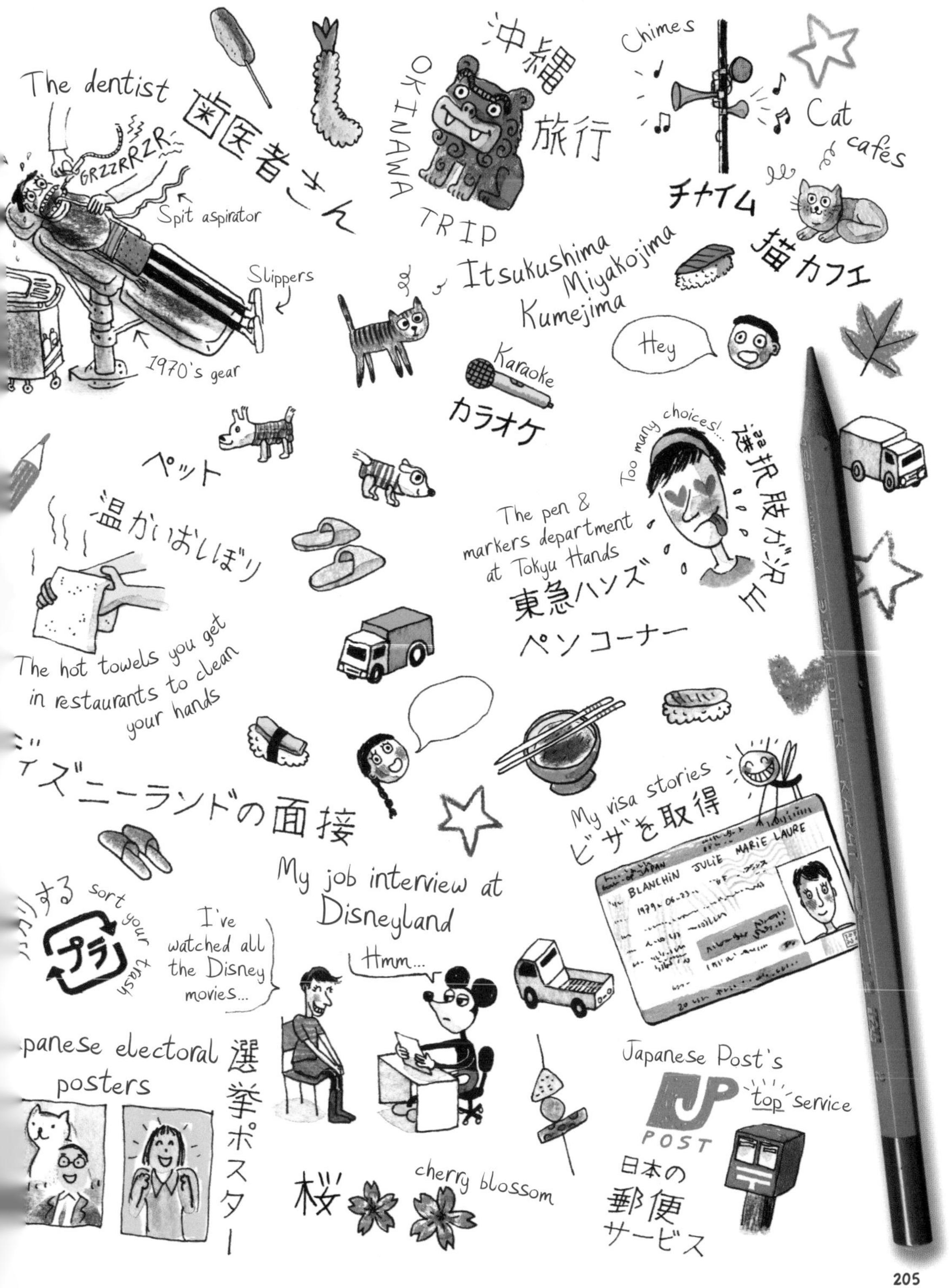

The dentist
歯医者さん
GRZZRRZR
Spit aspirator
Slippers
1970's gear
沖縄旅行
OKINAWA TRIP
Itsukushima
Miyakojima
Kumejima
Chimes
チャイム
Cat cafés
猫カフェ
Hey
Karaoke
カラオケ
ペット
Too many choices!...
選択肢が沢山
The pen & markers department at Tokyu Hands
東急ハンズ
ペンコーナー
温かいおしぼり
The hot towels you get in restaurants to clean your hands
ディズニーランドの面接
My visa stories
ビザを取得
JAPAN
BLANCHIN JULIE MARIE LAURE
My job interview at Disneyland
Hmm...
I've watched all the Disney movies...
sort your trash
プラ
panese electoral posters
選挙ポスター
Japanese Post's top service
JP POST
日本の郵便サービス
桜
cherry blossom

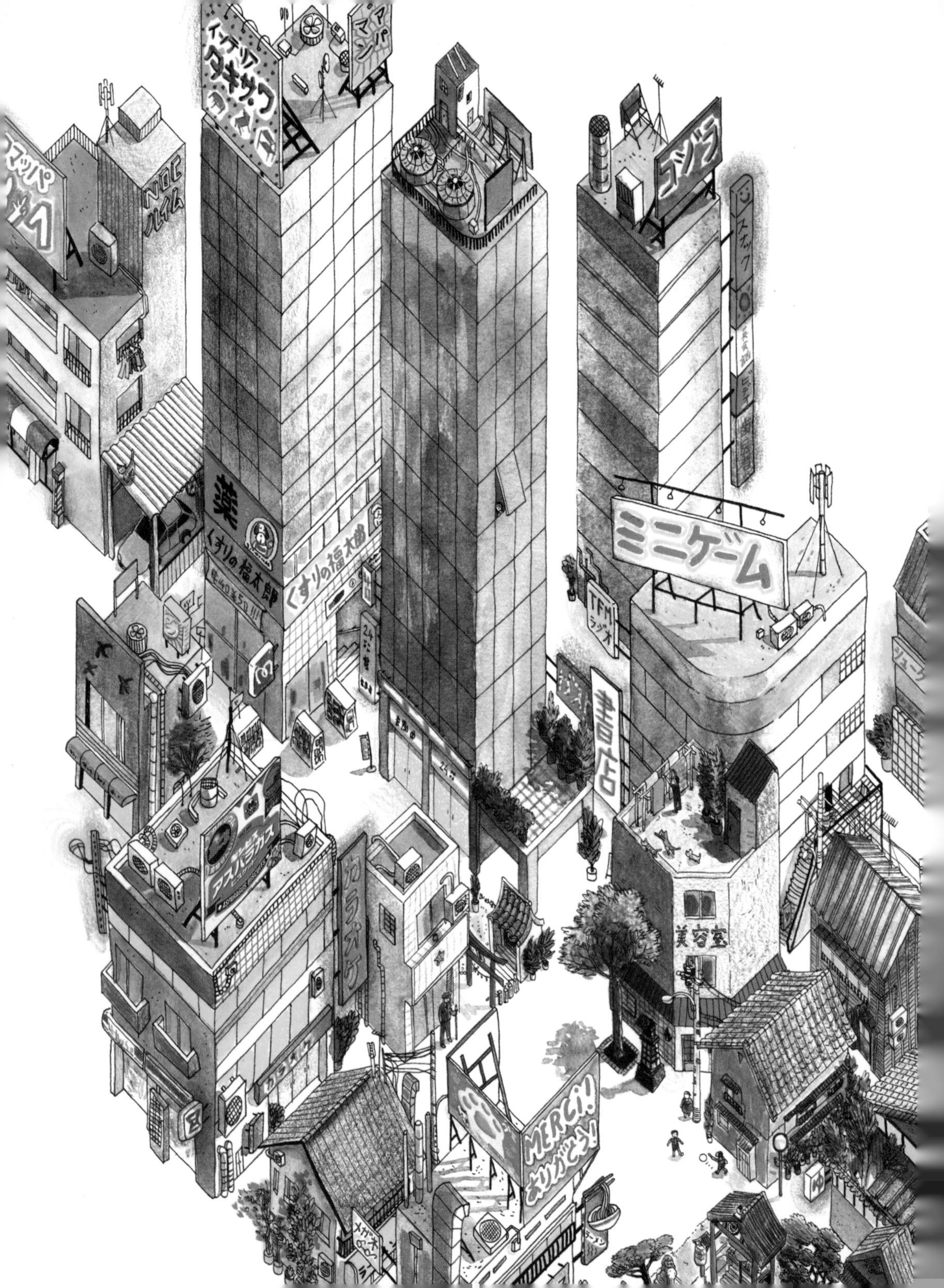

アパマン
ミニゲーム
薬
くすりの福太郎
くすりの福太郎
TFM
ラジオ
書店
美容室
カラオケ
アスパラガス
MERCI!
ありがとう!
スナック

Text and illustrations by Julie Blanchin Fujita.
Japanese translation by Issei Fujita.
Visit Julie's homepage at www.julieblanchin.com

イラスト、テキスト、デザイン：ジュリ・ブランシャン・フジタ
日本語の翻訳は藤田一世と共に。

Huge thanks to Issei, to my parents
Anne Marie and Gilbert,
to my parents-in-law Shigeko and Shizuo,
and to all my family.

一世と私の両親のアンマリとジルベール、
一世の両親の茂子さんと静雄さん、家族全員、
本当にどうもありがとうございました。

Originally published in French as *J'aime le Natto: une Aventure au Japon* by Hikari Éditions, Lille, France, 2017.

English Translation by Marie Velde ©2021 Periplus Editions (HK) Ltd

www.tuttlepublishing.com

ISBN 978-4-8053-1601-6

23 22 21 20
6   5   4   3   2   1

Printed in Malaysia
2010VP

TUTTLE PUBLISHING® is a registered trademark of Tuttle Publishing, a division of Periplus Editions (HK) Ltd.

Distributed by:

North America, Latin America & Europe
Tuttle Publishing
364 Innovation Drive, North Clarendon,
VT 05759-9436 U.S.A.
Tel: 1 (802) 773-8930
Fax: 1 (802) 773-6993
info@tuttlepublishing.com
www.tuttlepublishing.com

Japan
Tuttle Publishing
Yaekari Building, 3F
5-4-12 Osaki, Shinagawa-ku, Tokyo 141-0032
Tel: (03) 5437 0171; Fax: (03) 5437 0755
sales@tuttle.co.jp
www.tuttle.co.jp

Asia Pacific
Berkeley Books Pte Ltd
3 Kallang Sector #04-01
Singapore 349278
Tel: (65) 6741 2178
Fax: (65) 6741 2179
inquiries@periplus.com.sg
www.tuttlepublishing.com

Books to Span the East and West

Our core mission at Tuttle Publishing is to create books which bring people together one page at a time. Tuttle was founded in 1832 in the small New England town of Rutland, Vermont (USA). Our fundamental values remain as strong today as they were then—to publish best-in-class books informing the English-speaking world about the countries and peoples of Asia. The world is a smaller place today and Asia's influence has expanded, yet the need for meaningful dialogue and information about this diverse region has never been greater. Since 1948, Tuttle has been a leader in publishing books on the cultures, arts, cuisines, languages and literatures of Asia. Our authors and illustrators have won many awards and Tuttle has published thousands of titles on subjects ranging from martial arts to paper crafts. We welcome you to explore the wealth of information available on Asia at www.tuttlepublishing.com.